THE
DISNEY TOUCH

CCD Grant Funds 99-2000
Dr. Janet L. Barr, Director
Eastern Suffolk BOCES SLS
627A North Sunrise Service Road
Bellport, NY 11713-1540

THE
DISNEY TOUCH

Disney, ABC & the Quest for the
World's Greatest Media Empire

Revised Edition

❖

By

Ron Grover

IRWIN
Professional Publishing®
Chicago • London • Singapore

Times Mirror
Higher Education Group

Library of Congress Cataloging-in-Publication Data
Grover, Ron.
    The Disney touch: Disney, ABC & the quest for the world's greatest media empire / Ron Grover. — Rev. ed.
       p.   cm.
    Includes bibliographical references and index.
    ISBN 0-7863-1002-2
    1. Walt Disney Company—History.   2. Eisner, Michael, 1942–   .
I. Title
PN 1999.W27G76   1997
384′.8′0979494—dc20   96–20538

Disney store ISBN: 0-7863-1172-X

Printed in the United States of America
1 2 3 4 5 6 7 8 9 0 DO 3 2 1 0 9 8 7 6

To my daughter, Elizabeth,
who proves each day that wishes really can come true.

Preface

It was not the reaction that I had expected. "Isn't there any way I can talk you out of writing this book?" Michael Eisner asked as I entered his office.

To put it mildly, I was perplexed. From what I knew about Michael Eisner, the chairman of The Walt Disney Company is hardly a shy man. Few in Hollywood are. And, as any entertainment reporter will attest, few companies invite press coverage with the same gusto as Disney. Besides, Eisner's company had a terrific Cinderella story of rags to riches to tell. The problem was that Eisner seemed to have other ideas. "As soon as everyone starts writing books about how great you are," Eisner explained, "that's when things start to fall apart."

No one could fault Michael Eisner for his superstitious fear. Since he and Frank Wells arrived on the scene, the company founded on the wholesomeness of Mickey Mouse and Donald Duck had undergone a metamorphosis few in American business could duplicate. Once a lackluster theme park company, the Walt Disney Company of the 1990s is an entertainment giant. Earnings, which had fallen for three straight years before Eisner arrived, had increased eightfold under his direction. As a result, Disney, once derided by investment bankers as a chronic underachiever, had become a Wall Street darling.

By 1990, just about everyone in America knew Michael Eisner. His boyish face, framed by large lips and curly brown hair, has stared out from the covers of *Time, Newsweek, Business Week,* and dozens of other magazines. Along the way, Eisner also became one of America's highest-paid executives. But Eisner, as I would learn later, had steadfastly refused to cooperate on books before. His hesitancy only fueled my interest in writing this book.

As I researched it, I found that Michael Eisner can be deceptively charming. As host of the Disney Sunday night television show in the 80's, the company's chairman clowned with Goofy and Pluto and spouted self-deprecating humor. He is a devout family man who sprinkles Disney's annual report with references to his sons' latest school projects. But away from the cameras, out of earshot of reporters, Michael Eisner can be shrewd, pointed, and more than a little tough.

I also learned that Michael Eisner is unashamedly proud of his accomplishments. Almost certainly he wanted this book to be written. But like a good Washington politician, the Disney executive also knows something about spin control. If there was to be a book, he wanted to make sure that he and Disney's well-oiled press machine put a large dose of their own "pixie dust" into the mixture. And by protesting, even a little, Eisner wanted to inject his own measure of humility as well.

Erwin Okun, Disney's omnipresent senior vice-president of corporate communications, had already gotten Eisner's agreement for the book by the time I arrived at the company's Burbank studio. The ground rules were straightforward enough. This was to be my book, not a ghostwritten version of the story as told by Michael Eisner. Disney executives would give me ample time, but there would be no camping out on the company's doorstep. Disney was not going to open all of their closets for me to inspect. And at the same time, they were not going to have final say over the manuscript.

Ultimately, Disney's executives were generous, but certainly not lavish, with their time. Both Michael Eisner and company president Frank Wells gave me three hours. Jeffrey Katzenberg, Disney's indefatigable studio head, gave me one hour. So did theme park unit head Dick Nunis, just as he was heading off on one of his many trips to Orlando.

The amount of time I spent with other Disney executives varied, but none was too busy or too guarded. In all, I did more than 75 interviews and collected over 100 hours of tape. Ron Miller, Walt's son-in-law and the vanquished former chief executive, graciously gave me a rare interview. So did Sid Bass, the press-shy Fort Worth billionaire who rode to Disney's rescue in the depths of its 1984 takeover battle. Several other past Disney executives requested anonymity.

What evolved was a story of genius rediscovered. No one has ever questioned the pure ingenuity of Walt Disney. In a different way, in a different era, Michael Eisner and his team brought a similar freshness of thought and a dedication to succeed. Creativity was measured not only in new movie scripts and theme park rides, but in marketing strategies and in the financial transactions that shielded the company from excessive risk. From the latest Touchstone Pictures release to the chain of Disney Stores growing almost daily, no area of the company was untouched by the transition to a bold and creative new management team.

Without question, Michael Eisner set the tone. He is, even his critics admit, one of America's most creative executives. His ideas range from the brilliant to the silly. It was Eisner who pushed to make the blockbuster film *Three Men and a Baby* and to lure George Lucas to design theme park rides. Even as I sat with him for the first of our two interviews, he took a phone call from Bob Small, who runs the company's hotels. Eisner, just back from Orlando, wanted to lure honeymooners to the Walt Disney World complex. A doubtful Bob Small listened as Eisner outlined his plan for converting the top of Cinderella's castle, the landmark in the center of the Magic Kingdom, into an apartment for newlyweds.

I first met Michael Eisner in early 1987. At the time, I was researching the Walt Disney Company for what would become a cover story in *Business Week* magazine. It was that article that prompted this book. The first time I met Eisner he was officiating at the opening of "Star Tours," a space-age ride at Disneyland. Since then, I have had the opportunity to talk to him several times, both in the course of working for *Business Week* and in researching this book.

Since our first meeting, I have closely followed Eisner and his company as it grew from the $1.4 billion company he inherited to one with revenues of more than $18 billion a year. Along the way, it has also built a fifth theme park, begun a sixth in Paris, and expanded the company into television stations, restaurants and even a record label. And in 1995, Disney took its biggest step, paying $19 billion to buy Cap Cities/ABC.

In many ways, the revival of the Walt Disney Company was one of those lucky accidents of history. When Michael Eisner and Frank Wells arrived, the entertainment industry was on the rebound. The box office was sizzling, and new markets for home video and cable were fast expanding. The children that baby boomers had put off having were suddenly reaching the age at which they could enjoy Disney's toys and films. But it took a special group of executives to see the potential and act upon it. Team Disney was that group.

In writing this book, I have tried to be objective. Michael Eisner and the executives he gathered around him were no saints. Driven to succeed, the new managers could be curt and occasionally brusque. Ruthlessly focused on the bottom line, they were tough-minded managers and callous negotiators. When things didn't go their way, they weren't afraid to head into court. People were fired, others quit rather than work at the new Disney. No company, I found, can be built on fairy tales alone.

Making revisions for this edition of *The Disney Touch* was especially difficult. Things had gone shockingly bad for Disney in the mid-90's, starting with the financial weakness of Euro Disney and the company's eventual restructuring to avoid its failure. Even more difficult was the calamitous 1994, when Frank Wells was tragically killed, and Jeffrey Katzenberg quit in one of the messiest "divorces" in recent Hollywood history. Disney executives, especially chief financial officer Richard Nanula, were gracious in talking about the rescue plan for Euro Disney. But neither Eisner nor Katzenberg would comment for this book on their feud, which has boiled over to become a messy legal fight.

The hiring of Michael Ovitz as president, and the acquisition of ABC are covered in a separate chapter. Both are too recent to have their impact fully judged, although both will certainly become major elements of Disney's future successes and failures.

Finally, this is not a complete book about The Walt Disney Company. I have chosen to devote only a few pages to Walt's life and to the 1984 takeover battle that prompted the hiring of Eisner and Wells. It was my purpose to focus on the resurrection of Disney's fortunes after the two men arrived in Burbank. The company's history before Michael Eisner is important only for the perspective it provides by which to judge his management team's accomplishments. Those areas that I chose to largely exclude have been well covered in Bob Thomas's painstakingly researched *Walt Disney: An American Original* and in John Taylor's excellent *Storming the Magic Kingdom*.

Ultimately, I found, the person with the Disney Touch was really Walt Disney himself. A man of unlimited vision and far-ranging talents, he created an entertainment empire rich with assets that could sustain his company even through two decades of uninspired management. As a result, the company that Michael Eisner and Frank Wells inherited was still one of the world's best known and loved. More important, The Walt Disney Company was endowed with staggering real estate assets and some of the world's most marketable characters. Michael Eisner, Frank Wells, and the dozens of Disney executives who joined them added their own Disney Touch—brilliantly finding new ways to exploit those assets and new markets to conquer.

Acknowledgments

After spending well over a year researching and writing this book, I have learned at least one great truth. Writing can be a lonely exercise. Even so, I was fortunate to have the help and support of a great many kind and generous people. Like most nonfiction books, this one could not have been completed with them.

Because this is a revised version of the book, some of the cast of characters changed in the five years since I first wrote it. Unfortunately, some of those who were the most gracious with their time are no longer around to read of my warm feelings and sincere gratitude. Erwin Okun, perhaps Hollywood's finest public relations executive, died not long after my book was published. A man of grace and understanding, he provided great counsel and understanding. And he opened a great many doors for me in writing the book. I shall miss him. His successor, John Dreyer, has proven just as helpful and gracious, again pestering Michael Eisner and others on my behalf. Like Erwin, he is a good man and friend.

The biggest door both men opened for me remains that of Michael Eisner, chairman of The Walt Disney Company. Over the years, he has always been gracious with his time, even when events surrounding him were at their darkest. Without question, this book could not have been written without him. Although he knew that this was to be an independent work, Eisner not only agreed to several interviews but made many of his top executives available to me. My sincere thanks.

Frank Wells was similarly gracious, giving me three early-morning hours at his Beverly Hills home for my first edition. I spoke with him often in the following years, and perhaps only too late understood that he was the glue that helped hold this company together. His tragic death only proved how true this was.

Without exception, Disney's executives were also generous with their time. Among those who shared their insights with me, and to whom I owe great thanks, are Roy Disney, Jeffrey Katzenberg, Rich Frank, Dick Nunis, Joe Shapiro, Bo Boyd, Dick Cook, John Cooke, Robert Jacquemin, Steve Burke, Arthur Levitt III, Bob Levin, Jack Lindquist, Bill Mechanic, Ricardo Mestres, Larry Murphy, Richard Nanula, Peter Nolan, Paul Pressler, Marty Sklar, Bob Small, Rich Johnson, and Ed Nowak.

My thanks as well to those tireless Disney press people who helped me compile the mountains of documents and press releases that I needed: Chuck Champlin, Hilary Clark, Howard Green, June Moriarty, Tania Steele, Andi Sporkin, Dave Herbst, Daniel Wolf, Kristin Hogan, Tom Deegan, Terry Press, and the late Ed Pine. Disney's archivist David Smith and his assistants Rose Motzko and Jennifer Hendrickson were a plentiful reservoir of historic trivia and useful retrospective.

My special thanks to Gary Wilson, who gave me several hours of invaluable information at his Malibu home, and to Disney board members Stanley Gold and Ray Watson. Both shared their thoughts on Disney's takeover struggle and the course of events that brought Michael Eisner and Frank Wells to the company.

Sid Bass gave me a rare telephone interview, for which I am especially grateful. Al Checchi graciously took time out from running Northwest Airlines to give me his unique appraisal and invaluable insight. So, too, did a number of people in Hollywood's creative community. Among those to whom I owe special thanks are Sam Cohn, Robert Cort, Bud Crystal, Garry Marshall, Paul Junger Witt, Gary Wolf, Roland Betts, Tom Bernstein, and Jerry Zucker.

Those who passed Disney's way and relived those days for me included Chuck Cobb, Richard Berger, Jim Jimirro, Stan Kinsey, John Tishman, Tom Wilhite, and Rita Henderson. Thank you all. A special note of appreciation to Ron Miller who is, above all, a sincere and honest man. Some of those who have helped the most have asked that their contributions not be acknowledged, and I will honor their request. I only hope they all realize how much in their debt I am. Thanks as well to my bosses at *Business Week*, Steve Shepard and Keith Felcyn, for giving me time off to write the book. My added appreciation and thanks to my colleagues in the Los Angeles bureau—Larry Armstrong, Katie Kerwin, and Eric Schine—for quietly putting up with me and my lingering preoccupation.

No book can be completed without the faith and understanding of its editor. My thanks to Jeffrey Krames, a man of boundless enthusiasm, who remained a gentleman under occasionally trying conditions. I could not have waded through my own tangled sentences without the help of Doug Lowell and Maryanne Conlin, each of whom provided both inspiration and a sharp eye. And none of this would have ever found its way from my computer to a typed page without the able assistance of Sharon Miller, a cherub working 2,000 miles away.

Above all, I offer special thanks to those who are closest to me and whose support is immeasurable. My warmest thanks and love to my parents, to Susan, and Coli, and, above all, to Elizabeth.

Ron Grover

Contents

❖

Chapter 12

Introduction

The skies above the fabled Waldorf-Astoria Hotel were turning gray, the first indications of the massive snowstorm that would soon envelop New York City and much of the East Coast. But for Michael Eisner, the still boyish-looking 53-year-old chairman of The Walt Disney Company, it was a sunlit day of retribution.

Two years earlier, Eisner, the man who had saved an American institution in 1984, was suffering through one of the worst years of his, or any, executive's life. Gone were the accolades of a decade's worth of record earnings, of a revived Walt Disney empire of theme parks and merchandise, of blockbuster animated films and a thriving chain of Disney Stores.

The company whose earnings had grown ninefold in a decade, and, in the process, had reclaimed its place as one of America's most admired companies, was beset by tragedy and turmoil. Eisner's two closest allies, Disney president Frank Wells and studio chief Jeffrey Katzenberg, had both departed, the first in a skiing accident, the second in a storm of recriminations. Earnings had slid in 1993 as the company's biggest bet, the $5 billion Euro Disney theme park, struggled against debt and consumer apathy.

Now, as Michael Eisner stood at the podium at the front of the packed Waldorf ballroom, not far from the Park Avenue home he had grown up in, all of that was forgotten. Soon, Disney shareholders would vote overwhelmingly in favor of a $19 billion merger with Capital Cities, parent of the ABC network, a deal he had nurtured for years by building a film and TV production company that had set the standard by which other companies were measured. The vote, and another by Cap Cities' shareholders meeting at the same time elsewhere in the city, would immediately brand Michael Eisner's Walt Disney Company as the preeminent entertainment company in America, if not the world.

A month later, when the Federal Communications Commission gave its final approval as well, Eisner stood atop an $18-billion-a-year media colossus, with Hollywood's most profitable studio, the most well-known theme parks in the world, a major TV network, and a cable operation that included ESPN, one of the most profitable properties in the new digital age. With mountains of cash and unlimited potential, Disney would enter the new world of the information superhighway with as many assets as any company in the world. There was every reason to believe him when he told his audience that day in early January that "I consider myself the most fortunate executive in the world to have the opportunity to once again lead The Walt Disney Company as it embarks on its next exciting and historic period of growth."

As he addressed Disney's shareholders, Eisner probably couldn't help thinking back to the summer of 1984, when he and Frank Wells had been selected by a takeover-weary Disney board of directors to rescue an American icon. And of the first steps he and Wells had taken to start down that road.

The date was September 26, 1984. Four days earlier the two men had been elected chairman and president of what was then called Walt Disney Productions. Then, as the rows of small homes and cluttered warehouses of Burbank disappeared from the windows of a Continental Airlines 727, the two men sat in a near empty first-class section, lost in conversation, oblivious to the stewardesses that bustled about. Disney's new executive team were on their way to Fort Worth to meet with Sid Bass, their new company's largest shareholder.

Only a month before, Michael Eisner and Frank Wells had been little more than strangers. They had known one another only casually, through occasional encounters at the social events and official functions of the entertainment industry. They were already veterans of the sharp-elbowed world of Hollywood. Both had come to the filmmaking capital as young men—Eisner from a sheltered childhood on New York City's Park Avenue, Wells from the regimentation of a navy family. Both had prospered, rising to the upper echelons of Hollywood's most powerful studios.

Tall, slightly rumpled looking, with thinning strands of curly brown hair and deep-set eyes, Eisner epitomized Hollywood's new era of creative executives. He had learned not from lavish movies but from television, starting his career by airing sit-coms and cartoon shows at the American Broadcasting Company. Later, at Paramount Pictures, he had helped the studio develop a string of hits, including *Saturday Night Fever, Raiders of the Lost Ark,* and *Terms of Endearment.*

Wells, as tall as Eisner, had the lean, hard look of an aging athlete. Dressed in the crisp uniform of the corporate lawyer, he wore a starched white shirt, striped tie, and dark-rimmed glasses. Unlike Eisner, who gestured wildly as he talked, Wells sat ramrod straight, his lips pursed as he spoke. A lawyer by training, Wells started his Hollywood career by waging legal battles on behalf of Clint Eastwood, James Garner, and other stars. Trained in the minutiae of legal documents and financial statements, Wells had relied on business sense rather than creative genius to climb the Warner Brothers ladder.

Eisner and Wells had been brought together during the summer of 1984. Nearly two decades after its founder's death, Walt Disney Productions was in the midst of a crisis that threatened its very survival. Saul Steinberg, Irwin Jacobs, and a host of lesser-known raiders had circled the company for months. While they did, the company built on pixie dust and a squeaky-voiced mouse swayed helplessly, all but done in by its own incompetent management.

Help had arrived in the person of Sid Bass. Along with his three brothers, Bass ran a $4 billion empire that consisted of real estate holdings, oil wells, and cable television companies. The roots of the brothers' fortune could be traced back three generations to a cousin, Texas wildcatter Sid Richardson, who had traded oil and gas leases from a pay telephone. But since the early 1980s, the Bass brothers had made themselves an even bigger fortune by buying and selling their stakes in companies under siege.

The Bass group also had 9 percent of Walt Disney Productions, acquired in June 1984 by selling their Arvida real estate company to Disney. The deal was designed to put a large block of Walt Disney Productions' stock into friendly hands. But as the Continental jet headed toward Texas, Eisner and Wells couldn't be sure that Sid Bass wouldn't sell off his Disney stake, once more throwing the company into confusion. Indeed, unbeknownst to Eisner and Wells, Bass had already been contacted by Harry Gray, the acquisition-minded chairman of United Technologies, who wanted to know whether Bass wanted to sell his Disney shares. At the time, Bass wasn't sure.

Cruising at 31,000 feet, Michael Eisner wanted to know everything he could about the company he had inherited. Sitting in the seat across the aisle from Eisner and Wells was Mike Bagnall, Disney's silver-haired chief financial officer. For all of his experience with the Steven Spielbergs and Eddie Murphys of the entertainment world, Michael Eisner still knew little of the financial intricacies of running a $1.7 billion entertainment conglomerate. Sid Bass, Eisner knew, would want more than shapeless ideas and long-term visions for improving the fortunes of Walt Disney Productions.

Eisner listened intently as Bagnall went through his hurried presentation. The picture was a bleak one. The company's profits had been sliding during the previous three years, shrinking from a high of $135 million in 1980 to just $93 million in 1983. Attendance at the company's theme parks in Anaheim, California, and Orlando, Florida, had fallen for three of the last four years. At Disneyland, its flagship park in Anaheim, attendance was at its lowest point since 1974. Debt had grown dramatically, and even sales of Mickey Mouse dolls were falling.

Worse than the bleak figures was the haunting reality that the creative spark that had once symbolized Walt Disney Productions had long since died. The company that produced such classics as *Snow White and the Seven Dwarfs* and *Mary Poppins* now churned out box office bombs like *Watcher in the Woods* with alarming frequency. Once a major player in Hollywood, Disney had shrunk to the status of a second-tier studio, capturing a meager 4 percent of Hollywood's box office take.

Even so, Eisner and Wells knew that they had inherited a company rich in possibilities. When he died in 1966, Walt Disney had left behind a treasure of old films and cartoons, from classics such as *Pinocchio* and *Fantasia* to old episodes of the *Wonderful World of Disney* television program. The company had also begun to scratch the surface of possibilities for its 28,000 acres in Orlando. The once isolated citrus-growing area of central Florida, both men knew, had become a resort mecca in the years following the opening of Walt Disney World in 1971.

It was after dinnertime when the airplane touched down at the sprawling Dallas–Fort Worth International Airport. Sid Bass had sent a car and driver for the three Disney executives. Swinging out onto Highway 183, the limo began its 20-minute trip downtown. Reservations awaited them at the Worthington Hotel, the wedge-shaped hotel that the Bass brothers also owned.

Early the next morning, Michael Eisner and Frank Wells would face the first major test of their short tenure at Disney. The three-hour plane trip had done more than transport them the 1,500 miles from Burbank. It had brought them face-to-face with the future of the company that Walt built.

CHAPTER

The House That Walt Built

By today's corporate standards, Walt Disney should have failed. He had little sense for numbers, and even less of how to stick a budget. For Disney, the son of an unsuccessful midwestern businessman and farmer, the world of business was embodied in ideas—ideas inspired by sources as diverse as the Mark Twain books he had read as a youngster growing up in Kansas City and the castles he had toured while in Europe as an ambulance driver during World War I. The ideas that sparked Disney involved talking mice, flying elephants, and the laughter of little children. In time, those ideas would enable him to create one of the world's best-known companies—a successful one based on more than two dozen ingratiating cartoon characters.

Young Walt Disney's first business venture ended in bankruptcy in 1923. Set up in a Kansas City studio, the young Disney drew crude cartoon strips for local theaters and sketched advertisements for a barber shop. Despite the disappointment Disney dreamed on. With only $40 in his pocket, and carrying a leather suitcase containing a shirt, underwear, and drawing materials, the 21-year-old cartoonist headed for a dusty former cattle ranch called Hollywood. He was able to borrow enough money from an uncle to set up a modestly successful business. He did well with two cartoon series, *Oswald the Lucky Rabbit* and *Alice Comedies*. The

Alice series featured the interaction of a young brunette actress with animated lions, tigers, and fish. Before long, however, another company began drawing *Oswald*, and *Alice* had run its course.

Searching for a new character, Walt toyed with several other ideas. It was allegedly during a five-day train trip with his wife Lillian from New York to Los Angeles in 1928 that Walt first developed the idea of "the Mouse." The exact origin of Mickey Mouse is obscured in legend, most of it created by Walt Disney himself. He had intended to name the character "Mortimer." But his wife Lillian, an inker at the studio before they were married in 1925, suggested the name "Mickey" instead.

Dressed in the red shorts and yellow shoes that would become his trademark, Mickey Mouse would eventually appear in three feature-length films and 120 cartoons, as well as on dozens of TV shows and millions of T-shirts. Mickey's endearingly benign countenance contributed to the immense popularity that enables him to continue spanning the generations. He appeared for the first time on November 18, 1928, in "Steamboat Willie," with Minnie Mouse as his costar. The two were soon joined by other Disney characters, starting with Pluto in 1930 and Goofy in 1932. Donald Duck made his first appearance in 1934. Five years later he eclipsed even Mickey in popularity; in World War II he was the symbol that appeared on more than 200 military insignias.

Walt was the unquestioned spark behind his company. It was he who dreamed up new characters and the story line for his cartoons. In the beginning, he also provided Mickey's squeaky voice. Not long after moving to California, Walt was joined in business by Roy, his older brother by seven years. Afflicted by tuberculosis, Roy was recovering in a West Los Angeles veterans hospital at the time Walt arrived. The two brothers called their new venture Disney Brothers Cartoon Studio. While Walt was the creative force working with the small crew of animators he had assembled, Roy provided the business acumen that his brother lacked. With a brief stint as a bank teller as his only financial experience, Roy nevertheless was able to cajole the bankers and investors to lend Walt the money he needed to transform his "silly ideas" into cartoons and films.

It wasn't always a smooth relationship, and Roy often was forced to dissuade his younger brother from spending more money than the company had. Even though Roy provided the business know-how, however, there was never any question about who was actually in charge. In 1926, three years after launching Disney Brothers Studio, the company's name was changed to Walt Disney Studios. Later, in 1929, the company became Walt Disney Productions.

From the beginning, it was Walt, with his intuitive knack for story-telling, who created the magic. A stickler for detail, Walt insisted that Disney cartoons be lavishly done, regardless of the expense. Invariably, he insisted that his company be among the first to use every technical innovation in the film industry. By setting "Steamboat Willie" to the music of "Turkey in the Straw," Walt created the first cartoon to feature synchronized sound. Four years later, he became the first to add full color. And in 1937, *Snow White and the Seven Dwarfs* became the industry's first full-length animated movie.

The cost of being the best or first in his industry often meant spending money that the brothers didn't have. Making *Snow White* very nearly threw the young company into bankruptcy. In order to scrape up the $1 million needed to complete the film, Roy invited a senior Bank of America lending officer to the studio to see early bits and pieces of the film. Convinced that *Snow White* would be a hit, the banker extended the needed money to the brothers. When the film was released, it sold more than $8 million worth of tickets, earning enough to pay off the loan and the company's other debts.

During most of its early years, however, Walt Disney Productions lost money. From the early financial struggles emerged a flexible and creative business plan that paralleled and enhanced Walt's genius for creating not only cartoons but also a wide variety of promotional efforts. These began on a business trip to New York in 1929. Walt was approached by a stationery company executive with a proposal to pay the company $300 for the right to imprint Mickey Mouse on school writing tablets. "As usual, Roy and I needed the money," Walt said later. "So I took the three hundred."

These writing tablets were the beginning of the cross-promotion of Disney's cartoon characters that eventually made Walt Disney Productions a model of what business schools would later call "synergy." By 1932, Roy and Walt had hired a Kansas City advertising man to license Mickey Mouse and other Disney characters. Within three years, Ingersoll-Waterbury Co. was selling more than a million Mickey Mouse watches annually. Within a decade, 10 percent of the company's revenues came from the royalties derived from the licensing of cartoon characters.

In the early 1950s Disney finally began earning profits on a regular basis. It was then that Walt embarked on plans for Disneyland, at the time his most ambitious venture. Roy had long since developed a tight-fisted approach to Walt's internal planning budgets. Predictably, he only gave Walt $10,000 of company money to use in planning the park. But Walt was so dedicated to his idea that he borrowed against his life insurance policy to raise an additional $100,000. To help him create more imaginative rides, Walt created WED Enterprises (short for Walter Elias Disney), a supersecret group of engineers and artists who worked in hiding in a Glendale warehouse. As with his early cartoons, Walt himself was the font from which most of the ideas sprang.

Built on the site of a former 182-acre citrus grove in Anaheim, Disneyland cost $17 million to build, many times the initial estimate. The brothers scurried to line up investors, the ranks of which eventually even included the small printing company that had been printing books based on Disney's characters.

But Disneyland's biggest backer was ABC, which invested $500,000 outright and also guaranteed a $4.5 million loan. In return, ABC owned 34.5 percent of Disneyland and won a commitment from Walt to produce a weekly prime-time television show called *Disneyland*.

The deal between Disney and ABC forever changed the company. Disneyland opened on July 17, 1955, with five separate themed "lands" such as Fantasyland and Frontierland. Within a year its gross annual revenues zoomed to $10 million, about one-third of Walt Disney Productions' overall sales. Besides selling Mickey and Donald stuffed animals, the park also helped to promote the company's vast library of movies, from the teacup rides based on *Alice in Wonderland* to the *Swiss Family Robinson* tree house.

None of the promotions, however, was as powerful as the *Disneyland* television show. The first episode aired on a Wednesday in October 1954, nine months before the park opened. As he would do for the next decade, Walt Disney introduced the show. With his gravelly voice and quiet charm, he beamed from the tube like a kindly uncle inviting his family to Sunday dinner. *Disneyland* was the sixth-ranked show on television in its first year, and it moved up to fourth place in 1956. It ran for 29 straight seasons. One of the show's first big hits, a three-part *Davy Crockett* series starring Fess Parker, inspired a national craze for coonskin caps—another coup for Walt Disney Productions, which held the licenses and collected the money.

The promotional power of the weekly TV show had a ripple effect throughout Walt Disney Productions. Not only did the show promote the Disneyland park; the steady airing of cartoons featuring Mickey,

Donald, and Pluto also sparked a leap in sales of Disney-licensed merchandise based on the characters. So captivated was Walt by television's allure that he launched the company's second ABC television show, *The Mickey Mouse Club*, in late 1955.

Walt Disney Productions had changed dramatically since the early days of "Steamboat Willie." With Walt providing the inspiration, the company turned out such classic animated films as *Snow White and the Seven Dwarfs* (1937), *Pinocchio* (1940), and *Cinderella* (1950). As the company's founder was drawn further into planning for Disneyland and the TV shows, however, the studio had begun to produce less memorable animated classics such as *Sleeping Beauty* (1959) and *101 Dalmatians* (1961). Walt had also produced live-action films in the early 1950s, but with mixed results. Not until 1964 did the company issue its first big hit that was primarily nonanimated, *Mary Poppins*. By then, Walt Disney had already turned to his most farsighted project. Planning to build a second theme park, he began secretly buying land in the citrus groves of central Florida. For $5 million, the company purchased a total of nearly 28,000 acres outside the tiny rural town of Orlando. Walt was unhappy because Disneyland had attracted a clutter of sleazy motels and fast-food joints to Anaheim. This time he intended to control development of the land surrounding his project. He planned not only hotels and restaurants but an entire city of the future. The Experimental Prototype Community of Tomorrow (EPCOT) was to be a complete and self-contained city, with its own schools, apartments, and shopping facilities. It would even have a computer-controlled sewage-disposal system.

In time, the Orlando land would transform Walt Disney Productions into an entertainment giant. It was also the founder's last big dream—one that would not be realized during his lifetime. On December 15, 1966, Walt Disney died of lung cancer at age 65, only weeks after the illness was first diagnosed.

❖

Like most people, Walt Disney had been unwilling to face his own mortality. And like most company founders, he had failed to prepare the way for his successor. For a while, the company was run by Roy Disney, who was 73 years old at the time of his brother's death. Roy lived to see his younger brother's dream realized in Orlando but died nearly three months after Walt Disney World opened on October 1, 1971.

Walt and Roy had prepared few executives to carry on in their stead. Having no sons, Walt had tentatively trained his son-in-law Ron Miller, a former Los Angeles Rams tight end, as one possible successor. The special attention Walt lavished on Ron Miller came to symbolize a split within the company between the "Walt men"—the creative people—and the "Roy men"—those more interested in business matters. The split would develop into a feud that would intensify after the brothers died. Tall, good-looking, and painfully shy, Ron Miller had started on the construction site at Disneyland in 1953. Pushing his son-in-law up through the ranks, Walt soon made Ron second assistant director on the movie *Old Yeller*. Later, Miller worked on the *Zorro* TV series, and he began producing his own film, *Never a Dull Moment*, four months after Walt's death. That same year, he was elected to the board of Walt Disney Productions, taking Walt's seat.

Ron Miller's elevation symbolized the split that had begun developing within the company even before Walt's death. While they were jointly running the company, Walt and Roy fought often. Usually their fights erupted over Roy's refusal to finance Walt's riskier projects, but once it was about a more serious matter. This particularly heated argument led to a feud so divisive that the brothers barely spoke for years. Over his brother's vehement objections, in 1953 Walt set up his own private company, Retlaw Enterprises ("Retlaw" stands for "Walter" spelled backwards), to collect 5 percent of the income generated by any merchandising deal signed by Walt Disney Productions. Roy Disney argued that the deal would look to shareholders like Walt was siphoning money from the company. By the 1960s, Retlaw's annual income was about $500,000, as increasing amounts of Disney merchandise were snapped up at Disneyland. Eventually Walt ended the feud by sending Roy a peace pipe for his 63rd birthday.

In 1977, Roy's son, Roy E. Disney, resigned as an executive with the company seven months after Ron Miller, a "Walt man," was named head of production. Before his resignation, Roy Disney had been in charge of a small studio unit that produced 16-millimeter nature films and reported to Miller. When Roy Disney resigned, his uncle Walt's company was being run by a triumvirate that included Miller, Card Walker, and Donn Tatum. But it was Walker, a 40-year veteran of the company and a "Walt man," who called the shots. After joining the company in 1938 as a mail-room messenger earning $15.95 a week, Walker began working with Walt on *Fantasia* as a cameraman. In time, he would rise to head the company's marketing efforts. Along the way, he also became one of Walt Disney's closest confidants.

None of Walt's corporate heirs, however, was prepared to lead the company into the 1970s. As in most family-run businesses, every aspect of Walt Disney Productions had been controlled by either Walt or Roy during their lifetimes. So immersed in the details of his projects that he used to time the rides at Disneyland, Walt was not a man who could easily share even the simplest decisions—and it was unquestionably Walt who set the course for the company that bore his name.

Once its founder was no longer around to plot the future, Walt Disney Productions became a prisoner of its past. Nowhere was that more true than in the company's film division. When Walt Disney died, Roy put Card Walker in charge of a five-person committee to run the company's film division. Both Ron Miller and the young Roy Disney also served on the committee, but it was Card who decided which films were to be made. Hollywood was in the midst of significant changes. But Card Walker was sure that Americans still wanted the same kinds of films that Walt Disney had given them in the past.

For a while Card's philosophy worked. In 1974, Disney generated more than $48 million from U.S. ticket sales for its movies, 21 percent higher than the year before. Disney's big new hits that year were *Herbie Rides Again*, the exploits of a precocious Volkswagen, and *Castaway Cowboy*, starring James Garner as a Texas cowhand who saves a Hawaiian plantation for a pretty widow. However, the biggest chunk of 1974 ticket sales came from a pair of reissues of films Walt had made, *Lt. Robinson Crusoe U.S.N.* and *Alice in Wonderland*.

Five years later, the company was in trouble. Even in its heyday, it had never commanded a large percentage of the box office. But by 1979, Disney's market share had shrunk to a dismal 4 percent, lowest among the seven major studios. That year, when Columbia Pictures released *Kramer vs. Kramer* and Paramount issued the first of its *Star Trek* movies, Disney countered with such forgettable fare as reissues of *The Love Bug* and *Unidentified Flying Oddball*. Its new movies weren't much better. With a lineup that included such bombs as *Unidentified Flying Oddball* and *The Apple Dumpling Gang Rides Again*, Disney's $40.3 million in film profits in 1979 were its lowest in a decade.

The problem was that America's viewing public had changed, but Disney hadn't. The families that used to line up for Walt Disney films now stayed home and watched television instead. The movies that were drawing crowds to theaters were decidedly more violent and crude than anything Card Walker would allow Disney to produce. Teenagers flocked to see *Jaws* and *Animal House,* not Disney's dimwitted comedies starring Don Knotts and Tim Conway.

What was worse, insiders knew that the company's problems ran far deeper. Lacking Walt Disney's creativity, Walker chose to become the guardian of the founder's legacy. Only those projects that Walt might have approved were endorsed by Walker. After a while, there was no one on the Disney payroll who would take the kind of chances that had previously been symbolic of Walt Disney Productions. Instead, underlining the company's creative lethargy, Disney executives would often ask: "What would Walt have done?"

On the lot, Walt's lingering ghostly influence paralyzed the creative process. "Walt was such a commanding presence," his nephew Roy Disney says, "that you could almost hear those fingers of his tapping on the chair, his symbol that he wasn't pleased with some idea you had." Rather than daring to tempt fate, Walt's corporate heirs chose to do nothing.

The huge success of *Star Wars* in 1977 had shown that it was still possible to make a hit film without sacrificing family values. But Card Walker and Ron Miller were not eager to fork over the huge salaries that they would have had to pay to create a similar hit for their studio. As a result, few top projects came Disney's way. Even when they did, the studio tended to pass them up. In 1979, Steven Spielberg and George Lucas, who had developed *Raiders of the Lost Ark,* were quickly turned away from Disney because each wanted a piece of the profits. At the time, Disney policy was not to give "points," the percentage of the film's proceeds that many other studios had already begun granting. In 1980 Spielberg got the same response again, after Disney executives had reviewed another of his films, *E.T., The Extra-Terrestrial.* The film, distributed by Universal Pictures, went on to become the biggest moneymaker of all time. After Universal released it, Ron Miller later recalled, Walker admitted he would have loved to make that film. "But I would have taken out the line when the kid says, 'penis breath,'" Walker told Miller.

By June 1980, Card Walker had turned his attention to an even more pressing problem than Disney's film company. Construction work at EPCOT Center in Florida was going badly. Labor shortages and design problems had sent costs skyrocketing. Initially estimated to cost less than $600 million, EPCOT Center was now being listed in official company documents as an $800 million effort. Walker knew that the costs would go even higher. Internal estimates put its price tag at $1 billion. After EPCOT Center opened in October 1982, the company admitted it had spent more than $1.2 billion to build and open the park.

By then, the company's earnings were in a tailspin. To find the money to pay for EPCOT's escalating costs, Disney had taken on massive amounts of debt for the first time in several years. Worse yet, it had been forced to scale back on badly needed work at the other two theme parks. By 1982, the company was spending a total of barely $48 million for upkeep at Disneyland and Walt Disney World, only slightly more than the $40 million it had been spending five years earlier.

The result was older rides and a tarnishing image of the fresh and innovative company that Walt Disney had considered crucial to continued success. The situation got still worse when, because of skyrocketing gasoline prices in the 1970s and an economic slowdown in the early 1980s, attendance fell at both parks. The opening of EPCOT Center arrested the trend at Walt Disney World for a single year. But by 1983 attendance was again slipping in Orlando.

Walt Disney, who had enjoyed a cozy relationship with executives of all three television networks, had abhorred advertising. If one of his parks needed a boost in attendance, he could always convince NBC, ABC, or CBS to air a special celebrating Mickey's birthday or a Disneyland anniversary. Even with attendance slipping, Card Walker followed Walt's lead. There would be no advertising at any Disney theme parks, he decreed.

Nor would there be many price increases. Like Walt, who initially had not wanted to charge any admission to Disneyland, Walker worried that raising ticket prices would soil Walt Disney Productions' reputation as a "friendly company." Walker's financial people assured him that inflation was rising faster than Disney's ticket prices. Unfazed, he argued that higher admission prices would only exacerbate the attendance decline.

"He had his own internal thermometer that told him when prices were too high or too low," recalls Stan Kinsey, a Stanford M.B.A. who had joined Disney in 1980. Faced with recommendations to increase ticket prices, Card Walker would often admonish his staff the way Walt had once admonished him: "They're going to say these guys are crooks. That they are going to take us for all we're worth." (Card Walker refused several requests for an interview.)

Without a Walt Disney to plan the project, however, the company was forced to cut back on some of Walt's most ambitious plans. Although Walker forged ahead on building EPCOT Center, he scaled back Walt's grand plans for a city of the future. A 1971 master plan that had, among other things, called for the building of single-family homes and condos on 1,000 acres, was shelved. So, too, were Walt's plans to build several additional hotels within the 28,000-acre complex. With Roy Disney planning the project, Disney had managed to build three hotels in Orlando. But under Card Walker, a half-dozen others were delayed when the 1973 oil embargo dampened tourism in central Florida. A decade later, however, new hotels, with nearly 40,000 rooms, had been built in Orlando. Those hotels grabbed the lion's share of the area's $2 billion annual hotel market. None of the new hotels were built by Disney.

❖

By early 1984, Walt's nephew, Roy Disney, was an unhappy man. The 1.1 million shares of Walt Disney Productions stock that he owned were worth roughly $55 million—$30 million less than they had been worth only a year earlier. The company that brothers Walt and Roy Disney had built was in trouble. Despite the vast assets created by the two brothers—the treasury of old cartoons, the theme parks, and the huge Orlando real estate investment—the company was struggling. Even as Wall Street was enjoying one of its biggest rallies in years, investors had lost confidence in Card Walker and Ron Miller.

Over Roy Disney's objections, Ron Miller, at age 50, had been elected the company's chief executive at a board meeting on February 24, 1983. At the same board meeting, Card Walker had announced his intention to relinquish his position as chairman. However, he wanted to hold on to his chairmanship until May, so that he could preside over the opening of Tokyo Disneyland, a theme park that was to be owned and operated by the Oriental Land Co. under a licensing agreement with Walt Disney Productions.

Card Walker, however, didn't trust Ron Miller to run the company by himself. Before announcing his retirement, the 66-year-old Disney chairman had enlisted Ray Watson, a well-heeled California real estate developer, as vice-chairman. The 56-year-old Watson had first started working with the company in 1964, when Walt had called him in to review EPCOT Center's plans. Walker arranged that, when he did step down in April, it would be Watson, not Miller, who would assume the chairmanship. "At the time, I thought I needed someone to help me with . . . the areas, like real estate development, that I really hadn't done much with," recalled Miller.

Roy Disney had never thought well of Ron Miller, but the two men did agree that the first thing that needed to be fixed was the company's film studio. For years, Miller had argued with Walker that the company needed to develop a second label, geared to teenagers and adults. To prove his point, Miller had commissioned the polling firm of Yankelovich, Skelly & White to do a research study. The report showed that the Disney name was clearly identified with children's fare; one Chicago teenager said he "wouldn't be caught dead" going to a Disney movie but "looked forward to the day when he could take his children to see one."

Keeping the Disney name off the new label became crucial to Ron Miller. In 1980, in fact, he had tried in vain to convince Walker to buy another Hollywood studio. Enlisting Morgan Stanley, the company's investment banker, Miller wanted to buy Twentieth Century Fox. At the time, Fox was experiencing financial problems of its own. But it had also recently released a blockbuster, *The Empire Strikes Back*, the second of the *Star Wars* trilogy. Even so, Walker balked at the $650 million price for Fox. A year later Denver oilman Marvin Davis bought it for $725 million.

Ultimately, Card Walker relented. Miller was given approval to set up a second label that, after more than a year, was christened Touchstone Pictures. Initially, Miller assigned 27-year-old Tom Wilhite to head the new film company. A fresh-faced Iowa native who had never produced a film in his life, Wilhite had been working at Disney as a marketing executive. But the man he really wanted to run it was Michael Eisner, president of Paramount. Eisner and Barry Diller, Paramount's iron-fisted chairman, had turned the once laggard studio into Hollywood's hottest film company by producing such hits as *Saturday Night Fever* and *Raiders of the Lost Ark*.

Miller spent weeks courting Eisner. The problem was that Eisner wanted to run not only the film unit but Disney's theme parks as well. "Michael wanted to be president of the whole organization," says Miller. "I wanted him to just run the studio."

By spring 1984, Touchstone Pictures, now being run by former Fox production executive Richard Berger, was ready to release its first film. *Splash*, the tale of a mermaid in New York, starred Darryl Hannah and Tom Hanks. The project had been selected by Tom Wilhite, after several other Hollywood studios had turned it down. Disney executives were petrified about the brief nudity scenes described in the script. Fearing once more for the company's all-American image, they said they would agree to make the film only if the nude scenes were eliminated. In the end, Darryl Hannah's hair was strategically taped to her breasts, a compromise that satisfied the Disney executives.

Splash was the high point of Ron Miller's short tenure as Disney's chief executive. It grossed more than $69 million at the box office, at the time the most a Disney film had ever made. Only one event marred its release. On the same day *Splash* opened, Roy Disney submitted his letter of resignation, removing himself from the Disney board. Within two months, he ignited the takeover bid that would drive Ron Miller from his job.

❖

The planning for Roy Disney's assault on Walt Disney Productions began in his large house in Toluca Lake, an affluent neighborhood not far from the company's Burbank headquarters. Since leaving his position with the company in 1977, Walt's nephew had bought a cattle ranch in Oregon and a string of radio stations. He had even made a run at Fabergé, failing in a hostile bid to buy the perfume company. Each of these deals had been put together by Stanley Gold, a Los Angeles lawyer who since 1978 had run Roy's company, Shamrock Holdings. Gold's diversification of the company's holdings had doubled the $100 million Roy Disney had inherited from his father.

In early 1984, Stanley Gold's intention was to take over Walt Disney Productions. To put his plan in motion, one of Gold's first moves was to call Frank Wells, at the time a consultant to Warner Brothers. Wells had been a partner at the exclusive entertainment law firm Gang, Tyre & Brown that had hired Gold out of law school. The two men hadn't worked together long. In 1969, Wells left the firm to join Warner Brothers as head of the studio's West Coast business operations.

In the intervening years, Wells had climbed the corporate ladder at Warner, and by 1977 he had become president and co-chief executive of Warner Brothers. Quitting in 1982 to pursue a lifelong ambition, Wells left for a year to climb the tallest mountains on the seven continents. Returning to Hollywood hadn't been easy for Wells, however. When Gold called, Frank Wells had gone through most of his savings during the climbs and had been given a largely ceremonial job at Warner. Gold persuaded Wells to join him and Roy Disney in a group that came to be called informally the "brain trust." Wells's first move was to introduce Gold and Roy to Michael Milken, the Drexel Burnham Lambert junk bond king. Meeting with the "brain trust" in the predawn hours at his Beverly Hills office, Milken told the trio that he could raise the $2 billion that it would take to wage the takeover battle. But paying off the debt would almost certainly force Roy Disney to sell off huge pieces of the company that his father had helped build. "It was something that I just couldn't do," Roy Disney would say later.

In the end, Roy Disney backed away from the takeover bid, instead buying nearly 700,000 more shares. That was enough to give him more than 5 percent of the company. But it was New York financier Saul Steinberg who took Michael Milken up on his offer. From the headquarters of his Reliance Group Holdings in New York, Steinberg was already running a potent takeover operation. Among the companies he had pursued were Chemical Bank and Quaker State Oil Refining.

Nearly every time, Steinberg's prey got away. But Steinberg, a master at squeezing "green mail" payments from his targets, sold his stock and walked away with millions of dollars. In late March 1984, the raider announced that he had bought a 6.3 percent stake in Walt Disney Productions. Two months later, he launched a bid to buy 49 percent of the company, a deal valued at $1.2 billion. The idea of fighting a modern-era takeover was terrifying to the Disney board, which had little experience in the fast-changing world of raiders and junk bonds. Quickly hiring Morgan Stanley as their advisers, the board stumbled through a leveraged buyout that would allow it to buy back its own shares. Later, they scrambled to find a friendly suitor to acquire a large block of stock, thus putting the stock out of reach of Steinberg.

Operating under the code name "Project Fantasy," Morgan Stanley's team of investment bankers contacted longtime Disney partners such as Kodak and Coca-Cola. They also contacted fellow entertainment giants like MCA Inc. The search for a friendly suitor eventually led Disney chairman Ray Watson to contact Arvida, a Boca Raton land development company that Sid Bass had bought the year before from Penn Central.

An architect by trade, Ray Watson had spent most of his professional life with the Irvine Company, a large agricultural concern that had turned much of its 100,000 acres of land into planned communities of shopping centers and tract homes. Part of Disney's problem, Watson believed, was Card Walker's reluctance to develop more than just a small portion of the 28,000 acres the company owned in central Florida. Together with Arvida, which had an impressive record of building resorts and apartment buildings, Watson hoped to aggressively develop the Orlando property. In a dramatic departure from anything Walt had envisioned, Watson also drew up plans to build a hotel on a seven-acre plot of the company's land across the street from its Burbank studio. Watson had settled on Arvida after calling a former neighbor who had moved from California to Boca Raton to work for Arvida. Within weeks Sid Bass's top dealmaker, Richard Rainwater, proposed an even bigger alliance. Rainwater, who had been following Disney's stock for weeks, offered the Florida real estate company to Watson in a stock swap that would put a large piece of Disney's stock in Bass's hands.

In May, the Disney board approved the stock swap that gave Sid Bass 3.3 million shares, or 8.9 percent of Walt Disney Productions, in exchange for Arvida. Bass wanted the Disney stock in part to save on a huge tax bill for the deal, valued at $300 million. As part of the agreement, Arvida chairman Chuck Cobb also joined the board to vote the Bass's interest.

The Arvida merger also set in motion a chain of events that would eventually topple Ron Miller and put Michael Eisner and Frank Wells in charge of Walt Disney Productions. Angered that the stock swap had diluted Roy Disney's stake in the company, Gold and Roy Disney threatened to sue Disney's board. To mollify them, both men and Roy's brother-in-law, advertising executive Peter Daily, were invited to join the Disney board.

Finally on the inside of the company, Stanley Gold agitated for a shake-up. Allied now with Sid Bass, the two men argued bitterly with Ray Watson over another merger—with Gibson Greetings. Like the Arvida deal, Watson wanted to trade Disney's stock for the greeting card company.

The planned deal would put 15 percent of Disney's stock in the hands of the company, then controlled by former Treasury Secretary William Simon. The aim clearly was to dilute Saul Steinberg's stock even further. But anything that diluted Steinberg's stock would dilute Roy Disney's and Sid Bass's as well. Pressure by Gold and Bass finally forced Watson to drop the second merger.

Ultimately, to steer clear of Saul Steinberg, the Disney board paid $325.5 million for Steinberg's stock in June 1984. But it still had to face another likely takeover threat, this one from Minneapolis investor Irwin Jacobs. As Steinberg was dropping his pursuit of Disney, Jacobs had bought a 6 percent stake and was contemplating another run at the company.

To reduce the likelihood of another takeover attempt, the board voted for a decisive management change. In September, the board asked for and received Ron Miller's resignation.

No one questioned that Ron Miller was largely a scapegoat for the company's persistently poor box office performance. During Miller's short tenure as chief executive, the company had launched the Disney Channel at a cost of $82 million. Already, 1.4 million subscribers had signed up for the cable channel. Before he was dismissed, Miller had presented a five-year plan to revive the company, a plan that included putting many of the older Disney classics on videocassettes for the first time. However, during his tenure the company had also produced such big-budget box office disasters as *Tron* and *Something Wicked This Way Comes*. Only Miller's dismissal, Stanley Gold had argued, would convince Wall Street that the company was serious about turning itself around.

❖

Stanley Gold had been prepared for Ron Miller's departure for months. His first choice to head Disney was Frank Wells. The former Warner Brothers president had been a key adviser to Gold during the takeover battle and had also been approved by Sid Bass and his team. For one crucial meeting with a member of the team, top lieutenant Richard Rainwater, Wells had flown to Rainwater's vacation home in Nantucket. Wells was the kind of buttoned-down executive with whom Rainwater had dealt for years, a man grounded in the fundamentals of the balance sheet. But Wells had his own ideas. "If you can get Michael Eisner, he's the guy you should hire," Wells told Rainwater. Gold and Roy Disney had already been in touch with Eisner. Considered one of Hollywood's most creative executives, Eisner's name had come up often in discussions with Frank Wells and other Hollywood insiders. In late July, Roy Disney had called Eisner, who was visiting one of his three sons at a summer camp in Middlebury, Vermont. Eisner was interested. By early September, he, too, had been drawn into the "brain trust" that included Gold, Wells, and Roy Disney. September was also a fateful month for Paramount Pictures, Eisner's home for the past eight years. Despite its string of box office hits, Paramount hadn't been a happy place since the death of its parent company's chairman, Charlie Bluhdorn, the year before. The chairman of Gulf & Western had projected the image of a hardened businessman given to frequent tirades. But he had also maintained an almost fatherly relationship with both Eisner and Barry Diller. Bluhdorn's successor, Martin Davis, had no similar affection for his two Hollywood executives.

On September 8, the day after Ron Miller was fired at Walt Disney Productions, Barry Diller decided to leave Paramount Pictures to join Twentieth Century Fox. Even by Hollywood's standard, the deal Diller signed was breathtaking. Diller was to receive a base salary of $3 million a year and was eligible to receive 25 percent of any increase in value he brought to Fox's assets. All he had to do was turn around the fortunes of a studio that Denver oilman Marvin Davis had bought two years earlier and had proceeded to run into the ground.

Diller wanted Michael Eisner to join him at Fox. But Eisner, who had worked with Barry Diller at both ABC and Paramount Pictures, was tired of operating in Diller's shadow. And increasingly, the two men hadn't been getting along. A clause in Eisner's contract gave him the first opportunity to take Paramount's top job should Diller leave. Although he was still talking to Disney, Eisner wanted to know where he stood with Paramount. Eisner learned that Diller was leaving Paramount on Saturday morning, September 8, during a tennis match in which his son was playing. By Monday evening, Diller called Marty Davis in New York to inform him he was leaving Paramount.

Davis wanted Eisner to fly to New York that evening to settle the question of who would be running Paramount. At 2:00 P.M. Tuesday, Eisner boarded a Pan Am flight for New York along with Paramount production chief Jeffrey Katzenberg.

The two men arrived at New York's La Guardia Airport at 11:30 that evening and took a cab to Gulf & Western's high-rise office building overlooking Central Park. By midnight, they were meeting with Davis in his penthouse office.

The meeting turned into a late-night showdown. Unbeknownst to Eisner, Marty Davis had asked Diller to fire Eisner a few weeks earlier. Davis complained that Eisner wasn't enough of a team player. For all of the hit movies he brought to Paramount, Davis also felt that Eisner was a "smart-ass," someone who didn't project the air of seriousness that it takes to run a company. "Marty told me, 'Michael is like a kid,'" recalls Rich Frank, who headed Paramount's TV division. "'If you put blocks on the floor, he will just sit around and play with them.'" Frank was aghast. "I told him, 'Then I would spend all my money on blocks, and put them all over the place and get 20 people just like Michael.'"

Davis later denied making the statement. But during the late-night meeting with Eisner at his office overlooking Central Park, Davis told the Paramount Pictures president that he was undecided about who would get the studio's top job. One idea, Davis suggested, would be for Eisner to report to Frank Mancuso, Paramount's marketing chief. Eisner was adamant that he wouldn't.

The meeting may have been inconclusive, but that day's *Wall Street Journal* was not. At 4:00 A.M., Katzenberg called Eisner at his hotel to break the news to him. The financial newspaper was reporting that Frank Mancuso would be named the studio's chief executive. Eisner would be reporting to a new boss, one that only the day before had worked for Eisner.

Davis had been quoted in the article saying that, under Diller and Eisner, Paramount hadn't sold enough prime-time shows or made enough hit films. Davis later denied that he planted the story. But the article clearly showed the Gulf & Western chairman's contempt for Eisner. Later that day, Eisner resigned, walking away with a large settlement on his contract, including a deferred payment to cover a $1.2 million loan the company had given him to purchase his Bel Air home.

Eisner had other offers. Diller still wanted him at Fox. Leonard Goldenson, Eisner's old boss at ABC, offered to give him $300 million to launch their own film company. But Eisner wanted the Disney job that Roy Disney had dangled before him in July.

Walt Disney had been a personal hero for Michael Eisner. But, he decided, he would go there only on his own terms. If he were to join the company, he told Stanley Gold at a meeting at Gold's Beverly Hills home, it would be as Disney's chief executive or nothing.

Gold knew that Eisner and Barry Diller had been increasingly at odds with one another in their last few months at Paramount. That alone convinced Eisner that he no longer wanted to be the number two executive at a studio. And, if he wasn't willing to work for Frank Mancuso, he certainly wasn't going to be the number two person at Disney. Besides, Eisner told Gold, Disney needed a creative person at its helm. It had been Walt, not Roy, who had endowed the company with the assets that had built the company.

Later, meeting at Frank Wells's Beverly Hills home, Eisner and Wells decided that they would seek the Disney job as a team. With his bent for creativity, Eisner would be the chairman and chief executive. Wells, more comfortable with the nitty-gritty and fine-print details of running a company, would be president and chief operating officer. "I love the business of business," Wells had told Disney's chairman, Ray Watson, at a meeting at Wells's home.

Sid Bass, however, didn't want Michael Eisner to run the company. Bass had been told about Frank Wells by Richard Rainwater, who admired his no-nonsense manner and business background. Eisner was a member of the Hollywood crowd, a group for which Sid Bass held no particular admiration. Richard Rainwater, who had once helped George Lucas in a business deal, had checked Eisner out with the *Star Wars* filmmakers. The reviews came back positive. Michael Eisner knew how to pick hit films, George Lucas said. But Rainwater still felt that he had no business experience. He lacked the depth, he told Sid Bass, to run a $1.7 billion company.

Eisner learned of Bass's reluctance from Frank Wells. During most of the Disney takeover battle, Wells and Gold jogged together at the UCLA track not far from Eisner's home. On this morning in mid-September, however, Wells had called Sid Bass before heading to the track. Together with Gold, Wells had changed the routine and jogged over to Eisner's house instead.

The two men showed up at 8:00 A.M., just as Eisner's three boys headed off to school. "It's over," said Frank Wells. "Sid isn't buying it." Eisner got a sinking feeling. But he wanted one last shot at the job. Deciding to make one last pitch, Eisner, his wife Jane, Wells, and Gold all headed for the den. There, Eisner dialed Bass's Fort Worth office.

"I think you're making a mistake, Sid," Eisner said into the speakerphone, his voice rising. "It's going to take a creative person to run this company." Pacing in front of the speaker, his arms flailing as his agitation grew, Eisner added: "Look at the history of America's companies. They have always gotten into trouble when the creative people are replaced by the managers." Walt Disney Productions, Eisner continued, couldn't allow that to happen to it.

"I thought that was a little high-handed," Bass recalled later. But, as he thought about it, the Fort Worth dealmaker said, the more Eisner's argument started to make sense. To run a company like Disney, Bass realized, Eisner would have to be given the freedom to choose the projects he thought best for the company. That made sense to Bass, who was now thinking of filmmaking as analogous to his own rough-and-tumble world of deal making. "In my business, you can't make a deal, and then say 'I'm going to take it to a committee,'" Bass said later. "He had to have the final word. That's when I first thought Michael was CEO material."

Wells spoke to Bass next, echoing his approval of the arrangement. That was good enough for Sid Bass, who had already trusted Wells's judgment enough to let him run the company. If Wells thought Eisner was the better man for the job, Bass would trust his judgment once more. Bass's endorsement proved to be the crucial factor in securing the two top jobs for Eisner and Wells. At the time, the brain trust had been furiously lobbying the Disney board for support. Eisner enlisted the support of board members Sam Williams and Ignacio Lozano. Wells had flown in Roy Disney's airplane to Arizona, where Card Walker was on a fishing trip. Besides this lobbying effort, there had been another encouragement: Steven Spielberg had called Ray Watson to lend his support to Eisner.

There were other candidates for the job. Dick Nunis, who was in charge of the theme parks, had written to Ray Watson proposing himself for the top job. Arvida head Chuck Cobb had tried unsuccessfully to enlist support from Sid Bass and Richard Rainwater for his candidacy. Disney chairman Ray Watson was leaning toward Dennis Stanfill, a one-time vice-president for finance at Times Mirror Corporation who had been chairman at Fox before Marvin Davis arrived. Board member Phil Hawley was pushing hard for Stanfill. But as the tide began to turn toward Eisner and Wells, Ray Watson decided to back the two men as well.

Sid Bass's strong endorsement won over any board members who were still undecided. By Friday, September 21, the night before the Disney board meeting, Stanley Gold's troops had won. The vote was unanimous. The last vote to fall into the Eisner-Wells column had been that of Card Walker, who had stood by Walt's side for so many years. Fittingly, it was Card who nominated Michael Eisner and Frank Wells to run the company. It was a choice, Walker thought, that even Walt would have approved.

CHAPTER

Someday My Prince Will Come

The 13-member board of directors of Walt Disney Productions — 12 men and 1 woman — met in special session five times during the summer of 1984. Each session was called because of a crisis. The sixth and final special session of the year began at 11:07 A.M. on Saturday, September 22. This time the session marked the beginning of a new era for the company.

As at each of the previous meetings, the board settled into their green chairs in the wood-paneled conference room on the second floor of the Animation Building. The room, like much of the company, had changed little since Walt's death. A slightly faded black-and-white photograph of a stern-looking Walt and his brother Roy peered from the bleached-wood wall.

For most of the summer, the Animation Building had been swarming with the crisis managers — lawyers, investment bankers, and worried Disney board members — all defending the company from takeover. Walt had planned the building, located in the center of the lot at the intersection of Mickey Avenue and Dopey Drive, as the focal point of the Burbank studio he built in 1939. The corner office that he had occupied for 26 years was on the third floor, not far from where the cartoonists worked. By early 1984, the cartoonists outgrew the working space and moved to another building. Only Disney's executives remained.

On this warm, sunny day in late September, the mood was far more upbeat than it had been for months. The company faithful were prepared for the transfer of power they hoped would permanently put the company out of the reach of raiders.

Ray Watson called the meeting to order. Only 9 of Disney's 13 board members were present. Three others were connected by telephone. Watson, the California land developer who had presided over Disney's takeover defense, opened by describing the company's vulnerability. Irwin Jacobs still held nearly 8 percent of the company's stock. More important, he was on the verge of buying up more, intensifying the likelihood of a hostile takeover.

Only someone with support from both the Walt and Roy sides of the family could pull the company together, the Disney chairman told the board members. Watson had initially favored former Fox chairman Dennis Stanfill for the job. But after meeting with Michael Eisner and Frank Wells, the Orange County land developer had switched his support to the slate proposed by Roy Disney and his attorney Stanley Gold. One by one, each of the Disney directors had pledged similar support for the duo.

"It is time to get on with the next chapter for this company." Card Walker's voice came from a speakerphone sitting in the middle of the 20-foot-long conference table. Walker, in Arizona on a fishing trip, had been visited the previous night by Frank Wells and promised Wells that he would nominate Eisner and Wells to run the company. By 11:40 A.M., the two men had been chosen to head one of Hollywood's most fabled and troubled companies.

Eisner and Wells had been awaiting news of the board meeting at Eisner's Bel Air home since early that morning. It was Stanley Gold, Roy Disney's lawyer, who called them to break the news. "Congratulations," Gold said excitedly into the phone. "Now it's time to get to work."

❖

In many ways, Michael Eisner was the antithesis of Walt Disney. Unlike Walt, whose father had struggled financially, Eisner had been born and bred in affluence. He had spent most of his young life in a sprawling third-floor apartment on Park Avenue in New York City. His grandfather founded the American Safety Razor Company, and then ensured his family's wealth by selling it to Philip Morris. His other grandfather, a friend of Teddy Roosevelt, had made his fortune with a clothing factory that made parachutes for the army and uniforms for the Boy Scouts.

Eisner's father Lester, a Harvard-trained lawyer, had expanded the family fortune by investing in New York real estate. A Republican contributor, Lester Eisner had also served as a top housing official in the Eisenhower administration.

At home, young Michael was taught self-discipline. He and his sister were required to read for two hours each day before they could watch one hour of television. Entertainment for the Eisner family meant Broadway. Starting with *Oklahoma* for Michael's second birthday, every special occasion was marked with a trip to the theater.

Above all it was formal existence. Strict etiquette was observed during dinner at the Eisner home, where Michael was required to wear a jacket and tie. At an early age he was shuttled to dance school where the young boys wore blue blazers and the girls white gloves with their party dresses. Tall and gawky, Michael Eisner didn't like the classes much.

Even in the midst of affluence, however, the young Eisner was taught the value of a dollar. The family car may have been driven by a chauffeur, but the car was a station wagon instead of a Cadillac. "My grandfather drove across the Willis Avenue Bridge to save the toll," Eisner once told a reporter. "My father believed I should know what I had, but one of the lessons that I learned was that you do not spend capital."

It was years before Eisner would gravitate toward entertainment. At the Lawrenceville School, the ultraexpensive New Jersey boarding school he attended, "Mike the eyes," as he was known, was a good student. He tried, and largely failed, at sports, playing on the junior varsity tennis and basketball teams with little success.

Eisner had fleeting success as an actor. He was a member of the Periwig theatric club, and in his senior year he won a lead role in *The Caine Mutiny*. But he developed a case of spinal meningitis two weeks before the show and never made the opening curtain. Although he recovered from the disease, he never won another acting part.

At Denison University, a small liberal arts college in Granville, Ohio, he enrolled as a premedical student. His teachers remember him as an average student, given more to lengthy philosophical discussions than to the grind of schoolwork. By his junior year, he was hit with the theater bug again, undoubtedly influenced by a pretty coed who was a theater major. Soon his premed studies were forgotten, and Eisner switched to theater courses.

Eisner, who was a basically shy person, had had enough of acting. Instead, he concentrated on writing plays. One, entitled *To Stop a River*, was written to impress the same coed. The play, about the loose morals of a woman from Columbus, was performed by the school's thespian club to mixed reviews. After graduating, Eisner spent two months in Europe, writing plays in longhand. His father's secretary typed the plays when Eisner returned to New York, but only one agent—who died soon after—would ever read them.

By now, it was time to get a job. Eisner had used his family connections to get his first job in show business, as an usher at NBC in 1963. After graduating, he was promoted to a job as a clerk who kept track of the number of times that commercials aired. On weekends, he worked for the NBC radio station, giving out traffic reports. Moving to CBS, he inserted commercials into their proper slots for children's programs, the *Ed Sullivan Show*, and *Jeopardy*.

Eisner's big break in show business came in 1966 when a young television executive named Barry Diller read one of the more than 200 résumés Eisner had sent out. At the time, Diller was a 24-year-old vice-president at ABC, then a fledging network. Launched a decade earlier by former Paramount attorney Leonard Goldenson, ABC was a distant third among TV's "Big Three." With only two dozen TV stations signed up as affiliates, the shows it aired covered less than 50 percent of the country.

With little to lose, Diller and Eisner could be innovative with ABC's programming. Together, they created such innovations as the movie-of-the-week and the miniseries. Eisner's greatest attribute for the work, it turned out, was that he genuinely enjoyed even simple forms of pop programming—sit-coms and cartoon shows. It put him at an advantage. When he was given responsibility for Saturday morning programming in 1969, Eisner didn't need to guess what kids wanted. He simply looked for what he liked.

At the time, Saturday morning was ruled by cartoons based on animal characters like Mighty Mouse and Atom Ant. Eisner wanted to try something different. He had heard about a singing group called the Jackson Five and flew to Las Vegas to hear them. He quickly signed the singing brothers to an ABC contract. The Jackson Five cartoon series caught on, as did another cartoon series that Eisner added based on the singing Osmond Brothers. Within three years, ABC had the top-ranked Saturday morning schedule.

Within five years, Eisner was put in charge of ABC's prime-time schedule. There, he put on shows like *Happy Days* and *Welcome Back, Kotter*. Critics panned the shows as cartoonlike in their appearance. Eisner used many of the same storytelling techniques that he had practiced for Saturday morning cartoons—the importance of story line, character development, and conflict.

By the time ABC emerged as the top-ranked network on the air, Eisner had left to join Barry Diller at Paramount Pictures. (Diller left ABC in 1974, Eisner two years later.) At Paramount, the two men earned a reputation as Hollywood's most creative executives. During their eight years together, Paramount turned out an unprecedented string of hits like *Raiders of the Lost Ark* and *Saturday Night Fever*. In 1978, two years after Eisner arrived, Paramount led the "big seven" studios with nearly one-quarter of the nation's box office, propelled by hits like *Grease* and *Heaven Can Wait*. For six years, the studio never fell below second in market share.

The Diller team at Paramount not only made hit movies. They also challenged the way Hollywood worked. By the 1970s, other studios had become little more than banks that financed projects brought to them by powerful talent agents—packages that arrived already assembled and ready to shoot, complete with directors, stars, and script. Paramount refused to pay the agents' prices. Instead, Diller demanded that his executives assemble each movie piece by piece, the way Hollywood did it in the past.

While other studios scrambled for big-name stars and directors, Paramount believed that for a movie to be successful it needed the right story line. The story lines could be embarrassingly simple—the underdog makes good, such as *Bad News Bears* or *Flashdance*, or a fish out of water, like *Beverly Hills Cop*. But the movies sold tickets, and lots of them.

There have been arguments since over who was responsible for Paramount's success during those years. Unquestionably, the studio reflected the personality of Barry Diller, a desk-pounding executive who was a throwback to the Samuel Goldwyn days of making movies. Polite meetings, Goldwyn felt, make polite movies that no one wants to see. At Paramount, Diller demanded tension. Meetings could be loud and angry. To make a movie, studio executives had to defend their projects with a passion that would convince Diller and Eisner that their plan was worth the millions it would cost to produce.

Diller and company could be just as brutal on superstar directors who worked for them. One who learned the hard way was director John Avildsen. Normal Wexler, a brilliant but sometimes eccentric writer, turned in what Paramount executives thought was a riveting screenplay for *Saturday Night Fever.* Diller gave it to Avildsen, who proceeded to rewrite the script. It didn't matter that Avildsen had just been nominated for an Oscar for his work on *Rocky.* His rewrite dampened the script, Diller and Eisner both thought. The superstar director was unceremoniously fired. Paramount went back to the original script. And they gave the film to director John Badham, who turned it into one of the biggest hits of 1977.

Paramount, the story went, was the only studio in town that gave you the green light for a movie and then dared you to make it. It was a culture that descended from Charlie Bluhdorn, the Austrian-born self-made millionaire whose Gulf & Western Industries conglomerate had saved Paramount from raiders in the late 1960s. Bluhdorn could be blunt with a short temper, and he railed against unnecessary expenses and bottom-line losses. No film was so expensive that Paramount needed to make it, he insisted. It was a lesson that both Barry Diller and Michael Eisner learned well.

Michael Eisner never lost the fear of spending money that was drummed into him by Bluhdorn and Barry Diller. After becoming Paramount's president, he insisted that his studio negotiate harder than any other in Hollywood. Early in his tenure at Paramount, Eisner learned about the script for *Airplane* over dinner one night with a friend.

Excusing himself from the meal, Eisner ordered production chief Don Simpson to find the script. But before Eisner would buy the rights to the comedy he insisted that the film be made for $3 million. Later, when its directors wanted to make changes that would increase the budget, Eisner threatened to pull the plug. "We had already tried every other studio in town," recalled Jerry Zucker, the comedy's director. "He knew he had us over a barrel." The film was eventually made for $3.5 million and returned more than $40 million to the studio.

Diller, who championed such high-concept films as *Reds,* was known for his elitist tastes. Eisner had the common touch, the ability to strike the right chord with the viewing public. Not all Eisner's projects worked out, however. He turned down scripts for the hit movies *Private Benjamin* and *The Big Chill* but approved the woeful *White Dog,* the tale about a failed attempt to deprogram a racist dog that only bites white people. But in an industry in which the failures outnumber the hits, Diller and Eisner's track record was among the best in Hollywood.

It was Eisner who convinced Barry Diller to make *Raiders of the Lost Ark* in 1981, despite the then-lofty budget of $17.5 million. At the time, every studio in town had passed on the project, wanting no part of the huge percentage of the profits demanded by its two creators, George Lucas and Steven Spielberg. Eisner saw a Saturday morning adventure show for the big screen and wanted it. The movie sold nearly $300 million worth of tickets, netting $115 million for the studio.

Trained in the classics, Eisner also found a way to adapt more traditional stories to modern-day entertainment. He approved the idea for *Footloose*, a tale about a town that outlawed dancing, because it reminded him of two works by Nathaniel Hawthorne: the classic *The Scarlet Letter* and a lesser known short story called "The Maypole of Merrymount." "My wife thought I was ridiculous," Eisner later told a reporter. "She told me that if I ever talked about any connection to Hawthorne, I was a schmuck." *Footloose* was only a modest hit, but it hardly diminished Eisner's reputation as an idea man. For years, Paramount executives retold the story of how Eisner got the idea for the blockbuster film *Beverly Hills Cop* after he had been stopped by a Beverly Hills policeman for speeding. (Several other Paramount executives, including its producer Don Simpson, have also taken credit for coming up with the idea.) During a one-hour layover at an airport, he came up with the idea for the TV show *Happy Days*.

Despite their ability to turn out hits together, no two people were as different as Barry Diller and Michael Eisner. Diller, short and bald, was a bachelor who reveled in fancy clothes and traveled the Hollywood scene with trendy friends like actor Warren Beatty and designer Calvin Klein. Eisner, tall and gawky, cared little about his appearance or the fast lane. Married with three young sons, Eisner would just as soon leave the office early to attend an Indian Guides meeting with one of his boys.

Diller and Eisner battled often. But even his boss admired Michael Eisner's toughness. The most oft-repeated story about Paramount's sharp-elbowed approach centered on Lawrence Gordon, who had produced the movie *48 Hours* for Paramount. Eisner ordered locks put on Gordon's Paramount office when he learned that Gordon had been talking to two other studios about his next film. It didn't matter to Eisner that he and Gordon were close friends. What mattered was that Gordon had a contract with Paramount and a moral commitment to their friendship. And in Eisner's view, that meant that his studio had the first right to see any new projects Gordon might develop. Gordon eventually sued Paramount, but the two sides later settled the case amicably.

Many people in Hollywood chose not to work with the Diller-Eisner team. But in the eight years that the two men worked together, Paramount's profits increased sevenfold. Paramount became a leader not only in hit movies but in network TV programs like *Cheers* and *Family Ties*, syndication, and home video.

Eisner's mixture of creative inspiration and tightfisted practices no doubt won the approval of the shell-shocked Disney board. So, too, did his track record at ABC and Paramount, two once-sickly companies that had responded to the tonic prescribed by Barry Diller and Michael Eisner. "I always came in at the bottom," Eisner told Ray Watson during his interview for the Disney job. "I liked that. You can't fall off the floor."

❖

Believing that Michael Eisner had the creative genius that Walt Disney Productions needed, the Disney board was also hoping that Frank Wells had the business acumen to cure many of the company's other ills. Unconsciously perhaps, the board was also recreating the original team of Walt and Roy Disney. Eisner, with his proven record for recognizing mass appeal, would be the font for the ideas needed to reclaim the "Disney magic." As Roy had done three decades earlier, Wells would provide the wherewithal necessary to translate the ideas into reality.

In contrast to Eisner, who had grown up in affluence, Frank Wells had been raised in the blue-collar tradition of hard work and unwavering devotion. The son of a navy commander, young Frank had, during his teenage years, moved with his family from Coronado, California, to Arlington, Virginia, and then back to California. To supplement his weekly allowance, he worked as a newspaper carrier, grocery delivery boy, and swimming pool attendant. Driven to succeed, he accumulated in only two years the 18 Boy Scout merit badges needed to become a Life Scout, acquiring that status a full year sooner than specified by the manual.

Not a naturally gifted athlete, he nevertheless made the Coronado High School football and basketball teams, winning a letter for basketball while playing on the 1949 team that took the league championship. At Pomona College, a small liberal arts school 30 miles outside Los Angeles, he was a third-string basketball player. Finding the prospect of graduating without a letter unacceptable, he made sure he got one: He played goalie on the school's experimental water polo team, which competed only with local colleges.

But it was as a student that Wells excelled. He majored in government and was elected to Phi Beta Kappa. In his senior year, he won the Renta Gurley Archibald Scholarship Award for the highest grade point average in the senior class. A chronic joiner of clubs and other groups, he was a member of the student-faculty executive council and chaired the judiciary council, which passed judgment on suspected cheaters. When the quality of the school's food service became an issue, Wells joined the dining hall committee.

Upon graduation, he went to Oxford's Brasenose College, where he studied jurisprudence as a Rhodes scholar. After two years in the army he enrolled in Stanford Law School, where he edited the law review and graduated with honors.

By 1960, Wells had begun his climb through the entertainment community. Moving to Los Angeles, he joined the law firm of Gang Tyre & Brown, a small but highly respected firm that represented such heavyweights as Bob Hope and George Burns. His first case was a notable one. He filed a lawsuit on behalf of actor James Garner, who wanted to get out of his contract with Warner Brothers.

Wells won the case, but later joined Warner Brothers. In 1969, he became the studio's vice-president of West Coast operations. The position brought with it a depth of new responsibility. In addition to overseeing many of the business dealings of the studio's talent, he was also responsible for supervising negotiations on contracts involving script acquisitions and film distribution.

By 1973, Wells was named president of Warner, running the business side of the company. In one of his earliest coups, he haggled for months with producer Alexander Salkind before signing a contract to produce the film *Superman*. Later, he signed the distribution deal that brought 1981 Academy Award winner *Chariots of Fire* to Warner Brothers.

By 1982, however, Wells had left Warner in a move that startled Hollywood and established his reputation as something of an eccentric. He wanted to pursue a lifelong ambition, a dream that had first struck him when he climbed Kilimanjaro during his days as a Rhodes scholar. Wells set off, with Utah ski operator Dick Bass (no relation to Sid Bass), to climb the tallest mountain on each of the seven continents. Bass succeeded. Wells, despite a near fatal fall, climbed all but Mount Everest. A severe storm forced him to turn back only one day before he reached the top. Well's mountain-climbing exploits were indicative of the occasionally offbeat activities that lurked behind his buttoned-down image. Well's daily work schedule began at 6:00 A.M., when one of his two secretaries would arrive at his Beverly Hills home. Her first job of the day was to cope with the many letters she found strewn about, a result of Well's habit of taking home a shopping bag full of correspondence. Later at Disney, he donned scuba gear to go underwater and cut the ribbon to open the Living Seas exhibit at EPCOT Center. He also surprised an annual meeting of 2,000 Disney employees who had gathered at a giant sound stage on the Burbank lot. From the rear of the sound stage, following a stunt woman dressed as Tinker Bell, Wells slid down a 200-foot wire to the stage.

❖

After getting Stanley Gold's congratulatory telephone call the Saturday they were elected to head Disney, Michael Eisner and Frank Wells got into Wells's gray Mercedes 450 SL to drive the eight miles from Eisner's home to the Lakeside Country Club, not far from the studio. A quick celebratory luncheon with Gold and most of the Disney board was planned at the club, with outgoing chairman Ray Watson the host.

Their first official day on the job would be Monday. By midafternoon, however, Wells and Eisner were unofficially at work at the Disney studio. Joe Flom, the Skadden, Arps law firm managing partner who had been advising the company during its takeover fights, briefed them on the Irwin Jacobs situation. The Minneapolis investor, Flom told the two, might soon buy more company stock to supplement the nearly 8 percent that he already controlled. A Jacobs takeover effort was still very possible, the lawyer told Eisner and Wells.

The end of the fiscal year was a week away, and the two new Disney executives also wanted to dig into the company's balance sheet. After their session with Flom, the new Disney team went straight into a second meeting, with another of Disney's outside lawyers. Joe Shapiro was a partner with the Los Angeles office of Donovan, Leisure, Newton & Irvine. Shapiro had begun advising the Disney team late in the takeover battle. He gave Eisner and Wells a run-through on the early numbers that the company expected to report. The two men went home with dozens of company documents.

On Sunday morning, the day after their election, the two new Disney executives again went into a high-level huddle, behind the gates of Eisner's large white home. There, the two men began to wade through the mountain of financial documents that Joe Shapiro had given them.

Later that afternoon, they took their families on a sight-seeing tour of the Burbank lot. With Eisner was his wife Jane and their three sons. Wells took along his wife Luanne.

The lot was practically deserted at the time. However, the two families did meet Erwin Okun, Disney's vice-president of corporate communications. Okun, a silver-haired former *Newsday* business editor and an IBM press relations executive, had come to Disney in 1981. During the takeover fights, Okun had been one of Ron Miller's closest allies. Even as the Disney board had been deciding Miller's fate, Okun had worked with Miller on a five-page defense of his actions.

On this Sunday afternoon, Okun was preparing his own résumé, confident that the new management would be cleaning house—and, in particular, getting rid of Miller's allies. Eisner and Wells, however, didn't have housecleaning on their minds, at least not yet. In fact, Okun was fated not only to be retained but elevated to senior vice-president three years later.

The stroll through Disney's campuslike lot was a peaceful one for the two new corporate executives. It was also the last time for several months that Michael Eisner and Frank Wells would have time for themselves and their families.

CHAPTER

Rebuilding the Magic Kingdom

T he Fort Worth headquarters of Bass Brothers Enterprises is an imposing building, a black steel-and-glass high-rise that looms over
Main Street. The Bass suite of offices on the 32nd floor is a testimony to
power and wealth. Paintings by Jasper Johns and Frank Stella decorate
the walls. Deep-piled oriental rugs and antique desks adorn many of the
nearly two dozen offices, each occupied by a high-powered deal maker
taking home at least $1 million a year.

Michael Eisner had been wanting to meet Sid Bass, Disney's largest
stockholder. He called Bass on Monday morning, September 24, 1984,
two days after he and Frank Wells were elected. On the surface at least,
the meeting was social. Eisner and Wells wanted to thank Sid Bass and his
organization for their support. Without it, Eisner knew, he might never
have won Disney's top job. But the new Disney executives also knew that,
for all their Texas gentility, Bass and his group would want to see results.
The first step would be to make a strong presentation, mostly to convince
Bass that he had definite ideas on where to take Walt Disney Productions.

On Tuesday, Eisner flew from Burbank to Fort Worth, along with
Wells and Mike Bagnall, Disney's chief financial officer. Bagnall had
been with the company for 23 years, working his way up from an
accountant. For most of the past year, Bagnall had weathered the

takeover battles with Ray Watson and Roy Disney. Only near the end had he been largely supplanted by Disney's investment bankers, Morgan Stanley & Co.

It took the three Disney executives less than 10 minutes to get from the Worthington Hotel to Bass headquarters. Once they arrived at the 32nd floor, Eisner and his small team were escorted to a cramped conference room down the hall from Sid Bass's office, where the Bass brothers, surrounded by a tiny circle of their closest advisers, often mapped out their battle plans. The walls were covered with white laminated boards that were often cluttered with the remnants of some Bass strategy, written with green markers on the white background.

Today, however, the walls had been wiped clean before Eisner and his small party arrived. Already seated at the oval conference table was Irwin Jacobs, the short, stocky son of a Russian Jewish immigrant who still held a large block of Disney stock. Sid Bass had wanted "Irv the liquidator" at the meeting, and had sent his private Gulfstream to Minneapolis to ferry the raider. The gesture was less a courtesy than a necessary accommodation. Jacobs had been fretting that, if the meeting ran long, he would miss the start of Rosh Hashanah, the Jewish New Year.

"Irv the liquidator" was still a problem for Walt Disney Productions. The raider held nearly 8 percent of the company's stock. More important, he was making sounds indicating that he wanted more; the week before, he had told federal regulators that he was contemplating a bid for the entire company. Eisner and Wells had been briefed on Jacob's bid on Saturday, September 22, the same day they were elected by the Disney board. Joseph Flom, the Skadden Arps partner who had been adviser to Disney during the attempted takeover, had put it succinctly to the company's two new executives: Be careful of Irwin Jacobs.

Now, four days later, the Minneapolis raider was waiting for them. Rising from his seat at the conference table, Jacobs quickly extended his hand to the two new Disney executives. "I've been looking forward to hearing what you two have to say," he said, grinning up at the two taller men. "Very interested."

Sid Bass quickly made the other introductions, to his younger brother Lee and the Bass's longtime top strategist, Richard Rainwater. An olive-skinned man with dark curly hair, Rainwater ran the Bass organization's nonoil properties. Attracted by Disney's huge Orlando land holdings, Rainwater had studied Disney's financial numbers earlier that summer. It was Rainwater, more than anyone else in Bass's inner circle, who had pressed hardest for the Texan to buy Disney's stock. The potential for development of the company's Florida property alone was staggering, Rainwater had told his boss. If that didn't work, he added, "We could always sell it off."

Following Rainwater into the conference room was Al Checchi, a tall, slender man with darting eyes and a cocky manner. Checchi had joined the Basses only two years earlier, yet he was already a member of the inner circle. While working for Marriott Corporation, the large hotel chain, he had tried to lure the Bass organization into a deal to finance Marriott hotels. Fast-talking and gregarious, he had caught Rainwater's eye. It was the 36-year-old Checchi who had negotiated the deal to sell Arvida to Disney in June.

The last man to enter the room was Chuck Cobb, at age 48 the chairman of Arvida. Cobb, another newcomer to the Bass team, was not a member of the inner circle. A former chief operating officer for Penn Central, Arvida's parent company, he had been running the real estate unit since 1972. In 1983, he had blocked a Penn Central plan to sell off the company by making his own deal, and had brought the idea of buying Arvida to Richard Rainwater. When Arvida was subsequently sold to Disney, Bass and Rainwater sent Cobb to the Disney board, where he could vote the Bass interests. Sid Bass had never met Frank Wells before, but Bass's top aide, Richard Rainwater, had met with him a month earlier. Rainwater liked Wells's earnest nature and his strong business track record. Michael Eisner, he worried, was too much a part of Hollywood, not firmly rooted in the fundamentals of business. Sid Bass had only reluctantly agreed to support Eisner for the top job. Sid Bass knew even less about Michael Eisner. The only thing he knew about the new Disney chairman was what he had read in a recent *New York Magazine* article. Entitled "Hollywood's Hottest Stars," the article had portrayed the Paramount Studios team of executives as the smartest, most talented, and toughest in the industry. The author, Tony Schwartz, had lavished praise on Paramount chairman Barry Diller as shrewd and hard-edged. Eisner had been given credit as the man who picked *Raiders of the Lost Ark*, *Flashdance*, and *Footloose*, all huge hits.

In the pictures that accompanied Schwartz's article, Diller was shown squiring Debra Winger to a social event. In his picture, Michael Eisner had posed with his wife Jane and their three sons at their Bel Air home. "He seemed like a family man, an executive type, responsible," Bass recalled later. "I thought if I was going to choose somebody to run this company I would choose someone like that."

Eisner had presented five-year plans before, both at ABC and at Paramount. But he had had little time to prepare for his presentation to the Bass group. Bagnall had spent hours, during the flight from California, briefing Eisner on the company's financial situation. Still it would be some weeks before Eisner and the new team of executives he intended to bring in would complete their own assessment of the company and its assets.

Eisner started his presentation stressing that he had faced a similar situation at Paramount. Annual profits had increased to more than $120 million nearly a decade later, up from $30 million when Diller and Eisner had joined. "We think we can do the same thing again with Disney," Eisner said.

In many ways, the new Disney chief told the group, Disney was a company ready to be exploited. The home video market, little more than an afterthought to Hollywood five years earlier, had become a major industry, grossing $2 billion a year for Hollywood studios. Other companies were making millions of dollars every year, putting out lightweight action films, horror films, and other B movies. Disney, with its wealth of animated classics and Mickey Mouse cartoons, had only begun to scratch the surface of its own potential.

Growing nearly as fast as home video sales were sales of syndicated television shows, the new Disney chairman told the Texans. The proliferation of independent television stations throughout the country had sparked a bidding war for old sit-coms and movies. In a shortsighted attempt to boost its year-old Disney Channel, the old managers had kept Disney's classics off the market, standing on the sidelines as the market exploded. "There's a couple of hundred million dollars there alone," Eisner told the Texas investors.

Writing in a green felt pen on the white walls, Eisner detailed his plans for getting Disney back into television production, and specifically onto Saturday morning television, where lesser companies were making a fortune with cartoon shows. The Bass team already knew much of what Eisner was presenting, but they also knew that Michael Eisner was a maker of hits. More than anything else, they wanted to hear how the new Disney chairman intended to turn the company into another Paramount Pictures. Most keenly interested was Richard Rainwater. In the past year, Rainwater had gotten to know several Hollywood producers, including George Lucas. "You're going to sign up George Lucas, Steven Spielberg, and guys like that, aren't you?" Rainwater demanded.

Eisner had worked with Lucas and Spielberg before, on *Raiders of the Lost Ark*, the very movie that had, in fact, certified Michael Eisner as one of Hollywood's golden boys. Eisner knew that both Lucas and Spielberg were going to make more hits in the future, but he warned the Bass group that neither man would come cheaply. In present-day Hollywood, a filmmaker of the caliber of George Lucas could demand—and get—15 percent of a film's profits along with a fee of $5 million more. "The trick in this business is to find the next Steven Spielberg or George Lucas," Eisner stressed. At Paramount and ABC, Diller and Eisner had discovered people like Garry Marshall, who created *Happy Days*, and James Brooks, who made *Taxi*. At Disney, said Eisner, again his idea would be to find potential superstars to sign them before they became able to command superstar salaries. Sid Bass, for one, was impressed. "These were smart guys," he told his associates afterwards. "One thing you can't hide is IQ."

The Bass organization had also been doing some figuring. Neither Eisner nor Wells knew much about real estate development or about running theme parks and hotels. The Texans, in contrast, had made a fortune from buying and selling hard assets, and knew how to evaluate their value and potential.

Disney was sitting on top of a mountain of choice Florida real estate. The Bass team had been flabbergasted because the previous management hadn't moved more aggressively to wring profits out of its theme parks and hotels. "The prices that the company has been charging at its theme parks are absurd," Sid Bass told Eisner and Wells. The $17-a-day ticket price for a day at either of the two theme parks—EPCOT Center or the Magic Kingdom—was ridiculously low, Bass said, especially compared to the $1,000 or more it often cost a typical family to get to Orlando and stay at a hotel for a few days. "Heck, it costs $17 or more to go to a tennis match and this is for a full day of entertainment," Bass stressed. "A skiing trip for the family was probably double the cost of going to Orlando."

Disney had also mismanaged its hotel business, the Bass group felt. Early in the takeover fight, when Ray Watson was first negotiating with Arvida, Al Checchi had flown to Orlando to tour Disney's hotel operation. Marriott, Checchi recalled, had signed a tentative agreement to build a hotel in Orlando in the early 1970s. When the oil embargo hit, Walker, fearing tourism would fall off as gasoline prices spiked, had called off the deal.

Checchi had helped finance the construction of several dozen Marriott hotels during his tenure. It had not taken Checchi long to notice the vast untapped potential of the Disney hotel operations—a potential that had been virtually ignored by the previous management. Disney had built no new hotels on its property since 1973. While Disney dawdled, Checchi said, Orlando was booming.

The number of hotels outside Disney's property had mushroomed from a couple of dozen in 1980 to more than 250. Still, guests would much rather be inside Disney's gates, Checchi stressed. While the Disney hotels were running at near their occupancy levels for most of the year, in nearby Orange and Osceola counties fewer than 70 percent of hotel rooms were taken.

"The prices the company has been charging down there in their hotels are absurd," Sid Bass told Eisner and Wells. A Hyatt Hotel outside Disney's borders, without benefit of being linked to the parks by Monorail, was charging as much as $10 a night more than a comparable Disney hotel, Bass told the new Disney executives.

Hiking ticket and hotel prices would have an immediate benefit to the company. A $1 increase increase in the admission price alone would increase the company's income by about $31 million a year. That would be enough to pay the production costs of two films.

Eisner and Wells agreed that the prices would have to go up. But they also knew that a dramatic increase in prices could prompt almost immediate complaints. Older Disney hands, including theme park chief Dick Nunis, had grown up in a corporate culture that placed such a high regard on customer satisfaction that they had shied away from abrupt price increases.

If the Disney executives didn't react, the press almost certainly would. Negative articles would surely follow, painting Eisner and Wells as opportunists eager to trample the image of kindly Uncle Walt. "They were afraid of a huge outcry in the newspapers, and afraid that people at the gate would throw a tantrum," recalled Sid Bass.

The meeting at Bass headquarters lasted nearly three hours, ending when the group had sandwiches and coffee together before the three Disney executives headed for home. Sid Bass felt he had gotten the right vibes from the new Disney management team. Eisner's plan for reviving the studio by competing for hot film properties without spending a fortune especially appealed to him. "I'm impressed with these guys," he told Rainwater outside the conference room after the session. "It's not often that you see management so open, someone who will talk like that to shareholders."

Rainwater concurred. The two men also agreed that they would give Eisner and Wells the time they needed to carry out their plan. "We're with you for five years," Bass told the two Disney executives before they headed off to the airport. "We're prepared to stand pat for five years before we sell anything we hold."

❖

Near the end of the meeting with Eisner and Wells in Fort Worth, Sid Bass had taken Irwin Jacobs with him down the hall to his office for a half-hour private meeting. "These guys know what they want to do," Bass told Irwin. He also reiterated what he had said to Rainwater about the openness of Eisner and Wells. "Plus, they're talented," he added. Bass told Jacobs he was willing to give the two men five years to put their ideas into action. "After five years, no one has a crystal ball," Bass said.

Bass also had a proposition for the Minneapolis investor. The two of them, Bass said, should jointly buy up more Disney shares on the open market. "No more fussing and fighting," Bass said. Jacobs said he was unsure what he wanted to do. He promised to call Bass after checking with the partners with whom he had made his initial Disney purchases.

Bass decided not to wait. A few days later he called Beverly Hills junk bond guru Mike Milken. With arbitrager Ivan Boesky, Milken had bought 1.52 million Disney shares during the heat of the takeover battle. Boesky had borrowed much of the money he needed to buy the Disney stock. Now, with Disney no longer deemed vulnerable to takeover and its stock falling, he wanted out. Paying $60 a share, $3.25 more than the stock was trading for at the time, the Bass group bought all of Boesky's shares.

Within moments after the Dow Jones ticker carried news of the Boesky transaction, Jacobs was on the phone to Bass, upset that Bass had moved without consulting him. He asked for half the stock. Bass refused. "I put up my own money and now, ex post facto, you don't get 50 percent," Bass said. By now, Bass no longer wanted Jacobs for a partner. He had been told that Jacobs was pressuring the Disney management to put a Jacobs intimate on the payroll as Disney's controller. "He wanted to be a bit of a thorn in management," says Bass. "He wasn't being as gentlemanly as he should be." Jacobs was also contemplating making another run for the company. He offered $65 a share for the Bass holdings, $5 more than the Basses had just paid for Boesky's position and around $8 more than the stock was then trading for on the open market. Bass declined. "I want to keep this stock; I think it's a good investment," he told Jacobs. Instead, Bass first offered Jacobs $60 a share for his 7.7 percent stake in the company, but then increased the offer to $61 a share.

A few hours later, "Irv the liquidator" accepted the offer, worth $181.1 million. "We are extremely pleased to have such enormously supportive investors owning such a large proportion of this company," Eisner and Wells said in a statement issued by the company after the Boesky transaction. By mid-October, the Bass group owned nearly 24.8 percent of the company.

❖

Two days after the Fort Worth meeting, Michael and Jane Eisner and Frank and Luanne Wells went to Orlando. Joining them later were Jeffrey Katzenberg and his wife Marilyn. Eisner and Katzenberg had worked closely together at Paramount. A week earlier, only hours after Eisner himself was hired by the company, Katzenberg had agreed to move to Disney to head the new studio operation.

In Orlando, the six travelers were met by Dick Nunis, Disney's burly and gregarious theme park head. Nunis had wanted to run the company, and had offered his services to Ray Watson during the final crisis days before Eisner and Wells were hired. A member of the Disney board as well, however, he had eventually voted with the other members for the Eisner-Wells team. Now Dick Nunis was playing tour guide to his two new bosses. "We've got a lot to show you down here," the theme park head said, his large hand gripping Eisner's.

Eisner and Wells wanted to see for themselves what they had inherited. At the time, the Orlando parks and hotels were contributing nearly two-thirds of the company's $1.7 billion in revenues. More important, according to the Bass group, increasing ticket and hotel prices was the quickest way to increase profits.

For the next three days, the Eisner group played tourist. Dick Nunis arranged for them to ride every ride, eat at every restaurant, and visit even the most remote souvenir stand. Each morning at 7:30 A.M., Nunis would send three cars for the group. Most evenings they returned at nearly midnight. Stealing away from the group, Eisner and his wife Jane visited the Hyatt Hotel that Sid Bass and Al Checchi had mentioned during the Fort Worth meeting. The Disney chairman wanted to see for himself whether the hotel measured up to a Disney hotel. Registering under his wife's maiden name, Breckenridge, the two checked into a room. Twenty minutes later, they left, dropping the key on the bed as they headed out the door. "You're right," Eisner told Sid Bass by phone that night. "They're charging a heck of a lot more than we are."

❖

The first days on the job were frenetic ones for Michael Eisner and Frank Wells. They could see that sorting out the maze of Disney programs and problems was going to take months, not days. Not long after they came into the company, they scheduled ritualistic staff meetings to bring them up to speed. Consumer products chief Bo Boyd, who had gone to Florida for a Disney tennis tournament with several of his international salespeople, quickly flew to Burbank. Theme park marketing chief Jack Lindquist flew in from England, where he was setting up an office to book tours to Orlando. Carl Bongirno and Marty Sklar, who ran the Imagineering unit, came over from their Glendale warehouse for lunch.

Eisner had to fly to New York to sign an agreement to market the Disney Channel to the half-million homes that get Cablevision service. The deal, which was thought to be potentially worth $75 million over the next decade, had been negotiated by Jim Jimirro, Ron Miller's Disney Channel head. On the six-hour flight back to California, Jimirro briefed Eisner on how the cable channel worked. Settling into Walt's old corner office on the third floor of the Animation Building, Michael Eisner began to return telephone calls, working his way through a pile of message slips that had been taken by Lucille Martin, the pleasant secretary who had worked for Walt near the end of his life and still ran the chairman's office. One of the first people Eisner called back was Sam Cohn, the New York–based vice-chairman of International Creative Management. Cohn was representing Paul Mazursky, the one-time Greenwich Village comic who had directed such hit films as *Bob & Ted & Carol & Alice* and had written *Harry and Tonto*. Cohn was peddling a Mazursky script, based on a French play, that Universal Pictures had backed away from making. The next day, the script for what became *Down and Out in Beverly Hills* was delivered to Eisner.

The new Disney chairman also called George Lucas. Eisner wanted to thank the *Star Wars* creator for his support during the takeover fight. Eisner had also promised Rainwater during the meeting in Fort Worth that he could call him soon after he returned to Burbank. Eisner asked Lucas to consider designing rides for the park, based on either *Star Wars* or *Indiana Jones*. Lucas found the offer intriguing. He

had grown up in Modesto, California, and had stood in line for Disneyland's opening in 1955. Within a week after he got Eisner's call, Lucas
made the trip to Glendale. There, accompanied by Imagineering head
Marty Sklar, he toured the rides the Disney engineers were planning for
the company's theme parks.

Frank Wells, meanwhile, was also returning telephone calls. One
came from Roland Betts, a New York lawyer who had tried to work with
Wells before. Representing director Richard Attenborough, Betts had
unsuccessfully tried to have Warner Brothers finance part of the costs of
making *Gandhi*. The film won the 1982 Academy Award, but few of its
outside investors made much money on it. Now Betts was running Silver
Screen Partners, a limited partnership that had raised $83 million to fi-
nance films to be made by Home Box Office, the pay channel. The
films had all flopped. With Disney eager to increase its film production,
Betts wondered whether Disney would be interested in a similar deal.

Bill Haber, a major partner of the powerful Creative Artists Agency,
called to see if Disney was interested in movie projects by former *Benson*
writer Susan Harris and her husband, Paul Junger Witt, who was the
producer of *Brian's Song*. They were also looking for a studio to back a
television show, the agent told Eisner, that NBC had already agreed to
air. The show, written by Harris, was about four older women living together in Miami.

Eisner and Wells had little trouble attracting proposals. Disney represented virgin territory, a studio with new leaders and plenty of holes to
fill. But Michael Eisner also knew that he and Frank Wells needed help.
Both men felt that Disney's existing upper management, never particularly deep in numbers anyway, had spent too many years being "Disney-
ized." The most important telephone calls Eisner had to make, the new
Disney executives also knew, would be the ones that would bring in a
team that could make their plans work.

CHAPTER

Team Disney

D isney's annual February meeting for shareholders has always been an elaborate affair. A glittery parade of Disney characters troops down the aisles, accompanied by upbeat music. Sometimes, the latest movie would also be shown. Mickey, dressed in black tuxedo jacket and red pants, hugs the children in the audience and poses with whole families that have come to hear how their company is doing. Minnie is there, as are Donald and Goofy, and maybe Snow White and the Seven Dwarfs. Traditionally, the shareholder meeting is held in Anaheim one year, in Orlando the next. A large arena is needed—large enough to hold the 5,000 or more stock owners who travel by car, plane, or camper to be there. To encourage Disney owners to spend a few extra days at the parks, the meetings are often held on either a Tuesday or a Thursday. Many shareholders do just what the company wants, shopping for Mickey Mouse ears and whirling around in rides like Space Mountain or the Mad Hatter Teacup.

The first shareholders meeting of the Eisner-Wells era, held at the 20-year-old Anaheim Convention Center across Katella Avenue from Disneyland, was no exception. Nearly 8,000 shareholders filed in to see the new management team. They cheered when Eisner told them that

George Lucas had joined the company to design rides and that Disney would soon be making Saturday morning cartoon shows for both CBS and NBC.

But Eisner and Wells were aware that the shareholders knew that the company had been through a troubling year. To add a little lightness, Erwin Okun, Disney's public relations vice-president, had put together a three-minute film to open the show. Stitched together from old Disney cartoons, Mickey's 1984 "Overture" portrayed New York investor Saul Steinberg as a snarling grizzly bear chasing Mickey Mouse, while Minneapolis financier Irwin Jacobs was shown as an angry bulldog snapping at Pluto's heels. Eisner and Wells were depicted as cavalry officers, riding to the rescue of the company.

In fact, from the moment they joined the company, the two men knew that they would need help in bringing Disney back from the brink to which the previous managers had sent it. Over the next few months, Eisner and Wells assembled a team of high-powered and successful executives unlike any a Hollywood company had ever put together before. This team was eventually dubbed "Team Disney."

To lure the best talent in Hollywood and the financial community, the Disney board had to reverse a philosophy predicated on years of low salaries and skimpy bonuses. Such cheapness was one of many carry-overs from Walt's era. The Disney brothers, like many family-owned companies, had refused to pay top dollar for talent. By the mid-1980s, however, Hollywood salaries were soaring. A director in Steven Spielberg's class could easily earn $5 million for a film, and hot box office actors were routinely pulling down $1 million or more.

So, too, were Hollywood's best executives. With bonuses, Barry Diller and Michael Eisner had each made more than $2 million at Paramount in 1983, while marketing chief Frank Mancuso was paid $800,000. In addition, Diller's contract had assured him 2 percent of Paramount's profits, while Eisner's had given him 1 percent of the earnings. When Diller went to Fox, his salary zoomed to $3 million with a bonus that would pay him 25 percent of the increase in Fox's stock value during his tenure.

Disney's pay scale, in contrast, was abysmal. Even when his contract was rewritten in early 1984, the salary of Disney chief executive Ron Miller had increased from only $390,566 to $500,000 a year, with no provision for bonuses and only some minor stock options. Disney's overall compensation structure was so low, in fact, that compensation consultant Graef S. ("Bud") Crystal refused to include Disney in his survey of industry salaries. His reasoning was that Disney salaries would pull down the industry average and affect other executive's ability to ask for higher sums." It had become legendary in Hollywood that those guys paid paltry salaries," says Stanley Gold. "You couldn't get competent people in front of the camera and behind the camera to work there. It was the place of last resort."

The salary issue had first been raised when Gold recruited Eisner and Wells as the management team he would try to sell to Disney's board. Gold, a longtime entertainment lawyer, knew that it would take hefty salaries to bring high-priced talent to the company. He also knew that the compensation package had to include a piece of whatever added profits the two could generate. Such arrangements were standard in the Hollywood that Disney had isolated itself from for so long.

The details of the final contract began to come together as Eisner and Wells drove to Gold's house at 6:00 A.M. in the morning on September 22, just before the board meeting at which they were hired. Sitting in the passenger seat as Wells drove, Eisner jotted figures down on a notepad. Neither man was interested in a lofty salary. Frank Wells, in fact, had offered at one point to take $1 a year in salary in return for a generous stock options plan.

Eisner and Wells were confident that Disney's stock, depressed in the aftermath of the failed takeover fight, would increase in value if the plans he and Eisner had discussed bore fruit. "We believe we can turn this company around and we're willing to gamble," Wells told Ray Watson during one session. "We'll take low compensation, but we want to be like investors. If we turn the company around, we benefit."

The contract that was eventually signed was based on Eisner's notes. He had been paid a $750,000 salary at Paramount and wanted the same at Disney. As Paramount's top executive, Barry Diller had gotten a bonus equal to 2 percent of any increase in the studio's earnings. By the same measure, Eisner wanted 2 percent of whatever improvement he brought to Disney. He also wanted stock options; he asked for 500,000 shares he recalls later, "because it was a nice round number."

Weeks later, the Disney board finalized the agreement. The salaries, $750,000 for Eisner and $400,000 for Wells, were modest by studio mogul standards. Eisner also got a special $750,000 bonus for "benefits he lost leaving his prior employment," while Wells was paid $250,000 "to partially reimburse him for obligations arising out of the termination of his prior employment."

Even with comparatively modest salaries, Eisner and Wells had an arrangement that gave them impressive upside potential. Each man would get a percentage of any increase in net income that the company provided beyond what it had managed during the Ron Miller and Card Walker regimes. During the previous five years, Disney's annual growth in net income had averaged just under 9 percent. Under their contracts, Eisner would get 2 percent of any amount over the 9 percent level—which amounted to roughly $100 million—while Wells would get 1 percent.

The two executives were eventually awarded stock option packages that were among the most lucrative ever granted by a U.S. company. Their contracts gave Eisner options on 500,000 shares and Wells 450,000. The two also won a special concession. Most companies set the price of the options at the market price when the options are awarded; Disney fixed the options at $55.60 a share, the average share price for the previous 50 days. That concession would make any stock price that much more lucrative to Eisner and Wells. (The stock options were increased to 510,000 for Eisner and 460,000 for Wells when the board of directors approved the contract in December, adding more shares to compensate for increasing the option price to $57.44 per share.)

To attract the kind of executives the company needed, Eisner and Wells told the board, they would have to loosen the purse strings. Reluctantly, the board agreed. In November, they approved a major overhaul of the company's meager bonus and stock options plans. A committee of the board's outside directors was empowered to issue options for up to 1.7 million shares, more than double the 800,000 shares the company had authorized in 1981.* The board also put in place a loan program for executives to lend them the money they would need to exercise stock options.

The board also give itself authority to award Disney executives hefty bonuses tied to performance. The first year, the board allocated $3.5 million in cash bonuses to be paid out during the next year. (In their first three years, the amount awarded was nearly $18 million.) Disney's stockholders approved the added incentive programs at the shareholder meeting in February.

These moves marked a radical departure from previous policies and practices of Walt Disney Productions. Besides the added stock incentives, Eisner and Wells also now had the ability to lure executives to

---

*Arvida had a separate $5 million incentive program remaining from before it was acquired.

Disney by offering salaries that would have made Walt wince. Nowhere was the need more pressing than in the movie studio. The previous year, Disney had released such duds as *Trenchcoat* and *Running Brave*. It was true that *Splash* was a hit in 1984, but the company had made only one other original film that year—*Country*, which took in less than $10 million, saddling the company with a substantial loss.

Michael Eisner had seen this kind of situation before. ABC had been languishing when he was hired, and so had Paramount Pictures. The turnaround at both places had been accomplished through a combination of hard work and innovative ideas. Eisner had an abundant supply of ideas, but turning those ideas into the hit films that Disney needed would also require creation of a corporate work ethic that bordered on the maniacal.

❖

The hardest worker Michael Eisner had ever seen was Jeffrey Katzenberg. Head of production at Paramount at age 31, Katzenberg was arguably Hollywood's most effective studio executive. Anyone who knew Eisner well also knew that Katzenberg often served as Michael Eisner's alter ego. Eisner deserved the credit he got for the ideas for *Footloose* and *Beverly Hills Cop*, but it was Katzenberg who put together the myriad details that turned the ideas into effective films.

Known in Hollywood circles as the "golden retriever," Katzenberg was a tireless worker with an unerring ability to sniff out an agent or director who had a hot script in the works. Renowned for his work ethic, the five-foot seven-inch Katzenberg was hard at work every day by 7:00 A.M. and routinely worked weekends and holidays. He was just as famous for his telephone calls, which numbered as many as 150 a day, each lasting no more than two minutes.

Katzenberg and Eisner also shared something of a common background. Both had grown up on Park Avenue, just a few blocks apart. However, in contrast to Eisner, who had gravitated to Broadway plays and loved to read the classics, Katzenberg was lured by politics. The son of a stockbroker, young Jeffrey (whose nickname was "Squirt") joined John Lindsay's mayoral campaign at age 15. Katzenberg was a tireless worker for Lindsay, often staying until 2:00 A.M. and organizing other students by bribing them with free pizza and soda.

After graduating from the exclusive New York prep school Fieldston, Katzenberg attended New York University for two semesters before dropping out to join Lindsay's staff on a full-time basis. Lindsay introduced him to Hollywood producer David Picker. Picker later introduced Katzenberg to Barry Diller, who hired him in 1975 as his assistant at Paramount. "But he was so aggressive and impossible, he ruffled so many feathers that I couldn't keep him," recalled Diller. Diller sent him to Paramount's marketing department, "to see if he could survive those vicious people."

Katzenberg thrived and rose quickly. Two years later, Eisner assigned him to the doomed Paramount Television Network, a short-lived attempt to start a fourth television network. When that flopped in 1978, Katzenberg was assigned to Eisner and given the chore of overseeing production on the first *Star Trek* movie. Although the movie came in well over budget, Katzenberg soon came to epitomize the Paramount credo of negotiating hard and working even harder.

Tales of his workaholic antics soon became legend. During his first week on the job, he timed the traffic lights on his way to work so that he could make the trip in under 20 minutes. At Paramount, known as Hollywood's most tightfisted studio, he also learned the art of keeping the lid on costs. During the making of the hit film *Terms of Endearment*, he rode director Jim Brooks so hard that Brooks called Eisner to complain. But no one argued with Katzenberg's results—not even Brooks. The director later credited Katzenberg with making the dozens of calls necessary to get actor John Lithgow to make the film.

By 1984, Katzenberg had become Eisner's closest friend and confidant at Paramount. When it became obvious that Gulf & Western chairman Marty Davis would pass over Eisner as Diller's successor, Eisner and Katzenberg made up their minds to go into business together elsewhere. Initially, Davis offered to give Katzenberg Eisner's former job as Paramount's president, reporting to new Paramount chief Frank Mancuso. Katzenberg never had any intention of taking the job. But worried that Davis would hold hostage a $500,000 bonus that Katzenberg had coming to him, he asked for more time to consider the offer.

Disney's September 30 announcement that Katzenberg would joint the company was anticlimatic. For several weeks, Eisner and Katzenberg had already been planning how they would revamp the ailing Disney studio. One Saturday in early September, the two, with Jane Eisner, had sat beside Eisner's pool to sketch out plans for dramatically increasing the level of production of new films. They also discussed the need to quickly put out many of Disney's older movies on videocassette. The videocassette plan was of particular importance to their overall strategy. "It's the greatest opportunity in this town," Katzenberg had stressed. The old Mickey Mouse cartoons by themselves, Katzenberg figured, could also be worth millions on the burgeoning TV syndication market.

Within days of Katzenberg's arrival at Disney, the third floor of the Animation Building was transformed back into a small studio, much as it had been in Walt Disney's time. Eisner moved Katzenberg into an office down the hall from his own and positioned two secretaries outside Katzenberg's door.

Katzenberg's office became a hub of activity. The young executive could put through dozens of telephone calls in an hour. "You wouldn't have a meeting with Katzenberg by yourself," recalls Stan Kinsey, who was the studio's head of financial operations at the time. "While you were trying to talk, he would be taking a call. Or telling his secretary to place another call. And there would be a line outside his office of two to three people, waiting to see him."

The calls were rapid-fire. "Just called to say we are thinking about you," Katzenberg would say quickly. He would end with, "Better keep Disney in mind," before going on to the next call.

With Katzenberg on board, Eisner could begin building up the studio. In addition to upgrading the film operations, Eisner wanted to get Disney back on network television. As when Walt first built Disneyland, a Sunday night show would help to lure people to the parks. Eisner, Wells, and Katzenberg soon invited ABC chairman Leonard Goldenson to Disney for lunch. Goldenson brought along his president, Fred Pierce, and his programming chief, Tony Thomopolous.

Goldenson and Pierce had once offered to set up Eisner with his own film company. Now he offered Disney his prized 7:00 P.M. Sunday spot. ABC, he told the Disney executives, would pay $20 million for 13 one-hour movies and 10 two-hour movies. Eisner accepted the offer. Disney ultimately would pick up about $5 million of the costs—a traditional setup in the TV industry. (Studios often pay a portion of the costs of making network shows, with the hope of realizing profits later by syndicating the reruns.)

❖

Work habits at the Disney studio were due for a change. The 1,400 staff members had grown accustomed to the slow pace of the Walker-Miller years. Ron Miller often took time out in the middle of the day to play cards, and frequently left at 3:00 P.M. for the nearest golf course. The staff tended to follow his lead. The Disney lot had taken on an air of indifference to the outside world, not unlike that of a university campus.

Eisner and Katzenberg brought the Paramount work ethic to Disney. Both Eisner's mustard-colored Mercedes convertible and Katzenberg's white Porche arrived at the Disney studio by seven o'clock every morning. Most workdays stretched late into the night, lasting until after Katzenberg's mandatory 10:00 P.M. script meeting. "If you don't want to come in on Saturday, then don't bother coming in on Sunday" became the Disney motto. Stan Kinsey was shocked on the day before Thanksgiving when Katzenberg asked him to stop by his office the next day. "But that's Thanksgiving," Kinsey recalled telling Katzenberg. "Why?" Katzenberg answered. "Do you have anything planned?"

This kind of schedule sent shivers through the staff. The message that rippled through the company was clear. Anyone who was not prepared to work as hard as the two new Disney executives would soon be looking for a new job. Richard Berger, the former Fox executive brought in by Ron Miller in mid-1983, was one of the first to go. Stan Kinsey left a few months later, quitting when Katzenberg took away most of his responsibilities.

By early 1985, Eisner and Katzenberg had fired more than 400 people, administering a severe jolt to a staff that had grown up under the paternalistic wing of Uncle Walt and his kindly company. Even as the studio's output had shriveled to a handful of films each year, employment had increased. Eisner and Katzenberg found that there were hundreds of back-lot employees—painters, carpenters, and other technical people—who were rarely needed on the set. Most of them were fired, along with a 12-person staff of still photographers, a holdover from the days when Walt had insisted that nearly every major event at his studio be recorded for posterity.

Eisner and Katzenberg also began to hire their kind of people. Most of them came from Paramount Pictures. Three weeks after Katzenberg moved to Disney, Paramount lawyer Helene Hahn came over as head of legal affairs for the film unit. She was followed by Paramount's former pay television head, Bill Mechanic, and by Ricardo Mestres, a Harvard graduate who had been one of Katzenberg's top production assistants. Not long afterward, Katzenberg hired David Hoberman, a one-time motion picture agent who had worked his way up from the William Morris agency mail room. Along the way, he had also worked for television pioneer Norman Lear.

One of the biggest catches was Richard Frank. A New York native, Frank had been general manager of Chris Craft's KCOP-TV station in Los Angeles when he first met Eisner in 1975. At the time, Frank wanted Paramount to help pay for television shows that KCOP-TV and it could syndicate. Instead, Eisner hired him to work on the ill-fated Paramount TV network. When that failed, Frank moved over to the studio's television production unit, launching Paramount's successful syndication operation with shows like *Entertainment Tonight* and *Solid Gold*.

Eisner and Katzenberg wanted Frank to help revive Disney's moribund TV operations, but when Eisner called Frank shortly after he arrived at Disney, Frank said he still had five years to go on his contract. Gulf & Western chairman Marty Davis, already infuriated by the loss of Katzenberg and other top Paramount executives to the Eisner team, at first steadfastly refused to let Frank out of his contract. Six months later, Davis relented. Frank began work for Disney in March. At about the same time, one of Frank's top assistants, Bob Jacquemin, who had headed the unit that had sold Paramount's syndicated programs to TV stations, was also hired by Disney. Jacquemin was put in charge of selling Disney's large library of old TV shows and movies.

By the spring of 1985, Team Disney was taking shape. Nearly 30 Paramount executives had joined their former bosses at Disney.

❖

Not every part of the company, however, needed dramatic overhaul. Even during Disney's darkest times, the theme parks had retained most of the sparkle and service that Walt had demanded. Disney University, which Walt had created to train new workers to deliver his own brand of service to the parks' guests, still turned out fresh-faced, eager workers for the parks.

"In many ways, Walt's shadow actually held the company together," explained Sid Bass. "I couldn't understand how a company that was this badly mismanaged at the top could be so fantastic at the middle management level. The executives at the park remembered how Walt had done it."

Keeping Walt's flame alive was Richard Nunis, who had begun working at Disneyland even before the construction was complete in 1955. Nunis, who had played football with Ron Miller at the University of Southern California, was first hired by Walt to help set up Disney University. There, he helped to train the 600 "cast members" who served the eager crowds that swarmed into Disneyland's opening day. After the park opened, Nunis helped to supervise operation of the Dumbo Flying Elephant Ride, Cinderella's Golden Carousel, and other rides in Fantasyland. He was running Disneyland by 1967 and the entire theme park operation by 1971.

Eisner and Wells already knew how they intended to wring more money out of the theme parks. As they had discussed with the Bass group in Fort Worth, ticket prices would have to be raised, and quickly. Nunis, both men also knew, would keep the parks running in the manner that its guests had come to expect.

❖

Unlike its parks, Disney's finance department desperately needed help. The 1984 takeover battle had exposed glaring weaknesses. The company's strategic planning operation consisted of a single person. Its chief financial officer, Michael Bagnall, was an accountant who had come to Disney from Price Waterhouse & Co. more than two decades earlier. Like most Disney employees during that era, Bagnall had risen through the ranks from Disneyland. Both Stanley Gold and Sid Bass had complained loudly to Eisner and Wells that Disney had been ill served by its finance department during the takeover battle. (Michael Bagnall declined to be interviewed for this book.)

By December, Eisner and Wells had been joined by Al Checchi, a Sid Bass lieutenant, who had arranged the sale of Arvida to Disney. The idea of having Checchi join Disney came from Richard Rainwater, Bass's top aide, during a meeting at Eisner's office just after Thanksgiving. The meeting was mostly a social call. Rainwater and Checchi spent a two-day vacation together, playing tennis and running on the beach in Southern California.

Both Rainwater and Checchi had bought stock along with Sid Bass. Together they owned about 1.5 percent of the company. "Michael, maybe you ought to have Checchi out here for some period of time," Rainwater told Eisner during a meeting at the Disney offices. "He knows how to finance things. He knows how to develop things."

Sid Bass had already called Michael Eisner to help pave the way for Checchi's arrival. Checchi and his wife, a California native, were getting tired of living in Fort Worth and wanted to move to Los Angeles. Checchi would only be there to help Eisner, Bass stressed, not to run the show.

Eisner knew Checchi only briefly, from their meeting in Fort Worth. An honors student at Harvard Business School, Checchi had helped develop complex financing plans for both Marriott Corporation's hotels and Sid Bass's takeovers. Checchi, Eisner realized, could also be invaluable, especially in helping to plan the development of Disney's 28,000 acres in Florida.

At the time Sid Bass and his group held nearly one-quarter of Disney's shares. Eisner didn't have much choice. "Michael was probably sitting there saying 'holy shit,' " recalled Checchi. "But I told him, Michael, this isn't what you think. This isn't a setup." Eisner may have been wary of his new associate, but he accepted him anyway. Although Eisner and Checchi came from different worlds, both knew how to cut a deal. Soon they even became friends. Eisner helped Checchi to get settled in California, and even arranged for two of Checchi's children to attend the same private school that Eisner's sons attended.

Checchi, who occupied a second-floor office in the Animation Building, worked on only a few deals. One of them, which ultimately fell apart, would have brought Disney together with Marriott to build 20,000 rooms and a mammoth convention center in Orlando. Even though the deal fell through, the months of talks between Disney and Marriott were valuable. Through these talks, Michael Eisner found his new CFO, Gary Wilson.

Wilson had been Marriott's CFO for 12 years. A former football player on the Duke University team that went to the 1960 Cotton Bowl, Wilson had been the key architect behind Marriott's dramatic growth. Pioneering the use of limited partnerships to raise funds, Wilson sold off pieces of the hotel to investors while keeping the lucrative management contracts for Marriott. The combination had helped turn Marriott into a company with $3 billion in revenues by 1984, five times its size a decade earlier.

The Disney chairman had initially rejected the notion of hiring Wilson, who commanded a huge salary. Instead, he had hired a New York headhunter to find a topflight chief financial officer. A Citibank vice-president, however, had turned down Eisner's offer, and a Wall Street investment banker had flunked an interview over dinner at the Bel Air Hotel. After interviewing John Dahsburg, a Wilson assistant, Eisner finally talked to Wilson himself.

Checchi had been pushing for Wilson all along. The two men had worked together since the mid-1960s, when Checchi's uncle, a Washington, D.C., financial consultant, had hired Wilson out of the University of

Pennsylvania's Wharton School. Wilson had taught Checchi everything he knew about hotel financing. Both Wilson and Checchi also knew Disney. As early as 1979, they had tried unsuccessfully to convince Bill Marriott to buy the struggling entertainment company.

During the 1984 takeover bid, in fact, when Saul Steinberg had been looking for partners to buy pieces of Disney, Wilson had flown to New York, eager to buy Disney's Orlando hotels. During a meeting at Steinberg's Reliance Holdings office, Wilson offered to pay Steinberg $200 million. After serious thought, Bill Marriott turned the offer down.

Michael Eisner didn't know if he would like Gary Wilson. Tall and imperious, Wilson could be arrogant and was fond of describing his own accomplishments. His attire, which included silk handkerchiefs fluffed in his suit pocket, struck Eisner as foppish. Still, the new Disney chairman admired success, and Gary Wilson had been successful. "The headhunter kept saying, 'You want someone like Gary Wilson,'" Eisner recalled. "Finally, we decided, 'Why not Gary Wilson?'"

Gary Wilson didn't come cheaply. Striking a deal that would ultimately make him the best-paid CFO in corporate history, he was promised a huge block of stock options. By 1987, the Disney board had given him options of 550,000 shares on top of a $500,000 salary and $3 million in bonuses. The stock alone would eventually be worth more than $60 million. By contrast, Mike Bagnall, who was forced to take early retirement in June 1985, had been paid $233,126 in salary and bonus in his final year.

For Gary Wilson, the move to Disney meant more than money. At Marriott, he knew he would never be president of the company. Bill Marriott was saving that spot for one of his sons or, at the very least, for someone who shared his Mormon religion. The situation at Disney seemed more promising. Frank Wells was 53 years old and had told intimates that he was contemplating retirement in five years. He wanted once more to climb Mount Everest, which he had failed to reach some years earlier. His retirement could leave the number two job at Disney open for Gary Wilson. In Gary Wilson, Disney got a man as creative in structuring financial deals as Eisner and Katzenberg were in putting film projects together. The company also got a CFO who would be able to direct the massive expansion program that Eisner and Wells envisioned for Orlando, Europe, and elsewhere, encompassing both hotels and theme parks. Wilson also benefited Disney in that he became a magnet, attracting to the Disney staff former Marriott financial executives who were eager for greener pastures.

❖

Team Disney was in place. Besides infusing Walt Disney Productions with new people, Eisner and Wells also brought a new management style to the company. At Paramount, Eisner had found that he worked best through group encounter meetings, not only when thrashing out movie script ideas but also in generating ideas for creative business projects. Not long after joining the company, he convened six of Disney's most creative talents for a Sunday morning meeting at his home.

The idea was to come up with a cartoon show for Saturday mornings, an area that Disney had inexplicably ignored while studios with less talented animators were prospering. Eisner refused to end the meeting until his executives came up with several ideas that he could sell to network executives. "I was kind of desperate and running out of time, and I wanted to get into the TV business in an animated way," says Eisner.

Eisner admits that the meeting became a grueling experience. "You bring a bunch of disparate people in the room, you don't let them out, you don't feed them, you give them a sparse amount of water," he says. "And finally all of the inhibitions are gone and they are no longer trying to impress one another and they are no longer trying to impress you. And some really good ideas come out of it." One idea that came of the Sunday morning meeting was a show that became *The Wuzzles*, the story of an uncharted island populated by funny creatures such as one that was half-elephant and half-kangaroo. Disney sold the show to CBS. Eisner's own contribution to the meeting was *The Adventures of the Gummi Bears*, a tale about mythical bears living in medieval times, which Disney sold to NBC. Eisner, however, did not get this idea out of the meeting itself. He had thought of it earlier, when his youngest son demanded that his father buy him some Gummi Bear candies.

The meetings, an idea that came with Team Disney from Paramount, were so successful that they took on a life of their own. They even acquired a name—the "Gong Show." Often a Gong Show was a command session; Eisner, Wells, or Katzenberg would demand that a

group of creative people come up with ideas. Each participant was required to contribute something to the meeting. Ideas that were rejected
were ushered out with a loud "gong."

"They could run through decisions quicker than anyone I have
ever seen," recalled Stan Kinsey. "They knew what they wanted, and
boom, boom, boom." The Gong Show meetings were a corporate culture shock for many Disney executives, who had rarely been put on the
hot seat. "If you weren't used to it, you could say these guys aren't very
sensitive to other people's feelings," says Kinsey. "If you're sensitive about
things, you quickly learn not to take it personally."

Nowhere was the change in management culture more noticeable
than in Disney's film operations. Trained in the hard-driven Paramount
way of doing business, the new Disney film executives made an unoffi-
cial rule that everyone must arrive early and stay late. Weekends were
rarely taken off. More than a little animosity rose between some of the
newcomers and the holdovers. Ideas generated by holdovers were routinely brushed off. As if to show their disdain for Disney's old ways of
doing things, recalls Steve Beeks, a financial analyst who had been hired
by the outgoing managers, the new Disney executives even refused to
wear anything with "the Mouse" on it. "They were ruthless," says former
studio chief Richard Berger, who left not long after Katzenberg arrived.
"They just said, 'We don't want to hear about anything from the past. It
is our company, and we'll do it the way that we want to do it.'"

CHAPTER

Lord Mickey Gets Richer

For nearly 20 years, tourists at Disneyland had been greeted by a huge sign proclaiming the 80-acre theme park "The Happiest Place on Earth." But on September 26, 1984, the Anaheim park was anything but happy. Nearly 1,800 disgruntled Disneyland "cast members," many of them carrying antimanagement placards, were marching outside the Magic Kingdom's gates.

The Disneyland strike lasted for 21 tense days. Still reeling from its expensive takeover fight, and also suffering because of slipping attendance, the previous management had told workers it would freeze pay for two years and cut benefits. The workers, many of them making less than the top wage of $9.70 an hour, had demanded a 5 percent increase.

Michael Eisner and Frank Wells, who had inherited the strike from the previous management, authorized Dick Nunis to take a tough stance. Within three days Disneyland had begun hiring new ticket takers, ride operators, and street sweepers. On October 15, the striking workers returned to work.

Fixing the company's theme park operations, however, was going to be more difficult than breaking the strike. Attendance at the company's theme park operations had decreased during three of the previous four years—a trend that was interrupted only briefly by the opening of

EPCOT Center in Florida in late 1982. At Disneyland, attendance had been especially bad, falling to its lowest point in a decade. The company still would earn $192.6 million from its theme parks in 1984. But erosion had begun. Margins at the park, once as high as the mid-20 percent range, had slipped to 18 percent by 1984.

Improving Disney, Eisner and Wells believed, would have to start with improving the performance of the theme parks. Income from the company's three parks — Disneyland in California, the Magic Kingdom, and EPCOT Center in Florida — along with the management fee from the Tokyo park, accounted for two-thirds of Disney's overall revenues and operating income. Equally important, the money that customers plunked down for tickets, sodas, and trinkets was a reliable source of cash that the company could use to finance the construction of hotels, new parks, and other projects that Eisner and Wells had in mind.

The Bass group, the influential Disney owners from Fort Worth, had already made known their disdain for the way Ron Miller and Card Walker had run the parks. Even as the company's earnings were falling, its managers had steadfastly refused to increase ticket prices at the parks, worrying that rising prices would only exacerbate the attendance decline. In Orlando, no price increase had been imposed since 1982, while only $1 had been added at Disneyland in the last two years.

Sid Bass, Richard Rainwater, and Al Checchi had driven home the necessity of increasing ticket prices, but the chore of determining how much to add and when to do so fell to Frank Wells. Eisner and Jeffrey Katzenberg were spending most of their time in Burbank, trying to rebuild the Disney studio upon the ashes of *Tron* and its other box office embarrassments.

By late 1984, Frank Wells ordered Dick Nunis to give him an extensive review of Disney's theme park operations. For years, Disney's management had aggressively surveyed customers as they left the park, asking departing guests to rate their day at the park on a scale of 1 to 10. During the Ron Miller era, these customer satisfaction ratings had fluctuated between 8 and 9, the Wells group found. Rarely, if ever, did they decline by much more than a few percentage points. Even after the infrequent price hikes, in fact, the ratings had sometimes increased.

The findings of the review were illuminating to Eisner and Wells. Customers' satisfaction with the quality and cleanliness of the parks and the courtesy of Disney employees was extraordinarily high. Even on the question about "value for the money you paid," it was a rare guest who marked anything lower than an 8. Clearly, there was room to increase prices.

For some years, Nunis and his staff had been pushing for price increases. Besides, as the Basses had pointed out, price increases at the parks had failed to keep up with inflation. After accounting for inflation, ticket prices had risen only 1 percent in real terms over the previous decade, during which overall prices had almost doubled. Even so, Nunis and his staff worried that if management tried to increase prices by too much, falling attendance would almost certainly be exacerbated.

After going over the results of the survey, Wells, backed by Dick Nunis, decided that he favored a small increase. That approach, the two agreed, would enable the company to evaluate the impact of current increases on attendance.

Bass associate Al Checchi, who had been working out of a second-floor office at Disney for nearly two months, disagreed vehemently. In Orlando alone, Checchi felt, the company had room to dramatically increase its prices. "Hell, you don't have any competition down there," Checchi told Eisner one day while the two were driving home in Eisner's small yellow convertible.

Sea World, Checchi argued, along with Busch Gardens and such oddball parks as Broadwalk and Baseball, had operated for years in Disney's shadow. It was Walt Disney World that drew tourists from New York, Chicago, and elsewhere. And, in any event, whenever Disney increased its price the others would follow.

Tourism had been increasing in central Florida for years and would continue to increase in the future, Checchi argued, especially as the economy picked up and gasoline prices stayed low. Checchi favored a $5 price increase, which would take the price up to $23, a huge jump from the current $18 price for a one-day ticket.

Ultimately, the decision was Eisner's. The Disney chairman worried that the stiff increase that Checchi recommended would generate negative headlines in newspapers around the country. It went against Eisner's instincts to allow a $5 increase. He worried that newspapers in Orlando and Anaheim would almost certainly play up a huge increase, leading inevitably to stories on network television and in newspapers with nationwide distribution—publicity that would not be good for business.

Still, Eisner knew how the Basses felt. The numbers were compelling. Every $1 increase in ticket prices would add $31 million a year to Disney's profits if attendance remained stable. Even if the parks suffered a 5 percent decline in attendance, the most the study projected, each $1 increase would add $26 million annually to Disney's profits.

Driving home one day, Eisner made a decision. He reached for his car telephone and called Frank Wells. It was time, the Disney chairman told Wells, to begin to increase prices substantially. He wanted both Anaheim and Orlando ticket prices increased by $5 within two years. However, to minimize negative press, the prices would be increased in several steps. The price for a one-day pass to Walt Disney World, for instance, would be increased by $1.50 during the upcoming summer season and by another $1.50 just before Thanksgiving. Price increases would get to the $5 level Checchi encouraged, but only after 15 months at Orlando and two years at Disneyland.

❖

Jack Lindquist, short, white-haired, and ebullient, had joined Disney in 1955 as a junior marketing executive at Disneyland. Working late into the night with Walt Disney and Card Walker, he had listened as they dreamed up ideas for promoting the parks. He had helped to arrange the 1959 tour by the University of Washington and the University of Wisconsin football teams, the first Rose Bowl competitors to visit the Magic Kingdom. The Rose Bowl tour had become an annual event, and each year reporters gleefully followed the teams around, sending reports on each ride back to hometown readers.

During Lindquist's time, Disneyland had gotten miles of lines of free press by inviting presidents and kings, and by arranging shows that featured vintage cars and floats from 25 nations. To grab the attention of television cameras for the park's 10th anniversary, Walt had the "Great Moments with Mr. Lincoln" exhibit shipped to Disneyland from the 1964 World's Fair. Guests were impressed by sounds and movements that seemingly brought the nation's 16th president to life. Besides, ABC was always around to televise events on the Fourth of July and other occasions.

The only thing Walt Disney Productions didn't need was paid advertising. During virtually all of Jack Lindquist's 29 years with the company, Walt Disney and later Card Walker preached that it was foolish to spend money for what came free. One extreme example was EPCOT Center: Although it had cost Disney more than $1.2 billion to open the new park in 1982, a meager $630,000 was spent for advertising to announce the opening, all of it devoted to listings of the opening events in local newspapers.

Jack Lindquist, who by now had risen to the position of executive vice-president for marketing, was in London when Eisner and Wells joined the company. Unlike Disney's other executives, who made a pilgrimage to Burbank to meet the company's new top executives, Lindquist stayed on the job after he got a mailgram from Eisner and Wells announcing that they had joined the company. He finally met them, two months later, in the first-class section of a Delta Air Lines jet during a direct flight from Burbank to Orlando. In going through some old memos, Eisner and Wells had found out that Lindquist had proposed to Ron Miller and Ray Watson a massive campaign of paid TV ads for the first time in the company's history.

The plan had grown out of a three-city advertising test that Lindquist and Dick Nunis had secretly conducted in spring 1984. Using $150,000 from Disneyland's promotional budget, the two executives had placed TV ads on local channels in Chicago and Houston, and traditional newspaper advertisements in Kansas City. The idea was to find out how much more effective TV advertising would be than newspaper ads. The results of the study were illuminating to the two Disney executives. For every $1 million spent on TV ads, an additional 154,000 guests would visit the park. It would cost about $6.50 to bring in a visitor who would pay $18 to enter the park and another $15 or $20 for food and souvenirs. A $10 million ad campaign would yield $55.4 million in revenues. Eisner and Wells's intentions of aggressively increasing prices meant that the prospective yield would be even larger within a few years.

Lindquist had submitted a plan to Miller and Watson that called for spending $19 million on television advertising for the Orlando parks, plus another $18 million to celebrate Disneyland's 30th anniversary, including a giveaway of 400 new General Motors cars. At the time Disneyland's annual attendance was under 9.9 million and was still shrinking, in its fourth straight year of decline.

Eisner and Wells already knew that they would be increasing ticket prices soon. They also knew that the kind of price hikes they were contemplating could have a chilling effect on attendance, especially if the country slipped into another recession similar to the one it had experienced earlier in the decade. At the time, Eisner was also negotiating with ABC to air *The Disney Sunday Movie*. But the first show wouldn't appear until early 1986. In the meantime, Eisner had lined up NBC to broadcast a two-hour special for Disneyland's 30th anniversary.

Only heavy spending for television advertising, Eisner and Wells decided, could create the desired impact on flagging theme park attendance. Advertising expenditures had always come naturally to Disney's new heads. Getting people into a theme park, they hoped, would be no different from getting them into movie theaters. If spending millions could make a hit movie out of an ordinary film, they reasoned, it could certainly maintain interest in America's most well-known theme parks. A few days after meeting Lindquist on the flight to Orlando, they approved his plan. In February and March, Disney would run commercials in the largest 51 television markets in the Midwest and the North Atlantic states to promote Walt Disney World. A special toll-free telephone number would be set up to take hotel reservations. GM cars would be given away during Disneyland's anniversary party. "They asked us, 'Is that enough, do you need more?' " Nunis recalls incredulously. "Now, *that* was a change."

❖

George Lucas knew Disneyland well. As a high school student growing up in the northern California town of Modesto, Lucas had been a race-car enthusiast, but he had been forced to give up the sport after his lungs were crushed in an accident. After he recovered, his parents sent him for a weeklong visit to Anaheim, including one day at Disneyland. Hooked, he returned often. When he enrolled in the Cinema School of the University of Southern California, he became a regular Disneyland visitor during weekends and summers.

After graduation, Lucas became a protégé of Francis Ford Coppola. He assisted the director on *Finian's Rainbow* in 1968 and on *The Rain People* the next year. He was one of many cameramen on the celebrated Rolling Stones concert documentary *Gimme Shelter*. His first big break came in 1973 when Universal Pictures gave him $700,000 to make *American Graffiti*, an autobiographical film about American adolescence in the 1960s. The film was a hit, but it was his next movie, *Star Wars*, that made Lucas an international star. Produced for the then hefty budget of $11 million, the 1977 film became the second biggest film of all time, netting Twentieth Century Fox more than $193 million.

Working out of a small rented warehouse in Van Nuys, California, Lucas and a staff of ten had developed many of the special effects in *Star Wars*. When the film scored at the box office, Lucas moved his operation to Marin County in northern California. There he established Sky-walker Ranch, a 2,600-acre complex where his five-building Lucasfilm empire took on the look of small studio.

By 1984, Lucasfilm's Industrial Light and Magic unit was among the entertainment industry's leading special effects operations. The unit had made Elliot's bicycle fly in *E.T.: The Extra Terrestrial,* had made a steak crawl in *Poltergeist,* and had given life to the Spaceship *Enterprise* in *Star Trek II: The Wrath of Khan.*

Lucas had also, by this time, begun to branch out beyond filmmaking. His company had developed THX, a supercharged sound system for theaters. He was also working on a machine that would combine action films with flight simulators to give customers at shopping malls the sensation of skiing or surfing.

Disney's WED Imagineering unit was working on similar technology. Charles R. Bright, a WED vice-president for concept development, had talked to a British company, Rediffusion Simulation Ltd. Rediffusion had combined a large aircraft simulator with a film showing clouds and mountains that seemed to whiz by. The 13-ton simulator, which had been used to train British Airways jumbo-jet pilots, could rise, fall, or dive by as much as 35 degrees even when loaded with several dozen people. Riders got the unmistakable feeling of actual flight.

The Imagineering unit had bought Rediffusion's technology but had never found the concept to make it work for Disney. The unit's idea people had considered putting up a building that would hold four aircraft simulators, each costing about $500,000. Riders would have experiences such as skiing, surfing, and free-fall diving. Ron Miller, like George Lucas, had even contemplated putting simulators in shopping malls around the country. Some Disney insiders even suggested that a simulator should be linked to a movie setting. That could help promote a film like *The Black Hole,* Disney's 1979 space film, they argued.

Miller had played host to Lucas at his Napa Valley vineyard in 1982. Over Miller's Silverado chardonnay, the two men had discussed teaming up to develop a flight-simulator ride. Lucas, who was going through a divorce at the time, had begged off. Two years later, however, when Michael Eisner called him, Lucas was ready to listen.

Eisner had already told the Basses during their September 1984 meeting at Fort Worth that he intended to get the rights to George Lucas's *Star Wars* films for Disney parks. Eisner's ideas on how to use the rights were still murky. But he knew that Lucas, with his ability to grab the video generation, could develop just the right tonic for the theme parks, which had grown old and tired. Like Disney's box office bombs, it's theme park rides were also unpopular with America's teenagers. At increasingly younger ages, kids were seeking the bigger thrills that were available in parks with daredevil roller coasters. Only a few miles away from Disneyland, the Magic Mountain theme park was offering a spine-crunching experience called "The Black Viper." "Kids were becoming more grown-up quicker," explained Frank Wells. "What would appeal to eight- or nine-year-olds in the 60s and 70s was now appealing to the six-year-olds. And the nine-year-olds were now where the 12-year-olds had been."

If designing theme park rides was something alien to Michael Eisner, the new Disney executive soon found his groove. Creativity was creativity, he used to tell other Disney executives. Executives trained in ferreting out ideas for movies that would appeal to teenagers should be able to churn out ideas for theme park rides as well. To prove the point, walking through Walt Disney World soon after coming to the company, Eisner ordered boats for a small lake where only ducks were swimming. By the next day, the lake was filled with tourists in the boats.

Eisner was banking on even more dramatic ideas from George Lucas. Two weeks after Eisner called him in September 1984, Lucas, accompanied by Marty Sklar, had toured the Imagineers headquarters. Only days earlier, Eisner and Wells had taken the same tour, scheduling their trip for a Saturday so that Eisner could bring along his 15-year-old son, Breck. Eisner's son was especially smitten by the idea of a half-mile-long water-flume ride that dropped riders five stories. (The ride, later christened "Splash Mountain," opened at Disneyland about four years later.)

During both tours, Sklar pulled out nearly everything the Imagineers unit was working on, including the flight simulator. Lucas at once focused on the flight simulator. However, he was not to be landed cheaply. One of Hollywood's shrewdest businessmen, George Lucas retains the rights to the characters in his films. To sign him, Walt Disney Productions had to make certain concessions. For one thing, Lucas insisted on a royalty on the sale of any shirts, toys, or other merchandise based on his ride. In addition, Lucasfilm's ILM special effects unit would get a $6 million fee for making the film that accompanied the ride.

With Imagineers' show producer Tom Fitzgerald, Lucas worked out a story line for what became the "Star Tours" ride. An intergalactic sight-seeing company (called "Star Tours") would whisk guests around the universe in a spaceship. Lucas also instilled a sense of danger and a light touch by making the ship's pilot a totally incompetent and nearly psychotic android named Rex, who steers the ship through a dogfight and other misadventures.

Building the ride, however, proved more difficult than designing it, and also more costly than anticipated. Disney set the original budget at $30 million, a figure that included a $3 million contingency for cost overruns. The opening date was planned for November 1986. From the start there were problems in synchronizing the movements of the simulator with the twists and turns of the movie. The original budget didn't include a new facade for the 20-year-old Disneyland building that would house the project. When the roof had to be raised to accommodate the movements of the simulators, Disney's workers found that the building's structural interiors needed reworking as well. Lucas added another $100,000 to the final cost by changing the music that accompanied the ride. Initial tests showed that the ride could easily induce flight sickness. Using an Imagineers worker who was especially prone to air sickness, Disney workers experimented with different flight lengths. From an initial 20-minute length, the ride was cut back to just over 3 minutes, then increased again to 4 minutes because Eisner was worried that riders might feel cheated if the experience was too brief. To further mollify nervous riders, the frenetic mannerisms of the pilot were also toned down. Instead of bordering on psychotic, Rex was programmed to be simply nervous and inexperienced. The changes delayed the "Star Tours" opening by more than three months. The ride would not open until January 1987, meaning that it would not be available during the 1986 Thanksgiving-Christmas season, traditionally one of the busiest times of the year at Disneyland.

To take up the slack, Eisner ordered the Imagineers unit to come up with something else quickly. The result was Videopolis, a huge open-air stage, dance floor, and 2,000-seat arena. Disney workers completed the project in four months, cutting it out of an open field not far from the "It's a Small World" ride. Videopolis was soon booking acts like the Jets and the Miami Sound Machine.

When design work on "Star Tours" was just beginning, George Lucas was also asked to start another Disneyland project. Record executive David Geffen had called Jeffrey Katzenberg with an offer. Geffen, one of Katzenberg's best friends, had been advising singer Michael Jackson on financial decisions since 1980.

Jackson, an unabashed Disneyland fan, came to the park as often as two or three times a month. Often, when he left his sprawling Encino, California, mansion, Jackson was in disguise, but he rarely wore a disguise when he went to Disneyland. Inevitably, he attracted crowds, which drove the theme park's security forces crazy.

Geffen and the young singer wanted to make a movie for Disney. Eisner and Katzenberg had other ideas. Michael Jackson, then coming off his hit album *Thriller*, was a hot item to the younger teenagers who were abandoning Disneyland in droves. There was no telling how many teens the moon-walking star could lure into Disneyland, Eisner thought.

Just before Christmas, Katzenberg brought the singer to the Imagineers' warehouse for a one-hour session. Several years earlier, the Imagineering unit had developed one of the most sophisticated three-dimensional camera systems in the world, a 65-millimeter system that had been used by Disney and Kodak to create several action films for the parks. Katzenberg and Marty Sklar wanted Jackson to star in a rock video using the technology. Jackson liked the concept but insisted that the technical aspects of the film must be done by either George Lucas or Steven Spielberg.

Rick Rothschild, an Imagineers designer, headed up the team that sketched out three different scenarios for consideration by Jackson and Lucas. Both picked the same story, in which Jackson would play a space traveler named Captain EO, who commanded a motley crew of inept characters. Captain EO's improbable mission was to bring music and dance to a distant planet and to break the spell of the planet's wicked queen.

Jackson wrote the music. Lucas brought in his old mentor, Coppola, and enlisted Angelica Huston to play the wicked queen. Rusty Lemorande, who had produced *Yentl* in 1983, was also enlisted to help out with the film.

As with "Star Tours," there were continual delays in getting the project together. Lucasfilm designed several spectacular special effects that, when added to those already contemplated by Disney, brought the number of special effects in the 17-minute film to a total of more than 150. Laser units were installed behind the screen, to be fired over the heads of the audience to simulate battle scenes. Smoke units also were installed to shoot streams of smoke into the theater when Jackson's "spaceship" landed. Coordinating the special effects with the film was an intricate and frustrating project for the Disney engineers. Special effects ultimately added more than $6 million to the original $11 million budget.

The final price tag for "Captain EO" was $17 million, about as much as Walt Disney had spent to build Disneyland in 1955. An imaginative *Orange County Register* reporter opined that "Captain EO" had also become the most expensive film in history. He figured that it cost more than $1 million a minute to make, compared to only $222,222 for the megadud *Heaven's Gate* and "a paltry $102,880 for *Cleopatra.*" The reporter added, "Then again, you couldn't go straight from Liz Taylor's asp bite to Space Mountain and Mr. Toad's Wild Ride."

❖

Planned by Walt Disney himself as the hotel of the future, the Contemporary Resort had been the first hotel built and run by the company. It was enclosed within the imposing steel-and-concrete A-frame hotel in an enormous open space called the Grand Canyon Concourse. With 393 rooms opening to the concourse, this structure enables guests to watch from the doorways of their own rooms as the Walt Disney World Monorail enters the hotel lobby from one side and exits from the other.

In March 1985, Eisner asked Ray Watson to assemble experts on a wide range of fields at the Contemporary Resort to discuss the future of Walt Disney World. The meeting, dubbed the "Futurist Conference," lasted two days. Among the speakers were Jim Rouse, a land developer who had built planned communities in Columbia, Maryland, and Reston, Virginia, and nationally recognized futurist John Naisbitt, author of *Megatrends.*

The vague outlines of Disney's hotel strategy emerged from the conference. After several twists and turns, Disney also decided to build an average of 1,000 new rooms each year for the next several years. That would more than double the number of hotel rooms owned by the company within five years.

Even before the Futurist Conference, Eisner and Wells were eager to build hotels. Al Checchi, working with Disney's new managers inside the company, had been playing the same role he had initially assumed in Fort Worth: He had been pressuring Eisner and Wells to begin building hotels as soon as possible. Hotels, Checchi knew from his Marriott days, could be incredibly lucrative. Profit margins for rooms and meals hovered easily around 60 percent, nearly three times higher than the impressive figures at Disney's theme parks.

More important, once guests registered at Disney hotels, they were virtually captive customers. Few could pass up the Disney trinkets in the gift shops. With free Monorails and bus service to take them to the parks, fewer still wanted to leave the comfort Disney provided to venture to competing parks outside the company's property.

Michael Eisner and Frank Wells had little experience with hotels. Soon after the Futurist Conference, they launched an intensive effort to familiarize themselves with the business. In late February, the two Disney executives had called Jay Pritzker, chairman of Hyatt Hotels, who was in Hawaii recovering from bypass surgery. Serious talks developed, however, in March, when Checchi took Eisner and Wells to meet Marriott Corporation chairman J. W. ("Bill") Marriott, Jr.

Checchi knew Marriott's Bethesda, Maryland, headquarters well. He had learned how to finance and build hotels while working for Marriott CFO Gary Wilson. Now, with Eisner and Wells looking to expand Disney's hotel operation, Checchi wanted to bring in Wilson and the Marriott team as Disney's partners. The deal, which Checchi worked on for months, would be mammoth. Disney would provide the land. Marriott, which was capable of finding the financing to build hotels, would assume most of the building costs. In all, the hotel company would build more than a dozen hotels with a total of nearly 20,000 rooms, as well as a 250,000-square-foot convention center. Marriott would be paid only a management fee for running the hotels, with the investors taking much of the profits. Disney would see profits from selling its products, along with a license fee. It would also get a large new source of customers for the parks.

The deal could be incredibly lucrative for Marriott. Internal projections by the hotel company showed that, for each 1,000 rooms the chain built, it could expect more than $100 million in revenues and up to $60 million in profits. The advantages of being Disney's partner were staggering. Inside the park, the company's hotels averaged 98 percent occupancy rates, and in prime season they were almost always sold out. At the time, the hotel industry was averaging a 45 percent occupancy rate nationwide, while Orlando's non-Disney hotels averaged 68 percent.

Word that Disney and Marriott were talking about joining forces prompted a quick response from New York–based Tishman Realty & Construction. Tishman had built most of EPCOT Center and had been signed by Ray Watson just a few months earlier to build two hotels on the Orlando property. The deal also made Tishman the exclusive hotel company for the property. When a series of anxious letters to Frank Wells didn't stop the Marriott talks, Tishman filed a lawsuit in Orlando, seeking $1.5 billion in damages.

Even before Tishman sued, however, the Marriott deal had begun to fall apart. The developers Disney had inherited from its Arvida acquisition had built hotels before, Eisner and Wells knew. Disney also had a strong record in running its own three hotels. More important, Eisner worried, there was no reason to let Marriott walk off with profits that could just as easily flow to Disney's bottom line. Before pulling out of the deal, Eisner demanded that Marriott also agree to build a $70 million pavilion at EPCOT Center. "When they agreed so quickly, I knew it must have been a great deal for them," Eisner said later.

Disney never signed the Marriott deal. The company's lawyers worried that protracted litigation with Tishman would stop, or at the very least, delay, Disney's hotel-building plans. More important, after negotiating with Marriott officials for months, Eisner and Wells were now far more confident that they knew enough to handle the hotel construction themselves.

The company also settled with Tishman. The builder got to build its two hotels but lost its designation as Disney's official hotel company. Eisner also insisted that Disney have the final say on every detail of the hotel that would be constructed on its land, taking back that prerogative from Tishman.

Now, armed with many of the plans that the Marriott team had developed jointly with Disney, Eisner and Wells decided that Disney would go into the hotel-building business. To do so, however, the company had to back away from plans that Arvida chief Chuck Cobb and Ray Watson had developed for some of the property. During Ray Watson's last months as chairman, he and Cobb began work on a master plan for the Orlando property.

Hearkening back to the city-of-the-future concept espoused by Walt just before his death, Cobb's plan included 10,000 condo or apartment units and provided space for up to 10 industrial parks. (Ironically, at about the same time, Eisner was toying with the idea of a theme park called the American Workplace, which would use miniature industrial plants as the main attraction. The Disney chairman even asked the Harvard Business School to study the idea further.)

Eisner and Wells were increasingly irked by Chuck Cobb and never took his plan seriously. The Arvida executive could be abrasive in his manner and was frequently condescending to the new Disney executives. Cobb's master plan would be expensive, the two men thought. And it would send the company into the home-building business, an area about which neither Eisner nor Wells knew much.

Instead, they decided to stick with Disney's strengths. The central core strategy idea was accepted, but the condos and industrial parks were put on hold. Instead, Eisner and Wells decided, it would be new hotels, not an industrial park, that would go up next to EPCOT Center. That, the Disney planners projected, would make it easier for guests to get to EPCOT and would keep them from leaving Disney's property.

By mid-1985, the company had moved forward with long-dormant plans to build a 900-room hotel and to call it the "Grand Floridian." The Victorian-style hotel was to be modeled on the kind of turn-of-the-century resort that might have been frequented by John D. Rockefeller or Teddy Roosevelt. The budget for building it was $120 million. A 2,100-room moderate-priced hotel was also to be built, with many of the rooms located in "villages" based on the Caribbean islands of Martinique, Barbados, and Trinidad.

Tishman and its partners, meanwhile, began construction on its pair of hotels, the 1,509-room Dolphin and the 758-room Swan. The special attraction of these two hotels is that they are across a lake from EPCOT Center, allowing guests to travel to the park by water taxi. As part of the settlement agreement, Eisner had insisted that Disney choose the architect for the $375 million project. He chose Michael Graves, a postmodernistic architect based in Princeton, New Jersey, who is known for outlandish designs. Graves lived up to his whimsical reputation, designing a 27-story pyramid-shaped hotel with a 55-foot-high cartoonish dolphin on top and a 12-story hotel topped by a pair of turquoise swans.

❖

Among the least known of Walt Disney's pioneering projects was corporate sponsorship. Desperate for money to open Disneyland, he had openly welcomed any idea that gave him a few extra bucks to help complete the dream. His biggest Disneyland sponsor, of course, was ABC, which received one-third of the park in return for $500,000. ABC also guaranteed a $4.5 million loan to help Walt complete the $17 million park.

Walt also made money by selling Coca-Cola an exclusive soda concession for Disneyland. Similarly, Kodak got exclusive rights to sell film by putting up some money for the park. A prospective corporate sponsor, however, didn't have to be a big name, and didn't even have to be terribly dignified, for Walt to sign it up. Hollywood-Maxwell Co., consequently, set up a corset shop on Main Street in Disneyland, not far from where Apple Valley Building Co. sold real estate from a rented storefront.

By the time Michael Eisner and Frank Wells arrived at Disney, the company was getting nearly $100 million a year from such participation agreements. Most of the money came from EPCOT Center, where huge companies like AT&T, Exxon, and General Motors had pavilions. Paying as much as $75 million apiece, the sponsors supplied all construction costs and 10 years' worth of operating expenses.

Eisner and Wells, however, decided that Walt Disney Productions could do even better at the corporate sponsorship game. Many of the sponsorship contracts had not anticipated certain ideas that Eisner and Wells had in mind. The job of squeezing out a few extra dollars fell to Frank Wells. His training as a lawyer came in handy in renegotiating the deals. Kodak, whose contract was one of the first Wells renegotiated, agreed to pick up some of the costs of making "Captain EO" and to renovate existing theaters at both Disneyland and Walt Disney World to accommodate added special effects. GM, which was sponsoring EPCOT Center's "World of Motion" pavilion and which also supplied the official cars of Walt Disney World, agreed to a program of joint advertising.

Within two years of Eisner's and Wells's ascensions, Disney was getting $193 million from participation agreements. Some of the added money came from new sponsors, such as Metropolitan Life Insurance company, which agreed to spend nearly $90 million for a health-related pavilion at EPCOT Center. Mars, the New Jersey–based candy company, was signed as a sponsor for the "Star Tours" exhibit.

In some cases, Disney simply shopped around for better deals. In early 1987, the company kicked out Eastern Airlines as the official Walt Disney World carrier. The old deal with Eastern was expiring, and the airline, which was having financial problems, couldn't meet Disney's request for a substantial hike in payments. Instead, Wells signed Delta Air Lines, which agreed to pay $40 million during a 10-year contract in return for the "official airline" designation. Delta also agreed to participate in future projects, such as introduction of 70-millimeter films at the Magic Kingdom. Delta later supplanted PSA as the official Disneyland carrier as well, adding another $2 million a year to the agreement.

❖

By January 1987, Disneyland hardly looked the same. Disney had lined up rock groups like The Jets and Paul Revere and the Raiders for Videopolis. And more than 500 video monitors had been installed for an all-night New Year's Eve party attended by over 2,000 teenagers.

Crowds were also lining up for the "Captain EO Show," which had opened in September with all the hoopla of a gala Hollywood-style movie premiere. Jack Nicholson was at the premiere, as were Jane Fonda, Debra Winger, and Whoopi Goldberg. George Lucas and Francis Ford Coppola helped Eisner to dedicate the new Magic Eye Theater. Michael Jackson was nowhere to be found, although Disney officials suggested later that he was in the crowd, disguised as a little old lady.

On January 6, 1987, Disney also opened the "Star Tours" ride. Assisted by George Lucas, Eisner cut the ribbon with a special laser beam developed by the Imagineering unit. Mickey Mouse, dressed in a silver space suite, stood alongside *Star Wars* robots R2D2 and C3PO. By midmorning, Disneyland guests were waiting in lines for up to an hour to take the spaceship ride.

With the exception of the $1.2 billion the company had spent to open EPCOT Center in 1982, Disney had never spent more money on its parks than it had under Michael Eisner and Frank Wells. In 1987, when both "Star Tours" and "Captain EO" were operating, the company spent more than $280 million on upgrading and adding to its theme parks, nearly double the company's expenditures in 1984. In 1987, Disney broke ground for its most expensive ride to that point,

"Splash Mountain," a giant water-flume ride based on the 1946 Disney film *Song of the South*. By the time it was completed, "Splash Mountain" would cost more than $80 million.

Luckily for Disney, the crowds kept growing. Ticket prices were increased five times at Walt Disney World during the first two years of the Eisner-Wells tenure, and three times at Disneyland. By 1987, a family of four now had to pay $91 to spend a day at Orlando's Magic Kingdom, compared to $62 two years earlier, whereas inflation was creeping along at less than 4 percent a year. Even so, attendance at all three Disney parks had been increasing. In 1987, 36 million people would walk through the Disney turnstiles, 5 million more than in 1984.

Everything seemed to be working in the new management's favor. The economy was just pulling out of a recession when Eisner and Wells joined Disney and it began to grow impressively. After several years during which a strong dollar had kept tourists away, a weakening dollar also started to work in favor of the new management. Whatever the reasons, Disney's balance sheet began to sparkle. Theme park profits nearly tripled, growing from $196 million in 1983 to $548 million in 1987. Operating margins, which had fallen to 18 percent when Eisner and Wells arrived, were now a robust 30 percent.

More important, the company's cash flow—ready money available to spend on new projects—had more than tripled. With over $1.1 billion a year of fresh cash coming in each year, the company was able to build new hotels and new rides as well as a third theme park in Orlando—The Disney MGM Studios Theme Park—and it was able to do it without taking on any new debt. By 1987, Disney was also spending more than $30 million a year on advertising. Gone was Card Walker's conservatism, along with the company's aversion to spending money on advertising. The advertisements typically featured Mickey Mouse waving from the top of the EPCOT Center dome or frolicking down Disneyland's Main Street.

But Disney's most memorable advertisement happened by accident. The night before "Star Tours" was to open, Michael Eisner and his wife Jane were having dinner with astronauts Gordon Cooper and Donald Slayton, along with Jeana Yeager and Dick Rutan. A month earlier, Yeager and Rutan had made headlines by piloting their spindly-winged *Voyager* aircraft around the world on a single tank of fuel.

During their dinner, Jane Eisner asked Rutan what he intended to do next. "Well, next we're going to Disneyland," replied Rutan. The idea sounded like a great TV commercial to Jane Eisner, who quickly retold the story to her husband. The Disney chairman then called Disneyland marketing director Jack Lindquist. "He told me to find a way to use that line in some ad, somewhere," recalled Lindquist.

The Super Bowl was being played two weeks later at the Rose Bowl in Pasadena, California. The National Football Conference champion New York Giants easily routed the Denver Broncos. When the final gun blew, Giants quarterback Phil Simms leaped into the air and ran toward the sidelines, his fist raised in triumph. But before he left the field, he stopped and waited for a cameraman to get positioned. "Phil Simms, you just won the Super Bowl," the announcer asked the athlete. "What are you going to do next."

Stopping in mid-celebration, the blond quarterback turned to the camera and yelled: "I'm going to Disneyland."

CHAPTER

Down and Out in Burbank

H ollywood was in chaos in 1984. Blockbusters like *Beverly Hills Cop* and *Gremlins* helped to catapult the film industry to a record $4 billion at the box office. But there was turmoil at six of the industry's seven major studios. Denver oilman Marvin Davis had bought Twentieth Century Fox three years before and had launched a major shake-up at the studio. Major shake-ups were also under way at Universal Pictures and MGM/UA Communications, and a new management team had just settled into Columbia Pictures. At Paramount Pictures, the team that had created *Raiders of the Lost Ark, Grease,* and *Saturday Night Fever* had been dismantled just as *Beverly Hills Cop* was making its way to theaters.

The situation at Disney, across the Hollywood Hills in Burbank, was not much better. The studio that Walt built had nearly come to a halt. It was true that Ron Miller and Richard Berger, who ran the studio, had produced the hit film *Splash.* But *Splash* had been the exception rather than the rule. The film had been proposed to Disney production chief Tom Wilhite in 1983 only after every other major studio had turned it down. More typical of Disney's filmmaking abilities was Disney's only other new film that year, *Country.* It would bomb shortly after

Eisner arrived. So would the upcoming schedule of movies that the new team inherited, a motley assortment of films that included *Baby, The Journey of Natty Gann,* and *My Science Project.*

The Walt Disney Productions that Michael Eisner and Jeffrey Katzenberg had inherited was a boutique operation, capable of producing no more than three or four new films a year. It had few ties to the Steven Spielbergs and Ivan Reitmans of Hollywood, and fewer to the likes of John Hughes and John Avildsen. Box office superstars like Eddie Murphy and Sylvester Stallone wouldn't be caught dead on Dopey Drive.

Even with soaring theater ticket prices, earnings from Disney's film unit had been sliding for nearly a decade. In 1982, the company had made only $19.6 million from its movies, and most of that had come from reissues of the classics that Walt had made decades earlier. By contrast, in 1976 Disney movies had generated nearly $54 million in profits. The worst year had been 1983, when write-offs for such poor films as *Something Wicked This Way Comes* and *Trenchcoat* had saddled the film unit with a $5 million operating loss.*

One thing that Michael Eisner and Jeffrey Katzenberg knew was how to make hit films. Their track record at Paramount had shown that. But the move to Walt Disney Company also gave them the opportunity to step out from under Barry Diller's shadow.

The relationship between Eisner and Diller had begun to deteriorate just as the Paramount situation was coming unraveled. Eisner, insiders said, felt that Diller was damning him with faint praise at every opportunity. When things had begun to fall apart with Marty Davis, Eisner felt, Diller had deserted him.

When Diller went to Fox, neither Eisner nor Katzenberg had taken Diller up on his offer to go along. Diller, distant and challenging, had alienated many of his production people at Paramount. One by one those production people had jumped to Disney and joined Eisner and Katzenberg instead. Eisner could be as tough and hard as Diller when the chips were down. But he was also more fatherly, a compassionate man who talked lovingly of his family.

Eisner and Katzenberg could start from scratch in remaking the Walt Disney studio. Ron Miller and Richard Berger had already fought the battle with Card Walker that led to the creation of Touchstone

---

*The film unit had lost a total of $33.4 million, of which $28.3 million was attributed to start-up costs for the Disney Channel.

Pictures. The new label had come about only because new Disney chairman Ray Watson, who was an advocate of the change, had approved it. With the new label, Disney could make the kind of racier films that were appealing to modern audiences without soiling the Disney name for wholesome entertainment.

The creation of Touchstone Pictures, however, was not by itself the solution to the problem. With Card Walker at its helm, Disney's board of directors still controlled the films that the company could make, and their directions were clear. They would not allow the kind of sex-filled and violence-laced films that Columbia Pictures or Twentieth Century Fox could make. Ron Miller could make *Splash,* the board said, but had to cut all but the briefest glimpses of nudity.

Eisner and Katzenberg had come to Burbank with an entirely new mandate. The seven-month siege by Wall Street raiders had softened Disney's board to the kind of dramatic changes that were long overdue at the Burbank studio. Touchstone Pictures, Disney's two new film executives knew, was a blank page for them to fill with the kinds of movies that Paramount would clamor to make.

Eisner and Katzenberg also knew that, unlike Ron Miller, they could attract the kind of topflight talent that could make those pictures at Disney. So intent was Eisner on luring Hollywood's hottest producers, in fact, that he ordered Disney's Imagineering unit to draw up plans to bulldoze most of the studio's "back lot." Gone would be the old Flubber Street and the Spanish mission from the *Zorro* series. In their place, Eisner proposed building low-slung bungalows and lakes as an inducement to the industry's better filmmakers to relocate to Burbank.

The idea for bungalows never moved beyond the early planning stages. Instead, Eisner approved a $500,000 renovation of the Animation Building, covering the linoleum floors with beige carpets, repainting the army green walls white, and hanging expensive David Hockney prints in the executive suites.

Elsewhere, Disney also needed work. Disney's distribution system, which had maintained its salesmanship and contacts through years of successful reissues of Disney classics, was serviceable. But the marketing operation was weak, and there were few new scripts or projects that impressed Eisner or Katzenberg. "The cupboard was very bare," Eisner would say later.

Two weeks after coming to Disney, Michael Eisner, Jeffrey Katzenberg, and Frank Wells spent several days sorting through scripts and nearly completed films. They discarded several dozen scripts completely.

One of these, *The Poison Oracle*, had been written by Academy Award–winning author Peter Stone and was based on Peter Dickensen's novel about a young scientist embroiled in the investigation of a sultan's murder. Even with these impressive credentials, the trio felt the script was not worth producing.

Eisner, Wells, and Katzenberg also spent hours in the third-floor screening room at the Animation Building, looking at completed or nearly completed films. The films, the first batch turned out by Richard Berger for Touchstone, were ambitious but flawed. *Country* had been budgeted at $13.8 million; though it boasted Sam Shepard and Jessica Lange, it had little commercial appeal. Disney had spent $23 million to make *Return to Oz*, a film laden with high-tech special effects that was more a spoof than an update of MGM's 1939 classic *The Wizard of Oz*. Berger had brought in George Lucas to try to save the project near the end of production, but the film was still a disaster. Disney's new executives estimated that the five films ready for release would lose a total of $112 million. In all, Disney wrote down $166 million for the last quarter of 1984. The write-downs included $20 million in legal and other costs during the takeover fights, and more than $4 million to settle contracts with Ron Miller and Ray Watson. Also included in the write-downs were the costs of abandoning several projects at the theme parks, including pavilions that were to have been built jointly with the Israeli and Spanish governments.

Writing off the previous management's work is traditional in most businesses. By doing so, Eisner and Wells could saddle the previous management of Ron Miller and Card Walker with the expected losses. That would give Disney's new managers a clean slate, allowing Eisner and Wells to be judged on their own accomplishments.

The write-offs were large enough to slash Disney's earnings nearly in half for 1984. That caught the attention of the Securities and Exchange Commission. Not long after Disney reported the write-downs in mid-November, the company was ordered by the SEC to send several dozen of its internal documents to Washington. After several weeks of review and a hurried trip east by Mike Bagnall, however, the government dropped the matter.

By then, Team Disney was beginning to settle in at the Burbank studio. Unquestionably, the tone was set by Jeffrey Katzenberg and his workaholic nature. Executives were expected to be at their desk by 7:00 A.M. and to work late into the night. Mandatory story meetings were held at 10:00 P.M. Marketing meetings took place on Sunday morning. Each

Monday, members of Team Disney were expected to report on the half-dozen or more scripts that they had read over the weekend. "It was a crisis mentality," said former production head Richard Berger, who stayed on for several months after the new team was hired. "They were hell-bent to hit the ground running."

Local wags began to call Disney "Paramount in the Valley." There was no mistaking the Diller influence. As at Paramount, the power of the story was stressed over the box office charisma of hotshot actors. A star, no matter how popular, would inevitably bomb if the script was weak, the Disney executives felt. But a strong story line rarely failed.

At Paramount, Diller had contemplated hiring his own staff of writers rather than paying the lofty fees a hot script could command. At Disney, Eisner and Katzenberg hired three dozen writers, paying them $75,000 a year to rewrite old scripts or to turn fresh ideas into usable stories. It was a throwback to Hollywood practices of the 1940s, when talent was stockpiled by Samuel Goldwyn and Jack Warner. Only this time, instead of box office stars, Disney intended to stockpile promising young writers and near-hit producers.

Daniel Petrie, a writer for *Beverly Hills Cop*, came aboard, along with Tony Ganz and Deborah Blum, who had worked on Ron Howard's movie *Gung Ho*, and David Bombyk, a coproducer on *Witness*. None of these writers had played major roles in the huge hits, nor had Lauren Shuler, who had worked for John Hughes on *Pretty in Pink* at Paramount. She was signed to a three-year deal.

One of Team Disney's biggest deals was signing Interscope Communications. The company was headed by Ted Field, an heir to the Marshall Field department store fortune. Field had one moderate hit to his credit, *Revenge of the Nerds*, which he had made for Fox. Along with former Fox production executive Robert Cort, Field was willing to absorb the often hefty costs of buying and developing story ideas and scripts. The agreement was that Disney would make a film only if it liked Interscope's script; in return, Interscope would get a generous percentage of the profits.

All of Hollywood, both Eisner and Katzenberg knew, would be watching for the first Disney project of the Eisner era. Success was necessary. Anything else would validate people who had heaped most of the credit for Paramount's success onto Barry Diller's shoulders. The first film that Disney would do would also send a signal to the rest of the industry that Team Disney had overcome the corporate lethargy that had plagued Disney for more than two decades.

❖

As soon as the airplane carrying Jeffrey Katzenberg landed at San Francisco International Airport, the new head of Walt Disney Studios telephoned back to Burbank. During the hour-long flight, Katzenberg had finished reading the script for *Jerry Saved from Drowning*, a remake of a 1932 French film by Jean Renoir. The film was about a bum who jumps into the Seine and a bourgeois who saves him from drowning. The script Katzenberg read had rough spots, but Katzenberg had liked what he read. "This film has possibilities," he said crisply. At the other end of the telephone line, Michael Eisner agreed. "This is the one," said Disney's new chairman.

Sam Cohn, International Creative Management vice-chairman, had sent Eisner the script for *Jerry Saved from Drowning* by Federal Express from New York the first week Eisner was at Disney. Cohn represented Paul Mazursky, a one-time Greenwich Village comic and bit Hollywood actor who later wrote for comedian Danny Kaye and the 1960s TV comedy *The Monkees*. Since the late 1960s, Mazursky had developed into one of Hollywood's most admired directors and had directed such films as *Bob & Carol & Ted & Alice* and *Harry and Tonto*.

Eisner had admired Paul Mazursky since 1978, when the director had won an Academy Award nomination for *An Unmarried Woman*. But Eisner had never been able to get together with him on a project at Paramount. The only reason Disney was getting a chance on this film now, Cohn told Eisner, was that Universal's new studio chief, Frank Price, had decided against doing the film.

Mazursky had written *Jerry Saved from Drowning* with Leon Capetanos. The two had also written *Moscow on the Hudson* together. The setting for the French film had been Paris, but Mazursky and Capetanos had decided that Beverly Hills would be right for their rewritten version. They also decided to have the bum, Jerry Baskin, stay in a house owned by a wire-hanger king named Dave Whiteman and his wife Barb.

Making this film was a risky decision for Disney. Mazursky's films had a cult following but had never been big hits. Moreover, Eisner and Katzenberg objected to the cast that Mazursky envisioned for the film. The 55-year-old director wanted to play the role of Dave Whiteman himself. He also wanted to get one of his best friends, Jack Nicholson, to play the bum. Hiring Nicholson would make the film prohibitively expensive, Eisner initially told Cohn. Although Nicholson did eventually get a chance at the film, he decided against it, choosing instead to both act in and direct *The Two Jakes*, the long-awaited *Chinatown* sequel.

"Jack Nicholson would have been great in the role," recalled Michael Eisner later, "but we just weren't in a position at the time to make a deal with someone like him."

Neither Katzenberg nor Eisner believed Mazursky was a strong enough actor to carry the lead role, but the Disney chief executive did heartily approve of another suggestion. Bette Midler, said Paul Mazursky, would be the perfect actress to play Barb Whiteman.

❖

Bette Midler was no stranger to Michael Eisner. The Disney chairman remembered "The Divine Miss M" from her days as a singer in New York clubs, when her rich voice and bombastic personality had made her an underground star. Later, Eisner signed her to a deal with ABC-TV. In late 1984, however, Midler was in the depths of a personal crisis. The fiery singer-actor, who had left her native Honolulu in 1965 for Broadway, had won a Grammy for her 1972 album, *The Divine Miss M*, and was a frequent guest on *The Tonight Show*. Her film career had an equally auspicious start. She was nominated for an Academy Award in 1978 for her first film, *The Rose*. (It was Sally Field, however, who won the award that year, for *Norma Rae*.)

By 1982, however, Midler's career had hit rock bottom. In making the prophetically titled film *Jinxed*, Midler had feuded with the producer, the director, and her costar Ken Wahl. "*Jinxed* was the worst experience of my life," Midler told *Rolling Stone* in a 1982 interview. "It drove me to a nervous breakdown." The film was also a bomb, and Midler's highly visible fights had made her practically unhirable.

Despite these problems, Eisner and Katzenberg wanted her. In the right film, with the right script, she could still be a star, they thought— and *Jerry Saved from Drowning* could be just right for her. At the time, Midler was asking for $750,000 to do a film, plus a small piece of the profits. As much as they wanted her, Disney wouldn't pay more than $600,000, Katzenberg told her agents. "Her career is in the fucking toilet," the Disney studio chief explained.

Midler had nowhere else to go, and so she signed with Disney for $600,000 with a small share of the profits. "The Divine Miss M" had just met "the tightfisted Mr. K." Eisner and Katzenberg were determined to make films at Disney, as they had at Paramount, for less than the industry average, then running at about $17 million for a major film. One way to do this was to hold down the costs of developing and finding new scripts. The other was to hold down the rising salaries of Hollywood stars and directors. By 1985, even second-tier actors could command $1 million or more per film, and heavyweight directors like Steven Spielberg were getting as much as $5 million for a single film. Team Disney had decided at the outset that it wouldn't pay exorbitant salaries. Disney refused to accept projects that were packaged by talent agents like Creative Artists Agency. Adopting the Paramount model, Disney paid first-time directors $50,000 a film, the amount established as "scale" by the Directors Guild of America. That was the price Paramount had paid Robert Redford when he made his directing debut with *Ordinary People,* as Eisner quickly reminded any directors who objected—and that was what Disney intended to pay.

The Disney pay scale extended as well to the in-house producers who shepherd projects from script to finished product. Other studios paid $350,000 a year, but Disney would pay only $250,000. Moreover, while other studios required no more than a film a year from their staff producers, Disney insisted on two each year. "Jeffrey has no hesitancy in saying, 'You should take less for the privilege of working for Disney,'" producer Dan Melnick recalled.

There were no similar guidelines for holding down payments to the stars who went before the camera. But in early 1985, when the producers of *Ruthless People* wanted to cast the singer Madonna in the film, Disney decided that the $1 million she was asking was way out of line. Instead, they cast Midler, paying her the same $600,000 she had earned for her first film.

Jerry Saved from Drowning set the precedent for Walt Disney Productions. Stars who were down on their luck could find a home in Burbank, as long as they were willing to do what they were told and to do it cheaply. At Chasen's and the other industry watering holes, Disney became known as "The Betty Ford Clinic" of Hollywood, a reference to the alcohol and substance abuse clinic established by the former First Lady.

Following Midler on the set of *Jerry Saved from Drowning* was Richard Dreyfuss. Even more than Midler, the 36-year-old Dreyfuss fit the "Betty Ford" mold. A one-time Academy Award–winning actor, Dreyfuss had also fallen on hard times. The son of a Brooklyn attorney, Dreyfuss moved to Los Angeles with his family at age nine and got his start acting in amateur productions at the Beverly Hills Jewish Center. His first professional role was a bit part in the 1967 film *Valley of the Dolls.* He rose to prominence as an ambivalent college-bound boy in the

1973 hit *American Graffiti*, and at 29 he won an Oscar for the 1977 film *The Goodbye Girl*. He was also in two of the biggest hits of all time, *Jaws* and *Close Encounters of the Third Kind*.

By 1984, however, unable to shake an addiction to cocaine, Dreyfuss was virtually an unemployed actor. He worked only sporadically. In one of the few roles he was able to get, the lead in a poorly made film called *Whose Life Is It Anyway*, Dreyfuss played an unrewarding role as a paralyzed man confined to a hospital bed. In 1982, he crashed his Mercedes against a tree in the Benedict Canyon section of Los Angeles and was arrested for possession of cocaine and the drug Percodan. "I became a drug addict, I was arrested and I was a failure," Dreyfuss told *Newsweek* magazine five years later. Eisner remembered Richard Dreyfuss from Eisner's ABC days, when the network ordered a pilot for a television show based on the 1970 hit, *Catch 22*. In the TV version, Dreyfuss, then a rising actor just off his *American Graffiti* success, played the Alan Arkin role of Yossarian, the pilot flying on the edge of insanity. "We knew he was great," Eisner recalled. "It was just that no one else knew it at the time that we knew it." Whether Dreyfuss was great or not, his $1.2 million asking price was more than Disney was willing to pay. The one-time Academy Award winner was signed for $600,000.

Nick Nolte had no sad story to tell. The 44-year-old Omaha native was a solid actor, having started with *Return to Macon County* in 1975, and having been in such hits as *North Dallas Forty* in 1979 and *48 Hours* in 1982. Good as he was, the gruff-sounding blond actor had never had a starring role. Disgusted with the way he was being treated in Hollywood, he had moved his permanent residence to his wife's hometown in West Virginia. Eisner and Katzenberg, however, had worked with him at Paramount during the filming of *48 Hours*. They liked the diligence with which he practiced his craft, and he could be signed for little more than what Dreyfuss was being paid. "There was no way to overestimate their stinginess," said ICM agent Sam Cohn, who represented both Dreyfuss and Nolte.

By April 1985, Eisner and Katzenberg had signed Nolte to play the part of the drifter, and Dreyfuss and Midler as the Whitemans. Nolte, a serious method actor, practiced for his part by spending hours at the Union Rescue Mission in downtown Los Angeles, and had stopped bathing and brushing his teeth by the time filming began. Midler joked that to prepare for her role she "walked all over Beverly Hills and shopped till I was blue." The cameras began to roll for the first film of the Eisner-Wells regime on May 20. Disney built a 5,000-square-foot set in Burbank, complete with a landscaped yard and swimming pool, that served as the principal location for the film. Even with three well-known stars, the film's budget was a relatively modest $14 million.

❖

Nervous and edgy, Frank Wells pulled his blue Mercedes off Sunset Boulevard onto a side street to use his car telephone. It was May 2, 1985, and the Disney president had just finished his morning run on the track at the University of California at Los Angeles. The news that Wells had heard on his car radio was unsettling. E. F. Hutton, one of Wall Street's most trusted companies, had just pleaded guilty in a massive check-kiting scheme that involved many of the 400 banks with which it did business. There would also be a $10 million fine.

The news was no doubt a black eye for the securities industry, but for Frank Wells it struck even closer to home. Only the day before, E. F. Hutton brokers had begun selling shares in a limited partnership designed to raise the $100 million that Disney would need to reemerge as a major movie studio.

"Do we have a problem?" Wells curtly asked as soon as he got Roland Betts on the telephone. Betts, a 38-year-old former Wall Street lawyer, had put together the Silver Screen II partnership for Disney. A stocky man with wavy black hair, an easy smile, and the backslapping manner of a former athlete, Betts is the consummate salesman. But Betts was worried. Silver Screen, his first attempt to sell the public shares in a moviemaking venture, had been less than a success. The $83 million that it had raised in 1983 for Home Box Office had been the most ever raised by a limited partnership. But the Time Inc. cable channel had been a bust at producing films, churning out such flops as *Flashpoint* and *Heaven Help Us*. Few of Betts's 150,000 clients had seen any profits.

Betts and his partner Tom Bernstein had sought out Eisner and Wells not long after the two had been hired by Disney. Wells had told a *New York Times* reporter that they were still undecided on how they would finance their movies. Eisner's track record at Paramount, Betts figured, would make him a far better partner than HBO. Besides, with the support of the Bass organization, the Silver Screen people figured, there would be additional pressure on the new team to succeed.

Betts had called Frank Wells shortly after Wells and Eisner had started work. The two former lawyers already knew one another from previous film dealings. In 1981, Betts had tried to get Wells to help finance *Gandhi*, directed by Betts's client Richard Attenborough. Wells had passed, and Columbia Pictures had picked up the opportunity. The film went on to win the 1982 Academy Award. But Columbia, which had only the U.S. theatrical and video rights, barely made any money. "Frank Wells turned out to be pretty savvy," Betts recalled.

As structured by Silver Screen, Betts's investors would bear all the costs of making Disney's movies in return for a hefty percentage of the profits. It was the kind of deal that appealed to Michael Eisner. At Paramount, Eisner's mentor Barry Diller had actively sought out investors for his films, something rarely done at the time by other major studios. A group of banks had put up 25 percent of the costs of making *Flashdance*, for instance, in return for one-quarter of the profits.

Getting someone to share the risk was the type of good business that Charlie Bluhdorn had drilled into the heads of both Eisner and Diller. There was less pain in sharing the profits than in swallowing the entire loss, the Gulf & Western chief had preached. "I like to sleep at night," Eisner admitted later. "If you don't instill in your people the ability to fail there's no reason why they have to take the whole ship down with them."

Eisner, Wells, and Jeffrey Katzenberg had other reasons to look for partners who might soften the blow of failure. The three men all had lucrative provisions in their contracts tied to the profitability of the company. A box office flop of the magnitude of a *Heaven's Gate* or *Howard the Duck* would blow a hole in Disney's profits. Sharing the downside risk made economic sense for the three executives' own pocketbooks.

In mid-October, Wells flew to New York to see Betts in his office on Madison Avenue for the beginning of negotiations. Almost from the start, it was a roller-coaster relationship. Betts, still smarting from his lackluster experience with HBO, drove a hard bargain. "We didn't know if Eisner and Katzenberg were the reasons for Paramount's success, or whether it was Barry Diller," he says now. "There was just no way of knowing."

Eisner and Wells also drove a hard bargain. Making movies allowed companies to take lucrative tax credits, and the Disney team didn't want to share them with Roland Betts's partners. Betts also wanted Disney to repay the costs of any box office flops. Eisner refused. If any film failed to make money for Silver Screen, Disney would return only the money it collected from its portion of any film's revenues.

Three months after Betts first approached Frank Wells, he and Disney reached an agreement. Disney would find the script and put up at least $5 million for marketing and distributing the films. Betts's investors would pay up to $20 million per film and share in up to half the profits that the movies got from theaters and 25 percent of videocassette sales. Disney would also get most of the money from cable, network, and syndicated television. If any films were unsuccessful, within five years Disney was required to repay Silver Screen its initial investment in the film.

To turn the agreement into the money Disney needed, however, E. F. Hutton's vast network of brokers would have to sell the offering. "When Hutton Talks, People Listen," was the brokerage house's famous advertising slogan—and at the time Hutton was enjoying a hot streak of its own. In March 1985, Betts arranged for Eisner, Wells, and Katzenberg to speak to Hutton's 400 most successful brokers at a meeting at the Sheraton Yankee Clipper hotel in Fort Lauderdale, Florida. The elaborate affair, complete with lavish meals and generous door prizes, including cars, was Hutton's reward for its top moneymakers.

To prime the audience, Disney flew dozens of dancers from Orlando to Fort Lauderdale to put on a glittery show. Costumed characters mingled with the crowd, posing for pictures and handing out prospectuses with Mickey Mouse on the cover. The main attraction though, was the new Disney management. Speaking from the stage of the ballroom, Eisner, tall and engaging, charmed the Hutton brokers with stories of how Paramount had made *Raiders of the Lost Ark* and *Beverly Hills Cop.* Wells, following Eisner, talked about working with Clint Eastwood and signing the deal that brought *Chariots of Fire* to Warner Brothers.

The show seemed to stop, however, when Katzenberg took the podium. For all his fabled abilities with temperamental stars, Jeffrey Katzenberg had little experience in speaking before an audience. Now, reading from three-by-five index cards, he spoke in a monotone for nearly an hour about the films Disney had in production. For each film, he went through numbing details of virtually every facet of production.

"Those brokers were fidgeting and itching," recalled Betts. "I thought we had lost the whole damn thing." When Katzenberg beat a quick retreat to his room to resume his nonstop telephone calls to producers and stars, Eisner and Wells began working the room like politicians on the make. Going from table to table, they congratulated the brokers on their success and encouraged them to sell shares. "You from

Texas?" Wells asked one broker. "How much you think you can sell down there, $2 million?" Wells remembers it well: "It was just like a stump speech. We did what we could to put the thing over."

That included more than just glad-handing. Unlike the prior Disney management, which had carefully shielded its characters from excessive public exposure, Eisner and Wells were not afraid to throw Mickey and Donald into the hard sell. Not only did the Mouse appear on the offering's front cover, but a 10-minute videocassette hawking Silver Screen II used Disneyland as a backdrop. In front of Sleeping Beauty's Castle stood a salesman in a tuxedo, arm-in-arm with Mickey, Minnie, and Donald. Film clips from Disney classics such as *Snow White* and *Fantasia* were sprinkled throughout the video, as was Mary Poppin's one-word exclamation, "Supercalifragalisticexpialidosious," which was used to describe the offering.

A somber-looking Michael Eisner gave a short pitch about the quality of the movies he intended to make, but the parting shot that no doubt lingered in the minds of E. F. Hutton brokers showed Mickey riding in the open-air backseat of an antique biplane, his thumb extended upward in a gesture that symbolized "terrific."

The show Disney put on worked. The combination of the best-known movie company in America with Wall Street's most highly regarded firm brought in an impressive $14 million on May 1, 1985, the first day the offering was available.

Wells was a happy man for one day—but then the bomb was dropped. With news of its check-kiting problems, E. F. Hutton quickly tumbled from the ranks of Wall Street's mighty. By May 3, sales of Silver Screen units had virtually stopped. Betts and Bernstein worried that the Disney management would pull out. After all, recalled Bernstein, "Here we were, having put Mickey on the cover of the prospectus and then having him dragged through the mud."

Instead, Wells told the Silver Screen duo that Disney intended to stick with them. In fact, the Disney team really had no choice. The public offering was Wall Street's first look at the company's new managers. This was 1985, less than a year after Eisner and Wells had been brought into the company. Pulling the limited partnership off the market would only prove what some Wall Street analysts privately feared—that the new Disney managers were no better able to cope with the changing world of high-stakes finance than their predecessors has been.

Eisner and Wells went back on the speaking circuit. The two men visited E. F. Hutton conferences wherever they could. Eisner gave a pep talk on a special telephone hookup to the nearly 1,000 E. F. Hutton offices around the country, answering questions for more than an hour. Sales soon picked up.

The offering had one more near disaster to overcome. On May 29, nearly a month after the offering began, Massachusetts regulators canceled all sales in the state, citing improper registration. Pennsylvania, North Carolina, and Puerto Rico soon followed suit. When Massachusetts canceled, ironically, Tom Bernstein was pitching the offering before 400 brokers and their families at the Westport Theater in St. Louis, Missouri. Disney characters milled through the crowd, lending a carnival atmosphere as they posed for pictures with the brokers' kids.

After returning to New York, Bernstein learned that Silver Screen had similar problems in Maine, Michigan, and Arizona. The offering, in fact, had been improperly registered in a total of 15 states by the law firm that Silver Screen had hired. Betts and Bernstein soon hired another law firm, which withdrew the tainted registrations and refiled the offering.

Despite the myriad problems, response to the initial offering had been so strong that Betts and Bernstein decided to increase the offering from $100 million to $200 million. When the Silver Screen offering closed in September 1985, a year after Roland Betts and Frank Wells began discussing it, it had raised $193 million. By the end of September, Disney had received $58 million, the first installment of the $170 million it would eventually receive from the offering. (The balance went for various commissions and legal fees.)

❖

While Roland Betts and Tom Bernstein were parading Mickey and Donald at carnival-like sales meetings throughout Middle America, Michael Eisner and Jeffrey Katzenberg were building a studio. In a process they had begun while casting for the script that became *Down and Out in Beverly Hills*, the two Disney executives were still aggressively pursuing Hollywood's downtrodden, untested, and over-the-hill.

They signed Judge Reinhold, who had played the supporting role of a bumbling younger police detective in Paramount's 1984 smash *Beverly Hills Cop*, to a two-picture deal for $250,000 a film. Aging stars Burt Lancaster and Kirk Douglas were signed for *Tough Guys*, a movie about a pair of old bank robbers who try for one last score. The two actors wanted to work together and were willing to work for scale, the minimum $1,200 weekly salary established by the Screen Actors Guild. Each was also to receive a share of the profits, with a cap of $1 million. The film was only a modest hit, and neither actor received anything close to the maximum.

Disney also decided to build its stars by choosing actors from TV shows that had made their mark on the American viewer. Eisner and Katzenberg both felt that whatever following a TV star had would almost certainly carry over to the movie theater. The strategy wasn't new to Hollywood, but few stars had managed to make the transition. Bill Cosby, for example, whose star appeal on the tube was superb, had bombed miserably in movies.

Even so, Eisner and Katzenberg believed that name recognition from the small screen would work to their advantage. One of the first stars they signed was Shelley Long, a one-time member of Chicago's Second City improvisation troop. She had just left the hit TV show *Cheers*, on which she had played the obnoxiously erudite waitress Diane Chambers. Her movie career had had only mixed success. She had made such lukewarm films as *Night Shift* and *The Money Pit*.

Long was soon followed by literally scores of other TV stars from Paramount-produced television shows, including Danny De Vito of *Taxi*, Robin Williams of *Mork & Mindy*, and Ted Danson of *Cheers*. Tom Selleck, who also signed with Disney, had starred in *Magnum P.I.*, made by Universal, but Selleck had passed Paramount's way as well. He had once been the lead candidate to play *Indiana Jones* in the George Lucas trilogy but had left the film when CBS picked up the television show.

TV stars seemed a natural fit for the films planned by Team Disney. The typical upcoming Disney film looked more like a 90-minute sit-com than like a traditional movie. Story lines were simple and vaguely reminiscent of *I Love Lucy* or *Laverne and Shirley*. In *Down and Out in Beverly Hills* a bum meets the wealthy; in *Outrageous Fortune* two women chase the same man.

As they had at Paramount, Eisner and Katzenberg bared their knuckles to keep costs under control. The studio refused to make films with costly special effects or lavish battle scenes. Travel was kept to a minimum, and whenever possible, filming was done in and around Los Angeles. Many of the scenes were interiors that could be safely tucked into Disney's studio, where outside interferences could be minimized.

"They are very clear [about] what movie they want to make," recalled Robert Cort, who produced the 1987 *Outrageous Fortune,* one of the first films of the Eisner-Katzenberg tenure. At the outset, Cort recalled, an anxious-looking Katzenberg deputy, Marty Katz, was keeping close tabs on Cort and director Arthur Hiller. If an extra scene was needed, Katz had to be consulted. Any problems that arose were immediately transmitted to Katzenberg, who would hurry down to the set to prod the director. Ultimately, *Outrageous Fortune,* which had been projected to cost $19 million, came in about $100,000 under budget.

Even with Team Disney's economics, and even with the flood of money that was beginning to come from Silver Screen, Disney spent $84 million on film production in 1985, more than double the $31 million it had spent the year before. As part of the Silver Screen deal, Disney received a $22 million loan to pay some of the costs of the four films the Eisner team inherited—*The Black Cauldron, Return to Oz, Natty Gann,* and *My Science Project*—none of which would make much money. Under the terms of the Silver Screen deal, however, Disney didn't have to begin repaying the loan for five years. That, Eisner and Katzenberg hoped, would give them more than enough time to begin churning out their own moneymakers.

Many of the Eisner-Katzenberg early film, including *Down and Out in Beverly Hills,* were made from scripts that other studios had commissioned and then discarded. These are dubbed "turnarounds" by Hollywood insiders. It was a time-proven place to find movies. In the past, the industry's scrap heap has produced such box office winners as *E.T.: The Extra-Terrestrial,* which Columbia Pictures had turned away.

Katzenberg scoured the list of turnarounds for whatever he could make money on. One he found was *Ruthless People,* a script that Columbia had commissioned but then decided not to make. Eisner read the script and gave it to Jim Abrahams, David Zucker, and Jerry Zucker, who had directed *Airplane* for him at Paramount. The trio had come to Hollywood from Milwaukee a decade earlier to try making comedies.

Their first effort was *Kentucky Fried Movie,* which was only a modest hit, but their second, *Airplane,* became one of the Cinderella stories of modern Hollywood. By 1984, however, the three friends had bombed out twice, with a low-brow film, *Top Secret,* and a short-lived TV series, *Police Squad.* Zucker, Zucker, and Abrahams signed a two-year deal with Disney on May 1, 1985. Within a week, they were at work on *Ruthless People.* With a budget of $17 million, Disney signed

Midler to play the lead female role of Barbara Stone. Danny De Vito became her loathsome husband, Sam. Judge Reinhold was cast to play a bumbling stereo salesman who kidnaps Milder. The salesman's wife and accomplice was played by Helen Slater, whose previous movie had been *Supergirl.*

The filming of *Ruthless People* began at the posh Los Angeles restaurant L'Orangerie in January 1986. By then, Disney had more than a dozen films in various stages of production. Mark Medoff, who had won a Tony award for his play *Children of a Lesser God,* had been signed to write his first screenplay. *Off-Beat,* a $12 million film, starred Judge Reinhold as a meek library clerk who impersonates a New York cop to impress the woman he loves. *Risky Business* producer Steve Tisch had been signed to make *Big Business,* starring Lily Tomlin and Bette Midler, each playing a double role as twins who were mismatched at birth. *Diner* director Barry Levinson had come aboard to make *Tin Men,* starring Danny De Vito and Richard Dreyfuss as a pair of feuding aluminum siding salesmen in Baltimore.

❖

At Paramount, his colleagues had referred to him as "the Godfather." Quiet and diplomatic, Frank Mancuso, the studio's 50-year-old head of marketing, had known how to squeeze money out of anything Barry Diller and Michael Eisner made. He had orchestrated the marketing campaign for *Flashdance* by releasing both a rock video of the film for MTV and a sultry poster of its star Jennifer Beals. When other studios were releasing action films for the summer of 1982, he had countered by putting out *An Officer and a Gentleman* in July. The only love story in the theaters, it became a huge hit.

Paramount's marketing team had remained fiercely loyal to Frank Mancuso during the 1984 studio revolt. Of the nearly five dozen Paramount executives who had followed Michael Eisner to Disney, none had come from Paramount's well-regarded marketing crew, despite Team Disney's attempts to lure them.

Marketing was an area of Disney that badly needed help when Eisner and the rest of Team Disney arrived. At the time, other studios spent an average of $6.5 million to advertise and market their new films. Disney spent less than $3 million. Walt had never advertised heavily, as Card Walker had often reminded Ron Miller and Richard Berger. Disney's idea of publicity was also minimalist. When *Tex* had opened in

1982, for instance, Walker had ordered an eight-person publicity team to visit 74 cities in three dozen states with a 23-minute film clip in an attempt to drum up free articles in local newspapers. Disney had even put out a press release to trumpet the event. Still, the film sold less than $6 million worth of tickets.

Since mid-1983, Disney's advertising and promotional work for its films had been supervised by Barrie Lorie, who had come with Richard Berger from Fox. Neither Eisner nor Katzenberg was particularly impressed by Lorie, and he left for MGM shortly after they arrived. Since Eisner and Katzenberg couldn't hire anyone from the Paramount team, they did the next best thing. They gave their advertising account to a new entertainment unit that was just then being set up at the Los Angeles office of Young & Rubican by Gordon Weaver and Stephen Rose.

Weaver and Rose had left Paramount just before Eisner and Katzenberg left, amid allegations by the studio that the two marketing executives had improperly received kickbacks from companies that did advertising and promotional work for Paramount. On April 29, 1990, after leaving the advertising agency, Weaver and Rose were indicted by a federal grand jury for failure to file proper tax returns. They had allegedly failed to report income from the alleged kickbacks. Among the payments that were said to have been involved were the free use of a summer home by Weaver and a new Mercedes-Benz for Rose. Both men denied the charges at the time.*

Eisner and Katzenberg knew about the allegations. But at Paramount, Weaver and Rose had been key members of a Paramount marketing team that was renowned within the industry as Hollywood's best. Disney's two new executives especially admired the work Weaver and Rose had done in promoting such films as *Raiders of the Lost Ark* and *Star Trek*. They decided not to let unproved allegations get in the way of their hiring the best marketers available.

Hiring Weaver and Rose allowed Disney to get into mainstream film business without changing the whole marketing department overnight, but both Eisner and Katzenberg knew that, as the studio's film output increased, they would need someone on staff. Someone would have to handle the day-to-day job of putting together the advertising campaigns and promotional efforts that were increasingly important in selling films.

---

*Rose and Weaver later pled guilty to reduced charges and received suspended sentences.

In mid-June, the company hired Robert Levin, who had been a senior vice-president with the Chicago-based ad agency Needham Harper. Levin had handled the Sears and Exxon accounts for his agency. Rich Frank, the studio's second-ranking executive, knew Levin from their days together at the University of Illinois. But the closest thing to show business experience that Levin had was a 1960s campaign for a snack food called "Screaming Yellow Zonkers."

❖

Jerry Saved from Drowning, retitled *Down and Out in Beverly Hills*, was scheduled to open January 31, 1986. The film, Walt Disney Production's first R-rated movie, was previewed by an uncomfortable Disney board of directors at their November meeting. The board members were used to the mild-mannered Disney fare of the past three decades. Hearing Bette Midler swearing like a New York cabdriver was shocking to several board members. Even more shocking were the love scenes between both the husband Dave Whiteman and the bum Jerry Baskin with the family maid in the movie. Jerry also has an affair with his benefactor Dave's wife. "The sex scene with the maid had a lot of eyebrows raised," recalled Ray Watson, the former board chairman who retained his seat on the board.

No one, however, asked Michael Eisner to change the sex scene. "This company had the reputation of being a censor," Eisner announced to the board. "I don't like the language either, but you have to keep creative people." Sanitizing *Down and Out in Beverly Hills*, the Disney chairman told the board, would send the wrong kind of signal to Hollywood's creative community. Word would go out that, for all its brash talk, Disney had not changed—and such talk would inhibit the company's chances of hiring the creative people it had to have in order to succeed.

Team Disney was worried, however. A screening of the nearly completed film before a test audience at a Los Angeles theater had gone badly. Both Eisner and Katzenberg thought that the film was too long and that the scenes were jumbled. Mazursky was ordered to reedit it and to cut more than 20 minutes of rambling footage. By Thanksgiving he had shortened the film by 23 minutes, making its pace quicker and more to the Disney team's liking.

Worried that it would get trampled by such possible 1985 blockbusters as *Rocky IV, Back to School,* and *Jewel of the Nile,* the Disney brass decided not to release the film during the traditionally lucrative Christmas box office season. Instead, they planned a January 31 release, hoping that it would do well at a time when other studios usually release their weaker films.

Disney's marketing team had decided to pitch *Down and Out in Beverly Hills* as a hip urban movie, geared to rich liberals on both coasts. Spending lavishly, Disney orchestrated sneak previews along with New Year's Eve parties in 36 cities. Door prizes, including a free trip to Beverly Hills, were to be given away.

Jeffrey Katzenberg returned from a five-day vacation in Hawaii on the afternoon of one of the parties, which was to be held at the AMC Theater in Los Angeles, across the street from the stately Century Plaza. Katzenberg walked in to find distribution chief Dick Cook busily handing out extra tickets for the larger-than-expected crowd.

When the film opened in 800 cities a month later, it got mixed reviews. "The movie is sloppily constructed and occasionally [a] little vague," wrote *New York Magazine*, "but it's juicily, irresistibly funny." "The hokey scenes tend to outnumber the authentic scenes," wrote Joseph Gelmis in *Newsday*. "It's a gagfest rather than a serious comedy."

Despite the reviews, the movie worked. During its opening weekend, it sold more than $5.7 million worth of tickets, putting it ahead of *The Color Purple* and *Out of Africa*. The second week, when box office numbers usually fall off, *Down and Out in Beverly Hills* took in $6.2 million. The film ultimately sold more than $62 million worth of tickets, second only to *Splash* in Disney's history. Six months later, *Ruthless People* topped that record by taking in $71.6 million.

❖

By the time *Down and Out in Beverly Hills* opened, Wall Street was unabashedly backing Michael Eisner and Team Disney. The stock had slumped to below $60 a share in September 1984 when Eisner and Wells were hired, signaling the end to the takeover siege. By early 1985, however, the stock had risen to about $80, and even a little higher on occasion, on the strength of surprisingly high attendance at the theme parks. Strong support for the Silver Screen offering had added several more points. It hadn't hurt that Eisner and Wells had made several trips to New York, artfully stroking Wall Street analysts by giving them insights into how they intended to turn the company around. *Down and Out in Beverly Hills* seemed to symbolize the rebirth of Walt Disney Productions. As if to emphasize the difference in management style, the company's shareholders voted on February 6, 1986, to change the company's name to The Walt Disney Company. A month earlier, the board of directors had authorized a four-for-one stock split. The stock on February 6 was trading at $120 a share.

CHAPTER

Wishing Upon a Star

L ocals call Incline, on the shores of Lake Tahoe, "the Hollywood of Nevada." Barbara Streisand once owned one of the huge mansions that line Lake Shore Drive, an enclave of gated estates fronted by a private beach. Don Johnson is a regular on the tennis courts. So, too, is Leonard Nimoy, *Star Trek's* pointy-eared Vulcan, Mr. Spock.

By 1987, however, Nimoy had traded in his Starship *Enterprise* uniform for a director's chair. The 56-year-old Nimoy had already directed *Star Trek III: The Search for Spock* and *Star Trek IV: The Voyage Home* for Paramount Pictures. Both had been huge hits. Now, as the summer of 1987 drew to a close, Nimoy was in the film-editing room of his large Tudor home in Incline, cutting and splicing a Disney film, *Three Men and a Baby.*

On October 12, *Three Men and a Baby* was to go before a live audience for the first time. Nimoy and Robert Cort, the film's producer, had rented the 125-seat Incline Theater, with its worn red carpets and crackly sound system. The trial run, the two men thought, would let them know whether the film was as good as they thought it was. The first half hour of the movie erased whatever doubts they had. "The laughs were so loud that you completely missed some of the lines," recalled Robert Cort. By November 25, Disney knew it had its first blockbuster.

Opening in 1,100 theaters, *Three Men and a Baby* sold more than $10 million worth of tickets before the weekend was over. It was the second film in Hollywood history to lead the pack at the box office on Thanksgiving, Christmas, and New Year's Day. (The first had been *Rocky IV*, two years earlier). By late spring, *Three Men and a Baby* had been playing for an astounding six months and had sold nearly $168 million in tickets. At the time only 16 films had done better.

Three Men and a Baby marked a turning point for the Walt Disney Company. Until then, the studio had turned out a remarkable number of profitable films. *Down and Out in Beverly Hills* had been followed by *Ruthless People, Outrageous Fortune*, and *Stakeout*. In all, of the first 15 films produced by the Eisner team, all but *Offbeat* had been profitable.

Even *Ernest Goes to Camp*, a dim-witted comedy staring Tennessee-born advertising star James Varney, had sold more than $23 million worth of tickets. Varney and his mythical friend "Vern" were a hit in the South. The film had been made for just over $5 million. Eisner had sought out the hick star after visiting the Indianapolis 500 auto race in 1986 and hearing Varney get louder applause than Mickey Mouse.

By 1987, the film unit was a major contributor to Disney's bottom line. In the year that ended on September 30, 1987, film revenues accounted for $284 million, nearly five times the 1984 figure. Home video sales had boomed for *Down and Out in Beverly Hills, Ruthless People*, and *Tin Men*. The studio had accounted for more than $875 million in revenues and $130 million in earnings. After providing less than 5 percent of the company's profits during Ron Miller's last year, the studio now contributed more than 16 percent of the company's operating income. (In 1987, the company earned $776.8 million overall, 47 percent higher than the year before, with nearly $2.9 billion in revenues.) For all Disney's success, however, it still hadn't achieved a $100 million blockbuster, Hollywood's definition of success. In an industry that saves its accolades for home runs, Disney was a reliable singles and doubles hitter. By comparison, across the Hollywood Hills, Paramount ended 1986 with two blockbusters, *Top Gun* and *Crocodile Dundee*.

At Paramount, $100 million movies were affectionately referred to as "tent poles." The rush of dollars from a blockbuster, any Hollywood executive knew, could keep the studio tent standing, allowing it to overcome even a failure or two. A tent pole could usually be followed up by a sequel, with a built-in audience that would make it also a hit. Foreign and videocassette sales were also usually strong, and occasionally a television show could be based on a blockbuster. A further advantage was to be found in marketing a future film by playing a "trailer" featuring snippets of the upcoming film just before the tent pole that crowds had lined up to see.

Michael Eisner wanted a tent pole. The Disney chairman had thought he found one early on, with *The Color of Money*. The film, a 20-year sequel to the 1961 movie *The Hustler*, had the kind of star power that Disney had generally avoided. Directing the film was Martin Scorsese, the 44-year-old son of a Flushing, New York, clothes presser, who had won plaudits for his direction of *Taxi Driver* and *Alice Doesn't Live Here Anymore*. Paul Newman had made a return as the aging Eddie Felson, with Tom Cruise as the talented newcomer whom Felson attempts to coach.

The Color of Money had come to Disney in early 1985 from Eisner's old friend Michael Ovitz, who headed the Creative Artists Agency. Ovitz represented Newman and Scorsese, as well as Walter Tevis, who has written both the original book, also entitled *The Hustler*, and its sequel. Twentieth Century Fox, which made the 1961 movie, had the rights to the sequel. But Ovitz wanted Disney to have the film and convinced Fox to pass on the project.

The film was budgeted at $14.5 million, not high by Hollywood standards, but Disney would be obligated to pay profit percentages that would make it hard for the film to show a profit. In addition, because the deal came as a package—with the stars, director, and script all agreed to beforehand—it would also be difficult for Disney to make changes in the script.

Michael Eisner and Jeffrey Katzenberg, however, decided to take the film, believing that it would establish Disney as a major player in the industry. The teaming of Paul Newman and Tom Cruise was guaranteed to generate tons of publicity—and it did. The duo, portrayed by Disney's publicity machine as the aging heartthrob and his toothy successor, found themselves on the cover of *Life* magazine and were chronicled in a five-part series for NBC's *Today Show*. A full-length cover story was also featured in *Newsweek*, but was put inside the magazine to make room for a piece by Henry Kissinger on the first summit between Ronald Reagan and Mikhail Gorbachev. The Newman-Cruise story did appear on the cover of *Newsweek's* international edition.

The film got glowing reviews. *USA Today* critic Mike Clark gave it top rating—four stars—and said "no recent film remotely equals *Money's* first 90 minutes." Vincent Canby, writing in the *New York*

Times, called it a "most entertaining, original film with its own, vivid, very contemporary identity for being." *Newsweek* called it simply "a near masterpiece."

Disney's marketing crew also geared up, making four separate TV ads—including one featuring the love story between Tom Cruise and Elizabeth Mastrantonio to play during soap operas, one showing Tom Cruise for game shows, and one with Newman and Cruise for prime-time shows.

The Scorsese film, however, turned out to be too dark and moody for the general audience. The $52 million in ticket sales that *The Color of Money* generated hardly classified it as failure, but it fell far short of Eisner's blockbuster expectations. It would take another year for the Walt Disney Company to get its tent pole.

❖

Through most of their careers, Michael Eisner and Jeffrey Katzenberg had avoided bidding wars. At Paramount, Diller had preached, there was no script that the studio absolutely had to have. Eisner and Katzenberg believed in the same gospel, but by late 1985, an exception had floated toward Burbank from Paris. The movie, which had already been filed in France, was *Trois Hommes et un Couffin* (the title translated to *Three Men and a Cradle*). It was about three bachelors forced to raise a small infant. By the time Eisner and Katzenberg heard about it, so had most of Hollywood. At least two other studios, Paramount and Universal, were interested in buying it.

Robert Cort, the frizzy-haired former Fox production executive whose Interscope Company had signed with Disney earlier that year, was just finishing production of *Outrageous Fortune* when he heard about the film. An old girlfriend had just returned from Paris, where she had seen the French version. Cort's wife, a Hollywood agent whose firm represented comedian Bill Murray, Cort soon learned, had steered the film toward Frank Price, president of Universal Pictures, who wanted Murray as one of the three bachelors.

Cort finally located a French-language copy of the film at the French film office in Los Angeles. At 7:30 A.M. one Saturday morning, Cort brought the cassette to Disney's Burbank lot, planning to see it with Katzenberg. Because neither man spoke French, Katzenberg's office had Berlitz send over a translator.

Katzenberg wanted the film but knew that it would not come cheaply. "It was a complete dogfight," recalls Cort. Foreign film rights at the time were generally going for less than $100,000. But *Trois Hommes et un Couffin*, directed by Coline Serreau, was an early favorite to be nominated for an Academy Award as best foreign film, and everyone knew the bidding would go up.

The Disney bidding was handled by Eisner himself. The Disney chairman also knew about the film, having seen it while in Paris. Despite Disney's reputation for stinginess and for developing its own material, he had decided that this was one script that the studio must have. Even when the bidding went up to $700,000, a record for rights to a foreign film. Disney refused to back down. Eisner's final offer was $750,000 with 7.5 percent of the profits going to the film's executive producer, Jean Francois Lepetit, and 3.5 percent to 37-year-old writer and director Coline Serreau, along with a guarantee that she could direct the film. The deciding factor, it turned out, was Disney's concessions to Serreau.

Disney had won the film but inherited a problem. Serreau, for all her brilliance with the French version, proved too difficult for the Disney brass to work with. Insisting that the French script not be changed, she refused to allow rewrites that Cort and Katzenberg knew were crucial to bridge the cultural gap and make it easier for Americans to understand. Serreau also refused to agree to Disney's demand that a pair of twins play the baby. By having one baby nap while the other was on the set, Disney expected to cut down on production delays—a move they proposed would save several hundred thousand dollars.

Jeffrey Katzenberg knew that he had a problem. He had aggressively pursued *Cheers* star Ted Danson for the role of Jack Holden and had dogged *Magnum P.I.* star Tom Selleck for months before he would agree to play the architect. *Police Academy* and *Cocoon* star Steve Guttenberg had also signed on to play the cartoonist.

The casting was typical of Disney. None of the actors had ever been a huge star on the big screen, and they weren't going to command stiff salaries. In all, Disney had penciled in the budget at $13 million. But a feud with the director would almost certainly delay production, adding untold costs to the project.

Coline Serreau had to go. "It would have been war if those three had come to the set, and she was still there," recalls Cort. The three stars had been told that the script would be rewritten, but no one could get

Serreau to alter the film to meet American standards. "She had done a . . . translation, that was all," said Cort. Finally, Katzenberg and Ricardo Mestres stepped in. After a series of stormy telephone conversations, Serreau quit, citing health reasons, a month before production was to begin. With Serreau gone, Disney hustled to bring in Nimoy, whom they knew from Paramount. James Orr and Jim Cruickshank, a pair of Canadians who had written *Tough Guys* for Disney, were quickly flown to the set in Toronto where filming costs are cheaper than in the United States. To meet the projected Christmas release date, filming began even before the rewrites were complete.

In the end, Orr and Cruickshank rewrote most of the script. Sight gags were added, including the now famous shot of the baby urinating on the couch while Selleck tries to diaper her. The character played by Danson was changed from airline steward to actor, and the sound track was updated. "Good Night, Sweetheart," the lullaby that became the film's signature, was added at the last moment.

Disney executives knew that they had a hit as soon as they saw the first cut. The film tested strongly with women, in part, Disney executives felt, because it was "the ultimate revenge film."

Bob Levin had also prepared an extensive marketing effort for *Three Men and a Baby*. The studio had hired award-winning photographer Annie Leibovitz to shoot photos for the print ads. During one session, the infant unexpectedly urinated on Selleck. "Annie had the foresight to say, 'Stay like that, I'm shooting,' " recalled Levin. The sight of Selleck with a wet shirt became the focal point of the campaign. Television ads also included the urination scene.

Disney had initially planned to release the film in early December, but the Christmas season was getting crowded with such likely heavyweights as *Throw Momma from the Train* and *Broadcast News*. Disney knew that it had a solid film but feared that a film about a cute baby that included no sex and little violence could get lost in a crowd.

Once before, at Columbia in 1977, Cort had opened a film during Thanksgiving, traditionally a slow time for movies. The film was Steven Spielberg's *Close Encounters of the Third Kind*, one of the all-time biggest hits. Jeffrey Katzenberg and distribution chief Dick Cook decided to open *Three Men and a Baby* also on Thanksgiving in order to give it some time to generate momentum and positive word-of-mouth appeal.

Jeffrey Katzenberg promised to dance on the table of his third-floor conference room on Monday morning if *Three Men and a Baby* sold more than $4 million worth of tickets on the Saturday following Thanksgiving. At 7:00 A.M. Monday, the usual early-morning staff meeting gathered, and Katzenberg did his jig.

❖

On January 16, Disney achieved its tent pole, as *Three Men and a Baby* passed the $100 million mark. It had taken only 53 days to reach blockbuster status, a point Disney trumpeted in a press release. In a none too subtle jab at their former employers, Team Disney's press release also noted that it had taken Paramount Pictures' *Crocodile Dundee* 22 days longer. Disney also didn't take long to realize the benefits of its huge hit. Trailers playing before each showing of *Three Men and a Baby* introduced America to the next Disney film, a bawdy comedy starring a loud-mouthed comedian named Robin Williams. Within two months, *Good Morning, Vietnam* became Disney's second blockbuster, marking one of the few times a Hollywood studio had released back-to-back blockbusters. It eventually sold more than $123 million in tickets.

Jeffrey Katzenberg had first heard about the script for *Good Morning, Vietnam* as he was heading out the door at Paramount. The film had been brought there by Larry Brezner, a Hollywood talent manager whose firm's clients included Billy Crystal, Martin Short, and David Letterman. An outline for *Good Morning, Vietnam* had been plopped down on Brezner's desk one day in 1983.

The author was Ben Moses, a Chicago-based television producer who had been an Armed Forces disc jockey (DJ) in Vietnam in 1965. While there, Moses had met Adrian Cronauer, the jokester DJ on whom the movie was based. Moses and Cronauer had talked about turning Cronauer's story into a movie as early as the mid-1970s. But Cronauer, who later went to law school, had decided against it. In the early 1980s, Moses wrote a 60-page outline of the movie and sent it to Brezner, whom he knew through a friend. Brezner liked the outline but was never able to work out a deal with Paramount. One of his clients, however, Robin Williams, heard about the project. Eventually Brezner worked with *National Lampoon* writer Mitch Markowitz to tailor the screenplay to William's manic delivery.

In mid-1985, when Katzenberg learned that Paramount had broken off the deal with Brezner, he began working on the project. Within a few weeks, he and Brezner had struck a deal to bring the project to Burbank. (In November 1988 Martin Burke, a Hollywood writer who had written a screenplay based on his 1980 book, *The Laughing War*, sued Disney, claiming that Disney stole his idea. The lawsuit hasn't yet been settled.)

Team Disney had known Robin Williams for years. The son of a transplanted Detroit car salesman, Williams grew up in Marin County near San Francisco. In 1977, a struggling stand-up comedian, he was trying out his act at the Comedy Store, the best-known of the late-night clubs that dot Sunset Boulevard.

Happy Days creator Garry Marshall caught William's act and gave him a guest role on the TV show as an alien named Mork, who came from the fictional planet Ork and had become stranded on earth. When the season ended, Eisner and Marshall took the idea of a spin-off to ABC-TV, which bought the concept of *Mork & Mindy*. The show was an immediate hit, running for four years and ranking as high as third in 1979.

By the early 1980s, however, Robin Williams had fallen out of favor with American audiences. He had made seven films, including the modest-sized hit *Moscow on the Hudson*, but he had also made such monumental duds as *The Survivors* and *Club Paradise*. Worse yet, he got hooked on cocaine. (Eventually he testified in the grand jury inquiry into the death of his friend John Belushi because he had been with Belushi an hour before his death. Williams, however, was never implicated.) "There was a time that I was on everything but skates," he told the *Los Angeles Times* in an interview.

Disney was used to reclamation projects. It had already revived the careers of both Bette Midler and Richard Dreyfuss, and it intended to do the same with Robin Williams. The comedian had sworn off drugs and alcohol and was seeing a therapist. He had also reduced his usual $2 million salary demands. Disney paid him $1 million, plus 10 percent of the revenue Disney got from the film.

Katzenberg also surrounded Williams with the kind of creative people the comedian needed to be a success. *Good Morning, Vietnam* would feature a largely male cast. Disney hired Barry Levinson, whose specialty had been male-dominated films like *Diner* and *Tin Men*, to direct it. Levinson was also known as a loose and spontaneous director who could give actors the freedom to improvise. True to his reputation, he kept the camera at a distance and allowed Williams to be spontaneous. At several points, Levinson even threw away the script and let the zany comedian make up the routine as he went along.

What came out was unlike anything Disney had ever done before."The weather will be hot and wet," Williams says at one point to his radio audience. "Nice if you're in a lady, but not if you're in a jungle." The movie also featured a sound track from A&M Records with 1960s hits that enhanced its allure to the yuppie audiences that Disney had targeted.

However, Disney did have a marketing problem. Robin Williams was clearly a star, but his following consisted primarily of young males, especially those in college. "To the rest of the universe," recalled marketing chief Bob Levin, "he was just some crazy, silly guy." The situation translated into what industry experts call a "slow rollout." The rule in Hollywood is that a film usually does its best business within the first 10 days after its release. Because Robin Williams's appeal was so narrow, a full-scale release for the film risked the possibility that it would come and go before most of the audience even knew it was there.

Disney's strategy was to slowly build awareness for both the film and its mercurial star. The film was initially released in only three markets—New York, Los Angeles, and Chicago—at Christmas time. These three markets not only are close to major universities but also are crucial to feeding stories to the country's media outlets. Disney publicists also offered Williams to every talk show they could find. He appeared on shows in all three cities, as well as on *Good Morning, America* and *Today*. The key breakthrough came when Oprah Winfrey had him on her show. "A lot of women suddenly were looking at this guy, and saying to themselves, he's a funny guy," says Levin.

In a plan similar to that used for *The Color of Money* the year before, Disney's marketing team made two sets of commercials. For the younger audience, it aired commercials that featured Williams with his raunchiest material. The second set, geared to an older audience, featured less raunch and more of the story about the hero's work with illiterate Vietnamese peasants.

By January 15, when the film opened in more than 1,000 theaters around the country, lines formed around the blocks. Opening weekend was the biggest in Disney history, with nearly $12 million tickets sold nationally.

Jeffrey Katzenberg again had promised to dance on the table of his conference room if the film did well. As the early *Good Morning, Vietnam* tallies came in he did his jig, but this time, the Disney studio head went even further. He lay down on the table and screamed, "I've died and gone to heaven."

❖

The success of *Three Men and a Baby* and *Good Morning, Vietnam* made Disney's transition from the Ron Miller era complete. By 1987, the studio was no longer the boutique operation Eisner and Katzenberg had inherited. Thirteen films were in production for the coming year, including *Cocktail*, Tom Cruise's second movie for the company. Garry Marshall had been hired to direct *Beaches*, Bette Midler's first serious film for the company.

No longer Hollywood's weak sister, Disney had also increased its share of the box office. Rising from the 4 percent level at which they had hovered during the last seven years of the Ron Miller era, Disney films in 1987 accounted for a robust 14 percent of the record $4.3 billion of ticket sales that Hollywood's films generated. Only Paramount Pictures did better.

The next year, Disney moved even higher. With added ticket sales from its two 1987 blockbusters spilling over into the new year, it overtook Paramount to become the top Hollywood studio for the first time in its history. Paramount, after having finished first for two consecutive years, came in second in 1988. Any doubts about Michael Eisner and Jeffrey Katzenberg's value to Paramount Pictures had also long since been erased.

CHAPTER

Mr. Spielberg Comes to Toontown

G ary Wolf was training for the Boston Marathon. The bearded author of the book *Who Censored Roger Rabbit* had just finished a 15-mile run through the hills of Harvard, Massachusetts, when his telephone rang. Disney publicist Howard Green, a longtime friend of Wolf, was calling with unexpected news. Wolf's book, after five years of gathering dust on Disney's shelf, was going to be made into a movie.

Wolf's association with Disney began in 1980, when Ron Miller, then the company's head of production, saw the galley proofs of Gary Wolf's book. The book, which combined a Raymond Chandler–style tale of intrigue and deception with the story of a comic strip character come to life, would sell only modestly, but Miller wanted something for Disney's idle animators to work with. Over the objections of Card Walker and others, he paid $25,000 for the rights to turn Wolf's book into a movie. Roger Rabbit, Miller hoped, was just the kind of character who could flourish in the Disney stable. "It was the kind of movie," Ron Miller would say later, ". . . that Disney could do better than anyone else."

From almost the moment Walt Disney stepped off the train from Kansas City, no one in Hollywood was better at creating timeless characters. From Mickey Mouse, his first and most memorable character, created in 1928, to his last, the mad scientist duck Ludwig von Drake, created in 1961, Walt Disney's characters endured from one generation to the next. As they grew in popularity, so did the company that Walt built. First in short cartoons, then in full-length films, Walt's classic characters—Mickey, Minnie, Donald, Pluto, Goofy—became the asset base on which the company prospered. In all, he created or popularized more than 100 characters, including Cinderella, Snow White and the Seven Dwarfs, Bambi, and Peter Pan.

Walt's characters were also the basis for Disneyland and the glue that held together the Sunday night television show. Films like *Peter Pan* and *Sleeping Beauty* were released every few years, and they did as well the second or third time around as the first. By the time Walt died, the company was also bringing in more than $11.4 million a year from sales of dolls, toys, and other products based on his creations.

Just as the creative spark went out of Walt's movies when he died, there were also no new characters after his death. The most recent addition to the Disney stable, in fact, hadn't been created by Walt at all. Walt Disney Productions had made the short film "Winnie the Pooh and the Honey Tree" in 1966. But the honey-loving stuffed teddy bear and his friends, Tigger and Eeyore, had joined the company the year before when Ron Miller bought the rights from their creator, A. A. Milne.

By the time Michael Eisner and Frank Wells arrived on the scene, licensing had grown into a major business. More than $2 billion a year was coming in from products based on everything from G. I. Joe to the Transformers. Disney enjoyed a solid niche, but toys based on movies like *Star Wars* and *E.T.: The Extra-Terrestrial* were capturing the imagination of America's young. "There was nothing more important for this company than creating another character," recalled Michael Eisner later. "Those characters become the pump that kind of feeds the rest of the body."

Eisner made the search for a new character a top priority, calling a meeting of some of Disney's creative executives at his home within a week of joining the company. At the Sunday morning meeting, the Disney executives developed the ideas for the Wuzzles, a tribe of animals that were half-elephant and half-kangaroo, and for Gummi Bears, a family of bears with mythical powers. Both sets of characters found their way onto Saturday morning cartoon shows. *The Wuzzles* was on CBS and *The Adventures of the Gummi Bears* on NBC. Disney's animators also began work on *DuckTales*, a half-hour cartoon show that the company intended to offer for TV syndication in 1987. The show would reintroduce Scrooge McDuck's nephews, in yet another attempt to create new characters.

Characters introduced on television shows, however, rarely endure beyond a couple of seasons. It would take a breakthrough movie, with all the hoopla that a major theatrical release can generate, to make a new character part of America's consciousness. From the beginning, Michael Eisner and Jeffrey Katzenberg aimed to make a movie big enough to draw crowds and imaginative enough to create a memorable new character.

That movie, they thought, would be *Roger Rabbit.* Eisner, Katzenberg, and Frank Wells had seen one of nearly a dozen scripts that had been written for a *Roger Rabbit* movie not long after arriving, when they rummaged through the few projects that Ron Miller and Richard Berger had been working on. Berger, the trio had been told, had approached Steven Spielberg about doing a *Roger Rabbit* movie, only to withdraw the offer when the *E.T.* creator mentioned his fee.

By then, the Roger Rabbit idea had been through more starts and stops than a Disneyland ride. Wolf had modeled his rabbit on the Trix rabbit shown in TV commercials. He had intended the cartoon character to team up with real-life detectives to solve the mystery of who canceled his comic strip in the daily newspaper. Miller gave the project to Mark Sturdivant, a young Disney production executive, who assigned the script to Jeffrey Price and Peter Seaman, a pair of former advertising copywriters who had just come to Hollywood to try their hand at screenwriting.

In time, a total of 11 *Roger Rabbit* scripts were written, including a dreadful one that had the rabbit leading a platoon of cartoon soldiers against Nazis in wartime Germany. The concept was offered to several topflight directors, including Roger Zemeckis, who went on to direct *Back to the Future,* and Joe Dante, who received the offer just before he left to do *Gremlins.* Like Spielberg, none of the directors believed that Disney, with its narrow vision and skinflint reputation, had the ability to undertake an innovative project the costs of which were unknown. "They just didn't have the energy to pull together a movie this massive," Zemeckis said later.

The closest Ron Miller and Richard Berger would ever get to doing the *Roger Rabbit* movie was a small photograph in the 1983 annual report that included a caption saying "Work continues on the live action–animated *Roger Rabbit.*"

By early 1986, however, Team Disney had approached Steven Spielberg with an offer. Disney was willing to share the merchandising rights to *Roger Rabbit* and to give Spielberg's Amblin Entertainment production company a healthy percentage of the profits. In return, it needed Spielberg and his creative energies to pull off the project.

In the early stages, Disney and Spielberg didn't see eye to eye on the project. Initially Spielberg wanted to cast a strong actor, someone like Harrison Ford, in the lead role opposite the animated rabbit. He later changed his mind and approached comedian Bill Murray. Disney wanted to showcase Roger Rabbit, making him the central focus of any merchandising campaign. Roger Rabbit, they stressed, should be the star of the movie.

When Richard Berger approached Spielberg, Disney's film budget unit estimated that the film would cost at least $25 million to make. After talking with Spielberg, Berger realized that the costs would go much higher. Eisner and Katzenberg knew that as well. But they were desperate for a new character and were willing to pay to get one. Though they made an initial budget of $30 million, both men knew it could easily go over $40 million. Combinations of live action and animation had been tried in short sequences before, including those in the 1964 Disney film *Mary Poppins*, but combining the two for an entire film was a venture into the unknown.

Who Framed Roger Rabbit would become the most expensive film Disney had ever made. Costs mounted as Disney and Spielberg tried different ways to combine live characters and cartoon creatures so that they appeared to be in the same scene. By the time the movie was done, the production tab had jumped to $50.6 million. Disney spent another $32 million to promote and distribute the film. To help pay for some of the production costs, Disney had convinced Roland Betts to lift Silver Screen's $20 million cap and to pay $27.5 million of the costs, but the Silver Screen III partnership, sold to shareholders in late 1986, refused to pay Spielberg's percentage. Moreover, it demanded an accelerated reimbursement schedule from Disney. Speaking of the Disney executives, Spielberg said, "Through sheer tenaciousness, they convinced us that where there's a will and a big bank account, there's a way."

❖

Filming on *Who Framed Roger Rabbit* began on December 1, 1986, in Los Angeles' Chavez Ravine area, a dusty area near Dodger Stadium. Other scenes were shot around Griffith Park and in downtown Los Angeles, where storefronts along Hope Street were covered and repainted to make them look like 1947 shops.

Planning for the film began nine months earlier, when Spielberg brought in Robert Zemeckis, with whom he has worked on *Back to the Future*. To draw the Roger Rabbit character, Zemeckis enlisted Richard

Williams, a 53-year-old Canadian-born animator who was considered one of the best in the world. Williams had won an Academy Award for his 1971 cartoon "A Christmas Carol." Working from a studio in London, he had also done the cartoon lead-ins for the Pink Panther films, as well as scores of commercials. Williams signed with Disney in March 1986 after meeting with Zemeckis over drinks at London's exclusive St. James Club.

Roger Rabbit eventually became an amalgamation of rabbits from old Disney, Warner, and MGM cartoons. The mouth, for instance, came from Thumper in Disney's *Bambi* movie, and the neck came from the Bugs Bunny character famed cartoonist Tex Avery had created for Warner Brothers. The final version of Roger was drawn on the back of an envelope as Williams flew from London to New York.

Hiring Williams was the result of a delicate compromise between Disney and Steven Spielberg. Spielberg, who had just completed work on his own animated feature, *An American Tail*, worried that Disney's animators, depleted over the years, wouldn't be capable of handling all the animation needed for *Who Framed Roger Rabbit*.

For Saturday morning cartoon shows, animators hand-draw 6 of the 24 frames of film per second that go through the projector. Zemeckis insisted that his film would require at least 12 hand-drawn frames per second, which would make the quality similar to what Walt had demanded of his animators in *Snow White*. It would also be time-consuming, taking a team of 20 animators about a week to do each minute of film.

Negotiations were tense, but after several weeks Disney and Spielberg made a compromise agreement to set up a joint animation unit to be run by Amblin Entertainment. Spielberg was given the autonomy to hire a chief animator to run the unit. But for every animator that Spielberg and Zemeckis recruited, a Disney animator would also be used on the project. Eventually, Williams put together a team of 326 animators, half of them Disney employees, and set up a temporary animation studio in a restored Edwardian factory in north London. In the meantime, Spielberg was preparing for his next project, *Empire of the Sun*, which he was making for Warner Brothers. He left most of the day-to-day details of *Who Framed Roger Rabbit* to Zemeckis and to Frank Marshall, Spielberg's 39-year-old Amblin partner and longtime collaborator.

Spielberg himself played the invaluable role of securing the rights to the legions of 1940s-era cartoon characters that Disney wanted to use alongside Roger Rabbit. For $5,000 apiece, he got the rights to use Porky Pig and Daffy Duck from Warner Brothers, Woody Woodpecker from

Universal Studios, and even Droopy Dog from MGM/UA Communications. Earlier, Ron Miller had sent Mark Sturdivant to the same studios, to no avail. Spielberg succeeded in buying the rights because he had made huge hits for the studios involved, including such megahits as *Jaws* and *E.T.* for Universal and *Gremlins* for Warner Brothers. Old associations, however, didn't stop Warner from making some demands about how their characters would be used. As protective of Bugs Bunny as Disney is of Mickey Mouse, Warner insisted that Bugs appear on the screen only alongside Mickey and that he have the same number of spoken words.

Spielberg had given up his idea of casting a superstar like Harrison Ford in the lead. Frank Marshall had just seen Bob Hoskins in *Mona Lisa*, a performance that got him an Oscar nomination. The British-born Hoskins had earned a living playing small-time hoods in such films as *The Long Good Friday*. Small, squat, and rumpled, he was the perfect Eddie Valiant, the disheveled detective who helps Roger Rabbit solve the murder of R. K. Maroon. Stand-up comic Charles Fleischer had been lined up to supply Roger's voice, and had developed the Rabbit's uniquely stuttering speaking style. Christopher Lloyd, a Spielberg favorite from *Back to the Future*, was cast as Judge Doom, the sinister enforcer who tried to rid the city of its "toons."

The making of the film proved to be a technical nightmare. Spielberg's team had agreed that the characters would be three-dimensional. When the rabbit fell into the bathtub, real water would splash out. Furthermore, the cartoon characters would cast shadows, just as live characters do. These measures would give the various scenes a realistic look but would require a huge amount of animation work, many times more than creation of flat cartoon characters.

The filming of the live-action portions of the movie lasted for five months, and the complexity of the film required some innovations. Lucasfilm's Industrial Light and Magic crew built a special Vistavision large-frame camera, both to improve the image quality of the film and to produce frames large enough for animation work.

Many of the interior sets were built on platforms 10 feet high, to enable as many as 15 puppeteers to work underneath, using robotic arms and wires to manipulate props. With their help, pistols, trays loaded with drinks, and even lit cigars floated through the air awaiting the cartoon characters who would hold them.

The most impressive special effect was a rubbery taxicab, Benny the Car, which had to travel at least 40 miles an hour, to turn corners like a Porsche, and to do a 360-degree turn. George Lucas's ILM studio eventually made the car by modifying a Honda four-wheel-drive, off-road vehicle. The front seat was built to slide forward three feet, followed a few seconds later by the rest of the car—simulating the look of a rubber band snapping.

Almost from the start, the film's production schedule slipped, as more and more technical problems crept into the job. By mid-April 1987, even after working the crew in shifts so that they could put in 24-hour days for nearly a month, Robert Zemeckis finished photography two weeks behind schedule. Zemeckis and Richard Williams had already done a test run, putting the live action together with animation, on a 30-second clip in which Roger Rabbit was able to avoid a series of falling props. Still, Williams's crew was soon three months behind schedule.

By February 1988, only five months before the planned June 24 opening of *Roger Rabbit*, the film was still running weeks behind schedule. To the Disney executives, disaster seemed to be at hand. A frustrated Jeffrey Katzenberg flew to London several times to read Williams the riot act.

With Spielberg's grudging approval, Katzenberg took over production later that month, setting up an adjunct animation facility in Burbank to speed the process. Using 90 animators pulled off other projects, Disney completed a 10-minute key scene in which Eddie Valiant travels into the surreal world of Toon Town. Another 12-minute scene, in which Valiant was to have turned into a toon but then washed the paint off to return to normal, was eliminated from the picture altogether to save time. "The fact is that the Amblin people invited us to come in and try and help," Katzenberg said not long afterward. "Sometimes it's with tender loving care, and sometimes it's with a club."

By late April the film was back on schedule. Keeping to the film's June 24 schedule was crucial because of licensing agreements. A year earlier, Spielberg and Paul Pressler, the head of the licensing unit for Disney's consumer products division, had shown crude drawings of the film to several dozen product manufacturers in a soundstage on the Burbank lot. By mid-1988, Disney had signed 34 licensee agreements for more than 500 products from *Who Framed Roger Rabbit*.

The products included traditional kids' toys, such as 17-inch washable Roger Rabbit dolls in red overalls to be made by Hasbro, and $22 talking Roger Rabbit dolls for which LJN Toys had the license. There were also $240 Jessica Rabbit brooches and $294 leather bomber jackets appliqued with Baby Herman's picture above the line "Born to be Wild." LJN had even produced a sophisticated computer software game based on the movie. The only things that Disney declared off-limits were products that showed Baby Herman smoking his cigar or that overly glamorized Jessica's robust figure.

The introduction of most of the merchandise was timed to coincide with the film's opening. So, too, were two of the biggest joint advertising campaigns Disney had ever contemplated. McDonald's had committed $15 million for TV ads and for promotional tie-ins, including a series of plastic cups featuring the characters. Coca-Cola had geared a massive $20 million TV ad program for Diet Coke to the film's release. In both cases Disney helped to produce the TV spots, drawing Jessica and Roger at a McDonald's drive-in, for example. Disney animators had drawn a spot for Diet Coke that showed Jessica singing at the Ink and Paint Club that was featured in the film.

Weeks before *Who Framed Roger Rabbit* was to open, Disney's publicity machine was in full swing. Before the campaign was over, Disney spent more than $30 million on advertisements, including nearly $15 million in the first 10 days. Both figures were records for Disney. Katzenberg, in search of an even bigger media splash, had also done some hawking of his own. Taking along a 40-minute version of the film and a team of publicists, he had visited the New York offices of both *Newsweek* and *Time*. Whichever magazine would promise him a cover, he told them, could have exclusive rights to the story of how the film was made.

Newsweek was the first to promise a cover story. By giving reporter Michael Reese exclusive access to the production process and key players, Disney got the promised cover just as the movie was opening. The exposure was worth millions of dollars. "In a marriage made in Hollywood heaven," the article proclaimed, "Disney brings marketing savvy and a proud tradition of animation back to the groundbreaking days of Walt Disney himself; Amblin lends the Spielberg flair for razzle-dazzle story-telling that created such landmark films as *E.T.* and *Close Encounters of the Third Kind*." *Who Framed Roger Rabbit* never threatened *E.T.*'s all-time box office record. But on its first day it sold $1.8 million worth of tickets, the most ever for a Disney film. By the end of the first week, moviegoers had plunked down another $17 million. Two weeks later, it had sold more than $54 million worth of tickets.

In all, *Roger Rabbit* sold more than $154 million worth of tickets in the United States and another $174 million overseas. Disney's third $100 million blockbuster movie in a year, it also helped to catapult Disney into the top spot in Hollywood's box office race. By the end of 1988, Disney had captured nearly 20 percent of the domestic box office.

❖

With his pencil-thin mustache, narrow face, and gravelly voice, Roy Disney bore a remarkably strong resemblance to his uncle Walt. But despite his years of exposure to Walt when he was young, Roy Disney never developed a talent for drawing. Instead, he was fascinated first by airplanes, and later by sailboats. Starting at Disney in 1954, he was an assistant director on the documentary "The Living Desert" and then on "The Vanishing Prairie." Both eventually won Academy Awards in their fields.

Roy Disney never worked in the animation department. But he and Stanley Gold had played crucial roles in the chain of events that had led to Michael Eisner's hiring. Moments after Eisner was elected chairman, Roy asked to head the animation department. Michael Eisner quickly agreed.

At the time, the animation unit had atrophied from the nearly 400 people who had once worked there to just under 200. Stifled by Ron Miller and Card Walker, the brightest animators had left for other studios. The exodus started in 1979 when Don Bluth, claiming that the studio was skimping on the quality of its animation, walked out with 16 of his colleagues. Another young animator, Tim Burton, left later, going on to a career that included directing the hit movie *Beetlejuice* and the blockbuster *Batman*.

When Eisner and Wells came to the company, Disney's animators had been struggling for nearly a decade to complete *The Black Cauldron*. The first Disney film since *Black Beauty* in 1959 to be shot on huge 70-millimeter film, *The Black Cauldron* had been worked on by 68 animators. Nearly $40 million had been spent on a film that Roy Disney himself felt was too dark and forbidding to be successful.

Even so, as the new head of the animation department, Roy Disney supervised the final editing. Its release, on July 24, 1985, listed Ron Miller as an executive producer. The film was greeted by generally good reviews. But it did modest business at the box office, selling just over $21 million worth of tickets.

Roy Disney, like Michael Eisner and Jeffrey Katzenberg, was eager to churn out hit animated films. But *The Black Cauldron* was hardly the kind of movie on which the company had built its reputation. Its rerelease value at the box office was minimal and its prospects for video sales were dim. Certainly, it was not the type of animation film that would allow the company to create new characters, sell toys, or inspire theme park rides.

Rumors that Eisner and Frank Wells intended to shut down the animation unit began circulating at the Burbank studio almost as soon as the two men arrived. The two new executives, the rumor mill had it, wanted to guard against any future *Black Cauldron* fiascoes.

In fact, Eisner and Katzenberg had no intention of shutting down the animation unit. But still open was the question of how large a number of animators the company needed to employ. Increasingly, studios were hiring animators in Asian countries, where costs were cheaper. Moreover, kids were flocking to Saturday morning and afternoon cartoon shows.

Not long after settling into his third-floor office in the Animation Building, Roy Disney ordered many of the animators into his office to brief him on the projects they were working on. Reflecting his love for sailing boats, his newly decorated office looked like the inside of one of his championship sloops, with wood timbers, nautical maps, even a circular compass.

Behind his back, his animators worried that 54-year-old Roy Disney was nothing more than Walt's "Idiot Nephew," a person born into money and position who had little aptitude for business. Roy Disney knew about the snickering behind his back. But, nearly a decade after he had left the company, he was intent on proving them wrong. His first project, he told the animators that gathered around him, had to be something special. "I want to show these new guys that I'm part of the team," he told the group. "That we have something to contribute."

A week after Jeffrey Katzenberg arrived from Paramount, Roy Disney hauled him and Eisner down to his office to show them the early sketches and story boards for a project called *Basil of Baker Street*. The project, a tale of a family of mice who lived beneath Sherlock Holmes's London flat, had been started by a group of animators frustrated with the slow pace of working on *The Black Cauldron*. To mollify them, the studio had allowed them to start a new project. *Basil of Baker Street* was also the only animated film far enough along to move into production. By late 1984, when Team Disney arrived, the company had already spent $1.2 million on the project.

With the storyboards lining one of the building's narrow corridors, Roy Disney went through the story line. With him were John Musker and Ron Clements, two veteran Disney animators who had broken away from *The Black Cauldron* project. "I'm not sure that Michael and Jeffrey knew what they were looking at," said Roy Disney. "But they said go ahead anyway."

Basil of Baker Street was later renamed *The Great Mouse Detective*, but it was hardly a box office sensation. Set in 19th-century England, and without a flashy soundtrack, it sold only about $25 million worth of tickets. But during the year it took to complete the film, Roy Disney effectively lobbied for a larger presence for his animation unit. By early 1985, Eisner had set a goal of a new film every 18 months, a dramatic cut in the four to five years that it had previously taken Disney's animation unit to move a film from the story stage to final production.

As much as Eisner and Katzenberg respected the money and influence that Roy Disney had brought to the 1984 takeover battle, neither of the new Disney executives knew anything about his ability to pick winning film projects. His sole experience until then had been short documentaries, focusing on wild animals in their native environments. Katzenberg, on the other hand, knew how to pick winning projects. With a set of four-year-old twins at home, the new head of Disney's studio operation has also been immersing himself in classic cartoons, kids' stories, and Saturday morning cartoon shows. In time, he would even begin collecting antique "cels"—the huge transparent sheets animators draw on—from old Walt Disney animated classics.

Since Roy Disney wasn't likely to pick winning animated films, Katzenberg and Eisner took the lead. Eisner insisted that Disney's animators begin to write scripts for their projects, putting aside Walt's practice of storyboards to determine the plot. The scripts alone would save both time and money and improve the stories as well, he said. In late 1985 Katzenberg summoned Roy Disney and more than a dozen of his animators and producers to the conference room down the hall from his own newly decorated office for one of Disney's "Gong Shows."

"Gong Shows" were becoming commonplace at the Disney studio; they were a time when new ideas could be thrown out for discussion. Bad ideas would be met by a loud "gong" from either Katzenberg or one of his senior associates, the kind of demoralizing rejection that had forced Richard Berger and Stan Kinsey to leave the company.

No one dared to "gong" the opening suggestion. It was made by Katzenberg himself. Modeled on the Charles Dickens story *Oliver Twist*, it would be a modern-era tale of an orphan in New York City. Before he had left Paramount for Disney, Katzenberg had begun planning a musical version of *Oliver Twist*. He had even ordered some early musical scores prepared. But the project had died when Diller, Eisner, and he had left Paramount.

Disney's animators could see the possibilities. Instead of human actors, they would turn Oliver into a stray cat, taken in by a pack of quirky but friendly dogs. The film that evolved was *Oliver & Company*, for which Katzenberg approved an $18 million budget. Unlike other recent Disney animation films, which would feature the tired voice of Peggy Lee or Buddy Hackett, the new film would feature the voices of modern-day stars like Billy Joel, Bette Midler, and Cheech Marin. For the soundtrack, Disney also signed up singers like Joel, Huey Lewis, and Ruth Pointer.

At the "Gong Show," Ron Clements, who had just finished up *The Great Mouse Detective*, suggested doing a movie based on "The Little Mermaid," the Hans Christian Anderson fairy tale about a mermaid who wants to become human. "It sent an immediate wave of excitement through the room," Roy Disney recalled. "It was the kind of movie that Walt really would have made."

It was also the kind of film that Jeffrey Katzenberg had been wanting to do. It had been nearly three decades since Disney had made *Sleeping Beauty*, the studio's last animated film based on a well-known classic. For Katzenberg, *The Little Mermaid* became an obsession. As many as 400 artists and technicians worked on the project for the next three years, churning out 150,000 painted cels. The film's budget climbed to over $23 million. Katzenberg signed Broadway songwriters Howard Ashman and Alan Menken to do the musical score. The two had just done the score for *Little Shop of Horrors*, which featured the kind of upbeat, quirky songs that Katzenberg hoped would fit into the film.

To accompany the new activity, Eisner and Katzenberg told Roy Disney to begin hiring new animators. A new intern program was launched. Perhaps as important, the company spent $12 million to buy the kind of sophisticated computer equipment necessary to turn out the increased number of animated films the Eisner team required. The computers, which reduce the time it takes to do a scene by duplicating the background and other repeated scenes, had been pushed as early as 1982 by Stan Kinsey. At that time, however, both Card Walker and Ron Miller had decided that they were just too expensive—a decision that Team Disney countermanded.

While the animators were busy with their new machines and increased workload, newly arrived marketing chief Bob Levin was looking for ways to promote the new characters Eisner and Wells hoped would emerge from the animated films. Coming from Chicago, Levin had often worked with both the McDonald's and the Sears marketing teams. Having the country's largest retailer and its most famous fast-food restaurant on Disney's side certainly couldn't hurt the effort, Team Disney believed. Frank Wells, in fact, was already talking with McDonald's about sponsoring "Splash Mountain," the Giant $80 million water ride that Disney's Imagineers unit was designing for Disneyland.

McDonald's wasn't interested in spending as much money as the "Splash Mountain" project would have required. But the hamburger chain did sign on with Levin to promote Disney's animated film with toy giveaways and contests. McDonald's first Disney promotion would be *Oliver & Company*, for which the fast-food company would give out small rubber toy dogs representing four of the movie's characters. In all, McDonald's would spend more than $10 million on the giveaways.

In late 1987, Disney added Sears, signing a 10-year deal that gave the giant retailer exclusive right to market certain characters in the new animated films. The deal also included a $75 million commitment to sponsor a ride at the Disney–MGM Studios Theme Park in Orlando. (Sears backed out of the deal a year later, when it launched into a major restructuring to reduce costs.)

❖

Jeffrey Katzenberg had always liked a good power breakfast at the picturesque Bel Air Hotel. But one night in early 1987 the Disney studio chief sat in a dingy red vinyl booth at the Hamburger Hamlet on Sunset Drive. Munching fried onion rings and sipping a glass of his ever present Diet Coke, Katzenberg looked across the table at Warren Beatty, the Hollywood actor who was the town's reigning enigma.

A brilliant director and handsome leading man, the 52-year-old Beatty had been nominated for eight Academy Awards for his work behind the camera and another three in front of it. A man of seemingly unlimited libido, Beatty had also been sexually linked with many of Hollywood's most glamorous women. Brigitte Bardot, Liv Ullman, and Candice Bergen were but three of his many conquests. On this night in 1987, however, Warren Beatty didn't have a woman on his mind. Instead, playing with a salad at the Hamburger Hamlet, a favorite late-night hangout, he was pursuing a 10-year dream.

Unlike Beatty, whose nocturnal activities were well known, Katzenberg was a creature of the morning. Deals, in Jeffrey Katzenberg's view, were best made at early-morning breakfasts, not when the rest of Hollywood was settling into bed. But Beatty had suggested the nighttime meeting, and the deal the two men were discussing was no ordinary project. *Dick Tracy* was a film idea that had obsessed both men for years.

The Dick Tracy saga already had one of Hollywood's most tangled histories. Chester Gould's crime-fighting comic hero, who had first appeared on the pages of the *Detroit Mirror* on October 5, 1931, had been courted by Hollywood before. Both Republic Pictures and RKO Pictures had turned the hawk-nosed detective into a movie star, and in the early 1950s Ralph Byrd had played Tracy in a short-lived television series. Producer Michael Laughlin had tried to revive the movie idea in the mid-1970s, but no studio had been willing to make a commitment to the movie.

In 1977, the *Dick Tracy* movie finally seemed to be on the verge of getting made when producer Art Linson and director Floyd Mutrux bought the rights. Linson and Mutrux were Hollywood veterans, with such films as *Hollywood Knights* and *Aloha Bobby and Rose* to their credit. They also had an eager audience in Paramount president Michael Eisner and his young lieutenant, Jeffrey Katzenberg. Katzenberg and Eisner, who were at Paramount at that time, were looking for a summer film that they could build into the kind of annual moneymaker that the James Bond series had become for United Artists. The two had won Barry Diller's approval to make the film. But Diller worried about the film's hefty budget and told Katzenberg to line up another studio to help defray the costs. Katzenberg went to Universal Studios, which agreed to take the project off Paramount's hands, and sent the script to John Landis. Landis, whose film credits at the time included *The Blues Brothers* and *Animal House*, unsuccessfully pursued Clint Eastwood for the lead. When Eastwood declined, the young director shipped the script to Warren Beatty.

The story gets a little muddled at that point. Landis left the film to direct *Trading Places*. A parade of directors were shuttled in to take on *Dick Tracy*, including Richard Benjamin, who had directed *My Favorite Year*, and Walter Hill, who had *48 Hours* to his credit. Beatty was still interested, but he went to Paramount to make *Reds*, his 1981 tale about John Reed, the only American buried in the Kremlin.

Not long afterward, the Paramount team fell apart. Barry Diller left for Twentieth Century Fox, while Eisner and Katzenberg jumped to Disney. Universal, meanwhile, went through its own management shuffle. Studio head Ned Tannen, who had green-lighted *Dick Tracy*, left for Paramount. Beatty, dismayed, paid nearly $1 million for the rights to the project. He tried unsuccessfully to peddle it to directors Bob Fosse and Martin Scorsese before deciding to direct it himself.

By the mid-1980s, Warren Beatty was in the midst of a box office decline. *Reds* had been nominated for four Academy Awards and had won for him the award for best director. But making the film had been a nightmare. Originally budgeted at $23 million, it had actually cost more than $35 million. Worse yet, it lost several million dollars at the box office. After making such films as *Shampoo* (1975) and *Heaven Can Wait* (1978), Warren Beatty was no longer hot. His first film after *Reds* was *Ishtar*, a bomb of near mythic proportions.

Most of the blame for *Ishtar* had been heaped on Elaine May, the movie's mercurial writer and director. But as he sat in the Hamburger Hamlet, Jeffrey Katzenberg was acutely aware of many problems that could accompany a Warren Beatty project. Renowned in Hollywood for his methodical casting decisions and stoic perfectionism, Beatty made films that were routinely late and frequently over budget. The making of a typical Beatty film entailed endless script rewrites, dozens of reshot scenes, and more than a little turmoil on the set. What was worse, Beatty had often refused to accept suggestions from people at the studios that had bankrolled his films. In fact, he had ordered his lawyers to get an injunction to stop Paramount from editing *Reds* to make it shorter when it was to air on ABC.

Team Disney didn't like to operate that way. Budgets were sacrosanct, and directors were expected to stick to them. More important, if Disney financed a film, the Disney executives expected to be involved at every step, from script to final editing. Even with the well-respected Amblin Entertainment team, Katzenberg had stepped in when *Who Framed Roger Rabbit* began to fall behind schedule.

Michael Eisner, however, knew how valuable *Dick Tracy* could be for Disney and had made the first overtures to Beatty. *Dick Tracy*, like *Roger Rabbit*, represented a unique opportunity to build a franchise out of a single movie, Eisner felt. The tons of T-shirts, two-way wristwatches, and other Dick Tracy merchandise that Disney could license and sell were only part of the story. Dick Tracy, like Roger Rabbit, was the kind of character who could lure teenagers and young adults to Disney's theme parks.

Clearly, Disney could build on a *Dick Tracy* franchise, but Jeffrey Katzenberg would have to make the kind of deal that would fit into Disney's cost structure. It had cost Disney $20 million more than expected to complete *Who Framed Roger Rabbit*, and the studio chief hardly relished the thought of another overbudget epic on his hands. At Paramount, Eisner and Katzenberg had estimated that production costs on *Dick Tracy* would be $18 million. A decade later, the film would easily cost a minimum of $30 million.

Moreover, Katzenberg knew that the total costs would go even higher. The costs of promoting even run-of-the-mill films had skyrocketed in recent years, jumping to an average of $8.5 million by 1988. That was nothing compared to the costs of introducing a 59-year-old cartoon character to American teenagers who had never heard of the hawk-nosed detective or his slightly dated two-way wrist radio. The number of newspapers carrying the *Dick Tracy* cartoon, unlike *Superman* and *Batman* cartoons, had declined ever since the 1950s. By 1988 the *Dick Tracy* cartoon was carried by only one-third as many newspapers as at its highest point 15 years before.

On top of that, Warren Beatty was hardly a teen idol, capable of appealing to the under-20 crowd that is the movie industry's primary audience. To make *Dick Tracy* the kind of "event movie" that would force it into the country's consciousness even before it opened, Katzenberg knew, could cost $20 million or more in publicity. Warner Brothers, working on its own event movie, *Batman*, had budgeted $35 million to open that cartoon character extravaganza, on top of the $50 million or more that it spent to make the film.

Disney's legal executive, Helene Hahn, and superlawyer Bert Fields, who represented Warren Beatty, negotiated the deal during most of the next year. "We both came in with our different points of view," Fields said of the *Dick Tracy* negotiations. "There were clashes, and . . . tough positions [were necessary]." Ultimately, on the shaded porch behind Frank Well's Beverly Hills home, the deal was signed. Wells, Katzenberg, Eisner, and Hahn were there, along with Fields and Beatty. Beatty would get $9 million—$5.5 million for acting in the film, $2.5 million for directing it, $500,000 for producing it, and another $500,000 for rewriting the script. He would also be entitled to 15 percent of Disney's revenues for the film, merchandise, or anything else based on *Dick Tracy*.

Beatty also made major concessions. To keep the film costs under control, Disney agreed to pay $25 million toward its production. But costs overruns would come out of the director's own salary. In addition, the studio won Beatty's promise to make major efforts to promote the film, including granting interviews and going to talk shows. Publicity-shy and nervous around cameras, Beatty had refused to do any press interviews for *Reds*, a refusal that Paramount executives later blamed for the film's poor box office performance.

As its part of the deal, Disney promised to spend heavily to promote the film. Disney also agreed to pay 5 percent of the profits to Paramount and Universal, which still held some rights to the movie.

Photography was set to begin at the Universal Studios back lot on February 2, 1989. Beatty, who didn't like the script that *Top Gun* writers Jim Cash and Jack Epps, Jr., had written, had already been rewriting the script for months. He brought in Bo Goldman, who had written *Melvin and Howard*, to punch it up further. Beatty got the script he wanted but later lost an arbitration with the Writers Guild of America, which refused to let him have his name included in the writing credits. Instead, the script was credited to Cash and Epps, with Goldman listed as a "special consultant." Production was also marred by a legal suit, when Linson and Mutrux sued for credit as executive producers and for the 5 percent of the profits they said they had been promised when Paramount first signed the deal.

The suit was still pending when Beatty began to assemble the crew and cast for the picture. To design the comic-strip "look" of the film, Beatty brought in Vittorio Storaro, who had won an Academy Award for his camera work on *Reds*. Costume designer Milena Canonero had won Academy Awards for *Barry Lyndon* and *Chariots of Fire*. The elaborate prosthetic faces for Flattop, Lips, Pruneface, and the other gangsters were designed by John Caglione and Doug Drexler, whose credits included *The Cotton Club*, *Zelig*, and *Altered States*. Beatty persuaded Stephen Sondheim, the five-time Tony Award–winning Broadway composer, to do the sound track.

Picking the cast took Beatty longer. He had wanted Gene Hackman, Faye Dunaway, and Jack Nicholson to play roles in the film, but each had other commitments. He did line up several of his industry friends: *Ishtar* costar Dustin Hoffman, as well as Al Pacino, both of whom agreed to take scale payments of $1,440 a week. One casting choice that didn't work out was Sean Young, whom Beatty had selected to play Tracy's girlfriend, Tess Trueheart. Young and Beatty battled on the set, and three weeks into the production, he replaced her with Glenne Headley.

Rock star Madonna had read the script months before filming was set to begin. The vampish rock star, who had flopped in her latest two films, was hardly Beatty's first choice. Instead, the director wanted Melanie Griffith for the part of Breathless Mahoney, the curvaceous lounge singer who fails to pry Dick Tracy away from Tess Trueheart. Griffith, who was pregnant, turned down the part. Madonna was hired after she called Beatty at his Coldwater Canyon home and offered to do it for the same scale payment Hoffman and Pacino were getting.

Madonna, eager for a hit film after her two flops, unabashedly helped the film's promotional efforts. Timing the release of a new album to coincide with the film's release, she renamed the album *I'm Breathless*, and launched her "Blond Ambition" tour to publicize it. Disney was already in the midst of its own publicity blitz for *Dick Tracy*. Having the normally reclusive Warren Beatty available for interviews certainly helped. Building awareness slowly, the studio booked their star on a Barbara Walters special the night of the Academy Awards, a full three months before the film was to be released.

By the time *Dick Tracy* blasted into theaters around the country, Warren Beatty had turned huckster. His schedule included appearances on *20-20*, *David Letterman*, and Arsenio Hall's terminally hip syndicated talk show. On Larry King's cable TV show, he even answered telephone calls from the television audience.

"There is something sort of pathetic about it," wrote Anna Quindlen, a columnist for the *New York Times*. "Warren Beatty used to refuse to do this. He would not shill. Now he is shilling up a storm." Indeed, it seemed that you would find Warren Beatty everywhere you looked. He allowed a *Premiere* magazine reporter to visit the set during filming, a first for him. The same reporter visited him again at an orchestra stage in the old MGM studio at Culver City, while he mixed the sound track with the visuals. He gave *Los Angeles Times* critic Jack Mathews a nine-hour interview and a dinner at his favorite Chinese restaurant.

Time and *Newsweek* also were given lengthy interviews with the star. So, too, was *Rolling Stone*, almost certainly another first for Beatty. Just before the film opened, he also sat patiently through hours of interviews with local newspaper reporters in a suite at the Four Seasons Hotel in Beverly Hills that Disney had rented for him. "I just do what Disney tells me to do," Beatty explained.

❖

As Disney's managers had feared, the costs of making *Dick Tracy* continued to escalate. By the time the film was released on June 15, 1990, *Variety* reported that production costs had jumped to $46.5 million. Disney's elaborate marketing efforts and flood of TV commercials had added another $54.7 million, putting the costs for Warren Beatty's film at a staggering $101 million. Because Disney would get only about half the money taken in at the box office, the hefty price tag all but assured that the film wouldn't make a profit during its theatrical run. Indeed, it could take as much as five years for the company to recoup all of its costs—from videocassette sales and exhibition on cable TV.

With ticket sales of $104 million, *Dick Tracy* was hardly a bust. But after Hollywood's expectations that Disney had another *Batman*, the box office showing was also disappointing to many. Clearly, *Dick Tracy* was no *Batman*. Warner Brothers, after spending roughly the same amount of money to make its own crime-stopper movie, had grossed more than twice as much at the box office.

Dick Tracy also never became the new character for the Walt Disney Company that *Batman* became for Warner. The 85 licenses that Disney's consumer product units granted for the film meant more than $50 million in revenues for the company. But the amount of *Tracy* merchandise sold never approached the avalanche of T-shirts, lunch boxes, and other trinkets that followed *Batman*. Indeed, *Dick Tracy* merchandise even trailed those based on the Fox television show *The Simpsons* and the movie *Teenage Mutant Ninja Turtles*.

The *Dick Tracy* experience was not an isolated one for the Walt Disney Company. With Eisner and Katzenberg at the helm, the studio regularly turned out hit films. The new managers' first animated film, *Oliver & Company*, had sold a robust $53 million worth of tickets, at the time a record for animated films. The record would be broken a year later, in late 1989, with *The Little Mermaid*. The first Disney classic in nearly 30 years, the film took in more than $84 million at the box office. The 9 million videocassettes it sold was second only to *E.T.: The Extra Terrestrial*.

But *The Little Mermaid* was one of the few new Disney films that also created a character capable of being promoted outside the film theater. For months after the film was released, preteenage girls were buying up millions of dollars' worth of products featuring the mermaid Ariel. Other Disney characters hadn't fared nearly as well. Despite a $7 million advertising campaign by McDonald's, *Oliver* products didn't sell well. Neither, surprisingly, did *Roger Rabbit* trinkets.

The Disney managers tried to make use of their new characters. Roger became a permanent fixture at Disneyland. Disney's Imagineering unit was also ordered to begin planning rides for both the Anaheim and Orlando parks based on *Dick Tracy*, *Roger Rabbit*, and *The Little Mermaid*. A pair of *Roger Rabbit* shorts were prepared, each costing about $2 million, to play before high-profile Disney films. Almost certainly, a seven-minute *Roger* cartoon helped bring people to see *Honey, I Shrunk the Kids*, helping to make the 1989 film a huge hit.

The Disney animation unit continued to gear up for their next animated films. After finishing *The Little Mermaid*, directors John Musker and Ron Clements began work on *Aladdin*. The film, set for release in late 1992, would also include the *The Little Mermaid* songwriting team of Howard Ashman and Alan Menken to do the sound track.

By 1989, Disney was already on its schedule to produce a new animated film each year. Ashman and Menken were writing six songs for *Beauty and the Beast*, scheduled to be released in late 1991. Planning was also beginning on *King of the Jungle*, a tale of wild animals set in Africa, scheduled for release in 1993. A first-time team of Hendel Butoy and Mike Gabrile were finishing up work on *The Rescuers Down Under*, a sequel of the 1977 film. The film would be released in November 1990. In an effort to fill in the gap between major animated films, the company also created a new film unit called Disney Movietoons. Established to quickly turn out lower-quality animated films, it scheduled a full-length *DuckTales* movie as its first offering.

Disney's script writers were also at work on a new *Roger Rabbit* film. Set in Kansas, the "prequel" was titled *Toon Platoon* and would feature Roger as a young rabbit raised by human parents. Spielberg's team had again signed on to do the technical work for the project, which was set for release in 1993. Among the actors being sought to play opposite the cartoon rabbit was Tom Cruise. Warren Beatty, however, expressed no desire to do a sequel to *Dick Tracy*. Given the soaring cost of the original and its disappointing box office performance, no one at the Walt Disney Company was clamoring to change Beatty's mind.

CHAPTER

Riches Beneath the Castle

I t was in 1881 that an Italian schoolteacher, Carlo Lorenzini, writing under the pen name Carlo Collodi, first created the picaresque fairy tale *Pinocchio*. Not until 1940, however, did Walt Disney popularize the wooden puppet in his second animated film, an impressive technical achievement that cost $2.6 million—a staggering sum in those times. In the following years, *Pinocchio* became a steady moneymaker for the company. Released five times in the next four decades, the 87-minute film brought in more than $50 million. Pinocchio merchandise added millions more each year. The movie's best-known song, "When You Wish Upon a Star," won an Academy Award. "Pinocchio's Daring Journey" was one of the first rides Walt envisioned for Disneyland.

When Michael Eisner and Frank Wells joined the company in September 1984, however, *Pinocchio* was one of many Walt Disney treasures gathering dust in an air-conditioned building on the Burbank lot. Walt Disney, fearing that overexposure would dilute the effectiveness of his characters, had steadfastly refused to allow frequent showings of his classic animated films. So concerned was Walt about overexposing Donald Duck, who enjoyed immense popularity in the 1940s, that for a while he refused to allow the showing of even short cartoons that featured the duck.

Card Walker and Ron Miller had remained loyal to Walt's game plan. Fearing that overexposure would ruin the popularity of the films with theater audiences, the heirs to Walt's legacy had zealously guarded *Pinocchio, Sleeping Beauty, Cinderella,* and two dozen other Disney classics. Even as new markets blossomed, none of Disney's classics appeared on television or had been converted to videocassette. They were, Ron Miller would say later, "a piece of this company that you couldn't just throw around."

Miller, though, hadn't totally ignored the videocassette market, which had started to take off in the late 1970s. To explore the new market, Miller put Jim Jimirro, who supervised the sale of 16-millimeter Disney cartoons and nature films to schools, in charge of a committee to look into "ancillary markets" such as videocassettes and cable television. The committee, which included movie distribution chief Chuck Good and his deputy, Dick Cook, reported back in late 1978 with a pair of recommendations. At the time, cable television was available in roughly one-third of the nation's homes, and the market was growing rapidly. To tap that market, Jimirro's group suggested launching a family-oriented cable channel filled with old Disney cartoons and animated movies. To take advantage of the growing video market, the group also suggested that Disney begin a test program, first selling videos with short cartoons and later full-length animated movies.

Costs were already beginning to escalate for EPCOT Center, and Walker quickly dismissed the notion of launching a cable channel. Mike Bagnall, the company's senior vice-president for finance (who refused to grant any interviews for this book), had worked up some numbers on the emerging videocassette industry. The market, he projected, would almost certainly become a billion-dollar industry by the early 1980s. But the films that would fuel the boom, his analysts told him, would be bullet-riddled action films and X-rated fare. Kids, Bagnall had concluded, weren't going to be much of a factor.

Walker did give Ron Miller his approval to try the video market, at least with an initial test effort. In October 1980, the company sold cassettes of 10 of its lesser-quality live-action films through 87 Fotomat drive-through film kiosks on the West Coast. Even though the results were not spectacular, Disney released *Mary Poppins*—its first major film on videocassette—later that year. The next year it also released two of its worst animated performers, *Dumbo* and *Alice in Wonderland,* on video.

It wasn't much of a gamble. The company had already been forced to put the two movies on the weekly Sunday night show, filling the gap when Disney's TV producers ran short of programs.

By the time Michael Eisner and Frank Wells arrived, however, the great experiment had all but ended. In the previous three years, only three minor full-length animated films had been released on videocassette, and only a few short Mickey and Goofy cartoons. Still protective of the Disney library, Miller had begun buying lesser cartoons from outside producers in order to issue them on videocassette. One such cartoon introduced Americans to Luckey Luke, a lanky cowboy character imported from France. Luke proved to be anything but lucky for Disney. Another cassette, aimed at adults, featured faded singer and comedian Steve Allen.

During the September 1984 meeting with the Bass organization in Fort Worth, Eisner and Wells had stressed the wealth of possibilities that languished in the studio's dusty library. The library was so valuable, in fact, that during the takeover battle, analysts at Saul Steinberg's Reliance Group had estimated that it was worth $400 million. "If the library was exploited in a more aggressive manner," the report concluded, "the value could well be greater." Eisner intended to be as aggressive as he could, he told Bass. "The library has been allowed to sit for too long," the Disney chairman said. "It is time to begin exploiting it."

Everyone at the meeting had read the reports that had been prepared during the takeover battles. The Disney collection of old movies and animated films was one of the few unexploited libraries left in Hollywood. While other studios were digging into their own storerooms to bring out old movies on videocassette, Disney was sitting on 23 of the most highly regarded animation films ever made. Also stashed away were three decades of the Sunday night television show, a library of 200 one- and two-hour movies that included all the old *Zorro*, *Davy Crockett*, and *Swamp Fox* shows. Disney's studio had also produced 123 live-action movies, including such well-regarded films as *Mary Poppins* and *20,000 Leagues Under the Sea*. In addition, there were 500 short cartoons featuring timeless stars like Mickey, Pluto, and Donald, that could be sold to an expanding children's market.

At Paramount, Eisner had watched as the video market had gobbled up *Saturday Night Fever*, the *Indiana Jones* movies, and dozens of other movies. Overall, Hollywood studios had taken in nearly $1.5 billion from selling movies on videocassette. For a studio like Warner Brothers or Paramount, the new market could mean $400 million or more each year in added revenues. Disney, by contrast, had taken in less than $56 million from the video market in 1983—most of that from its shaky schedule of newly released films.

Michael Eisner, with three teenage sons of his own, knew that the baby boom that had begun in the early 1980s was producing a growing market for Disney's valuable collection of animated films and cartoons. Combined with booming VCR sales, it made an irresistible market for the new Disney management.

There was a practical reason to move quickly as well. Putting Disney's older movies on videocassette would generate a quick source of cash for the company. Both Eisner and Wells knew that it could be nearly 18 months before the films the new management wanted to make would be released to theater audiences. Even then, both men knew, there was no certainty that any of the new films would be a hit. The library, on the other hand, represented pure profits. The costs of making the films had long since been accounted for on Disney's balance sheet.

Selling those films on videocassette now would mean increased cash flow, swelling Disney's earnings and impressing Wall Street's analysts. A disgusted Wall Street had been discounting Disney's stock for years, while Ron Miller and Card Walker held on to its most valuable assets. Now, after jumping to as much as $68.50 a share during the takeover battle, the stock had settled back to around $53 a share. A jump in Disney's stock price would gladden Disney shareholders still shell-shocked from the takeover battle.

It would also make Sid Bass happy. Not least of all, it would make Michael Eisner and Frank Wells both happy and wealthy. Between the two of them, the two new Disney executives held options for 970,000 Disney shares. They also were entitled to bonuses based on improving Disney's earnings over the level recorded by Ron Miller.

Two weeks after returning from Fort Worth, Eisner ordered Bill Mechanic, one of the earliest Paramount recruits, to start cataloging the Disney library. Mechanic, with his long hair and bushy mustache, looked more the part of a film director than corporate executive. Indeed, he had followed Eisner to Disney in hopes of making films. But Mechanic had also spent years with Paramount's pay television unit and knew how to estimate the value of movies for the ancillary market.

In mid-October, Mechanic began the process of compiling the list of Disney movies and TV shows stored on the lot. Working with him was Jim Jimirro, who for the last two years had been in charge of both the Disney Channel and its video operations.

Most of the movies they found were in good shape, aside from a few scratches and a couple of rips in the originals. But none had been properly mastered. (*Mastering* is a technical improvement that is necessary for clean reproduction of film on videocassette.) The number of old treasures they found was impressive. "Everywhere we look we find another couple of hundred million dollars," Eisner told talent agent Michael Ovitz a few weeks later, when the two men and their families went on a week-long ski trip to Colorado.

Some sales could be made quickly. In another misguided attempt to protect the Disney Channel from its competitors, Ron Miller had refused to sell the rights to new Disney movies to any other cable channels. Mechanic's major job at Paramount had been to find the best cable deal for that studio's movies. He did the same for Disney, quickly selling off seven newly made Disney films to the Showtime pay channel. The seven, which included *Splash* and *Something Wicked This Way Comes*, brought in about $12 million during the first year of the Eisner-Wells regime. The company also rereleased cassettes of previously released classics, including both *Dumbo* and *Mary Poppins*.

In all, the company shipped out a million cassettes in 1985, at the time a record for the company. To help promote an upcoming summer special of seven older Mickey and Donald cartoons, Eisner approved the largest ad campaign the company had ever attempted. Before it was over, Disney spent $2.5 million on promotion of videocassettes. The company also slashed the prices on 125 previously released cassettes, hoping to entice retailers to buy the stacks of comedy classics that had been piling up on warehouse shelves.

❖

Michael Eisner was clearly getting restless. For three months, the Disney chief and his top staff had been debating the fate of *Pinocchio*. The film had been rereleased for the sixth time just months after Eisner and Wells arrived and had sold a tidy $26.4 million worth of tickets during the 1984 Christmas season. That gave it the third best box office gross a Disney animated film had ever received, trailing only *Snow White and the Seven Dwarfs* and *Cinderella*. For Michael Eisner, the box office gross only proved the value of the film on the home video market, which tends to take its lead from the number of tickets the movie sells.

Time was running out to make a decision on whether to release *Pinocchio* on videocassette. It was May 1985, five months after the film was released to the theaters. Most films are released on videocassette six months after theater audiences first see them, so Disney had precious little time left to take advantage of the marketing campaign it had launched for *Pinocchio*.

As they had discussed with the Bass group, Michael Eisner and Frank Wells were eager to push ahead and release *Pinocchio* on videocassette. But Eisner's management style required management meetings before making any major decision, and before he was ready to break with the company's traditional policy on videocassettes, the Disney chairman called together his top managers to discuss the entire situation.

Meeting in the wood-paneled third-floor conference room, Eisner gathered his Disney brain trust. In addition to Eisner and Wells, that meant studio head Jeffrey Katzenberg, chief financial officer Mike Bagnall, and Dick Cook, who had succeeded Chuck Good as the studio's distribution chief. Eisner had also invited Bill Mechanic and Stan Kinsey, the studio financial chief and one of the few Richard Berger holdovers still with the film unit. Joining the discussion for the first time was Richard Frank, who had just come over from Paramount to become Katzenberg's deputy as president of the studio.

Eisner asked Mike Bagnall to have his staff project how many *Pinocchio* cassettes the company could hope to sell. It was a rough estimate, Bagnall said, but under the right conditions a *Pinocchio* video could generate as much as $100 million in revenues over the next two years. But Bagnall, a holdover from the Card Walker years, also brought up the possible adverse reaction from that decision. "We could be killing the golden goose," he said. "We could ruin it for the rerelease market."

That was the problem that the Disney crew had been struggling with for weeks. "It was a threshold decision," recalled Rich Frank. "We had a good business in rereleasing. The question was, do you throw that business out of the window if you start putting the classic films on videocassette."

The numbers, the Disney executives all knew, were confusing. Stan Kinsey had estimated that the next four theatrical releases of *Pinocchio* would probably generate more than $125 million in ticket sales, bringing in as much as $75 million for Disney. It would be 28 years, however, before Disney would see the last of that money.

The loudest proponent for moving quickly to release the film on video was Rich Frank. Tall, with a neatly trimmed beard and a sharp New York accent, Frank could be quick to excite. Like most of Disney's top executives, the former TV station general manager had both stock options and a bonus tied to the company's performance. For Rich Frank, the odds simply stacked up too much in favor of a *Pinocchio* release to debate the point further. "The net present value of that money over the next 28 years has shrunk down to less than $25 million," he stressed. "If you go out and bring in $100 million in videocassette sales next month, that's $100 million right now."

Frank was also an outspoken critic of the sluggish manner in which Ron Miller had run the company. The two men, he felt, had nearly destroyed the company by sitting on its most valuable properties. "An asset isn't an asset if you don't use it," Frank said at one point during the meeting. "What the hell are we waiting for?"

Wells, along with Frank, had also argued to move quickly. Katzenberg, on the other hand, demurred. The Disney studio head, whose twin son and daughter were only three years old at the time, worried that overexposing Disney's classics would come to haunt the company later. "If by releasing them now, we've ruined them for future generations, than we have begun to dismantle the franchise that this company has been built on," Katzenberg argued.

Katzenberg advocated pricing the cassettes at a relatively high price to encourage consumers to rent them instead of buying them. Disney had been pricing many of its cassettes at as low as $19.95 apiece to encourage consumer sales, and the year before, *Tron* and a reissue of the *Dumbo* cassette had been priced at $39.95 for the same reason. If Disney intended to rerelease *Pinocchio*, Katzenberg argued, the film should be priced higher.

The argument continued for weeks. Rich Frank remained adamant, arguing that releasing *Pinocchio* might even enhance the Disney franchise by making the studio's characters more popular than ever before. Planting the Disney name in those homes, he argued, could also enhance the popularity of future Disney animated films. And they could generate even greater consumer demand for Disney's toys and other merchandise.

By late spring, Eisner decided it was time to make a decision. *Pinocchio* would go out on video that summer, six months after it had finished playing in theaters. But, as Katzenberg had suggested, the cassettes would be priced at $79.95, in order to generate the greatest possible revenue without putting so many cassettes into the public's hands that the next *Pinocchio* reissue might be affected. The pricing decision turned out to be a disaster. Released in July 1985, the videocassette sold just over 100,000 copies in its first two months, bringing in only about $5 million for the company. Worse yet, Disney was left with more than 300,000 unsold copies, representing nearly $12 million in unused inventory. Mechanic, who had been named head of the video operation the previous October, cut the price to $29.95 to sell the rest. Within a year, the company had sold all 300,000 copies, realizing $9 million profit from its experiment with *Pinocchio*.

The next Disney classic, *Sleeping Beauty*, was released on videocassette on October 14, 1986. This time, the company had learned its lesson. Despite a woeful performance at the box office, Disney priced the *Sleeping Beauty* videocassette at an affordable $29.95. Surrounding *Sleeping Beauty* with *Pinocchio*, *Dumbo*, and three other full-length movies in a special collector's set, the company also launched a $6 million media campaign for what it called the "Bring Disney Home for Good" promotion. Each of the cassettes were priced at $29.95.

The promotion sold a staggering total of over 5 million copies, including 1.2 million copies of *Sleeping Beauty* alone. By March 31, 1988, when Disney took *Sleeping Beauty* off the market, it had become the fourth-highest-selling videocassette ever released, behind the blockbusters *Beverly Hills Cop*, *Indiana Jones and the Temple of Doom*, and *Raiders of the Lost Ark*. The $21.6 million in revenues that Disney collected from video sales of *Sleeping Beauty* was more than double what the film had earned for Disney in the theaters a year earlier.

The video revenues provided an immediate boost to the company's earnings. In 1986 alone, home video revenues provided nearly $138 million, nearly double the 1984 level. In 1987, when the first stream of new movies from the Eisner-Katzenberg era began to be sold on videocassette, revenues increased to more than $235 million. Disney also adopted a two-tier pricing strategy. To promote sales of animated films, Disney priced the cassettes at $29.95. New releases were priced at $79.95 apiece, since consumers were more likely to rent than collect movies like *Down and Out in Beverly Hills*.

There was also no longer any question but that Disney would continue to put its movie classics out on video. In 1986, more than 35 percent of America's homes already owned videocassette players, and another million families a month were going out and buying them. By

October 1987, when *Lady and the Tramp* was released, the company had received more than 2 million orders before it began shipping. *Cinderella* was put out on video the next year, and *Bambi* in 1989.

Disney had also refined its marketing strategy for its video business. Video releases would be accompanied by impressive marketing campaigns. As initially ordered by Eisner, classics like *Lady and the Tramp* would be removed from the market after a year to keep stray cassettes from interfering with upcoming theatrical rereleases. To promote the *Lady and the Tramp* videocassette, Disney launched a $20 million marketing campaign. Besides buying heavy TV and print advertising, Mechanic arranged joint marketing programs with both McDonald's and the American Dairy Association. The hamburger chain offered $3 discounts for *Lady and the Tramp* cassette purchases, while consumers could save up to $4.25 on the cassette by buying milk.

With the *Cinderella* videocassette, Disney reached the $100 million sales plateau that Bagnall had first predicted by selling 7.5 million copies. *Bambi* did even better, selling 10.5 million copies and bringing the company sales total up to $168 million. At the time, only video sales for *E.T.: The Extra-Terrestrial* had done better.

❖

A happy group of Disney executives gathered at the Sheraton Premiere, a high-rise hotel in Universal City, just before Thanksgiving of 1986. The company had just announced earnings of $247 million for the year, nearly triple the profits in Ron Miller's final year. Video sales were starting to grow, and so were syndicated sales of Disney's old TV shows and movies to individual TV stations.

The explosion of independent television stations had created a booming market for syndicated programs in the early 1980s. While most studios were dusting off their old TV programs to satisfy that market, Walt Disney Productions has chosen to keep its library of older shows to itself. With the Disney Channel starting in April 1983, the company worried that many households would tune into free episodes of the *Wonderful World of Disney* on a syndicated program rather than paying over $10 a month to watch the cable channel.

Paramount, by contrast, has emerged as the industry leader in syndication. By 1984, Paramount was earning nearly $60 million a year by selling reruns of old shows, most notably *Star Trek*. Much of the credit went to Bob Jacquemin, a St. Louis, Missouri, native who had come to Paramount in 1978 after eight years of running his own TV sales organization.

Tall, with a large nose and the easy manner of a salesman, Jacquemin had sold 48 shows while at Paramount, including *Cheers* and *Family Ties*. He had also helped Paramount launch two new shows, *Solid Gold* in 1980 and *Entertainment Tonight* the following year. So committed to making the sales was Jacquemin that when smaller stations said they didn't have the receiving facilities to pick up *Solid Gold* from Paramount's satellite, Jacquemin brokered a deal with equipment manufacturers to get them the receiving dishes.

Jacquemin still had several months to go on his Paramount contract when Eisner called him in January 1985 to offer him a job at Disney. Jacquemin eventually joined the Disney team in mid-1985. But by then, the company already hired an assistant for Jacquemin. Judie Eden, from the Times-Mirror Corp.'s cable unit, had nearly completed cataloging the titles of more than 200 shows in Disney's library. Even though he was not yet with the company officially, Jacquemin also hired the Nielsen ratings organization to begin retrieving 30-year-old ratings books from a warehouse in San Francisco. The rating numbers would be needed to determine how well the shows had done when they initially aired on network television—a key selling point for station owners.

Like selling videocassettes, syndicating old Disney TV shows and movies was a quick way to increase the company's profits. On October 28, 1985, roughly a year after Eisner and Wells arrived, the company launched its first syndication package, called "Disney Magic One." Jacquemin sent his newly hired salesman out to station owners with a package of 25 movies and 178 hours of the Sunday night TV show. Among the movies were *Dumbo, Mary Poppins, 20,000 Leagues Under the Sea*, and *Splash*. By late 1985, the sales staff had sold the 25 movies to stations in 147 of the nation's 165 television markets and the Sunday night show's reruns to 125 stations.

The first revenues from the syndication package had begun to come in by late 1986. But when Jacquemin and 80 other Disney executives gathered at the Sheraton Premiere, the company was still missing out on "first-run" syndication shows—shows made especially for sale directly to TV stations. At the time, companies like KingWorld were making millions a year on "first-run" syndication shows like *Wheel of Fortune* and *The Oprah Winfrey Show*. Syndication shows were especially valuable to production companies like Disney. Not only could the shows be sold directly to TV stations and their advertisers, avoiding the "big three" networks, but the studio itself (not finicky network executives) could make the decisions about where and when the shows would air. For months, Jacquemin had been itching to get into the "first-run" business. In early 1985, Disney had nearly signed with Time-Life Inc. to do a news-magazine show like *Entertainment Tonight* that would be based on Time's *People* magazine. Disney and Time had initially agreed to share the costs of the $50 million show. In August, however, *Time* magazine chief Henry Grunwald backed out of the deal, worried that the show would siphon off readers from the magazine.

Another Disney show was actually produced the next year, but it bombed. *Today's Business*, an early-morning show that initially aired on 133 stations, was pulled off the air after Disney lost nearly $5 million. The show had starred Consuelo Mack and *Business Week* editor Bill Wolman.

Bob Jacquemin sat in the grand ballroom of the Sheraton Premiere for several days, listening to Disney executives give detailed reports on how their divisions had fared in 1986. Gary Krisel, head of the Disney TV animation unit, showed the assembled managers some color slides of a new show called *DuckTales*. At the time, Krisel was peddling the show, which featured Donald Duck's three nephews, to the three networks.

Jacquemin wanted the show for syndication. Disney already had a pair of cartoon shows on the networks, he told the assembled Disney executives. His own syndication operation hadn't yet found a successful show. This could be it. Besides, the syndication chief said, the cartoon shows now being syndicated in the afternoon—*Thundercats*, *G. I. Joe*, and the like—were geared to an audience of older boys. *DuckTales* could find a very profitable niche with girls and boys under age 10.

Within a week, Disney had shifted the show from its network unit to the syndication division. By early 1987, Jacquemin's sales staff had begun to line up orders for *DuckTales*. Disney's animation unit, however, was too preoccupied with making full-length animated films to handle the syndicated show. Instead, Disney hired TMS, a Japanese studio, to draw the first 65 half-hour episodes.

The half-hour weekly cartoon show became Disney's first hit show in syndication. In September of 1987, the studio began airing the first of the 65 episodes. Jacquemin's crew had lined up 121 stations, reaching more than 83 percent of TV households. Within a few months, it was the top-ranked afternoon kids' show in syndication, having captured nearly 11 percent of the market.

By 1988, the market for children's afternoon cartoon shows was the hottest syndication market in the industry. Warner Brothers and Fox were gearing up to enter the market. So, too, was Disney. With a half hour already doing well, Jacquemin encouraged Eisner to follow up on *DuckTales's* success. If station owners wanted to take the top-rated cartoon show, they should be willing as well to take a second Disney afternoon program, Jacquemin figured.

Eisner agreed. And ever before *DuckTales* had completed its first season, Disney had placed a second order with the Japanese studio to begin drawing 65 episodes of a second show. This show would be called *Chip 'n Dale's Rescue Rangers,* an updated story line using the pair of chipmunks who had made their animated debut in a series of Disney short cartoons in 1943.

The move into syndication would cost money. By late 1986, Jacquemin's unit was spending more than $70 million on new programming that wasn't likely to produce revenue—let alone profits—for at least a year. Disney outbid the Tribune Company for the rights to syndicate *Siskel & Ebert at the Movies.* The Tribune Company had originated the show, featuring two Chicago-based movie critics giving their opinions of the latest releases.

Disney also agreed to underwrite *Win, Lose or Draw,* a parlor game developed by actor Burt Reynolds. And it decided to spend more than $30 million to syndicate *Live with Regis & Kathie Lee,* a New York–based talk show featuring Regis Philbin and Kathie Lee Gifford. A year earlier, KingWorld had done the same with a Chicago-based talk show. The show featured a charismatic black hostess named Oprah Winfrey. With a little luck, Disney hoped to repeat Oprah's magic.

❖

In their first report to Disney's shareholders, Michael Eisner and Frank Wells went out of their way to laud the accomplishments of Ron Miller, Card Walker, and the other Disney executives who had just given up control of the company. "The farsighted team," the new Disney managers wrote, "clearly set the right track in positioning Disney's resources and directions for significant growth and improved returns on investment." They cited the Disney Channel as one example, adding that the channel is "a concept that we believe destined to become a leading revenue source in the years ahead."

Until they began planning the Disney Channel, which was launched on April 18, 1983, Walt's heirs had largely refused to venture beyond the company founder's own vision. New investments were reserved for EPCOT Center, which Walt had designed, or for the same kind of movies that the company had been making for decades.

Starting the new channel was anything but easy. In 1977, Jim Jimirro had made a proposal to start the cable unit, but Walker had turned it down because the company was concentrating its financial resources on EPCOT Center. A planned joint venture with Group W's satellite unit had fallen through in 1982 when Walker stormed out of a meeting with Group W executives. The Disney chief executive, those who attended the meeting later recalled, had refused to give Group W as much of the profits as it was demanding or to allow it any role in making creative decisions.

Left on its own, Disney spent $19 million to purchase the rights to two transponders on the Hughes Communication Galaxy I satellite, and then spent another $20 million on programming. Nearly half the programs were Disney retreads, from *Winnie-the-Pooh* cartoons for kids to *Love Bug* movies for young adults. Subscribers to the Disney Channel were the only people who could see *Cinderella* and some of the other Disney animated classics outside a theater. The channel also aired some new programs, notably *The New Leave It to Beaver*, as well as an original movie about baseball called *Tiger Town*.

In its first full year, the channel signed up more than 700,000 subscribers. It also lost $28 million, most of it in start-up costs. There were other repercussions as well throughout the company. In their attempt to boost the fortunes of the Disney Channel, Ron Miller and Card Walker had begun to systematically suffocate much of the rest of Disney's film and TV operations. Not only did the company refuse to syndicate any of its older shows; it also pulled the Sunday night TV show off CBS and even stopped selling its movies to other cable channels. "The idea was to give the Disney Channel as good a chance to make it as we could," recalled Ron Miller. "We were worried that people wouldn't want to buy Disney shows if they could get them for free."

By the time that Eisner and Wells arrived, the Disney Channel's losses had been trimmed. The channel had more than 1 million subscribers and was generating more than $77 million in revenues. Eisner had been briefed on the pay channel by Jimirro during a six-hour flight from New York on a luxury Regency Air airliner. Jimirro had negotiated an agreement with the giant cable system operator Cablevision Systems Inc., which had agreed to pay Disney a minimum of $75 million over the next 10 years for the right to offer Disney to its 541,145 cable subscribers. Eisner and Jimirro had gone to New York to sign the deal.

On the flight back, Jimirro, a compact man with dark hair and an infectious smile, had done his best to convince Eisner that the Disney Channel was on the verge of huge success. Subscribers, he said, had reached nearly 1.3 million. Within a year, it would be profitable. Moreover, the channel represented a tremendous opportunity to promote other pieces of the Disney company—the parks, consumer products, and upcoming movies.

Eisner was initially impressed enough with Jimirro to propose that the Disney board give him a special $80,000 bonus in late 1984. Within months, however, Eisner and Frank Wells had grown disenchanted with the longtime Disney executive. By April, they were casting about for a replacement.

Eisner had called John Cooke, the 42-year-old executive vice-president of Times-Mirror Cable Television, not long after joining Disney. The two men had known each other for five years, dating back to when Paramount and Times-Mirror had briefly discussed starting a joint pay television channel. By April, however, Cooke and Frank Wells were discussing a contract to bring the Times-Mirror executive to Disney. Jimirro unexpectedly resigned in June 1985, citing "superficial differences" with Eisner and Wells, clearing the way for Wells to hire Cooke.

The Disney Channel, Cooke soon found, was in far worse shape than its glossy numbers indicated. Although the service had nearly 1.8 million customers, the cable operation was losing a large number of the customers it was signing up. The Disney Channel, in short, was suffering from a condition that the industry calls "churn." For most companies, churn amounts to 5 percent of customers—people who tire of the service each month—or about 60 percent each year. The Disney Channel's churn rate was shockingly high—closer to 80 percent. "A lot of people were trying it because of the Disney name, but then they were dropping it later on," explained Cooke.

Cooke's first job was to overhaul the Disney Channel's programming. Ron Miller and Jim Jimirro had planned to spend $44 million in 1984 on new programming. Less than $5 million of that sum was allocated for buying outside programming. Although Jimirro launched 13 new shows—including the popular *Dumbo's Circus*—his acquisitions also included tired old programs like a Steve Allen variety show and a talk show with Dr. Joyce Brothers.

Initially Eisner gave Cooke license to increase the acquisition budget to $12 million a year, but within three years the budget grew to more than $50 million. The programs Cooke bought also had a decidedly different feel to them. Disney's executives found 100 "lost" episodes of *Ozzie and Harriet*, which became a big hit with yuppie viewers. The Disney Channel also became the home for Garrison Keillor's *A Prairie Home Companion*, rock concerts, and a new version of *The Mickey Mouse Club*. Unlike its squeaky-clean predecessor, this *Mickey Mouse Club* show featured rap songs, break dancing, and sexy teenage girls.

Cooke also instituted a far more aggressive marketing program. Under Jim Jimirro, the Disney Channel had been charging local cable companies more than $4 for each subscriber to the channel. That made the Disney Channel among the most expensive of an army of new pay channels that were introduced in the mid-1980s. Cooke slashed the cable operator's wholesale rate dramatically. By offering even lower prices to hotel chains around the country, he was able to line up the Stouffer, Hyatt, and Marriott hotel chains by 1989, along with Spectradyne, Inc., the Texas-based pay cable system for several other hotel chains.

The Disney Channel was gearing up just as cable was beginning to grab a solid hold on the American TV viewer. Improved programming and lower prices also translated into more subscribers. The system had its largest single month in late 1986, adding 138,000 new subscribers. By the end of 1987, the Disney Channel was growing steadily at a 20 percent annual rate and was reaching nearly 4 million households.

Tapping into the growing number of "strategic alliances" that Frank Wells was building with major corporate sponsors at the parks, Cooke also launched the channel's first joint promotional campaign. Mars Candy, which in 1989 began to sponsor the "Star Tours" rides, promoted the Disney Channel on wrappers for its M&M candy. Longtime Disney sponsor Coca-Cola also staged several promotions.

By late 1988, the Disney Channel was also achieving Eisner's goal of cross-promotion for other company ventures. Kids watching Winnie-the-Pooh or Mickey Mouse cartoons became a target market for Disney toys. Showing episodes of *The Mickey Mouse Club*, which had been filmed at the Disney-MGM Studios Theme Park, enticed 14-year-olds into pressuring their parents to take them to Orlando. When *Who Framed Roger Rabbit* was aired on the channel, specials on EPCOT Center were also run, along with anniversary shows celebrating the parks.

The Disney Channel also finally achieved the profitability levels that Eisner and Wells had anticipated. By 1990, it had more than 5 million subscribers and was earning more than $20 million a year.*

❖

Disney's annual report proclaimed that "1988 was a year when dreams became a reality" at its film unit. It was no doubt more than a little hyperbolic. But 1988 was the year in which the studio's revenues first passed $1 billion, a heady 31 percent increase over what the company had earned the previous year and triple the 1984 earnings. The Disney film unit was on a roll, as *Who Framed Roger Rabbit*, *Good Morning, Vietnam*, and *Three Men and a Baby* all passed the $100 million box office mark. Lost in the fine print of the annual report was an even more impressive number: Though the earnings from film production had received the most publicity, the video, TV syndication, and cable units together had actually been responsible for 60 percent of the studio's revenues.

The home video unit, sixth among Hollywood's major studios in 1985, had moved into the top-ranking position. Much of this success had to do with video sales of *Three Men and a Baby* and *Good Morning, Vietnam*, but the company had also received more than 4.8 million orders for *Cinderella* even before the videocassette was released. *Pinnochio* had become the hot-selling videocassette in Japan, and repackaged Disney cartoons were dominating the $276 million children's market in the United States.

Disney's TV syndication was generating $185 million in revenues three years after it had begun. *DuckTales* was the highest-rated afternoon show for children. By the end of 1989, Bob Jacquemin's sales team had

---

*Jim Jimirro disputes the characterization that the channel was losing money at his departure, and says many of his programs continue to be popular to its viewers today.

lined up 151 stations, covering 93 percent of the country, for *Chip 'n Dale's Rescue Rangers*. When the two shows began airing at the end of the 1989 season, the one-hour show was seen by more than 12 million children. The two shows ranked first and second among syndicated kids' shows.

More important, it was a strong enough showing for Disney to capture a robust $71 million in afternoon advertising revenues, nearly half the $185 million that was being spent on advertising for kids' syndicated programming. It was also strong enough for Disney to begin plans for a second full hour of syndicated programming.

Disney had mixed success with its other syndicated programming. *Siskel & Ebert* continued the strong ratings it had when it was with the Tribune Company. *Live with Regis & Kathie Lee* had good, if not spectacular, ratings. *Win, Lose or Draw* did well initially. But ratings for the show soon fell as other game shows began to crowd the market. Within two years, it was no longer on the air. The Disney Channel was an unqualified success. Viewership continued to climb, reaching more than 4 million by the end of 1988. Plans were being made to beam the channel to England and Ireland. Most important, the channel was making more than $20 million a year in operating profits.

Much of Disney's success in exploiting its ancillary businesses was simply good fortune. The markets for videocassettes were booming, kids were returning to syndicated programming, and more than half the country had signed onto cable television—three times the number just two years earlier. But there were no mistaking the new emphasis Disney's management brought to each of those areas. The days of coddling Disney's assets were clearly over.

❖

It began almost as an afterthought. But 55 years after a small stationery company had given Walt Disney $300 to put Mickey Mouse's picture on a school writing tablet, Eisner and Wells had come to a company that was collecting more than $110 million a year from licenses it granted manufacturers to use Mickey, Donald, Goofy, and the other Disney characters. And over the years, the characters had shown up on nearly everything from Winnie-the-Pooh dolls to a Disney ice show. By the early 1980s, profits from royalties on Mickey and Donald T-shirts and toys were more than twice as large as those from Disney's struggling film unit. In 1984 alone, earnings had fallen by 5 percent, at a time when the rest of the company's earnings had actually increased marginally.

Since late 1983, Disney's consumer products unit had been run by Barton ("Bo") Boyd, a 38-year-old antique car enthusiast. Like many Disney executives, Boyd traced his company roots to the theme parks, where he had started in 1968 as a buyer of plush toys for Disneyland. Eisner and Wells liked Boyd. Jovial and outgoing, he had fought to buck the stodgy trend that had permeated the company during the Walker-Miller years. But when the two new Disney executives had come to the company, they also knew that Boyd desperately needed help.

The first new executive Boyd elevated to help him was Steve Mc-Beth, an English literature major and former direct mail manager who had worked his way up at Disney since joining the company in 1980 as a production coordinator for the company's tiny education film unit. Installing him as head of the licensing division, Boyd instructed McBeth to aggressively seek new outlets for Disney products.

At the time, Disney was licensing more than 8,000 different products under 1,600 separate agreements. Within two years, McBeth had doubled the number of Disney products. More important, the company had gone well beyond plush toys and T-shirts. In short, Mickey went upscale. J. G. Hook designed a new Mickey & Co. label that featured trendy clothes for both men and women. Seiko's Lorus subsidiary upgraded the traditional Mickey Mouse watch by offering $350 models.

To old company hands it seemed as if nothing was sacred. Ron Miller and Card Walker may have been low to react to the changing entertainment world. But they had carefully guarded the franchises they inherited. Under Michael Eisner and Frank Wells, the rush to cash in on Mickey's popularity seemed to be commercialization run amok. Insiders grumbled when Gold Bond Ice Cream even began offering frozen treats shaped like Mickey and Pluto. "I get tired of seeing Mickey here and there and everywhere," says Ron Miller.

Three years later, Boyd hired Paul Pressler form Kenner-Parker Toys. As a 29-year-old vice-president in charge of finding the next hit toy, he had helped Kenner-Parker bring America such hit toys as Care Bears and Strawberry Shortcake. At Disney, the baby-faced toy executive was charged with the same chore. When Pressler joined Disney in early 1987, the company was riding the same wave of national popularity that was carrying the rest of the company. The advertising blitz that Eisner and Wells had approved for the theme parks almost always featured Mickey and the other characters. When hosting the *The Disney Sunday Movie*, Eisner would open each episode standing alongside Goofy or another character. And the Disney name and allure were being introduced almost daily to a new generation of kids through the exploitation of the company's library of old cartoons on videocassette or in the syndication market.

Not long after arriving at Disney, Pressler had stood alongside Steven Spielberg in a large cavernous sound stage on the Burbank lot. With nearly 100 manufacturers present, the new Disney licensing vice-president was lining up companies willing to pay 7 percent to 10 percent of their sales to make products based on Spielberg's upcoming *Who Framed Roger Rabbit*. Armed with nothing more than several dozen drawings and a short film clip, Pressler had signed up 34 companies to make nearly 500 Roger Rabbit products.

Roger Rabbit was a minor hit for Disney consumer products division. But soon Disney had their first homegrown merchandise hit in the animated film *The Little Mermaid*, a big hit with preteen girls. Pressler signed up more than 40 licensees based on the film, accounting for over $100 million in sales the first year alone. The next year, the company repeated its success with *Dick Tracy*, with 85 licensees signed on before the movie's June 1990 opening. The revenues from *Dick Tracy*, although not as strong as those from Bart Simpson, still accounted for nearly $150 million within a year of the movie's debut.

Creating hit movies was one thing, but Disney was one of the best names in kids' movies and the company was doing little to capitalize on the brand name. Pressler was put in charge of creating a Disney brand that would sell products, targeting different lines of products to different markets. The first new Disney "brand" actually came from outside the United States. Marketing executives at a Disney subcontractor in Brazil, Redibra, had licensed a line of "Disney Baby" baby carriers and disposable diapers. Geared to the mothers of infants, it had been a huge hit in the South American country in 1985. And by 1986, it had also been licensed in Japan, where the line had grown to more than 80 separate products featuring the infants Mickey, Minnie, Donald, and Pluto.

By late 1987, the Disney Baby products had arrived in America. In all, Disney licensed more than 40 U.S. companies to make Disney Babies products. Soon, Disney was designing its own products. In 1987, Pressler persuaded Mattel Inc. to sign up for a line of 30 infant and preschool products, including Disney rattles and a block set based on Disneyland's Main Street. In 1990, Mattel also launched a line of Minnie 'n Me dolls, small dress-up dolls that were aimed at Hasbro's "My Little Pony" line.

Disney's new visibility lured some of the better retailers, including J.C. Penney, Kmart, and Sears, Roebuck & Co. So did Disney's new eagerness to help promote its toys with national advertising. In one promotion, Disney and Nabisco jointly launched a $5 million in-store promotion tied to the Disney Channel's new *Mickey Mouse Club* show. The displays went up in 2,000 stores. Coupons on Oreo packages also awarded free trips to Walt Disney World. (Not all the relationships went smoothly. Disney broke off a 10-year arrangement with Sears when it felt the Chicago-based retailer, then in the midst of a major restructuring of its own, wasn't aggressively marketing the Disney products.)

To control every aspect of product sales, Disney needed to take the next step: owning its own retail chain. The idea was pitched to Eisner, Wells, and Gary Wilson in late 1986 by Steve Burke, a 28-year-old Harvard M.B.A. who had joined the company earlier that year as head of its newly created business development unit. Burke, a marathon runner who had helped General Foods develop its Grape Nuts cereal, was told to find new ventures for the company. But when he first brought Disney managers the concept of the Disney store, he recalls, "they thought it was small beer. Interesting, but just nothing that would show the kinds of returns they were hoping for."

Eisner and Wells had given Burke $400,000 to launch the first store at the Glendale Galleria, a few miles from the company's Burbank headquarters. Within a year, the store was generating an impressive $1,000 a square foot, or roughly $2 million annually. By the end of the first year, Disney launched two others, at a mall in Costa Mesa, California, and at San Francisco's Pier 39 waterfront shopping complex.

Not surprisingly, Michael Eisner had become an unabashed fan of the Disney store concept. Donning dark glasses and a baseball cap, the Disney chairman paid surprise visits to local outlets to check on their operations. He later selected the college-style sweaters that became the store personnel's "uniform."

❖

Before long, Disney stores had begun popping up at a rate of more than two a month. By the end of 1990, when there were more than 70 stores around the country, Disney was selling more than $120 million of products a year through its own outlets. The stores become so popular that former president Ronald Reagan, on a 45-minute Christmas trip to a

Los Angeles shopping mall, spent most of his time at the Disney store picking out Mickey, Minnie, and Thumper Rabbit stuffed toys for his grandchildren.*

By 1990, the Disney store merchandise, ranging from 50-cent Mickey Mouse erasers to a $3,200 diamond-studded Dumbo brooch, represented roughly 25 percent of the revenues of Disney's merchandise unit. The stores were generating over $20 million in profits. Almost by accident, Disney had also stumbled upon one of the company's strongest promotional vehicles. Each store was being visited by more than 1 million people a year, Disney's research soon found.

A TV monitor at the front of each store played a 30-minute video-tape promoting Disney's cable channel, an upcoming movie, or the latest videocassette. "It's a Small World" or other Disney music filtered throughout the store, and a giant Disney movie screen played the latest videocassette or syndicated TV program. Without any advertising, the stores soon were selling more than $10 million a year in tickets to the theme parks alone. And the stores soon became the third-leading place for Disney videocassettes to be sold.

By 1991, Disney stores were also popping up overseas. Eisner and Wells, eager to promote the company's $2 billion Euro Disneyland park near Paris, had ordered Burke to expand into Europe. Disney signed its first lease in mid-1990 with the Crown Estate, Queen Elizabeth's investment trust, to put a store in London's tony Regent Street shopping district. Stores were also planned for Paris and Tokyo to help promote the Paris and Tokyo theme parks.

The stores had given Disney a new way to reach the consumer, bypassing the nation's retail outlets. Ridding itself of the middleman no doubt was saving the company several millions a year. Disney was already working on yet another way. In late 1985, the company began testing a 24-page "Walt Disney Family Gift Catalog" with more than 200 mail-order products. A year later, the company was mailing 2.8 million catalogs every month, making it the fifth-largest children's mail-order catalog in the country.

Bypassing the retailer, of course, meant that Disney did not have to pay hefty commissions or surrender valuable profit margins. In mid-1988, it augmented its mail-order operation by paying $61 million to buy Childcraft Education Corp., a Princeton, New Jersey, company that

---

*And cartoon-decorated golf balls for himself.

owned two of the other five largest catalogs. Specializing in children's furniture and educational toys, Childcraft was mailing more than 6 million copies of its two catalogs each year. In 1988 the company generated $52 million in sales. Together with its own smaller catalog, Disney was suddenly reaching 8 million homes each month with its catalog and raking in more than $70 million a year in sales.

The retail stores and mail-order catalog were only two of the ways that Disney chose to find new ways to entice consumers to spend their money. In early 1990, the company produced its first album of original songs, the *Minnie and Me* album by 10-year-old Christa Larson. The next month, Walt Disney Records also released *Sebastian*, an album of reggae and calypso songs by Sam Wright, the voice of the animated crab in the Disney movie *The Little Mermaid*.

The two albums were produced by Marke Jaffe, a former director of marketing for A&M Records' children's division, who was lured to Disney in early 1990 to update the record unit. The record unit was operating separately from Hollywood Records, a unit of Jeffrey Katzenberg's studio, which had signed up such heavy metal acts as Pleasure Thieves, World War III, and Vanity Kills. It would be two years before Hollywood Records would have its first hit, and even that was a collection of old songs from the vintage group Queen, although the record label was never a great success.

The company was also moving cautiously into publishing. In 1989, it had taken over publication of a failing Italian magazine called *Topolino* that featured Mickey Mouse stories. Comic books were soon launched in Spain and Latin America. In the United States, Disney decided to put out eight separate comic books based on its *DuckTales* and other syndicated cartoon shows. By early 1990, the company decided to take an even bigger gamble. It hired Charles Wickham, a 52-year-old senior vice-president at Field Publications, publisher of the *Weekly Reader* children's newspaper, to set up the company's Hyperion Publishing operation in New York. Recasting Mickey Mouse as a high-adventure hero, the company had begun publication of the first of six Mickey Mouse Adventure storybooks. *Disney Adventures*, a book digest–sized book of games and puzzles, began showing up at market checkout stands by late 1990.

At the same time, Disney also showed up at the Frankfurt Book Fair with the first line of books under its newly created Disney Press imprint, a line that boasted some of the world's best-known children's authors and illustrators. By 1991, the unit expected to be publishing 24 different titles, including some based on the Muppets and others starring Mickey, Minnie, and the rest of the Disney characters.

C H A P T E R

The Empty Nest

W hile he was making cartoon shows for ABC in the mid-1960s, Michael Eisner used to force himself to watch Walt Disney's *Wonderful World of Color.* The show that Walt had started a decade earlier no longer enjoyed the lofty ratings of its first few seasons, but it was Eisner's only link to the company that Walt Disney had created. Much of the country was in a similar situation, for the Sunday night TV show was Disney's most visible public presentation, with the exception of the theme parks.

By the time Eisner and Frank Wells arrived at Disney, the show was no longer on the air. The last show, aired on September 23, 1983, had been a hastily compiled collection of old Mickey Mouse and Goofy cartoons. The introduction by kindly uncle Walt Disney had long since been replaced by a disembodied voice that greeted audiences with all the warmth and personality of an announcer for a detergent commercial. In its last season, the show, which had been renamed *Walt Disney,* finished in a tie for 73rd in the ratings.

Michael Eisner believed that Ron Miller's 1983 decision to pull the plug on the network TV show had been a colossal blunder. Unwilling to spend money on the television operation, Walt Disney Productions had allowed the company's most visible presence to atrophy. Few new episodes had been produced, and those few were poorly made and drew low ratings. Even so, the several million homes that still tuned in on Sunday nights got a visual message about the Disney company and about its theme parks and consumer products. The opening of the show, featuring Tinker Bell and a panoramic view of the Orlando property, "was like a one-minute commercial every week for us," said theme park head Dick Nunis.

In one particularly stormy Disney board meeting, Nunis had argued loudly against Miller's decision to pull the show off the air. Attendance at the theme parks was already falling, Nunis had argued. "If you won't let us advertise on television, at least let us have that show," the theme park chief pleaded. Miller, eager to rid the airways of anything that would compete with the new Disney Channel, was unmoved. "I just didn't get where he was coming from," Ron Miller would say later. "I mean, what the hell, no one was watching the damn thing anyway."

In 1984 Michael Eisner didn't know much about theme parks, but he knew a lot about making hit television shows. During his ABC and Paramount days, Eisner had shown an uncommon touch for predicting American viewing tastes. He developed the idea for the hit show *Happy Days* during a layover at Newark Airport. The pilot, appearing first as an episode of *Love American Style* in 1971, had rejuvenated the career of one-time child actor Ron Howard and inspired George Lucas to make his hit film *American Graffiti*. Seven years later, Eisner convinced ABC to take a chance on *Mork & Mindy*, a *Happy Days* spin-off. Expanding a guest appearance by San Francisco comedian Robin Williams, *Mork & Mindy* became a hit in its own right.

By 1984, Hollywood was also in the midst of a boom period for TV syndication. The explosion of new independent television stations, together with continued defections among network viewers, had triggered a seller's market for old TV shows. TV station owners were bidding up the prices of hit shows. Universal Studios could get $1.6 million for each of its 72 *Magnum P. I.* episodes. Twentieth Century Fox grossed more than $50 million annually from its M*A*S*H reruns. In all, Hollywood studios were collecting more than $400 million a year from the syndication market.

Disney, stuck in a backwater, had been blissfully ignoring the syndication market as well as the first-run network television possibilities. Trying to remedy the situation, Ron Miller had hired two old Hollywood hands to run the company's resurrected TV unit: Ed Self, a former ABC executive, and Bill Braderman, who had worked at Quinn Martin Productions. Neither man made much of an impact, and within a year, the company still hadn't had much of a nibble from network executives. Braderman and Self did not figure in Michael Eisner's TV plans for Disney. Eisner had a wealth of connections with network and production executives, and he himself would prime the pump to get Disney back into production. "This was my area," Eisner said later. "I had started on the ground floor at ABC and at Paramount. This wasn't all that different."

Eisner's first two weeks in office were filled with a flurry of meetings and congratulatory telephone calls. Among those who called was *Hill Street Blues* creator Steven Bochco, who was looking for a studio to help him finance the $300,000 he needed to complete a pilot for his new show, *L. A. Law*. Bochco was also asking for a huge piece of any syndication deal that Disney would eventually make for the show. It was a formula destined to work against Disney. Even with a modest hit, Eisner figured, the company would have to share most of its profits with Bochco. The most likely scenario, given the notoriously poor record of most TV shows, was a loss for the company.

If Eisner was wary of Steven Bochco, he was even more wary of Jerry Perrenchio. A one-time talent agent, Perrenchio and his partner, TV producer Norman Lear, had launched their own production company in 1974. Now, Perrenchio was offering Eisner the company, Embassy Communications, for $500 million. The company had obvious appeal, holding the lucrative syndication rights to *All in the Family*, *Maude*, and *The Jeffersons*. To Eisner, however, the price was staggering.

"I thought that anything that Norman Lear and Jerry Perrenchio would offer to me was obviously overpriced," Eisner recalled later. The company was sold to Coca-Cola's Columbia Pictures unit in 1985 for $485 million. There it became a big moneymaker. The next year it produced *Who's the Boss*, starring Tony Danza. The show, which became one of the biggest hits on television, was syndicated by Columbia in 1989 for more than $100 million.

One deal that Eisner did make was with Paul Witt, Tony Thomas, and Susan Harris. The three had been involved in such hit shows as *Benson* and *Soap*. Eisner knew Witt and Thomas from his days at ABC, when the producers had made the Emmy Award–winning movie *Brian's Song*. The three TV executives were now looking to branch out into movies, as their agent, Bill Haber, told Eisner in a telephone conversation.

Eisner was interested in signing them for a movie deal, but he was especially interested in a commitment NBC had given the three to air one of their new shows. The show, entitled *The Golden Girls*, was about four older women living together in Miami. As was customary in the television business, NBC had agreed to pay $200,000 of the $320,000 it would cost to produce each episode. The Witt-Thomas-Harris team was also looking for a "deficit-financing" deal for the show, in which a studio agrees to pay the remainder of the costs.*

In early spring, Disney signed its first substantial TV production deal, with Witt, Thomas, and Harris. The three-year agreement gave Disney first option on any movie or television projects that the trio developed, but the three TV producers also won a huge concession from Disney. The studio would have virtually no creative control over the shows the Witt-Thomas-Harris team produced. "We had something that Disney desperately needed, a pilot for a TV show," says Witt. "They needed an initial move to get them away from movies and theme parks, and one of the questions that they had was how to get shows on the air."

Disney paid a stiff price for *The Golden Girls*. The company was responsible for the entire $120,000 a week that NBC wasn't paying. On top of their regular producer's fees, Witt, Thomas, and Harris would get more than one-third of any profits the show made if it stayed on the air long enough to be syndicated. The show's four stars all got percentages as well. Haber's agency, Creative Artists Agency, got another 10 percent of any revenues generated by the show. Even if it was a huge hit, Disney would only get one-third of anything the program commanded.

The show had several of Disney's board members scratching their heads, recalls theme park boss Dick Nunis, who sits on the company's board. But Eisner was adamant that the show would work. "He told us, 'Everyone's got a grandmother,'" recalls Nunis. "Everyone will be watching it." Enough arms were twisted. Six months after coming to Disney, Eisner had his first network television show.

❖

Leonard Goldenson had given Michael Eisner his first job, acting on Barry Diller's suggestion. A former Paramount Pictures lawyer, the 76-year-old Goldenson had founded ABC-TV in 1951. To compete with

---

*Under "deficit-financing" deals, the producers and studios make money only if the show is successful enough to be syndicated after airing for three years on a network.

the bigger and more powerful networks, Goldenson had opened his network to young, aggressive program executives who didn't think like their established peers at NBC and CBS. This policy had lured such upcoming talents as Leonard Goldberg, Barry Diller, and Michael Eisner. It had also paved the way for youth-oriented shows like *Happy Days* and *Laverne & Shirley*—shows that transformed the fledgling network into a ratings powerhouse by the mid-1970s.

Even after Eisner and Diller left ABC for Paramount Pictures, Leonard Goldenson's network continued to do business with his one-time protégés. Later, when Eisner was pushed out of Paramount in 1984, Goldenson offered Eisner and Jeffrey Katzenberg $300 million to start a film production company in partnership with his network. That deal never came to fruition. But three months after Eisner arrived at Disney, he and Goldenson were finally back together. As it had done with Walt Disney three decades earlier, ABC would launch a one-hour Disney show.

Soon after New Year's Day in 1985, Eisner invited Goldenson and his two top programming executives, Fred Pierce and Tony Thomopoulos, to the Burbank studio. The three guests sat down for lunch with Eisner and Katzenberg in Disney's small executive dining room. "We wanted to do something to support their new administration," Leonard Goldenson recalled later. "We had a lot of history with them."

ABC's own Sunday evening show, *Ripley's Believe It or Not*, was languishing at the bottom of the ratings charts. The other shows the network had tried previously in its 7:00 P.M. slot, *Code Red* and *Those Amazing Animals*, had done no better. CBS's *60 Minutes* had dominated the time slot for years, but the audience that the show appealed to was getting older. ABC wanted something that would lure younger viewers and their parents.

The network, Goldenson said, was prepared to turn over its 7:00 P.M. Sunday night spot to Disney. ABC would pay $750,000 for each hour the studio produced, with Disney picking up the remaining $150,000 or more. In all, ABC was prepared to pay Disney more than $20 million for the 13 one-hour shows and 10 two-hour movies it wanted Disney to produce. Disney's costs would amount to about $5 million, an amount the studio would more than recoup if the shows were later syndicated. Even if they weren't, Eisner figured, some of the shows could also be reused on the Disney Channel. "It was the Disney franchise being reborn," says Rich Frank. "To us, that was worth a certain investment."

It took nearly four months for Disney and ABC to work out the details. Eisner wanted more money than ABC was willing to give, and wanted to make more two-hour movies than the network wanted. ABC, on the other hand, wanted more creative input than Disney's executives were willing to cede. The deal was finally signed in early summer. Rich Frank, who had just come over from Paramount, handled the final details. When the time came to sign the agreement, he and Eisner went to Fred Pierce's Century City office for the formality of putting their names on the contract. Most such signings are routine. But Pierce, who had been having troubles with his back, soon turned the conversation to a new set of stretching exercises his doctor had recommended.

Eisner at the time was also having twinges in his back. "All of a sudden, Ford is on the floor showing us the exercise and Michael is down there doing the mirror image of the thing," recalls Rich Frank. "And, out of the blue, the door comes swinging open and a secretary comes in. She sees the two of them stretched out on the floor, and Tony Thomopoulos and I in chairs watching them. I don't know what kind of story she told about what was going on there."

The fun ended there, however. ABC had wanted the show for its upcoming season, which would start in September 1985. The negotiating delay had put that in doubt. More importantly, Disney was only then in the middle of hiring the dozens of people it needed to gear up its depleted television production unit. With few writers or producers signed on, and no scripts prepared for the show, Disney couldn't meet the September deadline. Instead, ABC agreed to air the first Disney show in January 1986.

One big question was who would host the new show. Walt Disney himself had hosted the original show until his death in 1966. His reassuring voice and twinkling smile had been immeasurably beneficial to the company. The sight of Walt standing next to Donald Duck or introducing the latest Disney cartoon seemed to send a subliminal message that promoted the theme parks, consumer products, and even upcoming Disney movies.

As the final deal was coming together, Jeffrey Katzenberg and Rich Frank began compiling a long list of Hollywood actors as possible hosts. Among those on the list were Lloyd Bridges and Peter Graves. "There were just tons of actors," recalls Frank. "But the key thing we were concerned about was who would the American people trust." Katzenberg worried that an actor might be perceived as doing little more than simply reading his lines and might fail to provide the kind of warmth and credibility the show needed.

Eisner himself wanted Walter Cronkite, whose credibility rating at the time was among the highest of any public figure. But Cronkite, Disney soon discovered, would not be available for five years. The former CBS news anchor had just signed a long-term contract with CBS for a series of news specials.

Finally, Rich Frank recalled, "We all said 'Why not Michael, what's wrong with Michael.' I mean, he's very personable. He comes across as very likable, almost childlike." At first Eisner protested. Unlike Walt, who had spent most of his life acting out story lines for his animated cartoons, Eisner was ill at ease in front of large audiences. "I am not an in-front-of-the-camera type of person," he told Katzenberg and Frank. "I'm not an actor, and I'm not Walt." Katzenberg, too, was concerned. At the time, Eisner was 15 pounds overweight. The studio chief also worried that Eisner's hoarse speaking style was ill suited for television.

Running out of choices, Eisner finally agreed to do the show. "It was a strategic decision," Eisner said later. "We would at least show our guests that the company had a rudder." But before Katzenberg would agree to let Eisner before the cameras, the Disney chairman had to agree to go on a crash diet. A speech coach was hired. Eisner's wife Jane also was drafted to pick out several new suits for the Disney chairman.

On February 2, 1986, for the first time in nearly three years, Disney returned to Sunday night television. A newly trim Michael Eisner, dressed in a natty dark blue suit, introduced *Help Wanted: Kids*, a two-hour show starring *Laverne & Shirley* costar Cindy Williams and her real-life husband, Bill Hudson. "Good evening, I'm Michael Eisner," the Disney chairman began the show, as Mickey and Goofy stood at his sides. By the end of the evening, nearly 10 million homes had seen the show, almost twice the number that had seen Disney's last show more than two years earlier.

❖

Of the hundreds of producers and directors who made their way to Disney's Burbank studios, none got a better reception than Mel Brooks. The 62-year-old former stand-up comic, who had been born in New York City and whose real name was Melvin Kaminsky, was a faded legend among Hollywood insiders. In 1974, he had produced two blockbusters in a single year, the slapstick epics *Young Frankenstein* and *Blazing Saddles. Get Smart*, his 1965 spoof of spy television shows, had become a TV classic. His recent efforts, however, had been less successful.

One day in late 1988, Brooks showed up at the Burbank studio for lunch, bringing along Alan Schwartz, who had been his lawyer for 23 years and was also president of Brooksfilms, the comedian's film production company. Welcoming them in the executive dining room were not only Michael Eisner but also Jeffrey Katzenberg and Rich Frank. It was an old-fashioned Hollywood power lunch.

Michael Eisner had invited Brooks and Schwartz to the studio in hopes of getting Brooksfilms to make a movie with Disney. Brooks had just finished making the *Spaceballs* for MGM. It was a *Star Wars* spoof that became a modest-sized hit. Brooks, a short, rumpled man with unruly hair and a quick smile, wanted to get back into television. Brooks and Eisner had worked together in 1975, before Eisner left ABC for Paramount Pictures. But the show that Brooks had produced, *When Things Were Rotten*, a Robin Hood satire, had bombed. Three months after it first aired, ABC canceled it.

Earlier that year, Disney had finished production on the film *Big Business*, starring Lily Tomlin and Bette Midler in dual roles as twins mismatched at birth. Disney had spent more than $1 million to recreate the interior of New York's Plaza Hotel. Because the expense had rankled Katzenberg, he had ordered that the fake hotel hallways and room interiors be kept intact for possible later use. Brooks saw the hotel set during a tour of the studio lot and started talking about using it for a comedy show about an inept hotel manager.

The show was eventually titled *Nutt House*. With a commitment from NBC to air a show for the season that started in September 1989, Disney agreed to let Brooks make the show. Reaching back to two of the faded stars he had worked with before, Brooks cast Harvey Korman and Cloris Leachman as the leads. NBC aired the first show on September 8, 1989. Within five weeks, however, *Nutt House* was canceled by the top-rated network.

By the time *Nutt House* was canceled, it had become apparent that Disney's network television unit was the company's most noteworthy failure. Five of the first seven shows that the company had produced for the "big three" networks had flopped. Only *The Golden Girls*, which was first aired in 1985, had been a spectacular success, landing in the top 15 by the end of its first year. In 1988, the show also spawned *Empty Nest,* a sit-com about a widowed pediatrician and his two daughters. By the end of its second season, *Empty Nest* also was in the top 15, giving Disney the two top-ranked Saturday evening shows.

Disney's involvement in the two hit shows, both produced by the Witt-Thomas-Harris team, was minimal. By contrast, the other five shows had been developed by Disney itself, and none had lasted more than a single season. The procession of network failures had begun in 1986, with *The Ellen Burstyn Show,* followed the next year by *Sidekicks,* a short-lived action series on ABC, about an 11-year-old martial arts expert. The same season, ABC also quickly canceled *Harry,* a series starring Alan Arkin as a warehouse foreman. In 1987 CBS yanked *The Oldest Rookie,* the story of a deskbound cop who is reassigned to pound the beat in his middle age. CBS also canceled *Hard Time on Planet Earth,* a special-effects laden and expensive show about a time traveler deposited on earth. Even the low-rated Fox Broadcasting Company quickly dismissed one of the Disney shows. In late 1986 Fox chairman Barry Diller had ordered a *Down and Out in Beverly Hills* sit-com during a meeting at Eisner's large Bel Air home. Diller had heard that ABC was considering dropping Disney's Sunday night movie, and he wanted it for his network. Eisner preferred to try to keep the Sunday night show on ABC and offered Diller a show based on the 1986 movie as a substitute. The show was plagued by production delays. When the show was finally aired nearly a year later, it got abysmal ratings. *Down and Out in Beverly Hills* was unceremoniously canceled.

The Disney Sunday Movie was also a recurring problem. In its first season, ratings were poor and the show trailed far behind the Sunday night leader, *60 Minutes.* Trying to put the best face on the situation, the company reminded shareholders that, despite its generally poor ratings, the show ranked fifth among all shows for female viewers aged 18 to 49, a key demographic group for network advertisers. ABC executives, however, were less sanguine. The network agreed to take the show for another season, but later insisted that it be slashed to a single hour. Ratings still didn't improve.

In 1988, Disney moved the show to NBC, the top-rated network, and renamed it *The Magical World of Disney,* in an attempt to boost overall ratings. The change didn't help. Disney tried to revive interest in the show by changing the format and rotating three recurring stories. Actor Tim Dunigan was hired to reprise the *Davy Crockett* adventure series, and *Night Court* star Harry Anderson recreated the Disney's *The Absent-Minded Professor* movies. The third story featured an Alaskan wolf transported to the city. Later, Disney even borrowed stars from NBC's top-rated show, putting *Cosby* stars Keshia Knight Pulliam and Phylicia Rashad in an updated version of a musical based on the *Pollyanna* books.

In 1989, *The Magical World of Disney* ranked only 76th among that season's 96 shows. Early the next year, NBC executives pulled the show off the air. The only thing that lessened Disney's embarrassment was an agreement it was able to make with NBC that a revamped show might be aired later in the season if a place opened up in the network's schedule.

❖

The quick cancellation of *Nutt House* was a huge embarrassment for the company. Worse than that, it was also a large financial misstep for Team Disney. Even considering the license fee that NBC had given Disney, the show had cost the company more than $2 million to produce. Since only a handful of episodes had been made, it was a total loss. No TV station or cable channel was going to pick up the episodes.

By 1989, losses for Disney's network TV unit were beginning to mount. None of the half-dozen canceled shows had lasted long enough for Disney to use them in the syndication market. Counting the several dozen pilots the company had also made, Disney's losses approached $50 million.

Worse yet, the failed shows had left Disney managers with the stark realization that the Disney method simply wasn't working. At Paramount, Michael Eisner and Barry Diller were the creative forces behind the television shows their studio produced. They enjoyed a close working relationship with ABC, which still remembered them fondly for turning around the struggling network's fortunes. The trust ABC executives had in their former colleagues translated to commitments to air their programs.

Eisner and Diller had created the concept for *Mork & Mindy* during a half-hour brainstorming session with Garry Marshall. They sold it to ABC by stitching together a brief pilot out of a screen test for an unknown actress, Pam Dawber, and a segment of *Happy Days* in which Robin Williams played an alien from the planet Ork. "That was the best pilot I ever made," recalled Marshall later. "Ten minutes, and it couldn't have cost more than $500."

The creation of *Mork & Mindy* was an example of how Paramount could apply the formula it used for making movies to television shows. Like the story lines for *Beverly Hills Cop* or *Flashdance*, the idea for the television show had originated inside the studio. And like dozens of movie stars who got their start at Paramount, neither Williams nor Dawber were big names when the show began.

But the days in which a quickly developed concept and an inexpensive pilot could lead to a hit television show were clearly over by the time the Eisner team arrived at Disney. Jeffrey Katzenberg could still dictate the terms under which the studio would make its movies. He could control the writers, reshape the plots, and decide how and when the films would be released. But television was a different story. Control belonged to the network executives, who made the decisions on what shows would be made and when they would be shown.

By the mid-1980s, those executives were rushing to buy up programs being made by the industry's hot producers. As a result, producers and writers and not studios were controlling the television game. And the hottest production houses were controlling the television game. And the hottest production houses were being run by people like *The Cosby Show* producing team of Marcy Carsey and Tom Werner and *Perfect Strangers* creators Boy Boyett and Tom Miller. Even before they had seen a pilot, networks would hand out commitments to air programs made by a Steven Bochco or a Stephen Cannell.

When Eisner first arrived at Disney, he and Jeffrey Katzenberg tried to recreate the Paramount TV operation. Eisner was adamant about steering clear of expensive producers like Bochco and turned down multimillion-dollar deals like the one Jerry Perrenchio had offered. Instead, Eisner was intent on building the studio from within. Early on, Katzenberg lured away top Paramount TV executives like Mark Ovitz and Grant Rosenberg to beef up Disney's newly created TV operation. The men had helped Paramount create such TV shows as *Cheers, Family Ties,* and *MacGyver.*

At the outset, Disney tried to keep the same low-budget approach it had taken with its movies. By the summer of 1985, the studio began to collect a stable of young TV producers and writers who hadn't already had a hit TV program. Tom Greene, an assistant producer for Universal Pictures' *Knight Rider* show signed on. So did Barbara Hall, who had written a couple of episodes of *Family Ties,* and Lee David Zlotkoff, whose credits at the time included the *MacGyver* pilot.

As they had done with Bette Midler and Richard Dreyfuss, Eisner and Katzenberg also tried to revive the careers of faded movie stars by offering them television shows. One of the first they contracted was Ellen Burstyn, a 52-year-old former model and comedian whose career had been slipping since making the films *Harry and Tonto* and *Alice Doesn't Live Here Anymore* in the mid-1970s. Disney's writing team also created a show for Alan Arkin, a one-time folk singer and member of The Second City satirical group. The 50-year-old Arkin had never done a television show, and his movie appeal had long since passed.

None of the shows worked, however. By early 1989, the Disney team decided it was time to change the game plan. "We had worked through about four years saying we'll do it our way," says Rich Frank now. "Then we decided that we've been banging our head against a wall. Our way is just not going to work."

Disney's managers had watched while Columbia Pictures, Warner Brothers, and Universal were all signing lucrative deals with the best TV producers and writers in Hollywood. So, too, were the "big three" TV networks. ABC alone had signed both Steven Bochco and *Taxi* producer James Brooks to long-term contracts to make TV shows.

The deal for Brooks showed how costs were skyrocketing. The producer was guaranteed $65 million to deliver his next three shows to ABC. Bochco's deal was said to be worth $50 million.* In contrast, Disney was spending just over $5 million a year on its entire TV network operation. "We had to do something to compete with the networks," Eisner says. "They were competing for talent. And all the studios, seeing the golden harvest of the Bill Cosby numbers and *Who's the Boss*, were out there . . . So we went on a talent hunt, too."

Katzenberg proposed a four-year plan. During that period, the studio would spend roughly $25 million a year to line up the best talent it could. Within four years, the company would know whether the talent hunt had produced the hit shows and golden harvest it wanted. Reluctantly, Eisner approved Katzenberg's plan.

The first to sign with Disney was Terry Louise Fisher. A 36-year-old lawyer by training, Fisher had been Bochco's partner in creating *L. A. Law,* but the two producers had had a falling-out in 1989, when Bochco

---

*Both Brooks and Bochco also signed agreements with studios, Brooks at Columbia and Bochco at Twentieth Century Fox. The studios would finance the shows and get the rights to syndicate them in return.

had signed his ABC contract. The matter ultimately went to court, with Fisher suing before the case was settled. In early 1989, Disney signed Fisher to a three-year contract.

Fisher was soon followed by other high-priced talent. The company signed Matt Williams, a one-time writer on *The Cosby Show* who had helped to create *Roseanne* and *Another World* for the Carsey-Werner Company. Carsey-Werner had the top three television shows on the air. Because Williams and *Roseanne* star Roseanne Barr had been battling over future control of the show, Williams agreed to sign with Disney.

Disney also signed a contract with four members of the writing team that had taken over *The Golden Girls* when the original Witt-Thomas-Harris team moved on to other projects. The company was also able to sign Danny Arnold, a one-time producer of *The Real Mc-Coys* who had created *Barney Miller* in 1975 and its spin-off, *Fish*, two years later. Other TV deals brought in Ivan Reitman, the director of the films *Ghostbusters* and *Twins*, as well as *Eight Is Enough* creator Bill Blinn.

Before long, Disney found itself in the unaccustomed position of bidding up the price of talent. The studio's primary competition was Columbia Pictures, which was being fueled by the deep pockets of its new owner, Sony Corp. Jeffrey Katzenberg failed to lure *Married . . . With Children* producers Ron Levitt and Michael Moye away from Columbia. But Disney signed *Wonder Years* creators Carol Black and Neal Marlens, giving them a three-year, $15 million deal. In all, Disney signed contracts with more than $125 million to lure the hottest TV talent it could find. Disney also opened its checkbook to hire Garth Ancier, a one-time boy wonder with NBC. Ancier, like Eisner, was a graduate of the ultra-preppy Lawrenceville School in New Jersey. Later, he became a top assistant to NBC programming head Brandon Tartikoff and helped to develop both *Cosby* and *The Golden Girls* for the network. In 1986, Ancier had jumped to the new Fox network as head of programming, where he had developed the hit shows *Married . . . With Children* and *In Living Color*.

Ancier was available because he had lost out in a power struggle at Fox. Faced with losses, the network had begun to dump his sit-coms in favor of cheaper reality-based shows like *America's Most Wanted* and *Cops*. Heading for Disney, Ancier was given a five-year contract at $225,000 a year. He was also given primary responsibility for developing network shows for the company.

It didn't take long for Disney to see the results of its spending spree. Matt Williams developed the format for a show starring 57-year-old comedienne Carol Burnett and sold the show to NBC, which ordered six episodes of *Carol and Company*. Terry Louise Fisher produced a television movie for NBC, then was given $2 million to make a pilot for a show about lawyers called *Bar Girls*.

In all, Disney sold eight pilots to the "big three" networks for the season that began in September 1990. That was only one less than each of the perennial industry leaders, Columbia, Lorimar, and Universal, had sold. When the 1990 season opened, Disney had six shows on the air, three more than it had a year earlier.

Disney's executives knew that it would take time before their new crew of producers would generate any profits for the company. Traditionally, a TV show has to be on the air for three or more years in order to amass enough episodes for syndication. The company's biggest hit, *The Golden Girls*, didn't enter the syndication market until 1990, but the payoff was substantial. The show was syndicated for nearly $300 million. Disney stood to clear almost $100 million. Most of the rest of the proceeds went to the Witt-Thomas-Harris team.

❖

October 1990 was Black October for Walt Disney Company's television division. Only a month earlier, the company had high hopes for the six television shows it was airing on network television. Now, a month into the season, the cancellations had begun. The first to go was a Witt-Thomas half-hour sit-com, *Lenny*, that CBS temporarily pulled from the air. Two weeks later, NBC canceled *Hull High*, a musical show that had been put into the Disney Sunday movie time slot.

The quick cancellations were a lingering reminder that Disney hadn't yet overcome its TV unit's problems. There was also dissension within Disney's ranks. After months of feuds with Rich Frank, Garth Ancier left less than two years into his five-year contract with Disney.

The cancellations dug a financial hole for Disney. *Hull High* alone had cost the company $325,000 an episode to produce, resulting in a $1 million loss for the company during the show's short run. In a dramatic acknowledgment that its TV unit was still not working right, Disney decided to trim further losses by cutting back on its television operation.

At the company's mid-year budget review, Katzenberg recommended to Eisner that the company stop making one-hour shows. His reasoning was twofold: The syndication market for one-hour programs had cooled since the high-priced days of *Magnum P. I.* Moreover, each episode cost as much as $1 million to produce, forcing Disney to pay at least one-third the costs. When they failed, they brought with them huge losses.

By mid-September, Disney had informed the three networks that it would no longer accept commitments for one-hour shows. That meant eliminating Disney's nine-person drama department. It also meant giving up one show, *N. Y. P. D. Mounted,* that the company had agreed to make for CBS. CBS gave the show instead to Orion Pictures.

The company still had *The Golden Girls* and *Empty Nest,* the two Witt-Thomas-Harris team programs, on the air at NBC. Both were still in the top 15. Former *Roseanne* writer Matt Williams had a likely hit in *Carol and Company,* which followed the two Witt-Thomas-Harris shows on NBC's Saturday night lineup. NBC also was airing *The Fanelli Boys,* a sit-com about an Italian family that had been created by the four *Golden Girls* writers.

Moreover, Disney was still at work on several new shows for the "big three." NBC had ordered additional episodes of *The Magical World of Disney* for 1991, anticipating placing it again on its lineup. The company was also working on a half-hour comedy called *Dinosaurs* for CBS. The show, to be made in conjunction with Jim Henson Productions, would cost more than $1 million per episode to make and would feature lavish costumes and special effects.

Even with the 1990 cancellations, Disney had unquestionably made progress from the days when Ron Miller treated the television division as little more than a stepchild. But for all the television expertise that Michael Eisner brought with him from Paramount, Disney's television unit still stood out as the company's biggest failure. The $125 million that the company had spent to lure TV talent to the studio—a marked departure from how Team Disney liked to do business—was starting to show some results. But success still looked to be several hit shows away.

CHAPTER

New Lands to Conquer

A mong Los Angeles lawyers, none was better connected than Frank Rothman. He had been born in Los Angeles and during most of his nearly four decades had moved gracefully between the worlds of Beverly Hills celebrities and superstar corporations. Tall, with thinning hair and stylish wire-rimmed glasses, Rothman was a commanding presence in the courtroom. His courtroom brilliance had won a reduced sentence for David Begelman, the former Columbia Pictures president who was convicted of cashing forged checks. An antitrust specialist as well, Rothman had represented the National Football League, California's largest chain of grocery stores, and several major movie studios.

In the 1990s, Frank Rothman began to play in a different arena. Leaving the safety of his law firm in 1982, Rothman was appointed chairman and chief executive officer of MGM/UA Entertainment Inc.,* the struggling movie studio then owned by Los Angeles billionaire Kirk Kerkorian. Burdened by mountains of high-priced junk bonds, the studio was constantly flirting with financial disaster. Worse

---

*In 1986, MGM/UA Entertainment was renamed MGM/UA Communications Company.

yet, it seemed capable of producing only box office disasters—films like *The Pope of Greenwich Village, The Aviator, Until September,* and *Garbo Talks.*

The only thing MGM/UA had going for it was the glorious past of its Metro-Goldwyn-Mayer days. Having been started in 1924 by a merger between studios created by Hollywood giants Samuel Goldwyn and Louis B. Mayer, MGM became the industry's biggest and richest studio. With a roster of stars including Greta Garbo, Clark Gable, Jean Harlow, and James Stewart, the studio, MGM publicists boasted, had "more stars than there are in the heavens." Its films included such classics as *Gone with the Wind, The Wizard of Oz,* and *Ben-Hur.* The studio was so dominant that, by the early 1940s, MGM's famed "Leo the Lion" trademark represented the highest quality in entertainment.

In the mid-1970s, however, Kerkorian, the son of an Armenian fruit farmer, began to dismantle MGM's heritage. A reclusive billionaire who had built his fortune by buying and selling airlines and hotels, Kerkorian bought MGM in 1970 and added United Artists a decade later. But Kerkorian had only a superficial interest in the making of films and television shows. He slashed production budgets and began to sell off many of the studio's most memorable assets. In a move that seemed symbolic of his disregard for MGM's past, Kerkorian ordered a public auction of such Hollywood icons as the chariot from *Ben Hur* and the ruby slippers worn by Judy Garland in *The Wizard of Oz.* Kerkorian's biggest deal was selling MGM's historic 40-acre lot and the rights to 2,400 MGM movies to Atlanta TV mogul Ted Turner for a staggering $1.2 billion.

Before Turner came along, MGM was heading toward a $59 million loss. Struggling to cut the red ink, Frank Rothman was looking for anything of value that he could sell. In early 1985, he called Frank Wells. Both Rothman and Wells were entrenched members of the Beverly Hills legal and entertainment set and they knew each other well.

This time, however, Rothman wasn't making a social call. For $55 million, Rothman told Wells, the Disney Channel could have the rights to *Singin' in the Rain, Mutiny on the Bounty,* and other MGM classics.

Wells was eager to expand the Disney Channel allure beyond young viewers. Along with Disney Channel head Jim Jimirro, Wells negotiated with Rothman for weeks. In the end, Wells refused to pay MGM's price for the films. But Wells had another deal in mind. Disney was planning a major project, Wells told Rothman, something that could involve MGM.

At Wells's urging, Rothman drove to the Imagineering headquarters in Glendale in early February. There, the MGM chairman was quickly ushered into a large conference room where he was met by Imagineering head Carl Bongirno and executive vice-president Marty Sklar. In the middle of the large conference table sat a large model of a new theme park that the Imagineers had been planning for Orlando.

The model, which had been designed by Imagineering producer Bob Weis, contained areas for grandstands, walkways, and a tram ride through rows of studio sound stages. There were also areas for stunt shows and a pavilion where guests could take part in the filming of a television show. To give the planned studio tour added allure, Bongirno and Sklar stressed, Disney wanted to use MGM's highly visible library of movies, along with its logo and name.

The concept of a Hollywood-based theme park was hardly new at Disney, or for that matter, elsewhere in the entertainment industry. Less than 10 miles from Disney's Burbank studio, MCA Inc. has run it Universal Studios Tour since 1964, featuring a "Wild West" stunt show and a tour through parts of its working studio. The Universal attraction lured more than 3 million people to its 232-acre park in 1985.

Walt Disney had contemplated building an amusement park across the street from his own studio as early as 1948. He envisioned a park to be called "Mickey Mouse Park" that would have entertained kids and their parents with roller coasters, Ferris wheels, a railroad train, and western stagecoach rides. Radio and television shows would have been broadcast from a newly built theater, with admission-paying guests as the audience. Part of the attraction would have been a tour of the Disney studios.

Mickey Mouse Park never went beyond the drawing board. The city of Los Angeles refused to build a train to link the Disney amusement center to nearby Griffith Park—a key part of Walt's plan for his theme park. Walt Disney subsequently altered his idea into the concept of Disneyland and built it in an orange grove in Anaheim, 38 miles away.

The notion of a studio tour, however, continued to be knocked around at the Disney company. Theme park president Dick Nunis took along some early plans for a movie pavilion at EPCOT Center to one of his first meetings with Eisner and Wells. Eisner himself had come across some of Walt's old drawings for the studio tour while rummaging through some files at the Imagineering warehouse in Glendale.

Early in 1985, Eisner and Wells began eagerly searching for ways to develop Disney's Orlando acreage. A second round of price increases had already been ordered for 1985, raising the average ticket price for a day at one of the parks to $21.50. (It had been $17 only a year before.) Earnings from theme park operations would more than double by 1986, to nearly $404 million, because of the increased prices and the new TV advertising campaign. Eisner and Wells were already using some of the increased income to finance the construction of new hotels. But to fill the new hotel rooms and to entice tourists to spend an extra day in Orlando, the Disney managers wanted to add another theme park. "It was a management dream," said Frank Wells later, "to add another income-producing asset with the same infrastructure, the same roads and food service."

Even before Eisner and Wells arrived, Disney's Imagineering unit had been planning an entertainment pavilion that could be added to EPCOT Center. The pavilion would be modeled upon the "Spaceship Earth" ride at EPCOT, which portrays the history of communications from Egyptian hieroglyphics to state-of-the-art computers. The entertainment pavilion would use audio-animatronic figures and special effects to lead the rider from silent pictures to *Flashdance*. A robotic John Wayne would fire his six-shooter, and Humphrey Bogart would be seen bidding farewell to Ingrid Bergman at the airport in a scene from *Casablanca*.

One of the major points that Sid Bass and Richard Rainwater had stressed in Fort Worth in September 1984 at their first meeting with new Disney chiefs Michael Eisner and Frank Wells had been the need to develop Disney's Orlando property. The soaring costs of building EPCOT had frightened Ron Miller and Card Walker away from expanding further on the huge acreage just as tourism was escalating in central Florida. The typical tourists, Al Checchi had learned during his trip to Orlando in mid-1984, would spend a day or two at Walt Disney World but then would leave for Sea World or one of the other parks in the area.

Eisner and Wells wanted to expand the Imagineers' idea for a Hollywood pavilion at EPCOT Center. True to his Hollywood background, Eisner envisioned a separate theme park devoted entirely to rides based on movies. The new park would have its own separate gate and entrance fee, thus generating new revenues for the company. It would also encourage many guests to spend an added night at one of the Disney hotels. "The idea was to encourage them to increase their length of stay," said Wells, "It was two to two and a half days and we wanted to get it up to three or four days."

Walt Disney at the 1955 opening of Disneyland. © Disney Enterprises, Inc.

Disney Chairman Michael D. Eisner.
© Disney Enterprises, Inc.

Disney Vice-Chairman Roy Disney.
© Disney Enterprises, Inc.

Disney President Frank Wells helped
guide the company's fortunes for
nearly 10 years before his death in
a tragic helicopter crash set off management changes at the company.
© Disney Enterprises, Inc.

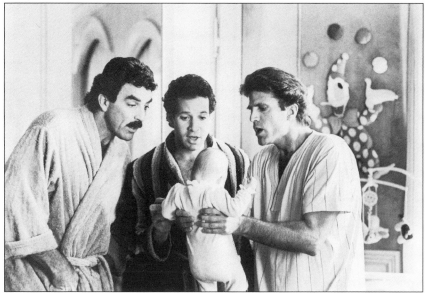

After winning a fierce bidding war for the rights to the French comedy, *Three Men and a Baby* became Disney's first $100 million picture.
© Touchtone Pictures.

Produced for $17 million, *Pretty Woman* became Disney's all-time most successful live-action film, grossing nearly $175 million.
© Touchtone Pictures.

Seven years after Ron Miller bought the rights to *Who Framed Roger Rabbit,* Eisner and Katzenberg convinced Steven Spielberg to produce the groundbreaking film. © Touchtone Pictures and Amblin Entertainment, Inc.

The Little Mermaid, Disney's first animated fairytale in three decades, launched a series of animated hits for the company.
© Disney Enterprises, Inc.

The 1991 film *Beauty and the Beast* became Disney's first $100 million animated release in the U.S. and launched the company's plan to create plays for broadway. © Disney Enterprises, Inc.

Released in 1994, *The Lion King* became Disney's largest grossing film of all time, accounting for an estimated $1 billion in worldwide revenues.
© Disney Enterprises, Inc.

After nearly three years of losses, profitability came to Euro Disney after a 1994 restructuring of the French theme park. © Disney Enterprises, Inc.

Eisner at Disneyland–expansion of Disney's U.S. theme parks was thwarted in Virginia but continues in Orlando and Anaheim. © Disney Enterprises, Inc.

Jeffrey Katzenberg helped resurrect Disney's film studio before a 1994 falling out with Michael Eisner prompted his departure to set up his own studio with David Geffen and Steven Spielberg.

Tom Murphy and Dan Burke created a media colossus at Cap Cities/ABC and sold it to Eisner for $19 million in 1995.

Super agent Michael Ovitz, Chairman of Creative Artists Agency, was hired by Disney in 1995 to help Eisner run the company after the acquisition of Cap Cities/ABC. © Disney Enterprises, Inc.

Disney's new managers were aware of the dangers of undertaking a huge construction project. The costs of EPCOT Center had ballooned in large part because of constant tinkering by Disney's Imagineering unit, which had been eager to improve and upgrade the rides. To control costs, Eisner and Wells decided to build a smaller park than the other two at the Walt Disney World complex. Unlike the Magic Kingdom and EPCOT Center, each of which could easily accommodate 10 million or more guests annually, the entertainment park would be built to hold fewer than 6 million.

Meeting several times at the Glendale warehouse of the Imagineers unit during the early months of 1985, Eisner approved several new rides to expand the park. Because Disney was also in the process of building up its animation department, Eisner suggested setting up a small animation studio at the new park, with an exhibit where guests could watch the cartoonists at work. Wells suggested developing an "Indiana Jones" attraction with George Lucas, who was already working on "Star Tours" for Disneyland. Eisner and his production chief, Jeffrey Katzenberg, also wanted to build additional movie sound stages in Orlando to accommodate Disney's growing movie and TV production schedule.

By the time Rothman saw the Disney model, the project had already grown dramatically. It now included not only a tour through the history of filmmaking but a mock television studio in which guests could take the part of Ethel Mertz in an *I Love Lucy* episode. Amateur singers could make their own rock videos at a recording studio.

What Disney still needed, however, was the MGM name and its vast array of movie classics. Rothman, who had the impression that just about everything that Kirk Kerkorian owned was for sale, agreed to begin talks. Frank Davis, an old pro and the company's executive vice-president, negotiated for MGM. Handling the negotiations for Disney were the company's new general counsel, Joe Shapiro, and Disney lawyer Peter Nolan.

The negotiations took about a month. In the end, Disney all but walked away with Leo the Lion's mane. Disney received almost free rein in use of the famous roaring lion and the treasure trove of old MGM movies. More important, it got those rights for virtually nothing. Under the 20-year agreement, Disney was to pay only $100,000 a year for the first three years and $250,000 for the fourth year. The annual fee would increase by $50,000 in every year thereafter, with an eventual cap of

$1 million for the yearly fee. Disney also got nearly unfettered ability to build several other studio tours, for each of which it would pay half the fee agreed upon for the Orlando park.

Disney's engineers estimated that the new park in Orlando would probably hold 28,000 people at a time, which translated into an annual attendance of 5 million people—well under the Eisner-Wells specification of a maximum of 6 million. The company expected to see revenues of at least $100 million a year, based on the 1985 one-day adult ticket price of $19.50.* The Disney executives knew that the guests would no doubt spend millions more on food, drinks, and merchandise.

The 31-page agreement that Disney and MGM/UA signed on June 27, 1985, also gave Disney the exclusive rights to use up to 250 MGM/UA films at any one time. Disney was prohibited from using newly released MGM films for the first year after the films were released. MGM also protected 35 of its classic movies, including *Gone with the Wind, The Wizard of Oz,* the James Bond series, *Rocky,* and several Woody Allen movies, by requiring Disney to obtain special permission to use anything from them. By September 1986, the granting of special permissions had begun. Disney requested and got the right to use portions of *The Wizard of Oz* and *Singin' in the Rain* for audio-animatronic characters sprinkled throughout The Great Movie Ride.

The MGM name became a forceful marketing tool for Disney. Under the agreement, Disney could use both the MGM name and Leo the Lion on stationery, advertisements, and posters, without giving MGM any additional compensation. MGM was to receive a modest 4 percent royalty on any merchandise sold at the park. But Disney retained the right to call the tour either "Disney-MGM" or "MGM-Disney." The only limitation on Disney's use of MGM movies was that no single excerpt from an MGM/UA movie could last longer than two minutes.

Disney executives were undoubtedly ecstatic. They had walked away with one of the world's most recognized names for just about nothing. MGM owner Kirk Kerkorian, who had not been in on the negotiations, was livid. The 68-year-old Kerkorian had peddled many things in his day, but one thing that he held sacred was the MGM name. He had used it for the MGM Grand Hotel that he built in 1978, and he would

---

*By the time the park was finished in mid-1989 the price of a one-day pass had increased to $29. Disney's first-year revenues for the park passed $200 million.

later use it in the name of his MGM Grand Air luxury service. He found it difficult to believe that his studio executives had sold off the MGM name to another company, and that they had done it so cheaply.

Peter Bart, who was an MGM/UA production executive at the time, recalls that Kerkorian showed up unexpectedly at a meeting of the MGM executive committee not long after the deal was completed. Normally cool-headed and almost meek in demeanor, Kerkorian berated the studio executives at the meeting and claimed he had never been advised that his underlings were negotiating to give away the MGM lion. "How could this happen? How could you give away our logo like this?" the studio owner yelled. The tirade stunned the MGM executives into silence. Few had ever heard the man they called "the boss" raise his voice.

Kerkorian ordered the MGM executives to find a way out of the Disney agreement, but their frenzied telephone calls to Frank Wells yielded no satisfaction. There was no way, short of litigation, the Disney executive told Kerkorian's people, that they were going to give back a logo that they considered so crucial to the success of the new studio attraction.*

❖

On July 8, 1985, inside the stately Florida capital in Tallahassee, Michael Eisner stood arm in arm with Florida Governor Bob Graham. Disney had already announced its plans for the Disney-MGM Studio Tour in a press release. Eisner and Graham decided to make another announcement, this time for waiting television cameras and eager reporters. Graham would soon launch his bid for the U.S. Senate and for him the publicity was a political windfall. The new park would initially give work to 750 Florida construction workers and would take on another 1,500 people as employees when it opened. More important, it had the potential to bring literally hundreds of millions of dollars into the state in the form of tourist money.

On cue, and using the same wording that Disney had used in its press release, Graham hailed the Disney announcement as "one of the most exciting business breakthroughs in this decade for Florida," proclaiming as well that it would "strengthen the position of Walt Disney

---

*In May 1988, MGM and Kerkorian's other company, MGM Grand, Inc., did file suit in an effort to invalidate the agreement. The lawsuit claimed that Disney had withheld its plans to build a working studio at the MGM park site, as well as not revealing its plans to build hotels so close to the tour. The suit is still pending.

World as the world's premier tourist destination." Eisner was only slightly less bombastic. "We are confident that the Disney-MGM Studio Tour will be a spectacular show." The MGM deal had been signed only 11 days earlier, but Disney was already preparing a marketing blitz. "I can think of no better way to tell the story of the history of motion pictures than in association with MGM," Eisner said. With a flourish, he added, "Both the lion and the mouse will roar."

The truth, however, was that it would be years before Leo or Mickey would do much roaring. Certainly neither was roaring as loudly as MCA president Sid Sheinberg. Sheinberg, a one-time law professor who worked his way up from MCA's legal department, is not a man to be trifled with. Quick to anger, he can also be unusually blunt—and in 1985, he had reason to be angry. MCA was also in the midst of plans for a studio tour in Orlando.

From Sheinberg's vantage point on the antique-decorated 15th floor of MCA's "Black Tower" headquarters building on the outskirts of Los Angeles, Disney's studio plans were nothing less than a broadside attack. "Disney's ability to decimate you by acting in a predatory way is chilling," the MCA president told *Orlando Sentinel* reporters during a meeting immediately after Disney's announcement. Creating a phrase that would become a battle cry for both companies as the war of words escalated in hostility, Sheinberg added: "Do you really want a little mouse to become one large, ravenous rat?"

MCA had initially announced its intention to build an Orlando version of its California studio in 1981. It had planned to put a working studio and tour on a site encompassing more than 400 acres, about 10 miles from EPCOT Center. The estimated project cost of $203 million, however, was so steep that MCA couldn't undertake it without backers. The company's search for backing had taken it to the Florida state government and Bob Graham. Prodded by Sheinberg, Graham had promised to recommend that the state's employee pension fund put $150 million into the MCA park. To bring added film production to the state, Graham had also said he would propose legislation that would enable the state to lend Universal $35 million a year for five years.

The course of events gets a little confusing at that point. Graham did make the promised recommendation to the state assembly. But a Tallahassee lobbyist named Bernie Parrish, who had once worked for Disney, began making the rounds of Florida legislators in an attempt to kill the bill. According to a front-page report in *The Wall Street Journal,*

Parrish demanded of a top aide to Graham, "Are you sure this is the kind of thing you ought to be doing? Disney's got a lot going in this state. What are you doing for [Disney]?" Disney disclaimed any current association with Parrish, and Parrish told the *Journal* that he was acting on his own. Within weeks of Parrish's blitz, however, a Florida legislative committee killed the MCA bill. Sheinberg was said to have contemplated taking legal action against Disney, but he never filed a lawsuit.*

The seeds of distrust between Disney and MCA, however, had been planted four years earlier. MCA executives regularly complained to reporters that Disney chairman Eisner actually stole the idea of the park from MCA. Eisner, MCA studio tour head Jay Stein has charged, first learned of MCA's Orlando park idea in 1981, when Sheinberg's company was looking for a partner to help finance the Florida theme park. MCA had taken the idea to Paramount Pictures when Eisner was that studio's president.

MCA and Paramount had worked together before, most recently in 1980 when the two companies had launched the USA Network on cable. Paramount had decided not to join MCA on the Orlando theme park project, but Eisner, Stein has charged, had become privy to MCA's plans. Eisner insists that he was never at the meeting at which the plans were revealed.

MCA officials also approached the Bass organization about becoming partners. Bass decided against joining the MCA studio tour venture but later formed a partnership with MCA to buy land near the proposed park. That joint venture dissolved shortly before Bass took a major financial stake in Walt Disney Productions. Sid Bass soon became a major Disney shareholder and a key proponent of development of Disney's Florida properties.

Michael Eisner brushed off the MCA charges as groundless. The position of Walt Disney Productions, its chairman announced, was that the MCA park would be welcome because it would help bring tourists to central Florida. Any tourists who made a trip to the MCA park would almost certainly spend at least one day at a Disney park as well.

Behind the scenes, however, it was apparent that Eisner and Wells knew that the MCA park presented a formidable challenge for Walt Disney World. Attendance at EPCOT Center had fallen off sharply almost

*Sid Sheinberg declined to be interviewed for this book.

as soon as the hoopla surrounding its 1982 opening died down. National TV ads, starting in 1985, had helped to arrest the decline. But the park was still crushingly dull. Initially designed by Walt as a city of the future, the park had taken on the formless quality of a "permanent world's fair." Its huge pavilions on energy, agriculture, and the seas were hardly the kind of draw that Disney needed to lure teenagers, many of whom had decided that the park was boring.

The MCA tour, on the other hand, wasn't likely to be boring. On the drawing boards was a ride in which a three-story-tall King Kong would lift and throw a tram full of people, as well as a stunt show featuring a shoot-out in the style of *Miami Vice* and an exploding helicopter. Compared with EPCOT, it would be thrilling stuff. Eisner knew that families with young children would still find their way to the Magic Kingdom, and some of them would stay another day to see EPCOT Center, but he also realized that teenagers and many adults could end up spending most of their time at the more exciting Universal Studios tour.

One way to lure free-spending teenagers would be to make EPCOT Center a little spicier, or at least more fun. Managers in the Card Walker era had refused to allow Disney characters to tread the turf in EPCOT Center, in a misguided effort to avoid competition between EPCOT and the Magic Kingdom. Eisner and Wells changed that edict, ordering Dick Nunis to put Mickey, Donald, and the other characters into EPCOT. The result was Goofy in a kilt and Chip 'n Dale in silken Chinese robes.

The Eisner-Wells team knew that they had to do more than provide a few new costumes for older characters in order to upgrade EPCOT Center's image with teenagers. EPCOT needed a healthy new dose of excitement. Eisner and Wells decided to put the three-dimensional "Captain EO" show that was being developed for Disneyland into EPCOT Center as well.

Wells also signed Metropolitan Life to provide more than $70 million for construction of a health-related pavilion at EPCOT Center. This pavilion would have more to offer than simply education. An altered version of the "Star Tours" simulator would take riders on a jolting ride through a human body. The battles in "Body Wars" would take place within the body's immune system, as "trauma troops" battled "infection fighters."

Disney also opened talks with the Swiss government about another showcase pavilion, with this one to feature a version of Disneyland's highly charged "Matterhorn" roller-coaster ride.

Disney's most overt attempt to grab the over-18 business was "Pleasure Island," a six-acre enclave of late-night spots that included a high-tech disco with 170 video screens, a country-and-western bar called the "Neon Armadillo," and a night club set in the middle of a roller-skating rink. Located on an isolated island, well away from the squeaky-clean theme parks, "Pleasure Island" could offer mixed drinks and racier entertainment. However, it opened more than a year later than planned. Besides that, it had been plagued by construction problems, and its price tag had run more than twice as high as expected, ending up at about $30 million. The biggest disappointment was that it took two years to become the huge hit with young adults that Disney had hoped for, and became one only after the admission price was slashed and a nightly New Year's Eve party was added.

To protect EPCOT's flank from MCA, what Disney really needed was a racier park of its own. By mid-1985, Disney's own studio tour was already taking shape in the nondescript Glendale warehouse where the Imagineeers unit worked. Besides the "Great Moments at the Movies" ride that the Imagineers unit had developed for EPCOT Center, the new theme park was planned to include "Video Theater," in which guests could participate in the making of TV shows. In addition, the park would have two stunt shows, one specializing in slapstick and the other "Epic," showing special effects such as boats sinking and bridges collapsing. Guests would also have the opportunity to tour a section called "Disney Archives," which would be computerized to answer questions.

As important as the variety and quality of the attractions was the necessity that Disney move fast. Though the company's public response to the MCA threat was a well-orchestrated yawn, Michael Eisner privately insisted that his company must beat its rival in the battle of studio tours. Hidden behind the easy smile and curly-haired exuberance of the Disney chairman is a strong competitor who doesn't like to lose. He especially didn't want to lose to MCA's Sid Sheinberg, with whom he had waged a running battle of words for months. "They invaded our home turf," he blurted out in an uncharacteristic moment during an interview for *Business Week.* "We will not be intimidated," he said on another occasion.

Eisner raised the stakes two years after first announcing the Orlando studio tour. In early 1987, Disney agreed with the city of Burbank to develop a studio theme park in Burbank, just a few miles from MCA's Los Angeles tour, on a 40-acre site that MCA had wanted to develop. MCA cried foul and filed a lawsuit against Burbank, alleging that Disney received preferential treatment. MCA also resorted to a few dirty tricks, mailing anti-Disney pamphlets to Burbank residents under the name Friends of Burbank. When the size of the project grew to $611 million a year later, Disney pulled out of Burbank. By that time, however, MCA was concentrating on Orlando, and also decided against Burbank.

In its race to beat MCA in Orlando, moreover, Disney held all the advantages. Since 1967, Disney's holdings had been governed by the Reedy Creek Improvement District, an independent quasi-governmental organization awarded to Disney by the Florida assembly. Disney's control of Reedy Creek meant that any Disney project could move forward without many of the regulatory reviews and licenses that MCA would need.

Moreover, while MCA was having troubles lining up financial partners in Orlando, the hike in ticket prices ordered by Eisner and Wells was already starting to have its effect. By 1988, the company was generating more than $1 billion a year in cash—more than double the amount of money it spent in 1988 to build the studio tour, a flock of new hotels, and new rides at Disneyland and elsewhere.

Eisner was determined to open his park first. Designing a park half the size of the one planned by MCA, he calculated, would enable Disney to have its park operating within three years, whereas MCA was estimating that it would take at least four to five years to get its park operating.

Marty Sklar and his team at the Imagineering unit initially estimated that the tour could handle as many as 1.5 million people annually. But within a year, the design team was adding so many new rides that to cover the added costs Disney increased its capacity projections to nearly 4 million. The time taken up by the actual tour of the studio was expanded from one hour to two hours. Disney also added "Catastrophe Canyon," which not only douses the tram in which guests ride in a torrential rainstorm but also subjects it to an earthquake, an oil-rig fire, and a 20,000-gallon flash flood. Plans for the animation building became more ambitious, and the structure that was eventually built was double the size of the one that had first been envisioned. Stunts were added to the "Indiana Jones" show designed by George Lucas. All the improvements, while they added enormously to the appeal of the studio tour, also caused the costs to rise substantially. The studio tour had been originally scheduled to open in late 1988, but its debut was delayed for six months. By the time it finally opened, the total costs had climbed to over $500 million.

❖

Most Americans first became aware of The Disney-MGM Studios Theme Park on March 29, 1989, during the presentation of the 1988 Academy Awards at the Shrine Auditorium in Los Angeles.* General Motors was hawking its new Chevrolet Lumina, and its commercials showed the new car along with Dumbo and other Disney cartoon characters. Even more important, the car was sitting in front of the gates to Disney's new studio tour, and the new park was also prominently mentioned by name during the TV spot. GM footed the bill for the $500,000 commercial. But it was Disney that got millions of dollars worth of free publicity.

The splash Disney made on Academy Awards night, thanks to GM, was only the beginning. By the time The Disney-MGM Studios Theme Park opened its doors to the public at 9:00 A.M. on May 1, the company had spent nearly $30 million in advertising and promotions. The opening was a classic "big event," and the attendant glitz and glamour drew on all that Eisner and his crew had learned about marketing during a decade in Hollywood.

Disney publicists had carefully planted articles in major publications, getting front-page stories in several major daily newspapers and a cover story in *Newsweek* magazine. Full-page advertisements appeared in *People* magazine, and *Time* and *Newsweek* had four-page spreads. A two-hour NBC special, produced by Disney and featuring a videotaped salute from former President Ronald Reagan, aired the night before the park's opening.

Years of promoting theme parks without the benefit of television advertising had sharpened Disney's marketing crew. For the studio tour opening, Disney offered airline tickets and hotel rooms to more than 3,000 members of the press. Even though the "Indiana Jones" stunt show wouldn't be complete for more than a month, and Disney was still fine-tuning its special-effects attractions, there were huge lines waiting when the gates opened. Half an hour later, the park had reached its capacity, and Disney officials began to close the parking lots.

---

*Disney changed the name of the theme park to The Disney-MGM Studios Theme Park during the planning and construction process.

Many of the guests had no doubt been lured to the opening by the parade of middle-American icons whom Disney had brought to Orlando for the opening. Bob Hope cut the ribbon, and Walter Cronkite said a few words. But the real stars came from Disney's own growing stable of Hollywood stars. Bette Midler, Robin Williams, and George Lucas all made appearances. Williams, playing a hick tourist clad in a Hawaiian shirt, was featured on a special film segment introducing guests to Disney's animation exhibit. Williams was transformed into one of the lost boys in Disney's animated film *Peter Pan*; Cronkite explained the steps involved in creating an animated film.

The hype Disney created for the opening worked. Throughout the summer, Disney officials were forced to close the parking lot early. Three months after the opening, the company announced that it would double the size of the park by 1992. During the Christmas season, so many people poured in that the park's closing hour was changed from 6:00 P.M. to midnight.

Wall Street also was impressed. The company's stock, trading at $85 a share just before the park opened, was trading at nearly $100 a share a month later.

Despite the success of Disney's new theme park, MCA was still a force to be reckoned with. On June 7, 1990, it opened its $630 million Universal Studios park. As promised, the MCA attractions were impressively violent. Attacking what it perceived as a chink in Disney's armor — that the Disney-MGM tour's rides were still too tame to lure rambunctious teenagers — Universal's Florida park attempted to give its guests shocking thrills. MCA audiences had a chance to recreate the bloody shower scene from *Psycho*, as well as take the tram ride that featured a three-story-tall King Kong lifting the trams up and hurling them to earth 30 feet below.

MCA also created an opportunity to needle Disney. A boat ride in Universal's man-made lagoon includes an attack by the killer shark from *Jaws*, complete with bloodied waters, human body parts, and a floating set of mouse ears.

Disney, however, still had a few tricks up its sleeve. Two days after MCA opened its gates, Disney brought the stars of its new movie *Dick Tracy* to "Pleasure Island." Siphoning off a large dose of publicity from the MCA opening, Disney staged the world premiere of the long-awaited movie at a small theater on "Pleasure Island." Reporters were transported to the island and given choice opportunities to interview Dustin Hoffman and Warren Beatty.

Disney's efforts were undeniably effective, but MCA turned out to be its own worst enemy. Even though the 444-acre MCA park was filled with violence-packed rides, some of them fell flat on opening day. The 28-foot-long Jaws failed to bare its teeth, and the 12-ton King Kong didn't snarl. National news shows televised lines of angry guests who were demanding their money back. A *Time* magazine article, although generally favorable, also dripped sarcasm. "Universal's Swamp of Dreams," its headline proclaimed.

Within five months, MCA filed suit against a company that had built three of its faulty rides. It would be at least a year before all of the Universal Studio's rides were working properly, leaving a lingering image of inefficiency in the minds of many tourists. For the moment at least, Disney had won the war of the studio tours.

CHAPTER

When Mickey Gets Grumpy

T here is little remarkable about White River, a tiny lumber mill town in northern Ontario. But the town of 1,200 residents claims to be the birthplace of Winnie-the-Pooh, the honey-loving bear made famous by children's author A. A. Milne. As local legend has it, Harry Colebourn, a veterinarian from Winnipeg on his way to London to serve in the army during World War I, bought a bear cub for $20 from a trapper at the White River train station. To remember his home town, Colebourn named the bear Winnipeg.

Not long after arriving in London, however, the veterinarian was forced to give his bear to the London zoo when his battalion shipped out for France. Colebourn's bear, whose name was quickly shortened to Winnie by zookeepers, became a favorite of Milne's son Christopher Robin Milne.

To commemorate what would have been the famous bear's 75th birthday in 1990, White River's elders decided to erect a 16-foot statue of Winnie. For White River, the statue was the ideal way to attract a few tourists and thus raise much-needed revenues. For The Walt Disney Company, which had bought the rights to Milne's character in 1961, it was an assault on the very foundation on which the company was built.

Within weeks of learning about it, Disney lawyer Robert Ogden dispatched a sternly worded letter to the tiny Canadian town, warning that it must steer clear of the fabled bear. As Disney's lawyers saw it, a statue would violate Disney's copyright and put White River in legal peril.

White River eventually won Disney's approval to build the statue, but not before a flood of letters found their way to Burbank. Each supported White River. "We got calls from people as far away as Australia who said, 'Go for it. Give it the good fight,'" recalls White River mayor Ollie Chapman. "Show them they're not God." Even after approving the statue, however, Disney insisted upon some restrictions. White River, Ogden told the town, could base its statue only on the drawings by the British illustrator Ernest Shepard that had appeared in Milne's books, not on the later drawings made famous by Disney's animators.

The Walt Disney Company's harsh response to White River's intentions was in keeping with the tightfisted character of the company that Walt Disney had built more than six decades earlier. Like most family-owned businesses, Walt Disney Productions had protected its property with an intensity that bordered on the fanatical. Early in his career, Walt had been nearly devastated when a business partner outmaneuvered him to win away the rights to one of Walt's first animated characters, Oswald the Lucky Rabbit. It was a lesson well learned. From that day on, Walt and Roy made sure that they would never again lose the fruits of their labor without a fight.

In the years that followed Walt shied away from having partners and insisted upon ironclad legal contracts for the few with whom he did business. He zealously guarded the copyrights on his characters, well before most companies policed the use of their property. Vehemently antiunion, Walt also withstood a monthlong strike by 300 of his animators in 1941 rather than give in to a union vote.

One of the first outside employees, other than animators, whom Walt hired was Los Angeles lawyer Gunther Lessing, a colorful character who had represented the Mexican outlaw Pancho Villa in the early 1920s. Lessing's first job, in 1930, was to represent the Disney brothers by getting the best possible distribution deal for their cartoons. A few years later, when Lessing formally joined the payroll, Disney put him in charge of a growing Disney team of lawyers whose duty it was to police the copyrights of Disney's stable of characters. In the years before such lawsuits were commonplace, Lessing would pepper the courts with petitions to stop unauthorized vendors from selling Disney's products.

The company remained vigilant in its defense of its assets in the years following Walt's death. Even so, when Michael Eisner and Frank Wells arrived in 1984, they brought with them a new and intensified resolve to protect the company from any efforts—real or imagined—to undermine its mission. To resurrect the company's fortunes would be meaningless, the new Disney managers believed, if those fortunes were not relentlessly defended from assault. Creativity was the soul of the Walt Disney company, but the legal department was its heart.

As long-standing members of Hollywood's hierarchy, Eisner and Wells had had much experience with the backbiting and overly contentious ways of the entertainment industry. No issue, it seemed, was too small or insignificant to warrant a flurry of lawsuits among Hollywood producers, directors, or actors. Wells had cut his professional teeth on such lawsuits. His career at a private law firm was launched when he grilled fabled Hollywood mogul Jack Warner on the witness stand in a successful effort to free Jim Garner from his contract with Warner. Not a lawyer, Eisner nevertheless was familiar with take-no-prisoners practices in the back alleys of Paramount Pictures. Under Barry Diller, Paramount employees, as well as outsiders who worked for the studio, were instilled with the company's own sense of martial-arts management.

At Disney, both Michael Eisner and Frank Wells knew, protecting the Disney image would be crucial to enhancing the future value of the toys, syndicated TV shows, and other projects the company had in the works. "One of my jobs is protecting the Disney image," says Eisner, "and being a little bit of the 'No, you can't do that' voice."

Eisner and Wells didn't waste much time building Disney's legal muscle. When the two men first arrived, the company had fewer than 20 full-time lawyers. Only two full-time attorneys were assigned to the task of signing new projects and stars, and the consumer products unit consisted of only one attorney. When Katzenberg moved over to run the studio, he brought Helene Hahn with him to build the Disney studio's legal office. Joe Shapiro, the Donovan Leisure partner who advised the Disney company during the takeover fight, succeeded retiring general counsel Richard Murrow two months later.

Shapiro quickly cleaned house, firing most of the 23 lawyers he inherited. Instead, offering lucrative incentive bonuses, Shapiro attracted his own brand of attorneys. To head the litigation unit, Shapiro brought in Ed Nowak from New York, where Nowak had worked at Simpson Thatcher & Barlett representing General Motors. Janet Johnson, a top

Simpson corporate attorney, also moved to LA, as did Joe Santaniello, who left American Home Products. By 1986, Shapiro had built up the Disney legal staff with attorneys who had the same brand of hardened experience that Gary Wilson expected from his financial crew. "The first thing I was told was to go out and start hiring strong people," recalls Peter Nolan, head of the consumer products legal staff.

It didn't take Eisner and Wells long to show their resolve. Like Walt before them, the new Disney managers refused to buckle to union demands. They stood fast during a 21-day strike at Disneyland that they inherited when they were hired. Later, they withstood the threat of strikes at Walt Disney World, instructing theme park chief Dick Nunis to threaten to replace striking workers in late 1988 rather than give in to demands for higher wages.

As the company grew, so did the number of legal fights in which it found itself involved. The bigger a company is, the more partners, the more activities, and the more opportunities to disagree it has. Few companies were growing as quickly as The Walt Disney Company. Fewer still had Disney's intensity of resolution to protect that growth.

❖

The sleek black furniture in Ricardo Mestres's Burbank offices projects the image of a cool, dispassionate studio executive. In late June 1990, however, the president of Disney's new Hollywood Pictures unit was anything but cool. Midway through the filming of *The Marrying Man*, the studio had begun having problems with Kim Basinger, the mercurial actress who was playing a nightclub singer in the film, which was set in the 1940s. The problems had started out as minor differences of opinion over the script and the songs that Basinger was to sing, but a Hollywood-style war of threatening letters and promised lawsuits erupted. At least one day of shooting had been lost as a result of Basinger's complaints, Mestres had been told by the Disney executives he dispatched to the Las Vegas set, and the actress seemed to have director Jerry Rees intimidated. Budgeted at $15 million, the film was already at least $500,000 over budget because of the delays.

Mestres had already begun to express his anger about the situation by sending angry messages to studio lawyer Helene Hahn, ordering her to fire off an angry salvo to Basinger's agent, Bill Block. Block, head of the Intertalent Agency, had responded with his own barrage of letters, defending Basinger and blaming Disney. It was Disney's fault for scheduling too tightly and for not having the script prepared on time, Block had claimed.

On this late-June day in 1990, as dusk began to darken the Burbank skies, the Disney executive got on the telephone with Bill Block for the third time that afternoon. Disney was considering filing suit against the actress, Mestres said sternly. "We have reached the point where there just isn't any goodwill left," he added, cutting off any possibility of rebuttal from Block. If there was one more incident, Mestres continued, Disney was prepared to invoke the pro rata provision in Basinger's contract and deduct $85,000 for every day Basinger set production back. "You just tell your client that if she gives us even the slightest problem from here on out, she will be getting the bill," Mestres said, and slammed down the telephone.

The next day Helene Hahn sent off her final letter, warning that Disney was prepared to move ahead and deduct the costs from Basinger's salary. The filming of *The Marrying Man*, which was scheduled for release in March 1991, finished in August—10 days late. Although Mestres's threat was never carried out, he had made his point. No star, no matter how big, was so crucial to The Walt Disney Company that he or she could not be replaced, prodded, or sued. "Nothing is more important than the story line," Katzenberg said, "except maybe bringing it in under budget."

With that philosophy, the Disney executives had gained a reputation as bullies. Michael Eisner and Jeffrey Katzenberg were graduates of Paramount Pictures, where bare-knuckle negotiating was the norm. At Paramount the two men had learned that budgets are sacrosanct—a basic tenet that, to Charlie Bluhdorn and Barry Diller, was the banner for a crusade. No one had picked up the banner more avidly than Eisner and Katzenberg.

Almost from the beginning, Team Disney had redefined the Paramount budget mania to suit the new studio philosophy that they were creating in Burbank. Under their direction, Disney often passed up high-priced stars and directors, rummaging instead through Hollywood's list of faded actors to find down-on-their-luck stars like Bette Midler and Richard Dreyfuss. Also steering clear of high-priced writers, Katzenberg hired three dozen handpicked, lesser-known writers. He paid them low salaries and pressured them to churn out scripts. One of the company's biggest early hits, *Outrageous Fortune*, had been written by Leslie Dixon, a first-time script writer.

To guard the bottom line, Disney routinely assigned one of its production executives to the set of a film, thus ensuring that Katzenberg's hand was felt by proxy. "We had Marty Katz with us almost the entire time that we were making the movie," recalls *Outrageous Fortune* producer Robert Cort. Katz, a top Disney production executive who had followed Katzenberg from Paramount, would pepper Cort and director Arthur Hiller with ideas on how to shoot a scene or refocus the story line, Cort recalls. As a general comment on Katzenberg and his production executives, Cort added, "They have a lot of comments. They may say a lot of things that one disagrees with, but they never say anything that is stupid."

Not every collaboration, however, worked out nearly as well as the one between Katz and Cort. In early 1987, Mestres and Katzenberg battled with Coline Serreau, director of *Three Men and a Baby*, for several weeks, not long before the shooting of the film was scheduled to begin in Toronto. Disney wanted Serreau to rewrite the script she had used to make the French version of the film. Immediately before the filming was set to start, Serreau left the picture, citing health problems. Around the Disney studio, executives joked that Serreau had been stricken with "Katzenberg fever." Whatever the reason, she was quickly replaced by Leonard Nimoy, and the script was speedily rewritten by James Orr and Jim Cruickshank.

Mestres was even more direct with Henry Winkler, the director who had once played the part of Fonzie on Paramount's *Happy Days* show for ABC. Winkler was signed in 1988 to make the film *Turner & Hooch*. Five weeks into the filming, the film was running behind schedule. What was worse, Winkler and Mestres were barely on speaking terms. Winkler was fired with only a week's notice, and was replaced by *Shoot to Kill* director Roger Spottiswoode, a journeyman filmmaker who Disney knew would get the film done quickly. He did just that, and the film opened in mid-July of 1989, as planned. It also went on to gross more than $69 million at the box office.

"They come in and make you crazy," is *Pretty Woman* director Garry Marshall's comment on Katzenberg's production executives. "They're always flopping around." During the filming of *Beaches*, Marshall recalled, he got so upset about the constant interference that he once stormed off the set in mock anger. "I wasn't going anywhere," says Marshall now. "I just went into my act. Pretty soon, everyone is so worried that you'll leave that they leave you alone." Despite his temper tantrum, Marshall says, Disney refused to accede to his demand that they fill the Hollywood Bowl with extras for one scene. The Bowl scene was rewritten to depict a rehearsal session for star Bette Midler.

With a string of hits in its column, Disney was able to flex its muscles with the nation's theater owners as well. Not long after the company's blockbuster 1988 year, Disney's distribution crew imposed new rules about box office receipts. Even if a theater decided to allow discounted tickets for children or senior citizens, Disney would refuse to accept anything less than the percentage it was entitled to for a full-priced ticket, distribution chief Dick Cook informed the theater chains.

To ensure that it got the highest percentage possible from each ticket, Disney also insisted that theater owners bid against one another for the right to show a Disney film. At the time, bidding was required in only about half the states in the country. Under the system, to secure the rights to a top film theaters would bid against one another, with the result that, for the better films, studios often would set as much as 52 percent of the price of each ticket as their "rental fee." Disney's distribution team was under orders by studio chairman Jeffrey Katzenberg to come as close as possible to that number, especially for the company's major releases.

As some theater owners around the country soon learned, Disney was also prepared to back up its demands. When one small theater—which operated largely without competition in its market—refused to pay the percentage that Disney wanted, Disney's sales force simply rented a local Elks' Lodge and showed the film on a bedsheet.

Within a few days, the theater owner increased his offer. The most visible fight that Disney picked with theater owners, however, was over the commercials that many theaters show before the movie itself. Stressing the diminished "enjoyment value" that came from watching a Coke or Chevrolet commercial before the movie, Jeffrey Katzenberg ordered distribution chief Dick Cook to tell major chains that Disney would refuse to book its films in any theater that continued the practice.

To buttress his point, Disney commissioned a public opinion poll to show what it described as growing dissatisfaction with theater commercials by the nation's moviegoers. Hollywood insiders said, however, that Disney's no-commercial policy was motivated more by a growing feud with Cineplex Odeon. Cineplex, a large theater chain that ran commercials, had boycotted Disney films when Disney insisted upon competitive bidding. Cineplex was also partly owned by Disney's longtime rival, MCA, and often ran commercials that promoted MCA's new Universal Studios park in Orlando.

At one point in 1987, Jeffrey Katzenberg also picked a fight with Hollywood unions, an area that studio executives usually consider taboo. Most studios usually allow the talks to be handled by the Alliance of Motion Picture and TV Producers, Hollywood's industry bargaining council. But during the increasingly acrimonious talks between the industry and the striking Screen Writers Guild, Katzenberg convened a special writers' meeting on the Disney lot. The meeting was ostensibly called to enable Katzenberg to present his views on the issues, but industry leaders later complained that the studio chief had told rank-and-file members that he wasn't confident that their union was giving them the whole story. Although Universal and Fox backed Disney on the issue, it was Disney's *Who Framed Roger Rabbit* that was singled out for picketing by the Screen Writers Guild. The writers' strike was settled after nearly five months.

The bad feelings engendered by various actions of the Disney company in other areas of the industry, however, occasionally did linger. For nearly two years, Jeffrey Katzenberg feuded with top entertainment lawyers Barry Hirsch and Bertram Fields. At one point, Katzenberg refused to take calls from Hirsch, whose client list includes Francis Ford Coppola. The Disney chief boycotted Bert Fields when negotiations with Fields's client Warren Beatty over the terms for making *Dick Tracy* bogged down. Both attorneys were later reconciled with Disney.

Some of the lawyers' clients, however, stayed on bad terms with the company. Disney battled with Hirsch over the salary demands of director Barry Levinson, who directed *Tin Men* and *Good Morning, Vietnam* for the studio. Levinson was paid $1.5 million to make the second film. After it grossed $123 million, the director asked for $4 million for his next Disney film. When Katzenberg refused, Levinson left for MGM/UA, where he directed the 1989 hit *Rain Man*.

Disney also lost David Zucker, Jim Abrahams, and Jerry Zucker, the trio that had made *Ruthless People* for Touchstone Pictures. Eisner and Katzenberg had given the three filmmakers their start at Paramount by financing *Airplane*. In 1987, when their Disney contract was up for renewal, the three returned to Paramount because they were dissatisfied with Disney's offer. "We felt we had made two films—*Airplane* and *Ruthless People*—that were substantial hits," says Jerry Zucker, "and we wanted an increase. They were doing great, their stock was up, and we wanted to participate." Disney's talks with the Zucker-Abrahams-Zucker team dragged on for months. Disney, which had paid the trio a total of $1 million for *Ruthless People*, refused to consider any increase at all—and certainly not the $3 million the trio was requesting. "Our agents and lawyers thought what we wanted was fair, but Disney never even got anywhere near it." The trio subsequently made two huge hits for Paramount, *Naked Gun* and *Ghost*. "I still like them, they helped us a lot," says Zucker. "But their attitude is, 'What have you done for us lately?'"

The bitterest parting occurred in August 1990, when David Kirkpatrick, a top production executive for both Touchstone and Walt Disney Pictures, left the company for Paramount. Kirkpatrick had been one of the many Paramount executives who had worked with Katzenberg at Paramount. But a year after he joined his former bosses at Disney, Kirkpatrick was forced out. The 39-year-old executive returned to Paramount in late 1990, only to be hit with a suit from Disney soon after leaving.

The suit, filed in Los Angeles Superior Court, alleged that Kirkpatrick had violated the terms of a two-year "standstill agreement." Among Disney's charges were that Kirkpatrick had illegally recruited another studio executive, Donald Granger, to join him at Paramount, and that Kirkpatrick had interfered with Katzenberg's negotiations with producers Ed Kaplan and Steve Tisch to buy the rights to their latest film, *The Dead Letter Department.*

Kirkpatrick's lawyer vehemently denied the charges and pledged to fight the suit. In a far more telling comment about Disney's hard-edged reputation, attorney Howard Weitzman told *Variety:* "Mouses that live in glass houses shouldn't call other persons louses."

❖

Rupert Murdoch is not a man to take defeat lightly. The son of a veteran Australian journalist and political kingmaker, Murdoch got his training as a journalist by covering the police and courts for the *Melbourne Herald.* A student at Oxford when his father died in 1952, young Rupert went home to manage a pair of small, unprofitable newspapers that his father had owned. By 1958, he had not only turned around his father's newspapers but used their assets to launch an expansion that would eventually include newspapers in Great Britain, Hong Kong, and the United States, along with the Twentieth Century Fox studio and TV network. In 1988, Murdoch's company, News Corp., had assets of more than $12 billion.

Seeking even further growth, Murdoch's ambition was to dominate the potentially lucrative cable television market in Great Britain. In 1986, Murdoch had begun laying the groundwork for the Sky Television network, a direct broadcast system that would beam TV signals from a satellite to British homes. He had put nearly $500 million into the venture by 1988.

Barry Diller, chairman of Murdoch's Fox studio empire, approached Michael Eisner in mid-1988 about the possibility of Disney's joining the Sky Television network. Both Sky Television and its chief rival, the British Satellite Broadcasting system, had been throwing around huge sums of money to secure the rights to show movies from Hollywood's leading studios. BSB, a consortium of leading British media and electronics companies, had paid $100 million for the exclusive rights to show 198 MGM/UA films and another $160 million for 175 Columbia Pictures films. Murdoch was willing to offer more than $200 million for the rights to show Disney films.

Disney's Rich Frank began negotiating with Fox and News Corp. officials during the summer of 1988. During the talks, Disney raised the notion of a joint venture in which Disney would use the satellite that Murdoch was planning to launch in early 1989 to beam the Disney Channel to Europe. The goals of the Disney executives were to help Disney's growing merchandise sales in Europe and to provide a needed promotional boost to the Euro Disneyland park, which was to be built near Paris in 1992.

By November 1988, Murdoch and Disney had reached an agreement to establish a joint venture. Disney would give Murdoch's Sky Television the rights to air the more than 30 films that the company's Touchstone unit had produced since 1985. The joint venture would have the right to use the Disney name and characters on pay television in the United Kingdom. Disney would begin operating the Disney Channel on Sky Television within a year, airing it a minimum of 18 hours a day, seven days a week. Disney was required to provide the channel with at least six hours a day of its own programs.

Almost immediately Disney began to argue that Murdoch's side was making decisions without Disney's knowledge. Each side had written up pages and pages of proposals about exactly how the joint operation should work. "[They were] really tough negotiations," recalled Rich Frank. "How would we split the money? How do you pick the movies to run? Who would be the director general? Who can hire him and fire him?" One key issue was how Murdoch would advertise Sky Television's other five channels in relation to the Disney Channel. "We're very protective of our characters," says Frank, "and we didn't want Mickey Mouse showing up [in] an ad next to an X-rated movie.

Disney was also chafed by the way Rupert Murdoch does business. Eager to get as many movie packages as possible, Murdoch jumped into the bidding war against BSB. When his British competitors went after Columbia's movie package, Murdoch wanted to raise his bid. Disney resisted, and the joint venture passed up the films. The company did successfully bid for a slate of films from Orion Pictures, but only after the Disney and Fox executives had stayed up all night to cut nearly $25 million off the eventual price. When Warner Brothers insisted on a guarantee from Fox and Disney to back up a Sky Television contract for several films, Disney balked.

"Rupert Murdoch works from hunch and gut. [His approach is] 'I want to buy this movie package, I don't care what it costs,'" according to Rich Frank. He went on to describe Disney: "We're a very straight business operation, and we look at the return on investment. We were saying, 'Let it go to BSB,' [but he said], 'I have to have it.'"

Disney's executives fumed when they would learn about a Sky TV decision only after it had been made, often in a newspaper account. Probably the final straw was an advertisement in one of Murdoch's London newspapers. Murdoch's papers are a string of racy tabloids, each of which usually features a photograph of a partially clad woman on page 3. When the ads started showing the women sitting next to the satellite delivery system, with the Disney Channel included, Disney balked. "You never talked to us about our approval for that," Frank angrily told the Sky Television staff after seeing the ad.

All the while, Fox executives were clamoring for the $75 million investment that Disney had pledged as its part of the agreement. Disney, arguing it was no longer being treated like a partner in the venture, refused to pay. On May 15, 1989, Sky Television sued, asking for $1.5 billion in damages. The suit charged that Disney had failed to reimburse Sky Television for its part of the $500 million Murdoch had spent to launch a French satellite early in 1989. It also says that Disney "failed and refused to provide adequate staffing for its participation . . . and refused to cooperate or even respond in a timely manner to provide approvals for others in carrying out the venture's business."

The suit was settled out of court two weeks after it was filed. The joint venture was abandoned, although Murdoch retained the rights to carry Disney's Touchstone movies on Sky Television. In return, Disney would get at least $100 million for the films. The Disney Channel was pulled from the Murdoch venture altogether. Both sides said that it was still possible for the Disney Channel to rejoin the News Corp. venture. Privately, however, Disney officials acknowledged that they were happy to be rid of the Murdoch connection.

The Fox deal showed how difficult partnership with Disney is, both for the other party and for Disney itself. "If you look back at the tradition of our company, Walt was always in control," says strategic planning head Larry Murphy. "Control was always the major thing, and [control is the] Disney way to do things. That can be interpreted as arrogant, but we just do things differently, and it makes it tough to do joint ventures."

Lorimar Telepictures was another company that found out what partnership with Disney is like. On November 25, 1987, Disney paid $8.4 million to Lorimar to buy a half-interest in Metrocolor Laboratories, a film-processing plant. Two months later, the companies expanded their joint venture. Disney would not only use Metrocolor to process its films under an exclusive five-year agreement, but would also, according to an option it signed, buy half the stock of Metrocolor's London affiliate, Kay Metrocolor Laboratories.

Soon Lorimar and Disney were at one another's throats. Lorimar, which was acquired by Warner Communications in late 1988, shut down its movie unit and stopped using the Metrocolor lab to develop its negatives. Faced with sharply reduced revenues for the partnership, Disney demanded that its 1987 agreement with Lorimar be reviewed. With Lorimar a new unit of Warner, Disney General Counsel Joe Shapiro argued, Warner Brothers was now required to begin processing its films with Metrocolor.

Warner refused. Moreover, when Disney tried to sell the lab to British-based Rank Organization in early 1989 for $130 million, Disney executives learned even more bad news. As part of a failed attempt to sell Metrocolor just before the Disney deal, Lorimar had promised New York investor Ronald Pearlman $38 million if the film processor was later sold off. That requirement, Shapiro charged, kept Lorimar and Warner executives from accepting the Rank bid.

When talks broke down, Disney refused to pay more than $8 million of its film-processing bills incurred during the dispute, prompting Lorimar to file suit in August 1989. Lorimar asked for $118 million in damages, in addition to the $8 million in unpaid bills. Disney countersued, seeking $48.8 million as its part of the failed Rank Organization deal. (The suit was eventually settled, with Disney walking away from the venture altogether.)

❖

The Walt Disney Company has never had much use for the 10,000 acres in western Osceola County, Florida, that Walt Disney bought in the early 1960s. Crisscrossed by swampy rivers and populated mostly by vultures and their prey, the land is unlikely to be used soon for resorts or a theme park. The land is just south of the Walt Disney World complex and has become the battleground for one of Disney's many fights with local authorities in central Florida. Twice in two years, Disney has sued Bob Daly, Osceola County's property appraiser, because Daly has denied the land the agricultural classification that Disney wanted for it.

Each year Disney pays approximately $38 million in property taxes, mostly in Orange County. But, by having its Osceola land classified as agricultural property, the company pays only about $600,000 annually on this land. Attempting to qualify for the agricultural classification, Disney planted more than 10,000 pine trees on the land and shipped in several dozen cows. Even so, Daly insisted that the land be reclassified. "The cattle production is not near what 10,000 acres should produce," he told local reporters shortly after denying Disney's application for the second time. The newspaper also reported that Disney alleged in its suit that the property was being used for "bona fide agricultural purposes, namely forestry and livestock operations."

An appetite for controversy and a clenched fist seem to be among the many characteristics that Michael Eisner brought with him to Orlando. The company had always enjoyed an uneasy alliance with local officials in Florida. Walt Disney World had benefited the area by turning a dusty citrus-growing region into the world's largest tourist destination and by employing more than 30,000 people annually. The Reedy Creek District that the Florida legislature established for the company in 1967, however, gave Disney unfettered power to develop its 28,000 acres, and often the company had developed its land with no consideration of the impact on neighbors.

Such tensions only increased with the arrival of Michael Eisner and Frank Wells. Their plans for expanding Walt Disney World lured more tourists to central Florida, causing further clogging of Orlando's already crowded roads. For more than two years, Disney and Orange County officials bickered over who would pay the costs of expanding the roads to accommodate the increased traffic. Disney finally agreed to pay $13.4 million, which was only a tiny part of the money that would be required.

Six months later, Disney was again at odds with the county. On January 2, 1990, Disney drew the ire of Orange County officials when it captured the entire $57.7 million in tax-exempt bonds available to the six-county central Florida area. Included was $19 million that central Florida officials had hoped would help them build homes for 1,200 blue-collar workers in the area. Local officials mailed their applications to the state bond authority, but Disney representatives hand-delivered Disney's application moments after the office opened, thus beating the local officials to the punch. Disney's Reedy Creek District, which already was saving more than $80 million a year in interest payments by holding $250 million in tax-exempt bonds issued over the previous two decades, wanted the money for expanding Walt Disney World's sewer systems.

Eisner hardly endeared himself to local officials when he jokingly called them "incompetent" for mailing in their bond application. Although the Disney chairman retracted the statement moments after uttering it, bruised feelings remained. The company did pay some of the costs of expanding the roads, which may have helped its reputation a little. A few months later, Disney also offered to help Orange County officials find a low-interest loan to build the homes.

❖

Michael Eisner was out of town, visiting the Orlando theme parks, when official Hollywood gathered at the Shrine Auditorium on March 16, 1989, for the Academy Awards presentation. The ceremony was to be telecast nationwide by ABC. In the audience, sitting in the 12th-row seats reserved for the official Disney party, were Roy Disney and Jeffrey Katzenberg. Snow White was also there, but in a less official capacity. Wearing the Disney character's signature blue-and-white shepherdess frock, an actress warbled a few notes during a lavish 11-minute opening ceremony. Sashaying through the audience, she brazenly flirted with the likes of Tom Hanks, Dustin Hoffman, and Ryan O'Neal. Her date for the evening was teen heartthrob Rob Lowe, with whom she sang an off-key duet.

Snow White's singing was not well received. "It reminded me that my brakes need new pads," wrote Andy Klein, of the Los Angeles *Herald-Examiner*. Disney executives were upset about more than the quality of Snow White's performance. The company, claiming it hadn't been informed that the Academy of Motion Picture Arts and Sciences intended to use the character, demanded an apology. Had one been forthcoming, "we could have considered the matter ended," said Frank Wells, who called Academy president Richard Kahn the morning after the show.

Even before Disney approached the Academy, the legal papers were being drawn up. Eisner, calling from Orlando, contacted Joe Shapiro at his office and urged him to turn on his television. Sufficiently alarmed, Shapiro mustered two of his lawyers, Ed Nowak and Peter Nolan, to draft a lawsuit. By 5:00 A.M. the next day, Nolan faxed a copy to Disney's outside lawyers for their review. At 3:30 P.M., Disney's lawyers filed suit in federal court, claiming copyright infringement and seeking an order prohibiting the Academy from using Disney characters without permission.

The Academy eventually did apologize. Disney dropped the suit, but the point had been made. The Walt Disney Company was prepared to fight to maintain exclusive rights to its characters. From the first, Walt Disney had been adamant about protecting the rights to his characters. In 1954, when Disney was riding the crest of its popular *Davy Crockett* show, Disney had ordered consumer products chief Vince Jefferds to send out telegrams to major department stores warning that they could be sued if they sold unauthorized coonskin caps.

"The issue of copyright is really inviolate," says Frank Wells. "You lose rights to [copyrights and trademarks] if you don't protect them. You're talking about things that the world focuses on." No company has been more vigilant in its protection of those rights than The Walt Disney Company under Michael Eisner and Frank Wells. Not long after taking charge of the company, they beefed up the consumer products legal staff and gave its head, Peter Nolan, a mandate to flood the courts with lawsuits against manufacturers that put Mickey or Donald on their products without paying Disney for the right.

By 1987, the company had filed 17 major lawsuits naming 700 defendants in the United States, as well as 78 other lawsuits overseas. The next year, it sued another 400 manufacturers of T-shirts and other merchandise showing Mickey Mouse and other Disney characters. Included in this suit were 149 New York–area merchants that the company contended were costing it $1 million a year in revenues. When *Dick Tracy* opened, the company filed suit against more than 1,500 vendors selling fake Tracy items.

Most of these actions were taken against back-alley manufacturers and fly-by-night vendors who slapped Mickey Mouse or Pluto on a T-shirt and sold it from a street corner. In its eagerness to protect Disney's heritage, the new managers also picked their share of embarrassing fights.

Though Disney had ultimately abandoned its effort to stop White River from erecting a Winnie-the-Pooh statue, it didn't retreat in its spring 1989 battle against three day-care centers in Hallandale, Florida, which had painted Disney characters on their outer walls. Arguing that use of the characters suggested that Disney had given a stamp of approval to the day-care centers, the company gave the centers one month to scrub the characters off their walls. The three day-care centers received letters of support from a Phoenix grandmother, a New York City doctor, and several dozen other people. "I've gotten so many telephone calls from people angry at Disney that I bet Walt Disney is turning over in his grave right now," Erica Scotti, who runs Very Important Babies Day Care, told the Associated Press. Gilbert Stein, Hallandale's mayor, added that he was "appalled at the harsh politics of a corporate giant that was built with the nickels and dimes of kids. I'd like to ban Mickey Mouse from the city limits."

For Disney, the tough stance was the only way it could protect its copyrights. The company's archrival, MCA, however, tried to reap a publicity bonanza for its Universal Studios Tour in nearby Orlando. It painted Flintstone cartoon characters over the Disney characters and threw a well-publicized party for the schoolchildren. "It's frustrating, I know, because these are children," Frank Wells said later, but we have no choice if we are to continue to own the rights to Mickey Mouse. It is among the most valuable rights this company has."

❖

"We are held to a higher standard in every area," Jeffrey Katzenberg told the *Los Angeles Times* in defense of The Walt Disney Company. "I am not sure our consumer is aware of this toughness, and I think our shareholders appreciate how concerned we are with the way we spend their money." By late 1989, it was difficult to find a Hollywood company with which Disney was not involved in a lawsuit or public relations fight. The company was still embroiled in litigation with MGM/UA over the use of the MGM name for its Disney-MGM Studios Theme Park in Orlando. MCA and Disney were still engaged in a war of words over their respective Florida studio tours. Time-Warner, which had bought Lorimar Telepictures, moved to settle the Metrocolor case. But so prevalent was Disney litigation that Alex Ben Block, the editor of *Show Biz News*, gave up the idea of putting out a special issue dedicated to Hollywood legal fights when he realized that "Disney was involved in almost every one of the fights."

News Corp. had dropped its suit over Sky Television, but early in 1990, Disney launched a new round of legal fisticuffs with Eisner's one-time boss, Barry Diller. The issues this time were afternoon cartoon shows and Disney's reign as the leading syndicator of kids' shows. After buying its own TV station in Los Angeles, Disney informed Diller that it would no longer sell its syndicated afternoon shows *DuckTales* and *Chip 'n Dale* to Fox's LA affiliate KTTV. An infuriated Diller responded by threatening to yank the two Disney shows from the five other stations Fox also owned. And in a broadside attack on Disney, the Fox chairman also ordered his production unit to begin work on its own afternoon cartoon series to sell to the 120 affiliates of its Fox TV network. Adding insult to injury, the show Diller wanted to make was *Peter Pan and the Pirates,* based on a Disney classic. Jeffrey Katzenberg had unsuccessfully blocked CBS from airing a Peter Pan cartoon show on Saturday mornings in 1989. He had pledged "all-out corporate war," the *Los Angeles Times* reported. But the original Peter Pan copyright had expired in 1986, and Fox claimed it had every right to use the character that Scottish storyteller John M. Barrie had created in 1911. Katzenberg had tried unsuccessfully to head off Fox as well by having Roy Disney try some quiet diplomacy. Fox network president Jamie Kellner, however, had insisted that his company would press ahead.

The problem began when Disney's salesmen reported overtures by Fox salespeople to Fox affiliates around the country, encouraging them to steer clear of Disney's two afternoon shows, *DuckTales* and *Chip 'n Dale Rescue Rangers*. About half of the Fox affiliates were carrying Disney's afternoon shows and were located in small markets where no other independents were available to buy the Disney programs. Moreover, Fox held great sway with those stations because it was delivering three nights a week of prime-time fare to them, including the hit show *The Simpsons*. "We just couldn't take it without a fight," recalled Rich Frank.

Claiming that Fox had "embarked upon an unlawful plan to drive [Disney] from the market," Disney instructed one of its lawyers, former Justice Department antitrust chief Stanford Litvak, to file suit against Fox. On February 21, 1990, the company filed suit in the federal court in Los Angeles, seeking unspecified damages from Fox. At the same time, Disney also filed comments in Washington with the Federal Communications Commission (FCC), which was then considering a request by Fox for permission to simultaneously operate its network and syndicate its television shows. (Under a 1970 set of FCC rules, networks were precluded from also syndicating TV shows.) "Fox's behavior in the market should clearly disqualify it from any consideration of such governmental favoritism," Rich Frank said in a press release that Disney distributed to highlight the action it had taken. It was unclear how much weight the Disney filing would have with federal regulators, but the company had again made its point. To the children of the world, the Disney name means fairy tales and adventure films. To both the company's partners and competitors, it can also mean legal fights and limitless opposition.

CHAPTER

Guarding the Kingdom's Coffers

T hroughout the 1980s takeover fever was sweeping America. Fueled by Michael Milken's junk bonds and put into gear by a booming stock market, the fever made it seem as if no deal was impossible. After having served for decades as high-priced but silent advisers, investment bankers were suddenly guiding the course of American business. *Business Week* called what was happening, "Monopoly in fast-forward: a frenzied blur of buybacks and spin-offs, mergers and acquisitions." The players were named Boesky, Icahn, Edelman, and Steinberg.

By the mid-1980s, "deal mania," as *Business Week* also described it, led to one multimillion-dollar deal after another. By leveraging corporate assets to the hilt, junk-bond financing allowed the investment firm of Kohlberg Kravis Roberts to offer $4.2 billion for Safeway Stores just three months after buying Beatrice Foods for $6.3 billion. Texas oilman T. Boone Pickens, a wildcatter turned raider, made unsuccessful runs at giant oil companies like Gulf Oil Corp. and Unocal Corp. The entertainment industry was hardly immune to the takeover frenzy. The march on Hollywood began with Saul Steinberg's ill-fated hostile attempt to raid Walt Disney Productions in 1984. Soon it spread to television. Capital Cities, a relative newcomer with a string of TV stations and a few magazines, swallowed the much larger ABC television network for

$3.5 billion. Australian empire builder Rupert Murdoch bought both Twentieth Century Fox and seven Metromedia television stations within a year, spending nearly $2.8 billion in the process. Even a couple of B-movie producers from Israel, Yolan Globus and Menahem Golan, could plunk down $134 million for a seedy midwestern movie theater chain.

By the time Japanese electronics giant Sony Corp. had successfully bid $3.4 billion for Columbia Pictures in 1989, a new vision had emerged for the entertainment industry. In this vision, shared by Sony and Murdoch, global media and entertainment conglomerates would bring together movie companies, cable outlets, book publishers, and magazine publishers under a single roof. Each operation would make the others stronger and more profitable than any one could be alone. Dominating the world market, one company would control an idea from its appearance in a book or magazine to its debut on television or the big screen, as well as its exploitation on videocassettes, cable, and in syndication.

During their first two years at Walt Disney Productions, Michael Eisner and Frank Wells spent most of their time restoring the company after the ravages of its own takeover battle. The company's debt had more than doubled in 1984, to nearly $900 million. More important, the time and attention that Disney's managers had been forced to spend on Saul Steinberg and Irwin Jacobs had sapped money that should have been put into upgrading Disney's theme parks and movie operations.

As 1987 began, Disney's turnaround was firmly in place. Relentlessly raising ticket prices, churning out hit movies, and aggressively marketing Disney's characters and animated films had transformed the company into a virtual cash machine. Not only had Disney eliminated much of its debt, but it was sitting on top of more than $340 million in cash—five times its reserves of the year before. Even after spending $507 million to build new hotels and the Disney-MGM Studios Theme Park in 1987 and to increase film production, the company was adding $270 million a year to its cash reserves. During the company's mid-year financial review in 1987, Disney chief financial officer Gary Wilson estimated that the company could easily borrow up to $2 billion to finance an even faster expansion.

It had been nearly two years since Wilson had come over from Marriott Corp. Michael Eisner had been drawn to Wilson in large part because of Wilson's reputation for putting together the financial plan that fueled Marriott's impressive expansion in the early 1980s. At Marriott, Wilson had supervised the hotel chain's construction of new units and the aggressive financial restructuring that had made Marriott into the nation's fastest-growing hotel company. Wilson was highly regarded for his financial acumen. But above all, Gary Wilson liked the challenge of putting together deals.

At Marriott, Wilson had pushed Marriott into the purchase of fast-food restaurants and airline catering businesses. With Al Checchi, he had nearly put together a $2 billion deal for Sid Bass and Bill Marriott, an attempt to buy the Conrail train system. Unknown to Eisner, Wilson had also once coveted Walt Disney Productions and had tried unsuccessfully to convince Bill Marriott to back Saul Steinberg's 1984 hostile bid for the company.

Michael Eisner was no less attuned to the fast-changing takeover atmosphere. He had watched with increased concern as his former boss Barry Diller and Rupert Murdoch had assembled the TV station group capable of transforming the lackluster Fox studio into a television network. Disney's longtime rival MCA had also bought a television station. And increasingly, studios were lining up to buy movie theater chains across the country.

Eisner knew that Disney, one of the few companies to enjoy a worldwide reputation, would be harmed if its international franchise was threatened as its competitors got bigger and more powerful. Even in the United States, expansion opportunities could be stifled if prized acquisitions went to Disney's competitors. "But what we didn't need was a headline about this deal being the biggest and the best," explained Eisner later. "Six months later, they would change the words and what was once the 'best' would be the 'stupidest.'"

For all his ambitions, Eisner was nonetheless tightfisted. His grandfather, he liked to tell subordinates, was a multimillionaire who would drive miles out of his way to avoid paying at one of New York's many toll bridges. Frugality had also been a constant companion during Eisner's early career, both at ABC and Paramount. "I learned at ABC that one dumb decision would bring the whole company down," says Eisner. "You've got to prepare not to have everything."

Eisner's tightfisted management style was no doubt a testimony to Charlie Bluhdorn and Barry Diller, both of whom could be excruciatingly tight with a buck.

Like Gary Wilson, however, Michael Eisner had also grown up in an industry where deals are king. Movie producers and TV show creators visited his third-floor office in the Animation Building with increasing regularity. By late 1985, a year after a foiled takeover had brought him to Disney, Michael Eisner decided it was time to go shopping.

❖

Michael Eisner had been at Disney just over a year when word spread through Hollywood that RCA, which owned the NBC-TV network, had walked away from a merger with Universal Pictures's parent company, MCA Inc. At the time NBC was the nation's third-rated network, still awaiting the rush of viewers that *The Cosby Show* would bring it. RCA, Eisner figured, might be hungry for another deal. The Disney chairman knew Grant Tinker, NBC's stately chairman and a well-regarded TV producer in his own right. Calling Tinker, Eisner asked if NBC was for sale. Tinker didn't know, but within weeks the Disney executive was discussing a deal with RCA chairman Thornton Bradshaw, the 68-year-old former Arco chairman who had been running RCA since 1981.

To keep the overall purchase price down, Eisner told Bradshaw he would buy NBC and then sell off RCA's consumer electronics unit. Bradshaw, nearing retirement, was agreeable but wanted to pass it by Felix Rohatyn, the Lazard Freres investment banker who had been advising RCA. Eisner never heard back from Rohatyn. By mid-December 1985, General Electric, eager to combine its consumer electronics operation and expand into broadcasting, bought RCA for $6.3 billion.

"If I had known more about the entertainment business back then, we might have made a real effort to buy it," recalled Gary Wilson later. Indeed, within five years, electronic companies such as Sony and Matsushita would be gobbling up movie studios to combine their VCRs and wide-screen television sets with Hollywood's movies and TV shows.

Disney's inability to respond quickly enough to the RCA deal demonstrated to Gary Wilson the need to upgrade the company's financial staff. When Wilson first arrived, Disney had no head of strategic planning, few M.B.A.s, and little analytical capability. Since 1983, in fact, the company hadn't even had a treasurer. Eisner and Wells had been shocked, not long after arriving, to find that the company had never even done a five-year business plan—the standard planning document for even the smallest companies.

Four months after Wilson joined the company, he hired Larry Murphy, a 33-year-old Marriott vice-president, to head Disney's strategic planning operation. Tall, with dark swept-back hair and a perpetual five-o'clock shadow, Murphy already knew Disney well. In 1984, Saul Steinberg and Gary Wilson had been discussing a possible role for Marriott in Steinberg's assault on Disney. Marriott had wanted Disney's Orlando hotels and other real estate, and had contemplated pledging $200 million toward Steinberg's raid on the company. Murphy had done a detailed financial analysis of Disney's assets for Gary Wilson at that time.

Murphy was the first of nearly a dozen members of the "Marriott Mafia" who joined Wilson at Disney. Another recruit was Neil McCarthy, an accountant who had worked under Wilson in Marriott's inflight catering business. McCarthy was put in charge of the company's accounting and tax units. Wilson added John Forsgren, who had been treasurer of Sperry Corporation, and Judson Green, a CPA who had been treasurer of Walt Disney World, to his staff. Richard Nanula, a recent Harvard M.B.A., who had impressed Eisner while working on a Disney-commissioned study on expansion plans for Orlando, was also hired to help Murphy assess potential acquisitions.

The Wilson team spent most of its first two years cleaning up the mess it had inherited from Mike Bagnall. Much of the $861 million the company owned in loans was refinanced, cutting the company's overall interest rate to 7 percent from 9 percent. The company also cut back on the $1.2 billion line of credit that Bagnall had arranged during the eight months of the 1984 takeover battle, slashing several million more in bank fees. For several months, Wilson also had his staff work up the numbers for a plan to sell off EPCOT Center to a group of investors, and then lease it back. The idea had first been proposed by Ray Watson in mid-1984. Wilson estimated that Disney could raise $1.5 billion by selling EPCOT. But Eisner, worried about bad publicity, decided to wait. Changes in the federal tax law in 1986 eventually made the deal less attractive. And when revenue from Disney's theme parks began to grow, Eisner decided to scrap the idea altogether.

The biggest rush of new cash Wilson and his team found came from Tokyo Disneyland. In 1986, Walt Disney Productions was getting $8 to $10 million each quarter in royalty payments. Card Walker had licensed the Japanese theme park to the Oriental Land Company in the late 1970s, when Disney was preparing to build EPCOT Center. The problem as Gary Wilson saw it was that the quarterly payments also saddled Disney with a huge tax bill.

Working with the Los Angeles office of the Long-Term Credit Bank of Japan, Wilson devised a plan to eliminate the company's tax bill from its Tokyo royalties while funneling more than $500 million into Disney's coffers. Calculating the future value of the royalty payments over the upcoming 20 years to be $723 million, the Disney chief financial officer arranged for New York–based Citicorp and the Long-Term Credit Bank to advance Disney that amount as a 20-year loan. The loan carried a low 6 percent interest rate, although Disney was required to reserve up to $145 million to cover any currency fluctuations that might affect its ability to make future repayments in yen. More important, Disney got more than $500 million in cash that it could use immediately to build hotels in Orlando.

Besides his financial legerdemain, Gary Wilson also brought to Disney a sense of financial order that the company had been missing since the days when Roy Disney had personally kept the company's books. Borrowing liberally from the Marriott strategic plan he had developed, in 1986 Wilson instituted what he called a "20-20 plan" at Disney. Each of the company's many operating units would be required to show 20 percent annual earnings growth over the course of the five-year plan. That would also translate into a 20 percent annual growth for Disney's earnings per share, a key indicator of how Wall Street would judge the company's stock price. The 20-20 plan also required that anything that the company wanted to buy would have to pay for itself in five years.

Wilson's requirements also established Walt Disney as a company that wasn't going to bid up the price of anything it bought. "We weren't going to get into any of those 'bet-your-multiple' deals," Wilson said. The success that Michael Eisner and Jeffrey Katzenberg had enjoyed in reviving the Touchstone Pictures label made the point equally clear. There was no need to pay the steep prices that were being demanded to buy existing companies, the Disney executives believed, when it could be just as easy—and far more profitable—to build a company from the ground up.

By mid-1986, Disney's financial staff had nearly 20 members. Several had followed Wilson from Marriott. Others had been recruited from other companies or prestigious business schools. Wilson had built the kind of financial operation that a company that brought in $2 billion a year needed. Wilson and his staff began to look around aggressively for the kinds of deals that other companies were making. With Disney Studios head Richard Frank, Wilson examined the TV library of MCA Inc. They also looked at the library of Lorimar Telepictures, the maker of the

TV shows *Dallas* and *Perfect Strangers*. When MGM/UA Communications, Inc., owner Kirk Kerkorian put his company up for bids, Disney was one of the first to ask for its internal financial numbers. "We looked at everything," Gary Wilson recalled. "You can't buy unless you look at enough things to know what's worth buying."

❖

Walter Yetnikoff was used to creative freedom and had a habit of going to his office after noon. The scraggly-bearded former lawyer had built CBS Records into the industry leader with acts like Bruce Springsteen, Billy Joel, and Michael Jackson. In 1986, however, Yetnikoff felt that he was about to get his wings clipped. The year before, New York investor Lawrence Tisch had taken a 25 percent stake in CBS Inc. to thwart the unwanted advances of Atlanta cable mogul Ted Turner. Installed as chairman, Tisch didn't take fondly to Yetnikoff's freewheeling ways.

Before long, Tisch was dismantling CBS's far-flung assets in order to concentrate on its network business. By making it known to investment bankers that he was willing to sell off the company's magazine and record units, he had created a virtual stampede. Triangle Industries, a New York–based packaging company, looked at the record company. So did Sony, which was looking to marry the world's largest record company with its own consumer electronics unit.

By mid-1986, Gary Wilson instructed Larry Murphy to begin looking at CBS Records as well. Disney's studio had worked with Yetnikoff earlier that year, when the CBS Records president had lined up CBS superstars Mick Jagger and Billy Joel for the *Ruthless People* sound track. The idea of acquiring a record company made sense to Disney. Both MCA and Warner Brothers already owned record units, and both made millions each year by capturing the revenues from sound tracks matched to their movies.

Gary Wilson was aware that the music industry was as unpredictable as the movie business. Indeed, CBS Records's earnings had fallen dramatically in 1985, when none of its better-known acts had released a major album. He also knew that, by contrast, the record company's profits had nearly doubled in 1986, rising to $162 million, on the strength of Michael Jackson's *Bad* album.

Murphy did a quick analysis of CBS Records. Under Disney's evaluation system, the company wasn't worth more than $700 million, he told Wilson and Eisner. "We were willing to go to maybe $1 billion,"

Wilson recalled later. In the end, Disney never had the chance. In a frantic effort to keep control of the company, Yetnikoff contacted the Blackstone Group, which represented Sony. The electronics giant, with the strength of a strong yen and a guaranteed outlet for CBS Records's music, bid a stiff $2 billion for the record company in late 1987.

It would be three years before Disney considered another acquisition in the record industry. This time, the companies were smaller and the prices cheaper, and two companies were under consideration. Dutch electronics maker NV Phillips had bought A&M Records for $500 million, while MCA had traded $500 million worth of its stock for Geffen Records. Disney looked at both and even had discussions with David Geffen, who insisted on taking stock instead of cash to cut his tax payments. Michael Eisner and Frank Wells decided that they were unwilling to dilute Disney's stock, which would cut its price to investors like Sid Bass. Instead, in late 1989, the company announced that it was starting its own record label, Hollywood Records.

As with Touchstone Pictures, Disney was prepared to build the company from the ground up. New rock stars seemed to crop up each week, Eisner and Wells thought. Instead of chasing after high-priced rock groups, Disney would simply create their own stars. To help pull this off, the company hired Hollywood attorney Peter Paterno, who had represented Guns 'n Roses and other heavy metal rock bands. "We're not joining the frenzy of media acquisitions," Eisner stated firmly.

❖

Jack Wrather, an entrepreneur who owned oil wells along with rights to the old *Lassie* and *The Lone Ranger* TV series, had been a close friend of Walt Disney's. He and Walt used to swap stories of fishing trips and deals gone bad. In 1955, Walt had granted a 99-year license agreement to his old friend that allowed Wrather to use the Disney name on any hotel in southern California. He only built one, the Disneyland Hotel, located on a 60-acre site next to the Disneyland theme park. The hotel opened in 1955, three months after the park itself opened.

By the time Eisner and Wells arrived at Disney in 1984, Jack Wrather had died and his company, Wrather Corp., was in deep trouble. Its oil and gas wells were losing money, and the company had been forced to sell off its old TV shows. The Disneyland Hotel was also suffering. In the three decades since its opening, the hotel had grown into a sprawling compound with three towers, 1,174 rooms, and 160,000 square feet of convention space—but the wallpaper was faded, the furniture was dirty, and the elevators were run-down. "The [worst] thing [is] that it still [has] the Disneyland name on it," Sid Bass told Eisner not long after the new chairman came aboard. "Whether you own it or not, when people aren't impressed with the hotel, you'll be the [one] getting the blame."

Disney was also under pressure to make a deal. In June 1987, Industrial Equity, an arm of New Zealand raider Ronald Brierley's network, bought 28 percent of Wrather. It also told the Securities and Exchange Commission that it intended to buy at least half the company. Not only would that put the company out of reach to Disney, Disney's executives knew, but it would also put the Disneyland Hotel under the ownership of a company that held no particular link to Disney.

With his background in hotels, Gary Wilson was the natural choice for the job of acquiring the Disneyland Hotel. Wilson gave the job to Richard Nanula, the Harvard-trained financial executive who had joined the company a year earlier. Nanula's first call was to Drexel Burnham Lambert, which was advising the Wrather family. Meeting at Drexel's Beverly Hills office a week later, Wilson and Nanula were told that it would cost Disney $145 million to buy the 72 percent stake of Wrather that Brierley didn't already own.

The hotel alone was probably worth no more than $100 million, Disney figured. But Disney had no interest in the two dozen oil wells and the oil property that the company owned. What Disney did want, in addition to the hotel, were the 26 acres the Wrather Company owned near Disneyland, along with its rights to the more than 300 acres in nearby Long Beach, California. Wrather had used the Long Beach harbor property only for two leased attractions, tours of Howard Hughes's giant *Spruce Goose* airplane and the ship *Queen Mary*, both of which were rather lackluster. The Long Beach property, Eisner and Wilson figured, could be useful in case Disney decided to build another theme park along with hotels in southern California. But at $145 million, the deal was far too expensive. The negotiations dragged on for months. In the end, Wilson approached Alfred Boyer, Brierley's operative in San Diego, about a joint bid for Wrather. Together, the two companies would buy the remaining 72 percent of the company for $109 million. Disney would pay $76 million for half the company, with Brierley paying the remainder. That would give each of the parties 50 percent of the company, although Disney would be given the right to run the Disneyland Hotel and develop the southern California acreage.

Boyer took the deal. But to get the lower price, Wilson resorted to the kind of strong-arm tactics that might have made Mickey Mouse blush. The main sticking point was Wrather's exclusive lease on the Disney-owned Monorail that connected the Disneyland Hotel to the theme park.

The Monorail was vitally important to the value of the hotel. With it, Disneyland Hotel patrons could get directly to the heart of the park, avoiding both traffic congestion and parking fees. Walt had given his friend Jack Wrather the Monorail lease for practically nothing, but the lease was coming up for renewal. In order to get the stock price he wanted, Wilson threatened the Wrather company with a major price increase in the Monorail lease if they sold to anyone else—a move that would make Wrather far less attractive. "He's relentless," one Drexel banker told a reporter later. "He's one of the toughest negotiators I have ever encountered."

Six months later, Disney bought out Industrial Equity's half of the company for $85.2 million. The Wrather purchase was the kind of deal that Team Disney wanted to make. The eventual cost was $161 million, but a three-month analysis of the property had shown that the potential far outweighed the risks.

A $35 million face-lift for the Disneyland Hotel would allow the company to raise room rates substantially. More important, by buying the Wrather company, the Walt Disney Company has reacquired the right to put the Disney name on future hotels it might build in southern California. That right, it turned out, was something the company desperately wanted as it made plans to build a second theme park—including hotels—in southern California.

❖

Chuck Cobb never seemed to fit in with Team Disney. After becoming an alternate high hurdler on the 1960 U.S. Olympic Team, the Stanford graduate had gone on to become chief operating officer of Penn Central. By 1984, the year Team Disney came to power, Cobb was running Arvida Corp., which was based in Boca Raton, Florida. That same year, Sid Bass traded Arvida, a resort and home developer, to Disney for 9 percent of Disney's stock.

Before Michael Eisner and Frank Wells arrived, Cobb himself had unsuccessfully campaigned for the top job at Disney. A member of the Disney board, he had envisioned the future of the company as lying in development of its extensive Florida real estate holdings. Even after Eisner and Wells took over the running of the company, the land developer refused to give up his self-appointed role as Orlando's guardian. Working with Ray Watson, the lanky 49-year-old Cobb had developed a master plan for Walt Disney World that included high-rise apartments, industrial parks, and even schools. "It was the kind of thing that Walt had envisioned," recalled Cobb later. "I saw tremendous potential there."

When they first came to the company, Eisner and Wells made a special point of flying to Boca Raton to meet with Cobb and his staff at Arvida headquarters. Not long afterward, Frank Wells showed Arvida executives a slide show of photographs documenting his mountain climbing, and he also attended Cobb's surprise 50th birthday party. Neither Wells nor Eisner, however, ever warmed up to Cobb, a free-speaking executive who often rubbed others the wrong way. At board meetings, Cobb frequently irritated Eisner and Wells by insisting on giving unwelcome lectures on the subtleties of real estate development. "He's an arrogant and stupid man," says Gary Wilson, who feuded with Cobb often. "None of us got along with him." Cobb, in contrast, says that he left the company with warm feelings for Eisner and Wells.

Within a year after joining Disney, the new managers were clearly disenchanted with Arvida and its blunt chairman. Increasingly, it was either Frank Wells or Gary Wilson who would make key real estate decisions for the company. Eisner and Wells had also rejected much of Cobb's plan to develop the Walt Disney World complex. "The disillusionment during the short honeymoon between the two companies began to disintegrate to the state of tolerant coexistence," according to Tony Ettorre, one of Cobb's longtime partners.

Moreover, the Disney management was getting nervous about real estate development in general. Disney was more comfortable with developing its own hotels than with building resorts for others, Eisner believed. He worried also that Arvida's 20,000 acres of property gave Disney far too wide an exposure to volatile real estate markets in southern California, Florida, and Georgia—exposure that could one day saddle the company with huge losses.

Already, the once-booming Arizona real estate market had begun to soften. Moreover, real estate development is notoriously cyclical, and companies make money only when they sell property. Indeed, the $65.7 million in earnings that Arvida provided to Disney in 1985 shrank to $41.8 million the next year when the company sold less property. Internal Disney estimates predicted that Arvida earnings would shrink even further in 1987.

By mid-1986, Cobb was looking for a company to buy Arvida from Disney and keep him in control. He contacted Florida Power & Light Company, a diversification-minded utility that had inquired in 1985 about the possibilities of buying Arvida. Disney wanted $400 million, roughly twice what it had paid for the company in 1984. In the end, the Florida utility backed away without ever making a bid.

Disney enlisted Shearson Lehman Brothers in November 1986 to help unload the company. By early the following year, Shearson investment bankers developed a plan for a limited partnership that would raise $300 million by selling 80 percent of the company to the public. Disney would retain the other 20 percent, and control the company.

Disney soon got a better offer. Gary Wilson contacted Chicago-based JMB Realty Corporation, which jointly owned a Boca Raton shopping mall with Arvida. Before Disney went ahead with Shearson's plan, JMB wanted to look at Arvida's books. On January 29, 1987, JMB made an initial offer to buy Arvida outright for $445 million. As part of the deal, Disney also agreed to lend JMB $143 million in a short-term loan until JMB could sell off some of the Arvida property. The deal took nearly nine months to close. And after JMB executives took a closer look at the assets, they decided to cut their price to $404 million.

Disney had rid itself of a company that no longer seemed to fit its needs. What was perhaps more important, it had sold Arvida at a premium price just before land prices in Florida started to slip. Disney's problems with Arvida weren't over yet, however. A group of 26 Arvida executives contended that Disney's board had voted them $12 million worth of stock options that had never been paid. Hiring a lawyer, the Arvida executives considered filing a lawsuit. Disney beat them to it. Three months after it received JMB's initial officer, Disney filed suit against the Arvida executives in U.S. court in Jacksonville, Florida. Disney argued that the options weren't due to be vested until November 1987, after its deal with JMB was scheduled to close. In June, Disney dropped its suit and paid the Arvida executives $8 million in exchange for their agreement to refrain from taking legal action. Chuck Cobb, who was not named in the suit, made a separate settlement. Disney paid him $2.1 million, and he pledged that he would not bring suit against the company.

❖

By 1985, it seemed, every company in America wanted to own a television station. Advertising revenues were soaring for independent TV stations. Network affiliates were worth even more. At the time, Rupert Murdoch was negotiating his $2 billion deal to buy the Metromedia TV stations from John Kluge. The Chicago-based Tribune Company would soon pay a record $510 million for a single station, KTLA in Los Angeles.

Rich Frank, who had managed a string of television stations before joining Eisner and Barry Diller at Paramount, could see the tide turning. In mid-1985, he and Eisner began shopping for television stations. That June, the two Disney executives flew to Akron, Ohio, to meet GenCorp chairman William Reynolds. GenCorp's broadcasting subsidiary, RKO General, owned three TV stations, including one in New York and one in Los Angeles.

Moreover, GenCorp was in deep trouble. In 1980 the Federal Communications Commission had ordered RKO to sell off the TV stations. The issue was RKO's qualifications for holding TV licenses, and a number of groups had raised challenges against the company. RKO's problems had begun in 1965 when Fidelity Television Inc., a Los Angeles citizens group headed by William Simon, who had once been director of the Los Angeles office of the Federal Bureau of Investigation, challenged RKO's eligibility to hold a license for its KHJ-TV station in Los Angeles. The case prompted challenges of the other RKO stations. The complaints charged that RKO's parent, then called General Tire & Rubber Co., had failed to tell the FCC about allegedly improper political contributions and foreign payments. Later, the FCC also charged that the RKO stations had improperly billed advertisers for $6 million in TV spots that never ran.

With all the troubles facing GenCorp, the Disney team hoped that they could buy the Los Angeles and New York stations cheaply. Owning a television station—especially a station located in a major city—would be a tremendous boon for the company's syndication operation. Armed with a television station, Disney could exercise firmer control over its broadcasting operations by airing its own cartoon shows and reruns. An important factor in the company's desire to buy a station was that television stations, unlike record companies and movie studios, are very difficult to start from scratch. The FCC limits the number of stations on the air by granting licenses, and most of the airwaves were already too crowded. "We probably analyzed every group of stations out there," said Rich Frank.

RKO's stations held tremendous potential. The New York station, WOR, served the country's largest market, with the potential to reach nearly 7 percent of the nation's 84 million TV households. The Los Angeles station, KHJ, served the second-largest market, with some 5 percent of TV households. Even with the myriad regulatory problems the station faced, GenCorp's financial staff told William Reynolds, the company should be able to get $400 million for the New York station and at least $300 million for the Los Angeles station.

The prices were far too high for Disney but not, apparently, for MCA and Westinghouse. GenCorp's investment bankers, Kidder, Peabody & Co. Inc., had been making the rounds to potential buyers. In November 1985, Westinghouse bid $307 million for KHJ. Three months later, MCA Inc. bid $387 million for WOR. Both deals had to be approved by the FCC. For MCA, the approval proved no problem, and nine months later the station's ownership changed hands.

The situation with the Los Angeles station was more complicated. As part of the deal, Fidelity Television Inc., the group that had initially challenged the KHJ license in 1965, was to get $98 million of the selling price to drop its litigation. GenCorp would get the other $209 million. Fidelity chairman Bill Simon had approved the deal, but FCC staffers were still concerned that GenCorp would be getting more than it should from Westinghouse.

A year after Westinghouse first agreed to the deal, the regulatory delay forced it to pull out. Westinghouse's decision had been rumored for weeks—and during those weeks, Disney president Frank Wells had been courting Bill Simon. Simon, Wells reasoned, was the key to the deal. If the 76-year-old Simon agreed to the deal, Wells figured, he could get the FCC to go along as well. "I took it as a project to get to know Bill Simon," Wells said.

Wells and Simon spent hours at Wells's home, talking over the history of Simon's quest for the KHJ license. In early March 1987, a month after Westinghouse had pulled out, Wells and Simon started talking price. At the time, Simon was in Washington, and Wells was in Orlando, looking over progress on construction of the Disney-MGM Studios

Theme Park. Wells was expected at home for the 55th birthday dinner that Luanne Wells had planned for her husband. Instead, Frank Wells headed for Washington.

Simon and GenCorp chairman Reynolds had been battling since the Westinghouse deal fell apart. Before heading to Washington, Wells called Roger Wollenberg, GenCorp's Washington-based attorney, to ask him to set up a meeting between Reynolds, Simon, and Wells. Wollenberg, a partner with the Washington firm of Wilmer, Cutter & Pickering, called Reynolds, who told him that he had a dinner scheduled for that evening in Akron but could make it for a half-day session.

The meeting took place in a fifth-floor conference room at the Wilmer, Cutter office near Georgetown. Wells said that Disney was willing to pay $320 million, slightly more than the Westinghouse offer. Most of the added money would go to the 52 investors in Simon's group, which included the estate of the late actress Donna Reed. To guarantee the deal, even in the event of a lengthy FCC review, however, Wells insisted that GenCorp accept a letter of credit for the entire $320 million in the event the FCC refused to approve the deal.

Reynolds and Simon accepted the offer and Disney announced the deal on March 9, 1987. The price was more than Disney had wanted to pay, but MCA also was interested in the station, and Wells wanted to head off the rival company. The Disney executives also figured that having a TV station in Los Angeles would give Disney a valuable way to promote Disneyland to schoolkids when they came home in the afternoons. Disney's contract with Murdoch's KTTV station in LA to air two of its afternoon cartoon shows, *DuckTales* and *Chip 'n Dale*, would soon expire. Within a year of buying KHJ, Disney was airing its cartoons on its own station as *The K-Mouse Hour*, advertising birthday parties at Disneyland along with Disney videocassettes and consumer products.

When Disney took control, the station was generating about $10 million a year in profits but was attracting only a minuscule audience. To alter its image, the company renamed the station K-CAL. The station's real problem, however, was its poor programming. Disney's cartoon shows helped lift the afternoon ratings, but the station was forced to spend large sums in order to line up reruns of shows like *Who's the Boss* for the key 7:00 P.M. evening slot. For prime time, Disney launched a bold experiment. Spending $30 million, Disney increased its news staff from 38 to 149 people and upgraded its equipment to offer a solid three-hour news block each evening.

A year after Disney bought the station, it had still not risen significantly in the ratings. Although its children's block handily won the afternoon audiences, prime-time viewers were slow to find the three-hour news programs. By late 1990, there were rumors in the broadcasting industry that Disney was considering substituting movies for the all-news evening format.

❖

On May 17, 1990, a harried Rich Frank began scrambling to put together a prime-time television special. Muppet creator Jim Henson had died the day before of a massive bacterial infection. Nine months earlier, the Walt Disney Company had agreed to pay Henson nearly $150 million in Disney stock for the rights to Kermit, Miss Piggy, and the rest of the Muppet characters. As part of the deal, Henson himself had agreed to a 10-year contract to work with Disney on TV shows and films.

With Henson's sudden death, the deal, which had not yet been signed, fell into uncertainty. Now, Disney executives began trying to put together a memorial for Henson in the form of a TV special. Longtime Henson collaborator Frank Oz agreed to direct the Disney special, which would use the Muppet characters in short film pieces. CBS was interested, as was NBC. Eisner, who had been out of town at the time of Henson's death, called New York to discuss the project with Henson's widow. A day into the planning, she decided against doing the show.

Henson and Eisner had met for lunch at the Bel Air Hotel in Los Angeles nearly a year before Henson's death. The creator of the Muppets knew Eisner from Eisner's ABC days, when Henson had made a pair of pilots for Muppet shows that never aired. Henson, tired of the administrative burden of running his growing company, wanted to sell his operation to Disney. To Eisner, the deal represented the opportunity to buy a library of five feature films starring the Muppets, as well as a total of nearly 300 episodes of three television series, *The Muppets*, *Fraggle Rock*, and *Muppet Babies*.

In many ways, the Muppet deal was a classic Disney acquisition. The Muppets were irreplaceable assets, characters that had been created by Henson's genius and elevated to their current popularity through years of nurturing. They were not the kinds of assets that could be created by forming a new division of Disney or giving an assignment to existing creative personnel.

Even before Henson's death, however, the deal had problems. Disney's animation people and the Muppet creator frequently disagreed over how to handle his characters. After his death, negotiations with Henson's five children bogged down completely. Henson, separated from his wife, had made provision for his company to go to his five children. But Henson's death saddled his children with huge tax bills. Combined with the generous payments Jim Henson had promised several of his key staffers, the kids faced sharply reduced payments from the sale.

Disney ultimately added more than $50 million in cash payments to make up the difference. But in the course of cataloging the new company's assets, Disney also learned that Henson had licensed the Muppet name for stores in Canada and elsewhere, diminishing Disney's exclusive rights to the characters. Negotiations with Skaden Arps, the Hensons' New York–based law firm, dragged on for months before the Henson children pulled out of the deal just after Thanksgiving in 1990. Disney, which had spent $40 million to put 3-D movies and a stage show at its theme parks, continued to negotiate a separate agreement to maintain those attractions.

❖

The Henson deal was the kind of acquisition to which Michael Eisner, Frank Wells, and Gary Wilson were attracted. Comparatively inexpensive, it would have been an asset that Disney could not easily duplicate. More important, perhaps, it would have had ongoing value for the company. Disney could have used the Muppets to enhance its other properties. Syndicated programming using the Muppets could have been aired, and Muppet rides could have been developed for the theme parks.

For the most part, Disney's acquisitions have been guided as much by price as by whether they will fit into the existing framework of the company. In 1988, the company paid $61 million for Childcraft, a New Jersey company that owned two of the biggest mail-order lists in the country. Building similar lists might have taken Disney years. Acquiring Childcraft's lists enabled the company to embark immediately upon an aggressive campaign to market its consumer products through mail-order catalogs.

However, Disney could also afford to be choosy. In 1989, the company turned down the chance to buy the troubled Cineplex Odeon theater chain because its price was too high. The same year, Disney had been offered Harcourt Brace Jovanovich's six theme parks, including its four Sea World parks. Eisner and Wells were intrigued by the idea of the Sea World parks, especially the one in Orlando, but First Boston, Harcourt's adviser, was asking $1.8 billion for the parks. Even when the asking price was dropped to $1.1 billion, Disney refused.

Eventually, beer company Anheuser-Busch, which also owns Busch Gardens, bought the six parks for just under $1.2 billion. Disney's decision to reject the Harcourt deal had boiled down to one fundamental question: Were the Sea World properties so unique that Disney could not create something similar or better, and at a lower price? At the time of the offer, Disney's Imagineers unit had already begun to plan the company's own version of a sea park and had chosen the old Wrather property in Long Beach, California, as its likely first site. The park was to feature audio-animatronic sea animals and water rides, and the idea was that eventually a similar one would be built in Orlando.

"Any concepts we had in mind would have just blown Sea World away," says Larry Murphy. "We just decided that we would have to spend so much energy just trying to make it Disney that it wasn't worth the effort."

CHAPTER

Hollywood Shuffle

To millions of American women, the sight of Patrick Swayze's seductive movements in the 1987 film *Dirty Dancing* was the stuff of daydreams. For Vestron Pictures, a tiny video company in Stamford, Connecticut, it was the ticket to box office nirvana. Set to a sultry 1960s sound track, the low-budget film grossed more than $160 million worldwide. For a brief while, it also propelled Vestron to unaccustomed heights as a major box office competitor.

But only a year later, the dancing—dirty or otherwise—at Vestron had stopped. In a mad dash to battle with the major studios, Vestron had geared up to produce 20 films a year. It signed stars like Jeff Goldblum, Jamie Lee Curtis, and Geena Davis. But Vestron never had another *Dirty Dancing*. Instead, deep in debt and facing huge production costs, the company drifted toward bankruptcy.

The Vestron experience was hardly unique. As Hollywood entered the latter part of the 1980s, it had become a graveyard for movie upstarts. The same companies that had so aggressively tapped Wall Street and the junk bond markets in the early 1980s were now struggling to avoid bankruptcy. The emergence of Twentieth Century Fox and Disney as major film studios had squeezed companies like De Laurentiis Entertainment and the Cannon Group. Created to make cheap movies to feed a voracious video market that the majors were now dominating, many smaller companies were on the verge of insolvency.

The law of Hollywood has always been that smaller companies flourish during the boom times. And they fail when things get tighter. The independents that made B movie horror and sex films in the 1960s fell from grace when TV networks began to air their own more graphic and violent films. In the late 1980s, history was repeating itself—only this time it was the major studios, eager to make action films as well as movies laden with special effects, that took over from the Cannons and the Vestrons.

Sitting in their newly redecorated white suites on the third floor of the Animation Building, Michael Eisner and Jeffrey Katzenberg could see the face of Hollywood changing. The industry, which had combined to produce more than 530 films in 1987, was scheduled to produce fewer than 480 in 1989. And the films that were getting made were going to cost far more money to produce. The average cost of making a film, $14 million when the two arrived at Disney, was fast approaching $25 million. Increasingly, studios were spending $50 million and more in hopes of achieving box office success. Smaller, less wealthy companies were doomed to continue to fail.

Disney itself was no longer immune to the explosion in film budgets. Its producers still ruthlessly policed costs on any project the company undertook, helping to keep the average costs of making its films below $20 million. But each year Disney's average budget crept closer to the industry average. More important, in their quest to retain box office supremacy, Michael Eisner and Jeffrey Katzenberg hadn't flinched when the costs of both *Who Framed Roger Rabbit* and *Dick Tracy* had climbed to $50 million. With the promotional costs added in, each of the films had cost more than $100 million to release.

The changing economics of the movie industry had increasingly dominated the weekly dinner that Katzenberg and Eisner scheduled to discuss studio issues. In 1988, the studio would be producing 12 new films, the maximum number that both Eisner and Katzenberg believed could be produced by one studio without sacrificing quality. The studio was scheduled to produce just as many in 1989. (Counting reissues of older films, Disney released 14 films in 1988 and 13 in 1989).

At the time, Disney was in the midst of its best year ever. *Three Men and a Baby,* which had been released during the Thanksgiving weekend in 1987, had earned more than $167 million. *Who Framed*

Roger Rabbit and *Good Morning, Vietnam* had each sold more than $100 million in tickets. Altogether, the company captured an industry-leading 20 percent of the box office. By the end of the summer, the studio unit would generate $825 million in revenues from its films, nearly 50 percent more than 1987.

The studio was already well into development for 1989 and 1990. Negotiations had just been completed for *Dick Tracy*, which was due to start production in early 1989. Australian director Peter Weir had been signed to direct *Dead Poets Society*, the story of a private boys' school that would star Robin Williams. Tom Schulman, who had written the script for *Dead Poets Society*, had just finished the script for *Teenie Weenies*, a comedy about an absentminded professor whose invention shrinks his children to microscopic size. (The movie would later be retitled *Honey, I Shrunk the Kids.*)

Dining at Morton's in LA in the summer of 1988, Eisner and Katzenberg were already discussing the next step. Disney's studio operation wasn't capable of producing more than a dozen new films each year. With Disney's near maniacal demand for total hands-on control, trying to make more than that 12 or 13 new films in one year would stretch Disney's creative executives too thin. Already, there were signs that the heavy production load was forcing Disney to turn out lower-quality films. In 1988 alone, the studio was preparing to release *The Rescue* and *Heartbreak Hotel*, two films that Disney executives feared would likely bomb.

As Katzenberg and Eisner saw it, the fallout of smaller studios provided an opening for companies like Walt Disney, which had built strong followings among theater chain owners. By 1989, in fact, the country's theaters were projected to have more than 22,500 screens, nearly double the number a decade earlier. To fill the added screens, Katzenberg proposed to Eisner that Disney create a second movie label—a mirror image to the company's successful Touchstone Pictures label—staffed with a handful of Touchstone executives and a dozen newly hired production executives. By late summer, Eisner had agreed.

Disney would be treading on relatively shaky ground. Studios that had tried to launch second film labels had routinely failed. In the most recent such attempt, Columbia's sister company, Tri-Star, had a sprinkling of hits like *The Natural* and *Short Circuit*. Tri-Star, however, never built much of a track record. Likewise, MGM was never the same company after it merged with United Artists in 1981, bringing the two studios under one roof.

Columbia and MGM/UA had failed, Katzenberg and Eisner believed, because they had relied on outside producers to make their films, often sacrificing quality for quantity. Disney could avoid that problem, both men agreed, by putting one of their top Touchstone executives in charge of the new unit. As they had done with Touchstone, Disney executives would supervise every aspect of the project, from the initial script to the final edit.

Jeffrey Katzenberg was already sitting on top of an uneasy hierarchy. Almost from the first month he was at Disney, Katzenberg had relied heavily on two top production executives, Ricardo Mestres and David Hoberman, to ferret out story ideas and oversee production. Mestres, a 28-year-old Harvard graduate, had come with Katzenberg from Paramount. The 34-year-old Hoberman, who had worked with television producer Norman Lear, joined Disney in early 1985 after three years as a film agent for the ICM Agency.

Both were tough-minded executives. On top of that, they were intensely competitive, each eager to find the next *Three Men and a Baby* for the studio. By mid-1988, the two men were openly jockeying with one another. The competition between the two had gotten so heated, in fact, that both Katzenberg and Eisner worried that one or the other might eventually leave to join another studio. A few months earlier, Katzenberg had elevated Ricardo Mestres to the presidency of Touchstone Pictures and had given Hoberman the responsibility of increasing the number of live-action films that the company could release under its old Walt Disney Pictures banner.

By late 1988, Eisner and Katzenberg were prepared to launch the new Disney film unit under the name Hollywood Pictures. The name was the same as that of the film company the two men had contemplated launching in 1984 in a partnership with ABC Television. Ironically, Eisner held the rights to the name, which he had registered with the California secretary of state just before joining Disney in 1984.

The new film company would be modeled on Touchstone. Under the plan, by 1992 Eisner wanted Touchstone and Hollywood Pictures to each be producing a dozen films a year. Like Touchstone, Hollywood Pictures would share a simple formula: light, bright adult entertainment with finely honed story lines and ruthlessly tight budgets.

The two labels also gave Disney the chance to give Hoberman and Mestres their own separate film companies. Under the new setup, Hoberman would be given control of both the Touchstone Pictures and the Walt Disney label. The new picture unit would go to Ricardo Mestres.

❖

Like Michael Eisner and Jeffrey Katzenberg, Ricardo Mestres had come to Hollywood from a background of wealth and privilege. The son of a partner in the prestigious New York law firm of Sullivan & Cromwell, Mestres attended Exeter prep school and Harvard University. But even at an early age, Mestres was smitten with Hollywood. During his junior year at Harvard, he wrote to Don Simpson, then Paramount's head of production, to apply for a job.

Hired during the summer of 1981, Mestres returned after graduation to a full-time job at Paramount. By 1984, he was put in charge of supervising production for *Beverly Hills Cop*. When Eisner and Katzenberg left Paramount to go to Walt Disney Productions, Mestres was one of the first Paramount executives to join them. Katzenberg had virtually trained Mestres, a baby-faced executive with a full head of curly brown hair and an infectious smile. Like Katzenberg, Mestres worked tirelessly at making calls to agents and actors. And, like Katzenberg, Mestres could turn cold and unforgiving when things went badly. Pictures under his supervision were tightly focused and even more tightly controlled.

When Eisner and Katzenberg put Mestres in charge of Hollywood Pictures in late 1988, Touchstone Pictures had two dozen production executives and a small army of business executives, lawyers, and accountants responsible for putting the deals together. On February 1, 1989, Mestres left the Animation Building and set up shop in a suite of offices in the less plush Roy O. Disney Building across Mickey Way. Along with him, Mestres brought one production executive, four lawyers, two accountants, and six businesspeople. Perhaps more importantly, he also took a half dozen projects that he had been working on at Touchstone Pictures.

Mestres's Touchstone projects included a script by Broadway playwright Neil Simon, *The Marrying Man*, and the script for *One Good Cop*, the story of a New York policeman named as guardian for his dead partner's three young daughters. One of the first calls Mestres made after moving to his new office was to talent agent Bill Block, who represented Kim Basinger. Mestres wanted Basinger to play the sexy lounge singer in *The Marrying Man*.

In February 1990, Mestres had Basinger for $2.5 million. Alex Baldwin was signed for $1.5 million to play opposite her. Mestres also began negotiations with the agents representing *Batman* star Michael Keaton to play the lead in *One Good Cop*. The Disney executive also bought his first script since moving over to head Hollywood Pictures.

For $150,000 he bought a script written by a pair of first-time screenwriters, Jill Mazursky and Jeffrey Abrams. The script was for a project called *Filofax*, about a con man who accidentally finds the date book of an uptight business executive and then assumes the executive's identity. *Filofax*, later retitled *Taking Care of Business*, was scheduled to be the first film to be released by Hollywood Pictures. In May, however, Katzenberg authorized Mestres to pay $400,000 for the script for *Arachnophobia*, a horror/comedy about spiders written by Don Jakoby, a former physics doctoral candidate. *Arachnophobia* was an expensive experiment for The Walt Disney Company. Eisner and Katzenberg had resisted making horror-type films, especially those that would carry expensive special effects and a lofty production budget.

Arachnophobia, they knew, would have both. Initially estimated to cost $18 million, the budget for the film had crept up to nearly $20 million even before the film went into production. Mestres assigned the project to Ted Field and Robert Cort, the producers who had worked with Mestres in making *Three Men and a Baby* and *Cocktail* for Touchstone Pictures. Within weeks, however, Mestres brought in Steven Spielberg to take over the special-effects-laden project.

Spielberg brought with him an even heftier price tag. Before long, the film's cost had moved up to $25 million. In addition, Spielberg demanded a large piece of the profits for his Amblin Entertainment to join the project. The superstar producer gave the job of directing the film to his longtime partner Frank Marshall, who had produced *Raiders of the Lost Ark* and several other films that Spielberg directed. Spielberg's major accomplishment, it turned out, was to charm the Venezuelan government into allowing the film crew into the country's environmentally fragile La Gran Sabana rain forest region.

By the time Disney had brought *Arachnophobia* to Amblin Entertainment in early 1990, Hollywood Pictures had nearly 85 projects in the works, 12 of which were already in active development. Despite the blowup Disney recently had with *Three Men and a Baby* creator Coline Serreau, the studio agreed to make her latest film, *Randall & Juliet*, a comedy about a black man and a white woman. Richard Dreyfuss signed to star in *The Proud and the Free*, a movie about the American Revolution based on Howard Fast's novel. Veteran film producer David Permut signed a long-term deal with Mestres that included a film on the life of Richard Nixon and another involving the rescue of a football team at the Super Bowl.

Like Touchstone Pictures, Hollywood Pictures also signed its share of faded stars. One was 65-year-old TV star Angela Lansbury, whose hit TV show *Murder, She Wrote* was starting to show signs of age. Goldie Hawn, whose career had also taken a downturn, signed a long-term deal.

❖

During Team Disney's first years, the studio's publicists scampered to give reporters an update whenever Disney's streak of profitable films grew. By early 1988 the studio's publicity men could boast that 18 of the first 20 films produced by the Eisner-Katzenberg regime grossed more than $20 million at the box office—the level at which most films are judged successful.

But by early 1990, the Walt Disney Company was in its deepest slump since Michael Eisner and Jeffrey Katzenberg arrived. The studio had cleverly released *Dead Poets Society* and *Honey, I Shrunk the Kids* in the summer of 1989, siphoning off viewers who skipped the lines for action-filled blockbusters like *Batman* and *Ghostbusters II*. Together *Dead Poets Society* and *Honey, I Shrunk the Kids* sold more than $220 million worth of tickets. *The Little Mermaid*, released at Thanksgiving, was an instant hit as well. It would ultimately gross $84 million, the most ever for an animated film. Undermining its own success, though, Disney had also released box office bombs like *Cheetah*, *An Innocent Man*, and *Gross Anatomy*. Even its Christmas film, *Blaze*, a heavily promoted film about former Louisiana governor Earl Long and his infamous love affair with stripper Blaze Star, had bombed. Made for $25 million, the film returned less than $10 million to the studio. The new year hadn't started off much better. Only $1 million worth of tickets were sold for *Where the Heart Is*. After selling more tickets than any other studio in 1988, Disney had fallen to third behind Warner Brothers and Universal Pictures in 1989.

By late 1989, however, Disney executives were completing work on a film that Jeffrey Katzenberg had bought from Vestron. At the time, the Stamford company was eagerly selling off many scripts that it no longer had the money to turn into pictures. One of those was *3,000*, a dark story that featured prostitution, a drug overdose, and a cruel business executive who uses and then discards a kind-hearted hooker.

Jeffrey Katzenberg bought the script for $200,000 and turned it over to Garry Marshall. Eisner and Katzenberg knew Marshall from their Paramount days when Marshall had been the creator of the hit TV shows *Happy Days* and *Laverne and Shirley*. Later, he had switched to directing films, with mixed results. *The Flamingo Kid* and *Nothing in Common* were unqualified hits, but *Overboard*, a lame comedy he made for MGM in 1987, had fizzled. Marshall's first project for Disney had been *Beaches*, the Bette Midler drama that grossed more than $57 million in late 1988.

Marshall's first love, however, has always been comedy. And Katzenberg had told the *Happy Days* creator to rewrite the Vestron script to turn it into a comedy. Working with writer J. F. Lawton, Marshall's rewrite changed the script into a Pygmalion-type tale of a prostitute who woos and wins the heart of a business executive. Marshall and Lawton got rid of the drug overdose. In its place, the new script added shopping sprees on Rodeo Drive and champagne sipping in a bubble bath. Before long the name also changed, first to *Off the Boulevard* and later to *Pretty Woman*.

David Hoberman and Frank Marshall, mesmerized by Julia Roberts's performance in *Mystic Pizza*, signed her for the then bargain price of $350,000 to play the prostitute role. The contract was signed before Roberts hit the big time with *Steel Magnolias*, her 1989 hit. "Disney is very good at grabbing people just as they need a comeback or are on the way up," says Marshall. "Now, she's asking three, four times that."

Initially, Disney had wanted to cast Sean Connery in the lead role of the ironfisted corporate raider. When Roberts was signed, however, the search began for a younger actor to play opposite the sultry actress. To keep the film within the $15 million budget Disney had set, Marshall tested several second-tier actors who could be signed for around $300,000. *Dead Calm* star Sam Neal was tested, reading with Roberts, as was British rock star Murray Head. Comic actor Charles Grodin also did a test for the film. In the end, none had the kind of chemistry with Roberts that Marshall wanted. Three months before shooting was to begin, Katzenberg sent the script to Richard Gere in New York. Katzenberg, as a junior production executive at Paramount, had hired Gere for *An Officer and a Gentleman* in 1982. Seven years later, although Gere's career was on the skids, he could still command a $2 million salary. Marshall wanted him, though, and Disney executives hired him, sending the budget for the film to $17 million.

To keep costs under control, most of the film was to be shot inside a single set, designed to look like a Beverly Hills hotel room. The special Los Angeles police squad assigned to film companies cordoned off two blocks of Rodeo Drive in Beverly Hills in late summer for Marshall to shoot exterior scenes.

Shooting didn't always go smoothly. Marshall, a mercurial man, can be explosive when working on a film. He and David Hoberman disagreed frequently. Marshall had wanted to rewrite a scene that takes place in a lavish restaurant, which would have added $150,000 to the budget. Hoberman rejected the idea, as he did when Marshall wanted to add extras for a scene at a polo match. Disney insisted as well that Marshall reshoot the final scene, which buttressed the film's happy ending.

While Gary Marshall was on the set, Jeffrey Katzenberg was back in Burbank working on the sound track for the new film. Sound tracks have long been an effective way to promote films. The airtime that local radio stations give to the songs from a sound track can be like a free three-minute commercial for the movie. Increasingly, sound tracks were also becoming huge businesses in their own right. MCA, which distributed the sound tracks from many of Hollywood's studios, made nearly $20 million alone from *Down and Out in Beverly Hills*.

Jeffrey Katzenberg had been part of the Paramount team that put together the sound tracks for the hits *Saturday Night Fever* and *Grease* at Paramount. Each of the albums had "gone platinum," selling more than one million copies each. Katzenberg, therefore, considered himself an expert on putting together the songs that accompany films. But under the terms of the deals that Paramount, like other studios, got from record companies, film units traditionally received only a small part of the profits.

Katzenberg intended to change that, starting with *Pretty Woman*. The Disney studio head had been growing increasingly impatient with how Disney's sound tracks were being handled. The company had spent a fortune promoting the album that accompanied *Ruthless People*, but hadn't seen much profit although the film had been a huge hit. Disney had also paid $800,000 toward financing the *Cocktail* sound track. But Katzenberg felt that Electra Asylum Records, which had the contract to distribute the record, had failed to market it aggressively enough.

Katzenberg had also fumed over the way Atlantic Recording had handled the sound track for *Beaches*. Almost from the beginning, the Disney studio chief had battled with the record company, claiming that Atlantic hadn't marketed the sound track the way Disney would have done it. Katzenberg was especially upset when the record company chose to highlight and promote "Under the Boardwalk" as the lead single. Katzenberg had argued unsuccessfully that Midler's recording of "Wind Beneath My Wings" was the best cut on the album. Although "Wind" ended up becoming a Grammy winner and the album was a best-seller, Disney felt it hadn't helped their movie much. Katzenberg didn't intend to make that same mistake with *Pretty Woman*. The Disney studio chief called record company executives interested in distributing the album and told them that Disney intended to be an equal player in all marketing decisions. The studio would put up $1 million to cover the costs of both producing and marketing the record. But, in return, Disney insisted on being in on all marketing decisions. Under the deal Katzenberg offered, his company would also get half the profits, to be figured after the record company collected its costs for distributing the album.

Accustomed to calling the shots on the distribution and marketing of sound tracks, most of the major record companies passed on the deal. In the past, they had all steadfastly refused to allow studios to share in the decision making or to take such a large piece of the profits. But EMI Records, which had a checkered past with sound tracks, desperately wanted this one.

EMI agreed to Disney's terms. It also lined the album with its own stars, including some heavyweights like Natalie Cole. But it also added a few relative newcomers like Lauren Wood. Disney insisted, however, that the album also include the Roy Orbison classic *Pretty Woman*. A Disney production executive had arbitrarily picked the Orbison song to accompany a rough cut of the film that was shown to Disney executives two months earlier. The song had obvious marketing appeal, Katzenberg felt. It also prompted him to rename the film *Pretty Woman*.

In a move calculated to avoid the rush of big-budget summer films, Disney planned the release of *Pretty Woman* for the spring. The promotional campaign kicked off in February, however, with the release of singles from the *Pretty Woman* sound track. EMI released Natalie Cole's *Wild Women Do* to both rhythm-and-blues and top-40 stations. The advance promotion helped both the sound track and the movie. The sound track went on to become a best-seller, with more than two million copies sold.

The movie, released on March 23, 1990, grossed a robust $11.3 millon in its first weekend. By early June, it had grossed $133 million and was still showing on nearly 1,000 screens around the country.

Before the summer was over, *Pretty Woman* surpassed *Three Men and a Baby* to become Disney's top-selling movie, and it was still in movie theaters as Thanksgiving approached. When it was through its theatrical run, *Pretty Woman* had sold more than $177 million in tickets in the United States and more than $200 million more overseas. At the time, only *E. T.* and *Indiana Jones and the Temple of Doom* had sold more tickets overseas.

❖

Almost single-handedly, *Pretty Woman* pulled Disney out of its nine-month slump. By the end of the summer, the studio was once again the top-ranked studio in Hollywood. *Dick Tracy* hadn't done as well as industry experts predicted, but it still grossed $105 million. Including two films from its new Hollywood Pictures unit, Disney released nine films during the summer, putting one of its films on 30 percent of the country's screens during the hottest box office season of the year. The rush of added films fattened Disney's balance sheet—the film unit took in $300 million in tickets during the summer months, $100 million more than its films had taken in during its banner 1988 summer. Even so, Disney had its share of disappointments. Although profitable, *Betsy's Wedding*, starring Alan Alda and Molly Ringwald, grossed only $19 million. At the outset, at least, Hollywood Pictures was also something of a disappointment. *Taking Care of Business*, its second release, grossed only $19 million.

The biggest disappointment of the summer, however, was *Arachnophobia*. Hollywood Pictures's first film grossed $52 million. Disney executives had predicted that the Spielberg-produced film would rival *Dick Tracy* in popularity. In an unusual mistake for its usually surefooted marketing team, Disney failed to fashion the kind of promotional effort that the studio had come to expect.

At first intending to promote *Arachnophobia* as a "thrill-omedy," Disney's marketers prepared trailers and television commercials that played up comical scenes of John Goodman as an off-beat exterminator. Two weeks after the film was released, however, Disney abruptly switched gears. Its new TV spots showed movie audiences recoiling in horror from the movie's most graphic spider scenes. Ultimately, the Disney marketing team's slow transformation proved too late. Although marginally profitable, *Arachnophobia* was nowhere near the blockbuster Disney had predicted.

❖

Disney had more to contend with than just disappointing films. By 1990, the age of superstar salaries was firmly entrenched. Sylvester Stallone could command $16 million for a single film, Tom Cruise more than $10 million. Even directors had become financial "superstars" in their own right. Steven Spielberg turned down $5 million from MGM/UA to direct

Rain Man, deciding instead to direct his own project, *Always.* By 1990, Hollywood had even seen its first $3 million script, a spy thriller called *Basic Instinct,* written by Joe Eszterhas, author of *Jagged Edge.*

Whether Team Disney liked it or not, it was being swept up in the frenzy. Not only had it cost the company $25 million to make *Arachnophobia,* but Disney was also forced to give Steven Spielberg a large piece of the profits. The studio only had to pay Tom Cruise $3 million to make *Cocktail,* but the young superstar also signed a "first dollar" deal—giving him 10 percent of Disney's revenue, or about $7 million more. Even *Innocent Man,* not one of the company's major films, had cost nearly $20 million for the company to make. Advertising costs had also skyrocketed, forcing Disney to pay nearly $90 million to promote its films in 1989, 50 percent more than for the same number of films in 1988.

In many ways, Disney's own success had contributed to its problems. In the mid-1980s, the company had been able to sign faded stars like Bette Midler and Richard Dreyfuss to cheap contracts. The hit movies those stars had made for Disney had revived their careers, enabling them to increase their contract demands. After starring in three hit films and earning less than $1 million for each of them, Midler negotiated a 1987 contract that guaranteed her $3 million a picture along with a generous piece of the profits. In addition, Disney agreed to make films that Midler wanted to produce herself. The three stars of *Three Men and a Baby* also signed generous contracts for the 1990 sequel, *Three Men and a Little Lady.* The deals ballooned the budget for the sequel to $30 million, more than twice the $13 millon it had cost Disney to make the original only three years earlier. Problems with coming up with an acceptable script eventually delayed the film's production schedule by over a year.

The combination of higher budgets and a string of lackluster films had conspired to stifle the profitability of Disney's studio operation. In 1989, Jeffrey Katzenberg's unit had profits of $256 million, a 38 percent hike over its 1988 earnings. But for the first time in three years, the studio's profit margin stopped growing. (In 1990, in fact, profit margins for the studio unit would decline to 14 percent from 16 percent the year before.)

No one was more concerned about the trend than Roland Betts. The Silver Screen founder had raised nearly $1 billion for Disney's filmmaking unit in three separate limited partnerships. The third offering, which closed in February 1988, raised $183 million. But almost immediately afterward, the New York lawyer began to have problems with some of the budgets for Disney's films. After forwarding Disney the money it needed to make the first 30 films Eisner and Katzenberg produced, Betts refused to provide the $21 million that Disney has asked the partnership to provide in the spring of 1988 to help them make *New York Stories.*

Woody Allen had developed the film for Orion Pictures, the studio for whom the one-time Greenwich Village comedian made most of his films. The concept of the movie itself was novel, with three separate directors—Allen, Martin Scorcese, and Francis Coppola—each contributing separate 36-minute segments. But to make the film the studio was required to give each of the directors a huge piece of the profits. Despite its longtime association with Woody Allen, Orion decided against making the film.

Katzenberg had been wooing Allen for years, and would see the director whenever Katzenberg was in New York on business. The Disney executive quickly picked up the project. But to make the film Disney was required to make lucrative deals with each of the directors. Together, the three would get more than 50 percent of whatever revenues the film might generate, Betts calculated. That was too rich for Silver Screen. "All of a sudden you have three directors who are just sucking the revenues out of the film," Betts explained later. "There was no way that we could make any money out of it."*

Increasingly, Betts was walking away from films that Disney was making. Silver Screen had refused to participate in the financing for *Stella,* a remake of the 1937 Barbara Stanwyk film *Stella Dallas* that Katzenberg agreed to make after Bette Midler brought it to him. Midler wanted to both act and to produce it. Betts balked when he learned that the Samuel Goldwyn Company continued to hold the foreign rights to the film. He also refused to participate on *Arachnophobia* because of the huge percentage Disney had surrendered to Steven Spielberg to serve as its executive producer. He walked away as well from *Three Men and a Little Lady* because of its price tag. "What good is it if a film makes $200 million and you never see a dime," Betts concluded.

By late 1989, Disney and Roland Betts were increasingly at odds. For nearly six years, the money Roland Betts raised had provided the financial safety net that Michael Eisner and Jeffrey Katzenberg needed to make their films. With Silver Screen paying all of the production costs, Disney was largely protected from huge box office losses. But to win that

---

*The film sold a woeful $11 million in tickets, but Katzenberg did sign Allen, along with Bette Midler, to do the film *Scenes from a Mall.*

protection, Disney executives felt that they had been forced to agree to terms tilted largely in favor of Silver Screen. Under the first Silver Screen agreement, Disney was entitled to receive 25 percent of the revenues it received from any film the limited partnership underwrote. But Disney was also required to repay Silver Screen for any losses on films that didn't recover the partnership's investment within five years.

Betts had negotiated the first Silver Screen partnership with Frank Wells and Ron Cayo, a holdover from the Ron Miller era. Since then, Gary Wilson had taken over the negotiations for the two following offerings. Betts and Wilson got along personally, and Wilson would often visit the Silver Screen founder at his New Mexico home. But the talks were often tense. Wilson demanded more money for Disney. Eventually he won an added $500,000 development fee for any film Disney produced, along with the right for Disney to assess Silver Screen a 13 percent overhead charge for each film produced — an amount that could add up to $7 million for some of Disney's more expensive films.

Silver Screen IV, the 1988 offering, contained only enough money to take Disney through mid-1991. Wilson and Betts met in late 1989 to talk about a new Silver Screen offering to provide the added funds Disney would need to cover the company's expanded production schedule. Disney needed at least $600 million more, Wilson told Betts. But before it would sign the deal, Disney insisted that Silver Screen increase the overhead payment and eliminate the provision requiring payments for films that lost money.

Looming over the talks as well was a potential added payment that Disney could still owe Silver Screen. Under a provision in each of the three limited partnership agreements, Disney had the option to buy back, beginning in 1995, Silver Screen's interest in any film the partnership invested in. The amount of the payment was based on a complicated formula that took into account future revenues the film could earn from syndication, foreign, or other sales. From where Roland Betts was sitting, that could mean tens of millions of dollars. If he and Disney didn't agree on a price, however, a set of appraisers would determine the eventual payment. And if Disney refused to meet the price, Betts was quick to add, "We'll just sell it to the highest bidder.

The talks didn't go well. Betts, worried that potential investors had soured on putting their money into the entertainment industry in the wake of big budgets and uncertain box offices, bought a piece of the

Texas Rangers baseball team and was contemplating other investments. Moreover, he could see the direction that Disney's film performance was taking, and was no longer sure that it would continue to be as profitable.

Eisner also knew that he could still get good terms in Japan. Increasingly, Japanese investors, lured by the popularity of internationally known American film stars, were flocking to Hollywood. In 1989, Japanese electronics giant Sony Corp. had paid $3.4 billion for Columbia Pictures. Another Japanese electronics manufacturer, Victor Company of Japan (JVC), had invested $100 million with producer Larry Gordon.

With business booming at Tokyo Disneyland, Eisner also knew that Disney's name carried a special allure for Japanese investors. Before Thanksgiving in 1989, he decided to test the Japanese waters himself. Along with Richard Nanula and Mike Montgomery from Disney's finance staff, Eisner had made the rounds of Tokyo's largest banks and securities firms in search of the same kind of deal that Gary Wilson had offered Roland Betts.

Within a few months, Montgomery, Disney's assistant treasurer, lined up a consortium headed by giant Japanese stock firm Yamaichi Securities to raise $600 million to finance the company's upcoming slate of films. Operating under the name Touchwood Limited Partners, the Japanese stock house would raise $180 million by selling units to individual investors. Yamaichi would then borrow the remaining $420 million from a group of banks headed by Citicorp. For Disney, the new partnership had some key advantages over the Silver Screen deal. Under the agreement, Disney would receive 65 percent of the film's profits—as opposed to the 37.5 percent it got from Silver Screen. Moreover, Disney took 17.5 percent off the top for its overhead—3 percent more than Betts gave it. And while Betts wasn't required to finance any film above $20 million, the Japanese offering allowed Disney free rein up to $35 million for each of the 20 films planned. Disney was also able to finance two films each with $50 million budgets.

One of the Japanese stock firms that had rejected Disney's overtures was Nomura Securities, another giant Tokyo firm. At the time, Nomura's U.S.-based subsidiary, Nomura Babcock & Brown, was negotiating with Ted Field and Robert Cort, the two producers who had made *Three Men and a Baby* and other films for Disney. The talks led to a deal in December 1989 in which Nomura agreed to underwrite future projects by Interscope Communications, the two producers' company. The only requirement was that Disney also match Nomura's investment.

By the spring of 1990, Cort and Nomura Babcock & Brown's managing director, Richard Koffey, were negotiating with Jeffrey Katzenberg and Helene Hahn. Disney agreed to match the Japanese investment in return for half of the revenue from any film Interscope made for it. Initially each side would kick in $50 million to $100 million, but the deal could eventually be huge. Under the three separate contracts signed, Disney could ultimately raise as much as $250 million for Interscope films.

❖

The final details of both the Touchwood and Nomura deals weren't completed until September 1990. By then, Disney's studio operation was gearing up to produce the 24 to 30 films a year that Michael Eisner and Jeffrey Katzenberg envisioned. For the first time since the two Disney executives arrived in Burbank that meant joining the bidding war for Hollywood talent.

From the beginning, Disney had concentrated on developing its own projects, with a stable of in-house writers writing scripts and first-time directors putting them before the camera. With so many films to churn out at once, however, the Disney formula slowly changed. Like other studios, usually reticent Disney executives were forced to pay for high-priced scripts. Working with *Alien* producer Gale Ann Hurd, Hoberman paid nearly $500,000 for the script to *Ultimatum,* a political thriller, outbidding Warner Brothers and Paramount Pictures in the process. Disney also paid $500,000 for *Hell Bent . . . and Back,* another hotly contested script.

The high-priced bids were an acknowledgment that theater audiences had come to expect big, glossy films like *Die Hard* and *Total Recall.* Unwilling to pay the huge costs of making big-budget films, Disney had tested the market—unsuccessfully—by distributing an independently produced war film, *Fire Birds.* Now, Katzenberg realized, if Disney were to continue to do battle with other major studios, that meant supplementing its traditional lower-budget comedies with more than a few of its own big-budget projects. To help Disney do that, the Disney executive signed *Rambo* producer Andy Vajna, a man renowned for his ability to make budget-busting films.

Vajna is a man for whom $60 million films are commonplace. So to keep a lid on its own costs, Disney limited its exposure to under $20 million a film. Under its deal with Vajna, Disney agreed to pay only half the costs of any film, up to a maximum $40 million budget. Disney also would pay all distribution costs in the United States, but would not get a share in any foreign sales for the film. Along with his contract, Vajna brought with him two big-budget projects, *The Stand* and *Princess of Mars*.

Disney signed other big-budget projects as well. Larry Gordon, whose films have included such expensive ones as *Predator* and *48 Hours*, signed to make *Rocketeer*, a $35 million action film about a superhero who fights to keep a secret rocket out of the hands of the Nazis. The studio also signed several highly paid actors. Sylvester Stallone, whom Eisner had once signed to play the lead role in *Beverly Hills Cop* at Paramount, signed a $5 million deal to do a comedy called *Oscar* that John Landis would direct. Tom Hanks, whose price tag had soared since he did *Turner & Hooch* for Disney in 1989, returned to the studio to make a film called *Significant Other* with Debra Winger. Bill Murray and Richard Dreyfuss were signed to make *What About Bob?*, sending the costs of that film to nearly $30 million.

By the end of 1990, the ramp up of Disney's live-action film operation was nearing full throttle. More than 100 films were in various stages of production. And, with Silver Screen backing away from all but those films with modest budgets, Disney's costs were going up to $258 million from the $65 million two years earlier. Katzenberg reunited actor Dustin Hoffman and director Robert Benton, the duo who made the Academy Award–winning film *Kramer vs. Kramer*. This time the two would be working on a $40 million movie version of E. L. Doctrow's book *Billy Bathgate*.

At the same time, Jeffrey Katzenberg was spending increasing amounts of time with the animation unit that had been revived by *The Little Mermaid*. Working from a nondescript office building in Glendale, Disney's animators were completing the retelling of *Beauty and the Beast*, with the song writing team of Alan Menken and Howard Ashman providing the soundtrack. Menken and Ashman won an Academy Award in 1990 for *The Little Mermaid* soundtrack.

In addition to *Beauty and the Beast*, Katzenberg had lined up other animated features. He had signed Robin Williams to provide the comic voice of a large blue genie in *Aladdin*, and he had enlisted rock star Elton John to provide the soundtrack for an animated feature based in Africa, called *The Lion King*. Indeed, Katzenberg became so smitten with animation that he began collecting vintage cels from previous Disney films for his Beverly Hills home.

By late 1990, however, the Disney studio chief could see the direction the company was taking. Back from the annual Christmas vacation he took with his wife and two children, Katzenberg sat down to pen what later became known as "the Katzenberg memo." In 28 pages, the Disney film chief railed about the high costs of filmmaking and the toll it was taking on the company's balance sheet. (In fact, in 1990 the company would see profits from only five of the 13 live-action films it released that year, with only *Pretty Woman* providing significant profits of the five.)

In 1991, the company would make great strides to rein in its costs. Film budgets were cut nearly in half, as the company relied more heavily on the Japanese funds and the Andy Vajna deal. But, with Katzenberg and Eisner both spending less time on the live-action side, the company had fewer winning films. In 1991, Katzenberg signed Robert Duvall and Anne-Margret for a musical, *Newsies,* about an 1899 strike by newspaper boys against publishing giant William Randolph Hearst. The company signed Woody Allen and Bette Midler to make *Scenes from a Mall,* directed by *Down and Out* director Paul Mazursky, and signed Kathleen Turner to play a hard-boiled Chicago detective in *V. I. Warshawski.* All of them flopped miserably.

By 1991, however, Disney's animated films were on a roll. Home video revenue from *The Little Mermaid* and worldwide ticket sales for *Beauty and the Beast* combined to provided a tide of profits that hid the results of Disney's poorly performing live-action films. Yet at the time, Eisner's attention was also diverted, as he was looking toward Paris where the company was preparing to launch its most expensive project to date. Eventually, however, both the film unit and the new Paris theme park would take their toll on the company and its chairman.

15

CHAPTER

A Kingdom under Siege

In January 13, 1990, nearly 3,000 partygoers reveled at a black-tie dinner honoring the grand opening of the Swan Hotel. The hotel, like much of what Michael Eisner had brought to the Walt Disney Company in the previous five years, was a wonderful mixture of fantasy and profit-minded practicality. As guests approached, they could see a pair of 28-ton swans resting in turquoise splendor over the fast growing Walt Disney World complex. Heroic seashell fountains sent streams of water into the air. Painted waves lapped at the windows. Inside, guests were greeted by two-dimensional potted palms and cutouts of parrots on perches holding lighting fixtures in their beaks.

The grand opening of the Swan Hotel that night was the highlight event of a four-day celebration that Disney's publicity crew, with their usual immodesty, had proclaimed "The Disney Decade." More than 1,500 reporters, their spouses, and even some of their children had been treated to a weeklong party, which had started in Anaheim, California. There the throng celebrated Disneyland's 35th anniversary with rock banks and three-story-high balloons in the shapes of Goofy, Roger Rabbit, and other Disney characters. At the Disneyland Hotel, Eisner, preceded by music and dancing girls, announced plans for nearly $300 million in new rides at the company's original theme park.

With even more fanfare than usual, Eisner also announced plans to move ahead with a second park in southern California, throwing open the competition between the cities of Long Beach and Anaheim for the anticipated $2 billion project. As if on cue, Anaheim mayor Fred Hunter bounded the steps from the audience to present to the Disney chairman a special proclamation in honor of "the partnership" his city had enjoyed for three decades with the company that Walt built.

As it turned out, the festivities at Anaheim were merely a warm-up. The press crew was transported in chartered jets to Orlando, accompanied by Disney characters and gallons of free cocktails. At the Disney MGM Studios Tour, the "Star Tours" ride was opened with help from George Lucas and *Star Wars* stars Mark Hamill and Carrie Fisher. Another star, Miami quarterback Dan Marino, officiated as a 30-ton turquoise dolphin was lifted atop the Dolphin Hotel that sits across a waterway from the Swan Hotel.

Accompanied this time by a dancing Roger Rabbit and Mickey Mouse, Eisner repeated his "Disney Decade" announcement at a Sunday morning breakfast in the Swan Hotel's green-and-pink ballroom. "We intend to do nothing less than reinvent the Disney theme park experience," the 47-year-old Eisner said as he began laying out plans for more than $5 billion worth of new projects. By the year 2000, company officials told the press, Disney expected to build four new parks, one each in Florida and Anaheim and two outside Paris. A fifth would be licensed in Japan. In all, Disney executives predicted, more than 100 million people would visit one of the Disney theme parks that would dot the world, nearly double the estimated 60 million "guests" who would go through the turnstiles in 1990 in Orlando, Anaheim, and Tokyo.

By then, Disney would be producing more than 30 pictures a year. Its consumer products division had grown to become a $1.6-billion-a-year enterprise, with its own mail-order operation and a 100-store Disney Store chain generating more than $200 million a year in revenues of its own. The company was moving into mainstream records and publishing, and had evolved into a major hotel operator with 30 hotels and over 26,000 rooms under the Disney name.

But fissures were already beginning to form just beneath the Disney facade of invincibility. Those cracks had begun to show in late 1990, as a nationwide recession and the Iraqi invasion of Kuwait had depressed the flow of tourists to Disney's parks in the fourth quarter. Disney could again report record earnings for the year, but for the first time in the

Eisner era the company failed to meet management's objective for 20 percent growth each year. In 1990, the company's earnings were up by 18 percent, to $824 million.

By 1991, Disney's six years of relentlessly upward earnings were over, and the Disney magic looked decidedly faded. The U.S. recession that had started in 1990 was quickly spreading to Europe and Asia. Fears of terrorist reprisals following the allied invasion of Iraq slashed air travel, and tourists were staying away from Disney's theme parks in droves. Revenues for Disney's parks fell by 5 percent and earnings by a whopping 31 percent. The theme parks' woes slashed Disney's overall earnings by 23 percent.

Worse yet, the diversified company that Eisner and Wells had struggled to create no longer looked in synch. The idea had always been that, by building up Disney's film studio and expanding both the theme parks and consumer products, the company would be all but immune from such a dramatic downturn. If the theme parks were struggling, the theory went, then earnings from the film studio would soften the decline.

This time, however, both the theme park unit and the studio were struggling at the same time. As Ricardo Mestres had feared, the turmoil on the set of *The Marrying Man* had carried over to the screen, and the film flopped badly when it was released in February. By then, nothing the studio touched seemed to work. Costs on *Billy Bathgate*, an adaption of the E. L. Doctorow best-seller, climbed from $25 million to $40 million. The studio spent nearly as much to make *The Rocketeer*, an action-adventure film from producer Larry Gordon. When they all flopped, Disney's live-action film unit was soon springing red ink. Only video sales of *Pretty Woman* and the classics *Jungle Book* and *Fantasia* kept the studio's earnings from falling as well. For the year, Katzenberg's crew earned $318 million, a scant 2 percent improvement over the previous year.

By late 1991, Disney's pixie dust was no longer spellbinding to Wall Street either. The company's stock price, which had jumped as high as $136 a share in late 1989, was soon trading at $86 by early 1991. The next year, as it turned out, would bring a new disaster. Twenty miles outside Paris the company was building a $4 billion theme park and resort on 4,800 acres of what had been a beanfield near the city of Marne-la-Vallée. To Eisner and Wells, the park represented planting the Disney flag on foreign shores. In the end, however, it became the company's biggest financial headache since the dark days of the early 1980s.

❖

Team Disney knew they were in trouble even before Euro Disney opened for business on April 12, 1992. Even while the company was negotiating terms with the French government for land and tax concessions five years earlier, placards denouncing the deal were springing up in the front of farmers' homes in the Ile-de-France region outside Paris where Disney wanted to locate the park and hotels. And in October 1989, when Disney launched a public stock offering in Europe to raise nearly $1 billion, things had gotten totally out of hand. To publicize the offering, Disney orchestrated a ceremony from the steps of the Paris Bourse, the French stock exchange. The podium was decorated with pictures of Donald Duck, Snow White, and other Disney characters.

Eisner and other Disney officials arrived at the ceremony in cars driven by actors dressed as Mickey Mouse and Pluto. A troop of Disney dancers, dressed in sedate red-and-white outfits, drew polite applause. In the crowd at the Bourse was a noisy group of 10 young Communist party members. Brandishing placards that said "Uncle Scrooge Go Home," the youths denounced the more than $6 billion in French government concessions. Instead, they argued, the money should go to education and the unemployed. As Eisner made the announcement, the Communists pelted the Disney executives with eggs and ketchup.

Despite the rude treatment, financing never proved to be a problem. A mixture of high finance and pure Disney-ana, the cover of the offering document issued by stock house S.G. Warburg included an artist's rendering of Cinderella's Castle, while Mickey, Minnie, and the rest of the Disney characters frolicked on the back. But the real sweetener was Warburg's incredibly rosy predictions. At the end of the first year, the offering document estimated, the park could generate nearly $1.1 billion in revenues and show a $400 million profit.

Priced at roughly $14 a share, the entire 42.9 million shares of the stock sold almost overnight. (Disney had a 49 percent interest in the project, worth $456 million more.) In the United States, the flurry of activity sent Disney's stock price up by $6 a share. In May 1990, less than eight months after raising $1 billion in the public offering, Disney raised another $770 million from a bond offering for the park.

The reasons for Wall Street's euphoria were clear enough. With operating profits of $400 million, Disney would collect $71 million in royalties and management fees even before its cut of the $55 million or so in dividends the new company was expected to pay. By the turn of the century, Warburg estimated, Disney would be collecting more than $766 million a year in management fees and royalties, on top of its dividend payouts.

Those numbers would prove to be hopelessly optimistic. By early 1990, 18 months into construction, costs were already starting to mount. Europeans, who had grown up in the shadows of great monuments and cathedrals, would never settle for anything less than the awe-inspiring, the Disney architects had argued to Eisner in the planning stages. The rides had to be bigger and better than any at Disneyland or Walt Disney World. Even the centerpiece castle in the Magic Kingdom had to be bigger and fancier than in the other parks. Initially estimated at $1.8 billion (or 10 billion francs), the park's price tag was on its way to being $157+ million higher.

Construction of the five hotels that would ring the park, estimated at $760 million, would eventually approach $1 billion. Unfamiliar with the French market, Disney made mistakes in selecting contractors, French construction-industry officials later said, with two general contractors filing for bankruptcy during construction. That forced Disney to pay twice for the work done by some subcontractors—once to the failed general contractors and again to the 20 or so smaller firms that carried out the work.

The problems with contractors alone added roughly $25 million to the costs. Disney also fiddled with the plans. A man-made lake in the center of the hotels, grew in size. So did the $165 million, 500-room Magic Kingdom Hotel, which would be built at the entrance of the park.

None of the added costs would have seemed unreasonable if the park had made money. Disney's marketing crew had done its part, signing up television stations in the United Kingdom, France, Holland, Scandinavia, and Australia to air a customized version of the Mickey Mouse Club that had run in the United States in the late 1950s, renamed "The Disney Club." To promote Disney, the show would typically be hosted by local talent and would include a half-hour animated series such as *DuckTales* or *Chip 'n Dale Rescue Rangers* dubbed into the foreign language. (By 1996, there would be 35 country-specific Disney clubs worldwide.)

For Christmas in 1989, Disney had joined with five networks to produce a $2 million Christmas special featuring Welsh singer Tom Jones and local celebrities from Germany, Italy, France, and elsewhere.

The stars may have been local, but the program was pure Disney: singer Julia Migenes warbled songs from Disney classics in front of the Eiffel Tower. One segment of the show took viewers from 15 European countries on a behind-the-scenes tour of construction work at Euro Disneyland.

But while Disney and its well-oiled publicity operation was stoking public opinion, a growing chorus of local intellectuals were deriding the new American import as nothing short of a "cultural Chernobyl," in the words of one. Protests continued during construction. And on opening day, local farmers, protesting French agricultural policies, threatened to block the entrance of the new park. The result was that, fearing traffic snarls or worse, many Parisians steered clear. Despite all the hoopla that Disney could muster, opening day fell short of the company's expectations when only about half the expected 60,000 people showed. "It wasn't the opening we may have wanted," Eisner recalled later.

Within months of the 1992 opening Disney's European executives were already projecting a $35 million deficit for the six-month initial fiscal year. Crowds were 5 percent below Disney's initial 11 million estimate for its first full year. For Disney, the results were financially distressing. The company would still book a $33 million gain on the royalties of Disney merchandise sold in 1992, and another $11.2 million from dividends and interest it held in the parent company, Euro Disney SCA. But Disney quietly agreed to defer its share of management fees for the park's first two years. Those fees could have amounted to hundreds of millions more. (In the two years before opening the park The Walt Disney Company had recorded $150.2 million in earnings on its share of the money that had been raised, and invested, by Euro Disney SCA.)

What had gone wrong? At the outset, Disney priced the park and the hotels more to meet its revenue targets than to meet demand. Park admission fees, for example, were higher than at either Disneyland or Walt Disney World—$42.45 for adults. A room at the Disneyland Hotel in Paris ran about $340 a night, about what the finest hotels in Paris were charging then. As a result, hotels were half-filled and guests didn't stay as long or spend as much as expected. In Orlando, they may stay four days, but in Paris Disney was lucky to get a second day out of many. In fact, Disney found that there was so much checking in and checking out—as guests would arrive early, rush to the parks and then check out the next morning before heading to the park the next day— that they were forced to install additional computer stations to handle the traffic.

Disney had also badly miscalculated the tastes of the European theme park guest. As in America, no wine was served, although many Europeans consider a glass of wine with lunch a given. Disney had figured guests would take the train; when they showed up in buses, there weren't enough parking spaces. Disney thought Monday would be a light day for visitors, Friday a heavy one, and added more staff on Fridays. It turned out to be the opposite.

In the hotels, Disney had been told that Europeans as a rule didn't eat breakfast. That turned out to be wrong, and soon there were huge lines as Disney tried to serve breakfast for 2,500 in a 350-seat restaurant. And, they didn't always want croissants and coffee as Disney had planned, with many of them ordering instead bacon and eggs. (Disney reacted quickly to that, however, and began delivering prepackaged breakfasts to guests rooms.)

"I guess we got greedy," Disney CFO Richard Nanula would say later. In retrospect, the company had been on a nearly unstoppable roll by the time the Paris theme park had opened, and to the Eisner crew it appeared as if everything they tried was nothing short of a rousing success. Paris changed that. In the end, it became clear to Nanula and others that the company hadn't done its homework. Whereas visitors to the American parks on average paid as much for merchandise and meals as they paid to enter the parks, Europeans were willing to shell out far less.

❖

Back in Burbank, Eisner and Wells were growing increasing nervous about the situation in Europe. By then Eisner, Wells, and the rest of Disney's top executives were sitting on the sixth floor of the new $28.6 million Team Disney building that noted architect Michael Graves had designed for the company. After five years of supervising the construction of Disney's hotels, Eisner had become increasingly fascinated by architecture. As one result of that fascination, the new Team Disney building had an architectural whimsy that seemed appropriate for the company — the 330,000-square-foot building combined a Tuscan-style palazzo with Greek courts. And for good measure 19-foot-tall terra-cotta statues, shaped like the seven dwarfs, acted as pillars holding up the roof.

There was little whimsy inside the building, however. Early estimates relayed to Burbank by Robert Fitzpatrick, the 49-year-old former Jesuit seminarian hired by Disney in 1986 to head the theme park project, were that the Euro Disney park was heading for a $1 billion loss in its first year. (Eventually, the park recorded a $350 million loss and a $650 million charge for accounting purposes.) Gray-haired, with a diplomatic countenance and easy manner, Fitzpatrick was well acquainted with the French. He spoke the language fluently and had a French wife. But Fitzpatrick, hired to head the project after serving as director of the arts festival that preceded the 1984 Olympic games in Los Angeles, was increasingly being viewed by the French as an American outsider trying to force American culture on the stubbornly nationalistic French.

To help Fitzpatrick, in late 1992 Eisner and Wells had dispatched Steve Burke, the 34-year-old Harvard M.B.A. and wunderkind who had joined Disney in 1985 from General Foods. Burke had emerged as a company hero for first suggesting and then launching the ultrasuccessful Disney Store chain. By 1992, the stores had spread to 173 locations, and roughly one a week was being opened. A Disney Store that had just opened in Paris was among the most successful of the 14 then operating in Paris.

A few months later the company also sent Mike Montgomery, the company's treasurer and a key player in several of Disney's more ticklish film financing ventures. Montgomery assumed the role of Euro Disney's executive vice-president and chief financial officer. Montgomery was to examine every aspect of how the company operated. To help Montgomery, Eisner dispatched legal counsel Sandy Litvack and CFO Richard Nanula to begin the difficult task of talking with banks, who now feared for the security of the funds they had loaned the Paris park.

Still, the Disney brass back home felt that to improve the park's image with locals, a Frenchman was needed to head the effort. On February 11, 1993, the company moved. The Paris park had just reported an $87.8 million loss. Fitzpatrick's status was changed to that of a consultant to the project. In his place, Disney elevated Philippe Bourguignon, who had been brought in the year before to run the park's day-to-day operations as president of Euro Disney.

The 45-year-old Bourguignon was just the French face Disney needed to head its new theme park operation. With business degrees from the IAE in Paris and the Aix-en-Provence, Bourguignon was chairman of the Paris chapter of the "Young President Organization." Before being hired by Disney in mid-1992, he had worked for 14 years with the Accor Group, the giant hotel operation that owned the upscale Sofitel Hotel chain and the far more downscale Motel 6 chain throughout the United States.

Even before Bourguignon's elevation, however, Disney was scrambling to find a way to cut costs, stoke attendance, and fill the hotels. With Montgomery and Burke running operations, the park cut 900 jobs, slashing an estimated $100 million a year in operating costs. That also allowed them to shut the Newport Bay hotel during the winter.

Food, drink, and souvenir prices were slashed by up to 25 percent, and attendance prices cut to $34. In a move that Disney execs felt could alone add up to 500,000 guests, the park spent nearly $100 million to begin construction of an improved version of Space Mountain, its Disneyland thrill ride.

Even with the moves to buttress Euro Disney's flagging operations, Disney executives knew the project was in trouble. A persistent recession had ravaged the French real estate market, all but killing the home company's plan to dot some of the remaining 4,000 acres in Marne-la-Vallée with condos, office buildings, and retail stores. The image of creating another Orlando, a Disney-owned and operated city, were fast fading. So were plans to open another theme park, modeled after the Disney-MGM Studio Tour in Orlando. (Disney had hoped the second "gate" would keep French tourists around for another day or two to help fill Euro Disney's hotel rooms.)

Above all, the financial model that Disney had used was out of whack. Inflation rates were half the 5 percent that Gary Wilson and his team had projected, cutting deeply into Euro Disney's ability to raise and keep prices high. And interest rates, prompted by the German Bundesbank's reluctance to reignite inflation, were nearly double the 5 percent the Disney crew had projected. Those steep interest rates were digging deeply into Euro Disney's balance sheet. In 1993 alone, the company paid a staggering $450 million for interest and principal on its $4 billion debt load.

The numbers were a total repudiation of the careful planning and tight-fisted negotiating that had characterized Team Disney's approach to the Euro Disney project. Mindful of the $1 billion cost overruns at EPCOT Center that had crippled Disney and fueled the 1984 takeover battle, Eisner had no intention of repeating the same mistake in France. "Frank and Michael don't really have huge experience with big projects," recalled Stanley Gold, Roy Disney's lawyer who rejoined the Disney board in 1987 after leading the 1984 revolt that brought in Eisner. "They have built some hotels, but nothing on this massive scale," he had said back then. "There are few people with experience with building $2 billion projects. That is the kind of place where they could get in trouble."

Ironically, Eisner had picked up the idea for a Paris theme park from the same Disney staffers who had been working with Miller and then-Disney chairman Ray Watson back in 1982. That year, Ron Miller, accompanied by eager French dignitaries, had taken a helicopter tour around the regions to the north and east of Paris. And in early 1984, both Miller and Watson had met in Orlando with a delegation of French tourism officials. Like Eisner, the former Disney executives were mesmerized by the size and spending potential of Europe.

In France, however, they had no intention of repeating the same mistake they made in 1980 when they had licensed the Disney name to the Oriental Land Co., a large Japanese railroad and real estate company. Oriental Land had owned the 204-acre park in Tokyo. Disney invested $2.5 million in the Tokyo project, but had only walked away with a 45-year contract that gave the company 10 percent of the admissions collected by Tokyo Disneyland, 5 percent of food and merchandise sales, and 10 percent of any corporate sponsorship agreement. By 1984, the Tokyo park was generating more than $50 million a year in management fees for Disney. Later in the decade, the Tokyo park began bringing in hundreds of millions of dollars each year for its foreign owners.

It had been Joe Shapiro's job to make sure the same thing didn't happen in Paris. In 1985, Eisner and Wells had dispatched Shapiro, Disneys' general counsel and a former partner with Donovan, Leisure, Newton & Irvine, to Paris to lead the negotiations with the French government. The 35-year-old Shapiro, a chain-smoking ex–New Yorker who once aspired to be a professional baseball player, lived for 15 months in the Bristol Hotel in Paris. Shuttling between his company's Burbank headquarters and Paris, the Disney lawyer negotiated the agreement with a French government that had fought hard to offer tax incentives and other benefits to keep the park from going to Spain—another contender.

The French saw the project as a job creator; estimates were that it would put as many as 40,000 people to work. The 10 million or more visitors to the park would generate billions of francs in revenue for the country's economy. The French offer included roughly 5,000 acres of land that the government promised would be classified at the rock-bottom price of $100 per square meter for new town developments. On top of that, the French said they would spend more than $400 million to upgrade and improve the country's highway system and extend the suburban rail line by 6.2 miles. The French also pledged to give the Disney project sharply reduced interest rates on nearly $1 billion in loans.

Negotiating against Jean-Rene Bernard, a high-ranking civil servant who had at one time served as France's ambassador to Mexico, Shapiro's job was to cut as tough a deal as possible. And despite a loud socialist minority in the country who had argued that the government's money would be better spent for housing and other immediate economic needs, Shapiro did just that. The most serious issue to confront the two sides was the preferential price at which Disney could buy the 4,841 acres. Ultimately, the French government agreed upon $5,000 an acre, roughly the land's value in 1971.

The signs of France's acquiescence can be found throughout the 400-page final agreement. Unlike other French companies, which pay a 18.6 percent tax on the cost of goods sold, the Disney park would have to pay only 5.5 percent. The buildings on the Disney project could be depreciated over 10 years rather than the usual 20 years French tax law ordinarily dictates. The state also agreed to expand roads, to extend the commuter rail line at a cost of $150 million, and to lend the new theme park project up to $770 million, or about 40 percent of the entire project. Euro Disney paid the entire $50 million cost for the station at the park. Joe Shapiro's job was done on March 24, 1987, when Eisner and French prime minister Chirac signed the mammoth agreement.

The work was only starting for Gary Wilson. Wilson, the former Marriott chief financial officer, had joined Disney two years earlier. And as he had done dozens of times at Marriott, Wilson structured the European deal as a series of limited partnerships designed to protect Disney from as much exposure as possible.

In France, the Disney-controlled project would then sell the property off to a financing company made up of individual investors. The sale would provide the funds to build the park and hotels. Then the financing company would lease the land back to the park under a 20-year contract. As it did in Tokyo, Disney would also collect 10 percent of the money spent on tickets and 5 percent on food and merchandise. Under its 30-year agreement to manage the park and hotels, Disney would get 3 percent of Euro Disney's revenues for the first five years, then 6 percent a year after that. On top of that, Disney would also get a large piece of the pretax profits.

❖

By mid-1993, it looked as if there might never be any profits for Disney to share. In Burbank, Eisner and Wells had just received word that Euro Disney would report a $200 million loss for the first six months of the fiscal year, and that the losses were likely to deepen. The key problem continued to be the park's $4 billion bank debt. The two Disney executives had just been briefed by Euro Disney's financial director John Forsgren, who told them that the company would be paying roughly $50 million more in interest rates than expected because it was paying floating rates on the majority of the debt—rates as high as 9.5 percent, nearly double the 4 percent that Disney had projected in its internal projections.

For Disney, that would mean taking a massive reserve—over $500 million—to cover its investment in the park's eventual loss. And it would only continue the wave of negative publicity that was engulfing the company at the time. "We had a real concern that if things continued like this [the bad publicity] could take the whole company with it," said Eisner later. No one was more alarmed than Richard Nanula, who had just been elevated two years earlier to the CFO slot. Nanula argued that not only was the size of the loss great but that the entire financial structure was now a drag on the venture. Without a massive restructuring, it would be years before Euro Disney could hope to stop the red ink.

Eisner and Wells put Nanula and Litvack in charge of devising a restructured deal. The debt load, Nanula had figured, needed to be slashed at least by 25 percent, to something closer to $3 billion. To take its place new equity would have to be raised. Those were the numbers, but getting there would be the difficult part. To raise added equity would mean improving the company's balance sheet, and to do that would require stemming the flow of funds. That meant the banks would have to agree to forego an interest rate payment they would soon be due. Disney, which was scheduled to receive a hefty royalty payment that year as well, had to be willing to cut its take as well.

With the advice of the investment banking firm of Lazard Freres, Disney made its proposal in October to the 60-bank consortium, represented by a joint steering committee that included Banque Nationale de Paris, Banque Indosuez, Deutsche Bank AG, and Barclays Bank PLC. "We showed them the size of the problem and what had to be done," Nanula recalled.

By the early 1990s, restructuring was a common way for overleveraged U.S. companies to seek refuge, and distressed companies with debt tied to now overvalued land routinely were begging for concessions. Donald Trump had just completed a massive restructuring of the debt on his Atlantic City casinos, and Rupert Murdoch had just pressured his banks into redoing the debt on News Corp.'s balance sheet.

The banks, however, were not as easily convinced this time around. In December, they told Disney they were willing to take on a small part of the restructuring. "Five or ten percent," recalled Nanula, "a sliver." For their part, they insisted that Disney put up more of the funds and agree to reduced royalty payments. Instead, the Disney brain trust decided to play hardball. "We figured that this was a declining asset the way that it was, and that the banks would rather have a worse structure and a plant that could operate than nothing at all," said Nanula.

Nanula and Litvack told the bankers they would provide enough cash for the Paris park to operate until March 31. Then, a new pressure point emerged. Euro Disneyland was planning its annual meeting for March 15. If there was no deal by the time of the Euro Disney meeting, the parent company was prepared to pull the plug and walk away, Nanula told the bankers. "We couldn't have Philippe standing up in front of an angry group of shareholders at the Wild West Show exhibit, where the meeting was to be held, without that deal," said Nanula later. "It would be a disaster." To increase the pressure, Eisner went public with the threat: that Disney might pull the plug after March. "Everything is possible today including closure," Eisner told the French magazine *Le Pointe*.

Faced with the possibility of Disney closing the park—and leaving the banks with nearly useless real estate and a theme park that wasn't paying its bills—the bankers eventually capitulated. On March 14, 1994, Euro Disney SCA and its consortium of 60 bankers announced agreement to restructure $1 billion in debt.

The plan gave Euro Disney some breathing room by giving it 24 months' forgiveness from paying interest on roughly $3 billion of the loans, along with a three-year postponement on paying back the principal. The banks also agreed to arrange for buyers of 51 percent of a $1.2 billion rights offering that would be used to pay down debt.

Disney didn't come away without having to ante up, however. The company agreed to put up an estimated $540 million for its 49 percent share of the $1.1 billion rights offering. It also agreed to waive its rights to management fees from 1992 to 1998, and to slash those fees from 6 percent to 1 percent of the park's net revenues. (The company can gradually increase the rates over time until getting back to the 6 percent rate in the year 2018.) Disney canceled $210 million in bills it had sent the park for various services, which gave the park $140 million in interim funds to pay its existing bills. The company also arranged a 1 percent loan to Euro Disney so that the park could buy back $255 million worth of rides and other buildings.

❖

As the deal was coming together, another potential rescuer was emerging in the faraway desert kingdom of Saudi Arabia. The talks were being followed there by 37-year-old Prince Al-Waleed Bin Talal Bin Abdulaziz Al Saud, a grandson of Saudi Arabia's first king. The Prince, educated at Menlo College in San Francisco, was a bona fide Disney nut who regularly traveled with an entourage to Anaheim and Orlando. Only months earlier, he had been in Paris and stayed for two days at Euro Disney.

Moreover, with a fortune estimated at nearly $10 billion, he was gaining a reputation as a shrewd investor with an eye for distressed properties. He had first attracted world attention in 1991 by shoring up ailing Citicorp and becoming its largest investor with an $800 million cash infusion.

Earlier in the spring, the Prince had asked his advisers at the Washington, D.C., consulting company Caryle Group to contact Disney. The call had come to Nanula from a Caryle principal, Steve Norris, a former Marriott official who had known Gary Wilson and strategic planning head Larry Murphy for years. The Prince was interested in taking a piece of the rights offering that was a part of the overall rescue plan, Norris said.

The negotiations were mostly handled long-distance by telephone, with the final details handled over a satellite hookup to the Prince's desert compound where he was working in the middle of the night. "We'd be in the middle of a key point and suddenly we'd lose the satellite," Nanula recalled. "Then I'd hear my secretary on the other line say, 'One minute, Your Highness,' and reconnect us. Happened several times." On June 1, the deal was done. The Prince agreed to buy up to nearly 25 percent of the rights offering by paying $247 million to buy shares from both Euro Disney's bankers and Disney. But even that deal had its last-minute twist.

Before agreeing to the compromise, Eisner had thrown in one last condition. To buy into the deal, the Prince would have to agree to a $100 million low-interest loan for Euro Disney to build a convention center that was then on the drawing boards. The reasoning was sound: The convention center would help fill the Euro Disney hotels that were still suffering huge vacancies. But the Prince's advisers, recalled Nanula, "were just flabbergasted." Nanula himself admits he thought Eisner had overreached and the Prince would walk away at the last-minute demand. Instead, two days later, he agreed to the final condition.

The transaction had reduced Disney's stake in Euro Disney to 39 percent, but had significantly eased the burden for Eisner. With the concessions, the park's $1.1 billion 1993 loss was slashed to $359 million in 1994, even though attendance in 1994 was off by 10 percent and occupancy at the hotels trailed Disney's initial projections.

By 1995, however, the numbers were certainly looking better. With interest costs slashed to $93 million from $265 million, the park announced its first profit, moving a relatively tiny $23 million into the black. Attendance was up by 21 percent, just short of the original 11 million target set by Disney back in 1985.

❖

Things were definitely looking up in Paris. But elsewhere in the Disney empire, there were still problems. After being launched with so much fanfare at the Disney Decade celebration in 1990, competing plans to build theme parks in either Long Beach, California or to expand in Anaheim were fast going nowhere. Talks with the Oriental Land Co. to build a second theme park in Tokyo, modeled after the Disney-MGM Studio Tour in Orlando, had broken up when the Japanese executives had summarily rejected the entire concept.

The first project to fall by the wayside had been Long Beach. In 1990, Eisner had ordered architects and ride designers at the Disney Imagineers workshop to begin planning a nautical theme park for a 350-acre plot of land near the Long Beach harbor. The idea was to include rides alongside the hangar that housed Howard Hughes's *Spruce Goose* and the 56-year-old one-time luxury liner, *Queen Mary*, both of which Disney had inherited as part of its deal with the Wrather Corp. to buy the Disneyland Hotel in Anaheim. The concept was to remake the entire area into an upscale resort, with five luxury resort hotels, a marina with 400 boat slips, and rides that had nautical themes. Included among them would be at least one ride based on Disney's animated hit *The Little Mermaid*, and another based on the vintage Disney film *20,000 Leagues Under the Sea.*

It wasn't long, however, before political opposition swarmed around Disney's plans for the $2.8 billion project, which Disney had initially named Port Disney and which was later renamed DisneySea. That opposition, which including fierce attacks by environmentalists and the state's Coastal Commission on Disney's plan to dredge the harbor, doomed the project to a lengthy regulatory process. After spending more than $70 million to design the plan and fight legislative battles, Disney threw in the towel in late 1991 and decided to concentrate instead on expanding its flagship Disneyland complex.

Disney had quietly been buying up land near Disneyland throughout the late 1980s in anticipation of expanding beyond the original park. The company had chafed for years as tacky souvenir shops and fast-food joints had crept to within yards of the Happiest Place on Earth. Worse yet, other than the Disneyland Hotel it had bought three years earlier from the Wrather Corp., most of the hotel revenues from Disneyland's visitors were going into other companies' pockets.

By early 1991, the company had bought a 23-acre abandoned trailer park catercorner from Disneyland and was negotiating to buy 58 adjoining acres of farmland. Together with the existing Disneyland parking lot, that would give the company more than 150 acres of property. The company held options on over 200 additional acres, and was still looking for more.

On May 9, Disney announced plans to spend up to $3 billion to build three new hotels, a six-acre lake, shopping malls, lush gardens, and a new theme park. The park, to be called WESTCOT Center, would be inspired by EPCOT Center in Orlando. As in Orlando, WESTCOT would have pavilions based on foreign cultures or science and a giant golden sphere called Spacestation Earth that would loom over the horizon.

In December, reeling from the political opposition to its proposal in Long Beach, Disney had decided to move ahead in Anaheim and abandon the *Spruce Goose* and *Queen Mary*. The problem was that Anaheim was proving far from its usual friendly self. Wallowing in recession and statewide budget cuts, the city was unable to come up with the kind of money that Disney needed to build freeway off-ramps, a parking garage, and street improvements to expand its existing park. The costs were starting to mount—$75 million to build an off-ramp, another $50 million to bury underground wires in the Disneyland parking lot.

The idea was to insulate the Disney parks from the outside environment, much as the company had done in Orlando. Trees would be planted and streets widened, with some cut off to outside traffic. To help that along, Disney quietly was looking to buy up some of the hotels that surrounded the Disneyland Hotel. Operating through a shell company called Ashley Properties, the company had bought the rights to the 242-room Grand Hotel in Anaheim out of bankruptcy court, with an eye toward renovating the 10-story tower just blocks east of Disneyland. Later it also bought the 502-room hotel, paying $30 million to Japan-based Tokyo

Corp. for the 11-year-old hotel. Together with the 1,136 rooms at the Disneyland Hotel, that gave the company 1,638 rooms within a few blocks of the theme park.

It took five years—and more than a little arm twisting—for Disney to get its way. The company delayed the Anaheim project twice, slashing its estimated price tag to $2 billion from its initial $3 billion figure, and it openly contemplated abandoning the entire project. But by July 1996, the city of Anaheim caved. The city of Anaheim agreed to a $550 million beautification program, including $150 million to expand the city's aging convention center.

By then, however, the Disney project had changed dramatically. Instead of WESTCOT, the company decided to build a $1.4 billion park called Disney's California Adventure that would recreate a Golden State vacation experience with such rides as hang gliders over California mountains and white water rafting down rivers. The park, which would be built on 55 acres of the Disneyland parking lot, would also offer rides that would mythically take place on California's beaches and in Hollywood. In Tinsel Town, for instance, park visitors would be able to make their own animated films.

In keeping with its Anaheim strategy to capture as many tourist dollars as possible, Disney also intended to build a 750-room "Grand California" hotel inside the new park, increasing the company's ownership to 2,300 rooms in the Anaheim area. At night, the company would also offer restaurants, nightclubs, and video arcades, much as it did in Orlando.

While Disney had been waiting for Anaheim to capitulate, the company had focused its efforts on Orlando, where they could control the environment within the nearly 30,000 acre complex. Not only did the company own the land, but by controlling the Reedy Creek District, they also controlled much of the regulatory process. There, the company decided to put its first new domestic theme park since the MGM Studio Tour opened in 1989.

The park, which would feature herds of live animals such as giraffes, zebras, and lions, would be housed on a 500-acre portion on the western edge of the property. By late 1984, the company had already begun site preparation for what would be called Disney's Animal Kingdom, to open in early 1998. All told, the park would be five times the size of the Magic Kingdom.

The company also had jumped into the sports business in Orlando, with plans to build a 200-acre amateur sports center at Walt Disney World that would include a 7,500-seat stadium and training sites for as many as 25 different teams at one time. In 1996 it became the spring training site for the Atlanta Braves baseball team. At the same time, construction was under way on the Disney Institute, a lakeside enclave that would offer as many as 80 different programs for families and their older children on such subjects as cooking, sports, and the performing arts.

Even as work was going on in Orlando, however, the company was looking to expand. Ultimately that would come back to haunt Eisner once more. The Disney chief had become fixated on American history when he had visited Williamsburg, Virginia. Jeffrey Katzenberg had traveled to Virginia with his family in 1992 to research the animated film *Pocahontas* that the company was planning. At the time, Eisner's oldest son was going to Georgetown, and the Disney chairman was spending a lot of time in Washington visiting with longtime friend Senator Bill Bradley.

Eisner had directed Disney Design and Development, the company's real estate unit, to begin scouting nearby Virginia and Maryland for a potential site for a theme park. The area, with an estimated 18 million visitors a year, was considered third only to Orlando and Las Vegas as a tourist attraction. And because the area had been luring tourists for years with its monuments and historical attractions, it already had plenty of hotels and the transportation needed to bring guests to a Disney park.

Disney Design president Peter Rummell and his crew eventually decided on a 2,400-acre parcel that Exxon had bought for a residential development in Prince William County 20 miles west of Washington, D.C. Exxon had abandoned the project a year earlier. In November 1993, the company signed an option for the land. But because the Virginia legislature only met during the first three months of the year, Disney announced the plan even before it had completed its economic analysis. "It turned out to be a real mistake on our part," said Disney CFO Richard Nanula later. "We didn't know much about the economics, and we sure hadn't counted on the political reaction that we were going to get."

The park that Disney announced on November 12, 1993, was estimated to cost $600 million to build and would feature rides based on historical events in America. Using Disney's audio-animatronics technology and the latest in simulator rides, the company's Imagineering unit developed rides that included a 19*th* Century settlement, an Indian village, and a World War II fighter aircraft.

The park, to be located in an area of exclusive homes where the likes of Washington Redskin owner Jack Kent Cooke and *Washington Post* owner Katharine Graham live, soon was in the epicenter of a howling protest by residents who feared that Disney would turn their enclave into another Orlando. Environmental groups worried that the construction would damage historical sites, the *Washington Post* editorialized against it, and Congress contemplated hearings. It hardly mattered that Virginia Govenor George Allen, fixated on the 3,000 jobs that would be created and the $1.5 billion in tax revenues that would be generated over a 30-year period, had given his approval.

Eisner, in the midst of negotiations with European banks, had sent Peter Rummell to announce the new park in Virginia. But soon, the Disney chairman was being called back east to become a key player in the second controversy to strike Disney's theme park unit in as many years. John Cooke, the Disney Channel president who had also taken over Disney's congressional operations, became a fixture on Capitol Hill. Disney also began lobbying local historians to join Disney's side. Eisner was even making the rounds to congressmen and sat down to lobby reporters at a hostile *Washington Post.*

To get his side on the record, Eisner wrote an op-ed piece for the *Post*, arguing that the park was a good idea. "At a time when too many Americans, particularly the young, have lost interest in our past and discount the relevance of history to present-day challenges," he wrote, "we felt we should do what we can to reconnect Americans with their heritage and maybe even show the world what a great country we are, a country of people from different lands, races, and religions all living together with a common language and a common goal."

Eisner's plea proved too little too late. On September 28, 1994, Disney decided to pull out of the Virginia project altogether. In making the announcement, Peter Rummell said the company would seek a new site for the historical-theme park, although Disney insiders said that the company was unlikely to want to risk the glare of negative publicity again in a new location. Instead, some of the ideas from Disney's America were being evaluated for a second theme park the company continued to plan for Anaheim alongside Disneyland.

At the time, Michael Eisner had other issues on his mind. By 1994, Disney was in the midst of the darkest year of the Eisner regime. Even though the problems in Paris were nearly resolved, back in Burbank Team Disney was falling apart.

16

C H A P T E R

Fallen Knights

Michael and Jane Eisner were having dinner Sunday evening at the Hollywood Hills home of their son Breck when the phone call came. Eisner's longtime secretary Lucille Martin, sobbing, had just spoken with the pilot of the Disney corporate jet in the mountain town of Elko, Nevada. "It's Frank," Lucille said somberly. "There's been an accident."

The news stunned Eisner. Rescue workers on the eastern Nevada slopes had radioed back that a helicopter carrying Wells and its pilot had crashed during foul weather near the top of Ruby Mountain. Both men had been killed instantly. Wells, known for his hell-bent skiing, had taken the Easter weekend off to be with his friend Clint Eastwood. The two, whose relationship dated back 20 years when Wells was at Warner and Eastwood was a top-rung action star, had spent the previous day schussing the slopes. Wells, Eastwood recalled later, was singing at the top of his lungs the Beatle standard "Hey Jude," off-key and with words not quite what Paul McCartney had written.

Back in Burbank, the Disney machinery was in gear. Eisner called Disney's corporate communications chief, John Dreyer, who hustled in from his home in La Cañada to issue a press release and start fielding press calls. Roy Disney was located, as were most of the other board members. For the time being, Eisner told them, nothing would change. Eisner would assume the president's title and count on Disney's existing management to help him through the transition.

It was an abrupt end to what had been one of Hollywood's smoothest working teams. Nearly ten years earlier, Eisner and Wells had been thrown together by an accident of corporate fate, when takeover artists had circled Disney and the two men had been hired to revive it. Since then, both had grown into their respective roles. Eisner had become the public face of the company, peering out from magazine covers, hosting the Disney Sunday evening shows, and writing the annual report to shareholders. The two men talked frequently, whether by phone or by hustling across the lobby that separated their offices on the sixth floor of the Team Disney building in Burbank.

Wells, far more comfortable out of the limelight, was happy taking a backseat to Eisner, making sure that the Disney machinery kept operating. If Eisner liked to troop down to the Imagineers workshop in Burbank to see the latest idea for a ride, Wells was there to make sure the thing would run. It was Wells who had persuaded AT&T to pony up $100 million for the new Indiana Jones thrill ride that was to open the next year in Disneyland. And it was Wells who had been dispatched when problems arose at Euro Disney or negotiations bogged down with a key star or director. When Eisner riled managers inside the company, as he was wont to do, it was Wells who would smooth over the matter.

Indeed, just days before his death, the 62-year-old Wells had been working the phones as Disney executives Sandy Litvack and Richard Nanula negotiated the financial bailout of the Euro Disney theme park with the French banking syndicate. Roland Betts, who had structured the first Silver Screen limited partnership to finance production of Disney's films, would recall seeing Wells—up before dawn as the two prepared to hit the slopes in Taos, New Mexico—working the phones to coordinate overseas strategy.

The Euro Disney refinancing would eventually be counted among Wells's finest saves. And if there was ever any doubt he was valued within the Hollywood community, the 4,000 people who gathered inside the cavernous Stage 2 on the Disney studio lot spoke volumes. It was the same huge warehouse-type building where Wells, six years earlier, had thrilled the Disney rank and file by entering their annual get-together by sliding down a 200-foot wire dressed as Indiana Jones.

On Monday, April 11, 1994, eight days after Wells's death, a more somber crowd awaited. Among those attending the services were Warren Beatty, Gregory Peck, Robert Redford, Steven Spielberg, and such Hollywood moguls as Warner Brothers studio chief Bob Daly and agents Michael Ovitz and Jeff Berg. It was perhaps only fitting that the Disney orchestra honored him by playing "Climb Every Mountain"—an especially poignant reminder of the spirit of the man who had once taken time off from a high-pressure entertainment career to climb six of the seven tallest mountains in the world.

"I was never angry with him—until last Sunday," Eisner said in his eulogy to his fallen comrade. "And I was angry at Frank because he was not around to help me deal with this difficult situation."

Ultimately, however, Frank Wells's death was but the beginning of what would prove to be an increasingly difficult period in the corporate life of the Walt Disney Company. Two days before Wells had taken off for Nevada, Eisner and he had agreed that Wells would sign a new seven-year contract to continue as president and chief executive. The final wording of the agreement was to have been completed the day after Wells returned from his skiing trip.

Signing his third contract had been a difficult decision for Wells. The long-time Democratic Party activist had contemplated a run for both the U.S. Senate and to be California governor. He was also keenly interested in environmental issues and had contributed $1 million to a 1992 ballot initiative to empower statewide conservation groups to purchase and protect added acreage of forest lands. At one point, recalled Eisner, Wells had even suggested that he take the largely honorary position of vice-chairman of the board to allow other, younger Disney executives to begin the move upward.

At the time of his death, Wells and Eisner had been discussing a wholesale reshuffling of the Disney management team. Companies, the two men felt, were like marriages. "They have to be renewed every seven years or apathy sets in," Eisner said later. Even while Wells and Eisner had been planning the changes, an exodus of key Disney players had already begun. Among the first to go was Disney CFO Gary Wilson. In late 1989 Wilson told Eisner he wanted to leave the company, and midway through that year he and his longtime friend Al Checchi led a group of private investors that bought Northwest Airlines for $3.7 billion. (Wilson had helped put the Northwest buyout financing together while in London working on the Euro Disney project.)

Eisner and Wells had arranged to keep Wilson with the company by agreeing to a five-year contract by which Wilson would continue to work as a adviser on acquisitions and financial issues. Although Wilson wouldn't be paid a salary, he would remain a Disney board member and be paid a special $2 million bonus. In addition, he would keep his options to purchase an additional 339,400 shares of Disney stock, worth roughly $35 million at the time.

Wilson was succeeded by Disney treasurer Judson Green. But soon other Disney executives left. Bill Mechanic, Disney's longtime video chief, jumped to Fox and became chief operating officer of Rupert Murdoch's studio operation. TV syndication chief Bob Jacquemin, citing personal problems, took a sabbatical. And in late 1992, Eisner's top public relations executive Erwin Okun, one of the few remaining holdovers from the Ron Miller era, died after a short bout with cancer. He was succeeded by John Dreyer, a longtime Disney PR man, who was heading the Orlando public relations machine.

Disney had quietly accepted the resignation of general counsel Joe Shapiro, another veteran of the 1984 takeover battle, who was also fighting cancer. To take on some of Shapiro's role as Disney's top political hand, Eisner began to rely more heavily on Disney Channel president John Cooke, an old friend of vice-president Al Gore and a frequent contributor to Democratic Party causes.

The departures had forced Eisner and Wells to elevate key Disney executives. Richard Nanula, Disney's 30-year-old treasurer and a veteran of the company's film finance ventures with Gary Wilson, had succeeded Judson Green as CFO when Green was dispatched to Orlando to run Walt Disney World. With Shapiro's illness, the company also began relying even more heavily on Sandy Litvack, a one-time Justice Department antitrust chief who had been hired as general counsel in 1991. Litvack, a hard-edged negotiator who had played football briefly in college, was a key part of the team that had negotiated the Euro Disney recapitalization. He was also increasingly being called on by the company as a troubleshooter whenever things began to go wrong. He jumped into several legal cases, and was actively involved in the ongoing negotiations with Anaheim over the Disneyland expansions.

The continued lackluster performance of Disney's theme park unit in 1991 and 1992 also made some changes more urgent. Dick Nunis, the 61-year-old theme park head who had started his Disney life as a training instructor for new employees at Disneyland in the 1950s, was

quietly eased upstairs. Nunis, who remained on the Disney board, became a senior strategist for the company in his largely ceremonial role of
chairman of the theme park unit. The actual day-to-day operations of
the parks were then entrusted to Judson Green, a one-time certified public accountant who had joined the company in 1981 and by 1987 had
cut his teeth with Gary Wilson structuring the Euro Disney financing.
Since then, he had risen through the ranks and was running most of the
theme park units anyway.

Steve Burke had already moved to Paris to help handle the Euro
Disney nightmare by the time of Wells's death. Paul Pressler, who had
joined Disney in 1987 and was a top executive in the consumer products
division, succeeded Burke as head of the Disney Stores operation. A few
years later, Pressler would be moved to head Disneyland, which was
falling behind the company's projections. (Burke would later move
again, to Cap Cities in March 1996, after Disney purchased that company in July 1995.)

Another person that Eisner and Wells wanted to move around was
CFO Richard Nanula, who both men thought was destined to one day
run a company like Disney. After Wells's death, Nanula was moved. In
late 1994, longtime Disneyland president Jack Lindquist announced his
retirement. That gave Eisner the opportunity to move Pressler over to run
Disneyland, and to give Nanula a shot at running the Disney Store operation. At the time there were 335 Disney Stores in eight countries, and the
company planned to increase the number to 600 around the world.

Months before his death, however, Wells had been confronted by
what would ultimately prove to be a problem without a solution: what to
do with Jeffrey Katzenberg.

❖

By the early 1990s, Katzenberg had come into his own. Gone were
the corporate suits and hard-edged negotiations that had characterized
his early years at Disney. A new, mellower Katzenberg presided over the
company's fastest-growing unit. His normal work attire tended toward
jeans and work shirts, and he was rarely out of sneakers. After years of
browbeating stars to sign the smallest contracts in Hollywood, he was
now openly courting superstar directors and big-name actors. He lined
up Robert Redford for *Quiz Show*, a tale of the corrupt game shows of
the 1950s. Whoopi Goldberg was signed to do *Sister Act*, which would
go on to gross more than $100 million and become a huge hit overseas.

TV production, long a problem for the company, was suddenly minting hits. Tim Allen's *Home Improvement* was a fixture in the ratings top 10, joined occasionally by Ellen DeGeneres's new show, *Ellen*.

By 1993, the 43-year-old Katzenberg lorded over a Disney operation that had generated $622 million in operating earnings. Moreover, the company was in the midst of a streak of animated films unparalleled in Hollywood history. *Beauty and the Beast* became the first animated film to generate more than $300 million at the box office worldwide, a record that was soon eclipsed when *Aladdin* zoomed past $350 million. And inside the company, Disney executives knew the best was yet to come with *The Lion King*, which would eventually go on to more than $700 million worldwide. With revenues from videos, sound tracks and royalties from consumer products, the animated films were soon delivering a huge chunk of the company's operating profits.

Much of that was directly the result of Katzenberg's hands-on style and intensified interest in the animation process. Twice a week the studio chief would head his black Mustang convertible toward the Disney Animation Building in Glendale to sit through storyboard meetings, review just completed scenes, and battle over songs, punchlines, and characters. Roy Disney may have convinced Eisner and Katzenberg nearly a decade earlier that animation was worth keeping, but it was Katzenberg who found a way to make it into a cash-generating machine.

For all this, Katzenberg believed he deserved a promotion. Jeffrey Katzenberg loved the Disney life. At Christmas, he would put on an ice cream worker's costume to scoop out frozen treats for employees at the company's Disneyland holiday party. Each September, he would take his wife Marilyn and their twins to Disney World in Orlando to ride the latest rides. But for all the studio's flashy numbers, Katzenberg could never get Eisner to believe he was more than the best film executive in the industry.

Katzenberg considered such statements faint praise, at best. And by August 1993, he was itching to make his move. The contract he had signed with Disney in October 1988 had a year to run, but with an unusual provision that allowed either side to give the other a year's notice that it wouldn't be extended. Eisner had no intention of giving Katzenberg notice, but the Disney chairman was unsure whether Katzenberg intended to test the waters elsewhere.

Eisner decided to find out where Katzenberg stood during the company's annual management retreat in Aspen that August. As the two strolled through downtown, they stopped in front of Boogies, a diner.

"What do you want," Eisner asked Katzenberg. Katzenberg answered that he wanted to be a partner, much as Wells had been for years. He told Eisner he considered himself "a builder" and that he "wanted new mountains to climb." Would Katzenberg want to be elevated to vice-chairman of the Disney board? Eisner asked.

"Does it make sense for Frank to be vice-chairman and me to be president?" Katzenberg asked.

"No, that would be perceived as a demotion for Frank," Eisner responded.

What happened next depends on who was telling the story. But as Katzenberg later told friends—and Eisner later denied—Eisner then said what Katzenberg wanted to hear. "If for any reason Frank Wells is not here—if he decides to run for political office, if he goes off to climb the summit—you are the number two person, and I would want you to have his job." Eisner had a different recollection of the meeting. "I can't say whether I did and it's unfortunate if this became a misunderstanding. I wish I had made the message clear."

What was clear was that Katzenberg was intent on expanding his portfolio of responsibilities. And to show Eisner how serious he was, he decided to draw the battle lines and trigger the one-year exit provision of his contract. The word came in a one-paragraph "Dear Frank" letter from Katzenberg's New York–based lawyer Arthur D. Emil on August 31. The words were shrouded in legalisms—with allusions to Paragraph 9(a)(i) of Katzenberg's October 1, 1988 contract—but the intent was hard to miss. By September 30, 1994, Disney's studio chief intended to leave the company.

❖

Michael Eisner did not want Jeffrey Katzenberg to leave the company. The studio chief, Eisner was fond of saying, was still the best "golden retriever" in Hollywood, and no one was his equal in sniffing out potential story ideas and turning them into hit movies and TV shows.

The problem was that the two men, who had been nearly inseparable during the early days of the Disney revival, had grown increasingly apart. After 19 years together, first at Paramount and for nearly the last decade at Disney, Eisner and Katzenberg were operating in their own power orbits. Eisner was in charge of running a nearly $9 billion a year company, one that at the time had problems with its Paris theme park and was weathering a nasty reception in Virginia for the park it hoped to build there. Unlike their earlier days, when Katzenberg could count on Eisner to read scripts and offer his notes, there were fewer and fewer occasions when the top man could focus on individual projects.

The two had a standing appointment to meet at Locanda Veneta, a trendy Beverly Hills restaurant, on those Monday evenings when both were in town. But with Eisner jetting to points east and west, those meetings were increasingly infrequent. Moreover, while Eisner marveled at Katzenberg's mastery of Disney's animation operation, he was less sanguine about the company's live-action films.

By 1993, Eisner and Wells were growing increasingly concerned about the growing number of flops the studio was turning out. That year, the studio had lost $36 million alone on its live-action films, with such disasters as *Life with Mikey*, a comedy starring Michael J. Fox, and *Super Mario Brothers*, a live-action version of the computer game that starred *Roger Rabbit* star Bob Hoskins.

In fact, of the 25 live-action films that the studio released in 1993, only ten had made money. Eisner and Wells knew that were it not for the gigantic success of the animated hit *Aladdin* and video sales for *Beauty and the Beast*, the studio would likely have lost money. (With the animated films, it earned $508 million in 1992, a huge jump from the $318 million it had earned the year before.)

Moreover, Eisner and Wells were growing even more frustrated by what they saw as a continuing trend toward mediocre live-action films. In fact, as Wells told Eisner in a review of the studio in early 1994, during the first four years of Katzenberg's tenure as studio chief, Disney had made money on nearly all the 35 live-action films it had released. That success had earned the company a healthy $791 million, even before the animated film profits began rolling in.

The problem was that since then Katzenberg had been putting more films into production each year as he geared up to make 30 films annually. Katzenberg, like many in the industry, believed that with foreign sales for films booming, and with new technologies coming on line for satellite and cable television, there would be a nearly endless appetite for Hollywood films. But the studio's ramp-up, Wells felt, had seriously diluted Katzenberg's ability to maintain the kind of total control over film selection and execution that had made Disney's films so successful in the first place. On top of that, Eisner was spending increasing amounts of time with Disney's other far-flung operations, meaning that he was less able to read scripts with Katzenberg.

As a result, as Disney began gearing up, its profits for live-action films began going down. In fact, of the 13 live-action films that were released by the company in 1990, when the ramp-up began, only *Pretty Woman* was profitable. In 1991, the studio had lost money on 11 of the 18 films it released. Contributing to the $42 million loss that year were V. I. *Warshawski*, starring Kathleen Turner as a private eye, and a film version of E. L. Doctorow's bestseller *Billy Bathgate*, starring Dustin Hoffman and Bruce Willis."

Wells especially was incensed over what he saw as a company unit that had lost its way. Of the near-perfect batting average the company had in its first four years, the studio was now making money on only about half the live-action films it was putting into the marketplace. Indeed, after making nearly $200 million a year from its live-action films in Katzenberg's early years, the company was making closer to $40 million a year, a huge swing in profitability that Wells saw as intolerable.

The solution as Wells saw it was to cut back on the number of films that the company was making. In his opinion, the company should be making no more than 15 films annually. With fewer films, Katzenberg could again maintain the kind of hands-on control that was the hallmark of Disney in the early years. It would be embarrassing to eliminate Hollywood Pictures, the Disney president had felt, although he felt that Katzenberg needed to find other ways to cut production for the good of the entire company. "If Jeffrey wants to be a team player, he'd cut back," Wells told Eisner.

At one point, Wells asked Eisner if they should renew Katzenberg's contract, which was coming up for renewal in two years. (As previously mentioned, under Katzenberg's 1988 agreement, Disney and the studio chief could each exercise a provision, ending the deal within one year.) Eisner favored what he told Wells was "rehabilitation" for his long-time friend and associate, getting Katzenberg the chance to become more of a team player. To start this process, the Disney chairman encouraged Katzenberg to ease out his own protégé, Ricardo Mestres, as head of the underperforming Hollywood Pictures unit. Launched in 1989, Hollywood Pictures had never been profitable. In 1993, Mestres was offered a deal to make films for the company as an independent producer, and he stepped down.

In addition to his concerns that Katzenberg's performance had slipped, Eisner was also growing increasingly tired of what he saw as Katzenberg's meddling.

The studio chief had argued loudly that the company needed to acquire a television network to avoid having its TV shows blocked from being aired. And when the company announced its intention to build a theme park in Virginia, Katzenberg had criticized Eisner for not making the trip back east for the announcement—relying instead of Disney underlings to handle the press questions. (Eisner later said that the announcement came as the company was in the midst of delicate negotiations in Paris, and he didn't want reporters to hammer away at him on that topic.)

Moreover, Eisner was worried about Katzenberg's personal life. He was especially miffed that his studio chief was spending so much time on an outside venture, a gourmet sub shop called Dive! that Katzenberg started with Steven Spielberg. Katzenberg had gotten Eisner's permission before moving ahead with Dive!, but it angered Eisner that the shop came as it did just after the company had abandoned plans for its own restaurant, Mickey's Kitchen.

Then there was the issue of David Geffen. The record mogul, who had been instrumental in signing singer Michael Jackson to do the "Captain EO" film for the park in the mid-1980s, was Katzenberg's best friend. Eisner and Geffen though, were hardly friends. And the Disney chief was certain that it was Geffen who had goaded Katzenberg into seeking the company's number two job in Aspen.

Eisner knew he had a growing problem with Jeffrey Katzenberg on his hands. Despite the numbers with the studio's live-action films, the animated films under Katzenberg were hugely successful and provided immense revenues for the theme parks and consumer products division. But Wells's job was never likely to be available to him, Eisner knew. The board of directors thought of Katzenberg strictly as a creative executive, a far cry from the kind of detail-oriented business executive that Wells was. Still, Katzenberg was a tremendous asset to the company—one that Eisner didn't want to lose. After getting back from Aspen, Eisner and Katzenberg began talking about what new challenges Katzenberg could take on within the company. Eisner gave him control of Hollywood Records, Disney's flailing effort at creating a pop music label. To help Katzenberg increase the film unit's output, Eisner agreed to let him spend $80 million to buy Miramax Films, the art film maker of such cult hits as *The Crying Game* and *Tie Me Up, Tie Me Down*. At the time, several other studios were also bidding for the company.

Eisner also asked the studio chief to take on Disney's attempts to become a major Broadway producer. The company had already signed an option to spend upwards of $35 million to renovate the old Amsterdam Theater, and Disney was in the process of assembling a cast to take the film *Beauty and the Beast* to the stage. By late 1993, Katzenberg and Eisner were making a weekly trip to Houston where the cast was fine-tuning the show.

Katzenberg was also put in charge of an internal task force that was looking at the new world of interactive telecommunications and examining how to enter the booming market for CD-ROM games. Katzenberg also began working with Disney Channel president John Cooke, who by 1989 had started to contact regional telephone companies, encouraging them to hook up with Disney to produce TV shows for the telcus to deliver via their telephone wires. Disney wanted to produce the shows for the venture, along with an animated "navigator," the on-line guide that helps TV viewers find the right show and order movies.

At the same time, Eisner had asked Frank Wells to begin the task of negotiating a contract renewal with Katzenberg. That alone was frought with risks. By declaring his intention to not exercise his option in August, Katzenberg had given up the rights to more than $100 million in stock options. That made Katzenberg a tough negotiator.

Moreover, Wells was still smarting from Katzenberg's bold move in Aspen to take the company's number two job. "Frank was hurt," recalled Disney board member Stanley Gold, Wells's running partner and long-time friend. "He said, 'That's a lot of chutzpah from Jeffrey.' " Katzenberg denies he was ever interested in Wells's job. "The idea that I wanted Frank Wells's job is complete nonsense," he said. "He was singularly the most supportive, encouraging, and generous champion that I had during my years at Disney." Indeed, just before Wells's tragic death, at least one board member had been told that the company expected to soon sign Katzenberg to a new contract. Unfortunately, Wells's death only made the situation worse.

❖

Since joining the company in late 1984, Eisner had insisted that the company's managers gather for a weekly lunch each Monday. But on April 4, 1994, the day after Frank Wells's death, the meeting was dominated by a single item. Handing out a one-page press release that would go out later that day, Eisner informed his management team that he was taking Wells's title as president and chief operating officer and would assume Wells's various duties.

For Jeffrey Katzenberg, who had arrived at work at 6:30 that morning expecting to hear from Eisner, the press release came as a complete surprise. "I don't think I blinked for the entire lunch," an obviously enraged Katzenberg told an associate later. After 19 years, after their talk in Aspen, after months of talks about a larger role within the company, Katzenberg thought he deserved more. "If he had assured me, privately, that it didn't mean anything, fine," Katzenberg said later. "But by his actions, Michael assured me that he meant everything. It told me that he wouldn't share with me." Katzenberg "didn't want to be treated as a golden retriever," David Geffen said later. "He wanted Michael's approval."

The two men met that night for their regularly scheduled Monday evening dinner at Locanda Veneta. Both were shaken by Wells's death, but neither brought up the subject of Wells's job that evening. Katzenberg said later that he thought it was Eisner's place to bring it up, but instead the Disney chief talked about some business matters and their appreciation for all that Wells had done for the company. Although Katzenberg normally sleeps well, that night he restlessly prowled his Beverly Hills home, convinced that Eisner was condescending toward him.

The next morning, for the first time in 10 years at Disney, a visibly angry Katzenberg stormed into Eisner's office to demand to Eisner's secretary that the two men have lunch that day. Eisner got the message and at 12:30, they sat down in a private dining room on the sixth floor of the Team Disney building. There, with portraits of Walt and his brother Roy bearing silent witness to the building storm, Katzenberg demanded that Eisner explain what was going on.

I don't understand what you're doing," Katzenberg said. "I don't understand why you're putting out a press release without talking to me. I don't understand why you said nothing at dinner. I don't understand why, after more than 18 years, you wouldn't first talk to me. If you don't want to do what was promised, I'm leaving."

A furious Eisner responded, "You're putting a gun to my head."

"No, I'm just holding you to your promise."

"Are you telling me that if I don't do this you'll leave?" Eisner asked.

"I just want you to do what you said you would do," Katzenberg responded. The two men agreed to let their tempers cool and to revisit the issue later. Still, later that day Katzenberg told Geffen that at the end of the lunch, he said to Eisner: "I am going to leave."

At Disney's regularly scheduled board meeting later in April, Eisner recounted his confrontation with Katzenberg to the company's astonished board members. Apparently never thinking he had actually offered Katzenberg Wells's job, Eisner had never told the board of the discussion in Aspen. Moreover, because Katzenberg didn't sit on the Disney board and had little contact with most of its members, he had done little to cultivate supporters.

Whatever the reasons, the Disney board was almost unanimous in its support of their chairman. "We had to digest an enormous loss. Frank's body wasn't even off the mountain yet," said one board member. "It exhibited bad taste and judgment." Another pointed to Katzenberg's success as a studio chief. "It would be a waste for him to do that job," the board member said. "In a large sense, Jeffrey's job as chairman was more important than Frank's job. It would be silly to dilute his effectiveness as chairman of the studio. Frank's job involved so much detail—hard, technical kinds of things."

Katzenberg couldn't count on Roy Disney or Stanley Gold for their support. Gold, one of Disney's most influential board members, was still smarting over how Katzenberg had treated Wells the year before in asking for his job. And Roy Disney, who had campaigned in 1984 for Eisner and Wells to expand Disney's animation operation, was upset that it was Katzenberg—and not he—who was reaping publicity from the emergence of such Disney animated blockbusters as *Beauty and the Beast* and *The Lion King*.

No, Eisner was told by his board, we are in no hurry to elevate Jeffrey Katzenberg at this point. Eisner responded by keeping Wells's office, across the sixth floor lobby from his own, empty for months. Katzenberg stayed in his own sixth-floor suite of offices down the hall. The two men decided to revisit the entire issue again in August, when they could both take time off from the demands of their jobs. Fate, however, fate was to again intervene in the Disney family feud.

❖

At 2:00 A.M. on July 15 Eisner awoke with shooting pains in both arms. The 52-year-old Disney chairman had just attended his first meeting at investment banker Herbert Allen's annual retreat in Sun Valley,Idaho. There, over golf and brandy, big-ticket deals are talked about by the likes of Rupert Murdoch, Sumner Redstone, and Bill Gates.

But sitting alone at his villa, Eisner was alarmed. Dressing quickly, he drove to a small local hospital for an electrocardiogram. The tests showed nothing unusual. Eisner, not wanting to have his health become a topic of conversation within the Disney organization, called his secretary, Lucille Martin, and instructed her to pay the bill from Eisner's own account rather than the company medical plan.

Lucille Martin did more than that. She also called Michael Engelberg, Eisner's internist, who five years earlier had given Eisner the idea for a film called *The Puppet Masters*. As Eisner was getting ready to carry his bags to the car, Engelberg called. After some small talk about Engelberg's film and other matters, the doctor asked Eisner how he had been feeling lately. Eisner, stunned by the quick turn in the conversation's direction, told his doctor about the late-night visit to the local hospital.

"Michael, why don't you go by Cedar for a test tonight," Engleberg suggested. "I'll set it up while you're flying in. That night Eisner checked into Cedars-Sinai Medical Center under an assumed name. After 15 minutes on a treadmill, the doctors told him to prepare immediately for emergency quadruple-bypass surgery. Early the next morning, Cedars heart surgeon Dr. Alfredo Trento performed the three-hour operation, reporting later that it "was a normal bypass procedure without any complications." A complete recovery was expected, and Eisner was told he could go home in a few days and back to work within three or four weeks.

The operation, as it turned out, proved to be far less eventful than its aftermath. Eisner's wife Jane had called agent Michael Ovitz, Eisner's best friend, who rushed to her side late Friday evening. Also alerted was cochairman Roy Disney, who took the company jet back from a castle he owned in Ireland when he heard the news. Katzenberg, as it turned out, only heard about it on Saturday morning, hours after the operation. Calling Eisner's home to report that *The Lion King* had just passed $170 million in its first month of release, Katzenberg got Jane instead. "Oh, Jeffrey, I meant to call you," she was reported to have said.

The press release that Disney spokesman John Dreyer issued that morning said that Roy Disney would assume control of the company and that he and Eisner had already been discussing business matters. It wasn't long before stories began appearing in the press that Katzenberg might leave the company if not given the company's number two job. Eisner appeared to fight back. In a month-old interview with *Newsweek*, Eisner said he was considering restructuring the company to be "modeled after Rupert Murdoch's News Corp. In other words: a powerful CEO without a strong second-in-command." *Time* reported that Eisner was considering looking outside the company for a number two man, while *The Wall Street Journal* opined that Sandy Litvack might be better suited for the troubleshooting and negotiating aspects of the job. Katzenberg, the *Journal* added, was opposed by many members of the Disney board and was no longer considered a top candidate for the job.

In fact, as he was being wheeled into the operating room, Eisner had given his wife Jane a list of potential candidates to succeed him in the event he didn't make it. Katzenberg's name wasn't on that list, which included Ovitz and former Fox chief Barry Diller. Not surprisingly, Katzenberg was despondent and retreated to his house in Malibu for the first month of August. "He was starting to say, I'm getting tired of not being dealt with," said his friend Jim Wiatt, the president of the talent agency International Creative Management. "He felt he needed to force a confrontation."

The timing couldn't have been worse. But 10 days after Eisner returned to recuperate at his Bel Air home, he invited Katzenberg to his home to settle the issue. Eisner hadn't liked reading in the press that Katzenberg wanted the president's job and was willing to leave the company if he didn't get it. That, he told Katzenberg, was the kind of pushing that he wouldn't tolerate.

Katzenberg interrupted Eisner, telling him first how much he had enjoyed working for both Wells and Eisner. "Having told you that, it is also time for me to move on," said Katzenberg.

"Have you taken a job?" Eisner asked.

"No."

"Is it something that we can discuss?" Eisner asked.

Katzenberg was prepared for the moment and responded quickly. "We can talk about it, Michael, but I suspect that the decision is carved in stone by other people. Roy Disney is hostile toward me. You think I want to go into a board meeting and know that I don't have the complete support of Roy Disney or Stanley Gold, or know that the only reason I'm there is that you shoved this down their throat."

It was clearly an ultimatum. In Katzenberg's mind, he had quit. To buy some time, Eisner asked Katzenberg to put down on paper what he saw as his strengths, what he would bring to the role of Disney president, how he might reorganize the company, the issues he saw confronting the company, and what strategy—including acquisitions or joint ventures— he might implement.

Over the next 10 days, Katzenberg drafted and redrafted his memo, finally distilling his ideas down to four pages. He never got a chance to give it to Eisner. On August 24, Eisner summoned Katzenberg to his office and handed him a draft of a press release that had been sent out earlier that day.

The press release was a stunning blow to Katzenberg, one that would reverberate throughout the entertainment industry. Titled "Disney Reorganizes Filmed Entertainment and Corporate Operations," the press release went to great lengths to offer Katzenberg "heartfelt thanks" for the "enormous contribution to the growth and success of [Disney's] animation, live-action motion picture, and television business over the past ten years."

The corporate revamping was swift and thorough. To decentralize the power that Katzenberg had once enjoyed, Eisner split the studio into two distinct entities. One would handle production of TV shows, the Disney Channel, and the company's new joint venture with telephone companies to provide video-on-demand services. The other unit would be strictly for the live-action movie business.

Eisner decided to turn over the live-action film unit to Joe Roth. The 45-year-old former chairman of Twentieth Century Fox had come to Disney in 1992 to set up a new film unit after a falling-out with Fox owner Rupert Murdoch. Roth, a one-time director, was well liked among Hollywood types and had green-lighted such hits as *Home Alone, Sleeping with the Enemy, Edward Scissorhands,* and *Mrs. Doubtfire.* After the Bette Midler megaflop *For the Boys,* which saddled Fox with a $30 million loss, Roth was unable to get Murdoch to commit to a contract extension. At the same time, Fox chairman Barry Diller had quit the company.

Insiders had believed that Eisner would turn over the studio operation to Richard Frank, Katzenberg's second-in-command at the studio and another of the ex-Paramount executives who had come to Disney with Eisner in the mid-1980s. Instead, Eisner had given Frank control of the newly created Walt Disney Television and Telecommunications unit.

Katzenberg's pride and joy, the animation unit, was formally returned to the control of Roy Disney, who had served as its figurehead chairman since 1994. But it was obvious that Eisner intended to exert more control over that aspect of the studio. Not only would Roth and Frank report directly to Eisner, but the Disney chairman intended to step up his efforts to meet with Disney's two top animation executives, Peter Schneider and Tom Schumacher.

Eisner also continued to hold the title of president and chief operating officer of the company. But to take on the added responsibilities left with Wells's death, he gave Sandy Litvack the new title of chief of corporate operations. Litvack was given responsiblity for the day-to-day supervision of the company's internal matters other than financial issues. CFO Richard Nanula would continue to report to Eisner.

Katzenberg asked Eisner if he could stay on to complete work on *Pocahontas,* the animated film that was to be released the following summer, but Eisner said he needn't bother. Within the largely cloistered Hollywood community, Katzenberg's abrupt dismissal was considered ruthless, even though the now departing studio chief had started the battle by triggering the provision in his contract that ended his employment at the end of September. Eisner told reporters that Katzenberg wanted a job that didn't exist—a president's slot that he had eliminated through the restructuring. "This is not a Shakespearean tragedy," he told the *Los Angeles Times,* "This is people moving on with their lives, and doing new and interesting things."

Katzenberg's departure became a misty-eyed affair because the outgoing studio chief had become genuinely liked by some of his charges. When *The Lion King* became Disney's top-selling film of all time, Katzenberg called each of the 600 animators and other staffers who had worked on the project to personally thank them. As a result, the Burbank-based animators threw a party in his honor at a local Los Angeles nightclub. And when Katzenberg took his family to Walt Disney World for his annual Labor Day weekend a week after his announced departure, the entire animation department surprised him with a keg of Diet Coke, his favorite drink.

The 250 members of the Orlando animation department lined up to wish him well and presented him with a huge drawing showing Katzenberg surrounded by the animated characters they had created together over the previous decade. As the animators lined up so that he could sign their *Lion King* books, Katzenberg's wife Marilyn stood to one side and cried.

But Disney hadn't heard the last of Jeffrey Katzenberg. Though his contract officially expired on September 30, Katzenberg believed that the company owned him potentially hundreds of millions of dollars in the profit participation that he enjoyed from such megahits as *The Lion King*, *Beauty and the Beast*, and even the upcoming *Pocahontas*. Hiring all-star litigator Bert Fields, Katzenberg threatened to sue his former bosses if they didn't ante up by September 9, but then delayed the demand.

On Saturday, September 10, Eisner tried to reach a compromise and visited Katzenberg at his Beverly Hills home. But Katzenberg was unmoved. He told the Disney chairman that he would wait for a settlement offer. By September 30, when Katzenberg left the company, no such offer had been made.

❖

Sipping a can of Diet Coke at a table in the front of a large meeting room at the Peninsula Hotel in Beverly Hills, Jeffrey Katzenberg was back. It was two weeks after he had vacated his sixth-floor office at the Team Disney building in Burbank. Now, as TV cameras jostled with one another for position and Hollywood's power elite sat shoulder-to-shoulder with dozens of reporters, Katzenberg unveiled what he promised would be the next great Hollywood studio.

The new venture didn't yet have a name, but it had heavyweight backers. Together with superstar director Steven Spielberg and record mogul David Geffen, Katzenberg intended to create a studio that would go toe-to-toe with the likes of Disney, Warner Brothers, and Hollywood's other powers. "The only rule is that there are no rules," said Katzenberg. "We intend to be our own sovereign state."

Over the next few months, the self-styled "dream team" of Hollywood moguls would get a name—Dreamworks—and literally mountains of money. Microsoft founder Paul Allen would kick in $492 million, while the family that owned Korea's Samsung Electronics would invest $300 million more. High-tech companies such as Microsoft and Silicon Graphics would launch joint ventures with the new studio. In all, Katzenberg's new studio would raise more than $2 billion in equity and credit to launch into film and TV production, animated films, records, and interactive games. Its first deal was to make Saturday morning cartoon shows for ABC, a direct shot at Disney's strength.

Despite an agreement with Disney not to lure employees over to his venture, Katzenberg was soon hiring those who had left Disney's employment or would soon be eligible. He tapped former Disney treasurer Michael J. Montgomery as his chief financial strategist, and a few months later added Disney's studio top lawyer, Helene Hahn, when her contract expired. More than two dozen Disney animators also joined the company, working on an upcoming film about Moses that was tentatively titled *The Prince of Egypt*. Before long, former TV syndication chief Bob Jacquemin signed up, as did Disney film marketing executive Terry Press.

Back at Disney, Katzenberg's departure prompted still other changes. To keep studio music chief Chris Montan from leaving to join Katzenberg, Eisner had to offer him a $3 million contract to make films and sound tracks for the studio. But other longtime Katzenberg aides were soon shuffled to lesser positions. Studio marketing chief Robert Levin was moved from the studio to fill a new position as Eisner's top public-relations adviser. Within a few months, he left the company.

So did newly designated TV chief Richard Frank, who announced in March 1995 that he intended to leave the company to "pursue new career interests." In his place, the company named 53-year-old Dennis Hightower, a Harvard M.B.A. and one-time Mattel executive who for the previous five years had been heading the company's consumer products operation in Europe and the Middle East. Frank would eventually set up his own TV production company with cable giant Comcast Corp.

Now that the Jeffrey Katzenberg issue had been resolved, Eisner was eager to move the company forward again. After its lackluster 1993, when Euro Disney's problems dragged down the company's earnings, Disney certainly looked healthier. It reported record earnings in 1994 of $1.1 billion and would break the $10 billion barrier in revenues for the first time. Now, it was time for the company to look beyond its traditional lines of business in films and TV programs, theme parks, and consumer products. It was time to go shopping.

CHAPTER

New Lands to Conquer

Michael Eisner was aboard the Disney Gulfstream 4 corporate jet, along with his wife Jane and two of his sons, the Sunday after Thanksgiving in 1993. The only Eisner missing was son Eric, had just spent the weekend in Jamestown, New York with Jane Eisner's sister Mary. Sitting in the comfort of the Disney jet, Eisner set about to write his annual letter to the shareholders. For years, Eisner's letter had been a celebration of Disney successes, with a smattering of family news in spots for emphasis, but rarely an insight to into the collective thinking of Team Disney.

On this day in 1993, though, Michael Eisner was clearly troubled. His week had been filled with Disney activities. The day before jetting off to New York, Eisner and his sons had seen the first audience screening of the animated film *The Lion King,* which that summer would become Disney's biggest film ever. And on Wednesday, the day before Thanksgiving, Eisner and his hockey-playing son had jetted to Winnipeg to see the Mighty Ducks, the newly formed Disney-owned professional hockey team. The weekend in Jamestown had been filled with Disney films, with the clan catching *Three Musketeers* Friday and *Cool Runnings* on Saturday.

But as Eisner and his family were heading to Houston, where casting tryouts would be held for Disney's upcoming Broadway version of *Beauty and the Beast*, the media world was changing fast. Paramount Communications, the company for which Eisner had worked for a decade, was in the midst of a takeover battle. On one side was MTV-owner Viacom Inc., and its hard-bitten chairman, Sumner Redstone, and on the other was Barry Diller and his TV shopping company QVC. Eventually, Viacom would win the company, spending more than $10 billion to marry Paramount's programming interests with the Viacom's cable properties. Clearly, the media world was fast consolidating, with once huge companies getting even bigger and control of what consumers see being put in the hands of fewer and fewer companies.

The Viacom battle was hardly the only disturbing sign of the coming new media order. Rupert Murdoch's News Corp. was spreading its satellites to Asia, Great Britain, and Latin America. Time-Warner, already the nation's second-largest owner of cable television systems, was launching its own TV network to battle not only the big three but a stronger Fox network and a start-up backed by Paramount Pictures. The biggest deal of all, an estimated $30 billion merger between cable giant Tele-Communications Inc. and Philadelphia-based Bell Atlantic, had been announced only a month earlier. (Ultimately, the TCI-Bell Atlantic deal would fall apart, as the two sides could not agree on significant control issues.)

As one of the industry's leading providers of films and TV shows, The Walt Disney Company already knew firsthand what the impending consolidation could mean. Earlier that year, the studio had signed a deal estimated at more than $1 billion to air its films over a 10-year period on TCI's newly launched Starz! pay cable channel instead of its longtime home at Viacom's Showtime channel. The channel was TCI's effort to compete with pay channels such as Showtime and HBO in hopes of driving down prices to its subscribers. But to Disney studio chief Jeffrey Katzenberg, the TCI deal represented a 40 percent hike over what Showtime was willing to pay for the films.

The TCI deal served notice that a new order of "gatekeepers" was emerging on the scene. Cable, which now reached 70 percent of U.S. homes, had the money and power to control what consumers would see. Telephone companies, emboldened by coming federal legislation that would allow them to own cable systems, would soon also have controlling power. And if both Warner Brothers and Paramount succeeded in launching broadcast TV networks, they would join Fox among Hollywood's seven largest studios as owners of their own outlets for TV shows. Would Fox, which had just ordered the TV show *Mont* from Disney, still be in the market for outside produced shows down the road? And what if NBC owner General Electric, as rumored, was in the market to buy its own film studio to cut the costs it was paying Hollywood to make shows?

The need for programming, Michael Eisner knew, would be intensified by the coming information superhighway. Most executives believed that high-speed computers, able to "digitize" films and TV shows, would soon compress the amount of space entertainment took when being sent through wires or over the air. That reduced space would give rise to excess space that would be filled by such interactive services as on-line data, movies that could be ordered up immediately, and tons of new channels. Eisner and The Walt Disney Company had always assumed that, as one of Hollywood's premier providers of that so-called content, the interactive world would continue to beat a path to their door.

But with the world changing around him, Eisner now worried that other gatekeepers would arrive on the scene. And if they couldn't keep Disney out, they could reduce the price the company could get for its products. Disney was already watching as the growth of its Disney Channel, which added 633,000 new subscribers in 1991 and 832,000 in 1992, had started to flatten out. (In 1993, only 650,000 new subscribers would be added.) Moreover, a company plan to start another cable channel had been put on hold as cable systems, swarmed with the launch of new channels, had begun to drop older channels and all but kill newcomers by refusing to give them space on the dial. Rupert Murdoch's fx cable channel struggled for months before catching on, and lost more than $50 million its first year because it was forced to cut deals below its costs to get cable systems to carry it.

Eisner let shareholders into his thinking in a rare passage of his 1993 letter. "We continue to remind ourselves that it is the software that is important, the software that we continue to produce in the form of Disney animated classics, live action movies, TV series and specials, animated cartoons and Disney Channel offerings," he wrote. But he also offered: "If we have any concern, it is only that no one business entity be allowed to control access to the new systems. Therefore, it is not impossible that we will be strategically affiliated with hardware providers, with computer makers, with telephone or cable companies, with domestic and international satellite companies or with other like concerns. We must protect our access to the home."

❖

Michael Eisner's letter to the company shareholders may have had the casual air of a man musing about the future. But Disney executives had been concerned for years about what they had seen as a fast-changing political and technological environment and where their company might fit in. Congress was contemplating allowing telephone companies into the television business to limit the hold cable companies had on consumers, and the idea of telcos one day delivering TV shows over their wires no longer looked technologically impossible.

For Disney, the idea took on special importance. By 1989, the Disney Channel was seen in more than 5 million homes, and that rate was growing at a steady if unspectacular 12 percent annually. But with more than 60 million households receiving cable, Disney was actually seen in only a small percentage of American homes. Moreover, the Disney Channel could not compete with such behemoths as MTV, ESPN, and CNN, which were large enough to dictate the terms by which cable operators would pay them to be carried. To grow, Disney needed to find a new outlet.

By 1989, Disney president John Cooke was promoting the idea that the company consider hooking up with a telephone company to deliver Disney-made TV programs. In a presentation to a Disney corporate seminar in Orlando, Cooke said it could take up to 20 years for telcos to fully compete with cable companies, but the size and financial ability of the telephone companies would eventually make them a worthy competitor. Cooke had already done his homework, and earlier that year he had met with top executives of the seven regional telephone companies that had once been AT&T. Several of them, including BellSouth and Ameritech, were especially interested in joining forces with Disney.

Cooke continued his pilgrimages to the telephone companies and by early 1993 he had narrowed his focus to two companies, Philadelphia-based Bell Atlantic and Ameritech, which was headquartered in Chicago. At the time, Disney's studio was providing movies as part of a Bell Atlantic test program in the Washington, D.C., area that supplied movies on demand. Ameritech was intrigued by offering an "electronic mall" or home-shopping service and had asked Disney if it wanted to be a partner in the venture.

Disney soon focused even more on Ameritech. The Chicago-based company served more than 13 million customers in Illinois, Indiana, Michigan, Ohio, and Wisconsin, as well as owning pieces of telephone companies in New Zealand and Hungary. But its markets in the Midwest were largely mature and, as far as phone services were concerned, showed little chance of real growth in the future. As a result, the telephone company was building a two-way cable television–type service that would allow it to compete directly with cable companies by offering many of the same TV shows that viewers were now getting from cable.

Ameritech was in the midst of a business plan to build TV systems that would reach about 1.2 million customers in the Chicago, Cleveland, Columbus (Ohio), Detroit, Indianapolis, and Milwaukee metropolitan areas. It would soon ask the Federal Communications Commission to allow it to launch what was then called "video dial tone" service to many of its customers. And by the year 2001, according to its internal projections, Ameritech expected to reach 6 million midwestern customers with its own TV service.

Ameritech knew a great deal about copper wires and switching stations. But as Congress began work on a rewrite of federal telecommunications legislation that would enable the telephone companies to offer TV shows and movies over their wires, the company knew pitifully little about the kinds of programming that would allow it to compete with the TCIs of the world. For that, Ameritech officials had told Cooke, the company needed help. (Ironically, at the same time, one of Ameritech's fellow Baby Bells, Bell Atlantic, had begun the same discussions with Hollywood agent Michael Ovitz, one of Eisner's closest friends.)

With Ameritech eager to join forces with Disney, Cooke brought in Wells and Disney strategic planning chief Larry Murphy to talk with executives at several phone companies. It was soon clear that the costs of developing programming to distinguish the telcos from the cable companies was so great that Ameritech would need partners, and Disney began to canvass other cable companies to line up other partners for the venture.

At about the same time as Ameritech came calling, Disney was making inquiries of its own within the media industry. A Disney planning group, headed by strategic planning chief Larry Murphy, had been examining the fast-changing nature of America's television networks. The 24-year-old federal Financial Interest and Syndication Rules, which had been upheld for decades by the Federal Communications Commission, were due to expire at the end of 1995. Those rules effectively banned TV networks from owning television programming, and had so far kept Hollywood and the TV networks from seeking mergers.

Michael Eisner had wanted to buy a network for years. Not long after taking over in 1984, the new Disney chief had briefly negotiated for the purchase of NBC from its then owner, RCA. Because Disney was producing just about no TV shows back then, it wouldn't run afoul of the FCC's so-called Fin Syn rules. In 1985, Disney had also looked at CBS before Larry Tisch bought a 25 percent stake in the network and assumed control. But by 1993, Disney was among Hollywood's preeminent TV production companies, with such hit shows as *Home Improvement* on ABC and *Blossom* and *Empty Nest* on NBC.

With the Fin Syn rules set to expire soon, a Disney planning group headed by Peter Murphy and Tom Staggs was urging Eisner to revisit the notion of acquiring a network. Among those arguing for a network deal was Katzenberg. Along with Richard Frank, Katzenberg had convinced Eisner three years earlier to invest heavily to expand Disney's TV production wing. Now, with hits such as *Blossom* and *Home Improvement*, Katzenberg worried that without a network of its own Disney would be producing shows that no one would buy.

Moreover, the network business, after several slack years, was robust once more as ad rates were increasing nearly 9 percent annually. Coupled with the hefty earnings that each of the three major networks enjoyed through the TV stations they owned, the network business was clearly a good one again. Eisner was no stranger to the network business, of course. A one-time programming executive at ABC, he had kept closely in touch with the fortunes of the business since joining Paramount and Disney. When he was in New York, he often dined with CBS chief Tisch and other network brass. With a trip to New York coming up later in the month, Eisner put in a call to Tom Murphy, chairman of ABC's parent company Cap Cities.

Murphy had ventured into the TV business in 1954 when, as a 29-year-old product and merchandising manager, he had bought a bankrupt UHF station situated in a former convent in Albany, New York. In 1961, Murphy had recruited Dan Burke, a fellow Harvard M.B.A., from General Foods. Together, over the years, they had built one of the best-run media companies in the world. They bought newspapers like the *Kansas City Star* and the *Fort Worth Star-Telegram* and in 1986 bought ABC for $3.5 billion. Murphy and Burke lured fabled investor Warren Buffett to help in the deal, and Berkshire Hathaway paid nearly $700 million for a 13 percent stake in the company. As a show of support for the new team, Buffet had also signed an irrevocable waiver to Cap Cities, giving Murphy and Burke the power to vote his shares.

By 1993, Cap Cities was on a uptick after two years of falling earnings. That year, it would have operating earnings of $862.1 million, a 19 percent increase over the prior year. Along with its TV network and 8 TV stations, the company owned the ABC radio network, 17 radio stations, 80 percent of ESPN, the world's preeminent cable sports channel, and a one-third interest in two other cable channels, Arts and Entertainment and Lifetime. It was clearly the kind of gatekeeper that Eisner's staff believed the company needed to own to keep its movies and TV shows in front of the public.

At the time, Cap Cities also faced an uncertain management situation. Murphy would soon turn 69 and Burke, at 64, was contemplating retirement. Wall Street had been speculating for months that, with the need for new management, Cap Cities' founders would be a natural fit with Disney's younger but proven management team.

In addition, Disney had in recent years become a steady supplier of hit shows for ABC's schedule, with Tim Allen's *Home Improvement* already a top-10 ratings hit and the studio about ready to deliver Ellen Degeneres's *Ellen*. The two companies were jointly producing another show, *Thunder Alley*, starring Ed Asner as a former race car driver caring for his daughter and her two children. In 1994, Disney had also begun airing movies as a key part of ABC's Family Movie show on Saturday evenings.

Eisner and Murphy began discussing a possible merger in September 1993. And, when Eisner and Wells scheduled a meeting on the Euro Disney restructuring in mid-October, Eisner called Murphy once more. This time, he wanted to discuss a possible merger of the two companies. Sid Bass, who at the time owned just over 6 percent of Disney's stock with 31 million shares, flew in from Dallas to join them in New York as well. Greeting them at Cap Cities' 66th Street headquarters were Murphy, Burke, and Warren Buffett, the company's largest single investor.

The Cap Cities side was interested in a deal. But the sticking point was price. The numbers that the strategic planning team had worked up for Eisner indicated that Cap Cities was worth roughly $15 billion, or around $700 a share. Tom Murphy wanted roughly 10 percent more, or nearly $17 billion. Moreover, both Murphy and Buffett wanted the price to be paid in Disney stock.

Meeting for dinner later, the Disney team went over the numbers. The 10 percent distance between the two sides was bad enough, but the idea of paying for the acquisition with a massive chunk of Disney stock was too much for Sid Bass. The thought of buying ABC died, at least for the moment.

Not long after, Tom Murphy seemed to throw cold water on the likelihood that the company would ever make a deal with anyone. "We have a history of not selling anything unless we're forced to by the Federal Communications Commission," he told *Fortune* magazine. Moreover, at the time, Wall Street analysts, noting that ABC's ratings were on the upswing and that the TV stations were enjoying healthy profits, were putting the value of the company at between $17 and $19 billion.

Eisner, however, was still interested. His attentions had been diverted through much of 1994, with the death of Frank Wells, Jeffrey Katzenberg's messy departure, and the still lingering negotiations to resurrect the fortunes of Euro Disney. But, with the Paramount deal still fresh, Eisner remained convinced that the company needed to own a network to guarantee its TV shows and movies a place to be seen in the future. And with new technology making it likely that cable systems could soon deliver hundreds of channels to customers in the United States and abroad, the Disney chairman especially coveted Cap Cities' stable of cable channels.

Eisner had been thinking of the problem of being blocked from the marketplace during the month he spent recuperating from his heart bypass operation during the summer of 1994. On his first day back on the job after his operation, Eisner had taken the first step, approving the structure of Disney's deal with the three telephone companies to create their own distribution network. Under the agreement, the four partners would invest a total of $500 million and have equal representation on a board of directors. Disney would become the de facto leader of the venture, however, and would be responsible for lining up cable channels and other programming until the group had its own management.

Disney's interest in buying a network had also become well known within the tight-knit entertainment industry by that time. In the summer of 1984, General Electric chairman Jack Welch had called Disney board member Stanley Gold to see if he could set up a meeting with Eisner to discuss a possible joint venture to produce television programs. GE executives had denied for years that they were interested in unloading NBC, which they had bought from RCA five years earlier. During that period, NBC had fallen from first to second and was flirting with third place among TV's big three broadcast networks.

NBC was also desperate to expand into cable as well. The company had recently launched a business and news channel, CNBC. The network had also been negotiating for months with Time-Warner about purchasing Time's 17 percent stake in cable programmer Turner Broadcasting System, which owned the highly profitable Cable News Network, the TBS superstation, and the former MGM film library for its movie channels. With investment bankers Allen & Co. as its advisers, NBC at one point had sweetened the pot by telling Time-Warner it was prepared to sell Time a 49 percent stake in NBC for $2.5 billion.

Eisner, Richard Nanula, and Stanley Gold traveled to New York to meet with Welch in September 1994. It didn't turn out to be much of a meeting. The Disney contingent, worried that Time-Warner could end up controlling the network, had come prepared to consider a bid for the entire network, which the strategic planning team had valued at roughly $5 billion. The two sides were also well aware of one another. For years, Disney produced such shows as *The Golden Girls* and *Empty Nest* for NBC. And earlier that year, the company had sold *The Crusaders*, a syndicated show produced by Westinghouse Broadcasting Co. and Providence Journal Co., to the seven TV affiliates NBC owned and operated.

But NBC had other ideas. The network's executives wanted to step up their efforts to produce their own programs. At the time, Disney had a deal to produce *Thunder Alley* jointly with ABC, and NBC wanted a similar arrangement. To secure the arrangement, they were willing to offer Disney the same deal they had floated to Warner Brothers—a 49 percent interest in NBC for $2.5 million, with NBC chairman Bob Wright continuing to run the network. "We wanted to own, not be partners," recalled CFO Richard Nanula. "I'm not sure that we're the best partners in the world." The Disney executives walked out of their meeting with NBC without an agreement.

❖

By mid-1995, the revamped management team that Michael Eisner had put in place following Jeffrey Katzenberg's departure was beginning to operate well. Working from Frank Wells's former office next to Eisner, was Sandy Litvack, the company's senior executive vice-president and chief of corporate operations. Litvack, a longtime Wall Street lawyer who had served in the Carter administration as assistant attorney general in charge of antitrust matters, had been elevated to what was Disney's top administrative job in the restructuring of the previous summer.

In his job, he handled many of the same chores that Frank Wells had before his death, making sure that the now huge and growing Disney machinery functioned smoothly. The company's health and human resources, legal, and government lobbying offices all reported to him, and Eisner would dispatch him to problem areas. It was Litvack, along with Richard Nanula, who had completed the job of refinancing Euro Disney. Litvack also negotiated with companies seeking to sponsor rides at Disneyland.

The 58-year-old Litvack, who had joined Disney in April 1991, was well qualified for the job. He joined the company as a senior vice-president and general counsel and a year later became head of human resources. A one-time college football player with a law degree from Georgetown University, he had been managing partner of the Wall Street firm Donovan, Leisure, Newton & Irving and later head of litigation at Dewey Ballantine. Still, despite his fast move up the ladder at Disney, he was hardly a Hollywood insider. Litvack and his wife Judith chose not to live in a Beverly Hills mansion, instead making their home in a high-rise condominium apartment in Westwood.

One of the key negotiations that Litvack took on was the still simmering lawsuit threatened by former studio chief Katzenberg. Katzenberg, who had hired super-lawyer Bert Fields to represent his interests, claimed that his contract with Disney required the company to pay him 2% of the profits for such hits as *Aladdin*, *Beauty and the Beast*, and *The Lion King*. The tab could run into the millions. Eisner, still furious at Katzenberg, had initially pledged not to settle. But he had turned to Litvack for some way out of the tangle without a lawsuit. For months, Litvack had tried to settle the matter with little success.

While Litvack was trying to deal with the studio's leftover problems, its current affairs were being handled by its new chairman, Joe Roth. The 47-year-old Roth was a ruggedly handsome one-time movie director with three films to his credit, including such lightly regarded fare as *Coupe de Ville* and *Revenge of the Nerds II*. Where Roth excelled, however, was as a movie executive. He had helped car dealer Jim Robinson create Morgan Creek Pictures, one of the industry's top independent producers with such hits as Kevin Costner's *Robin Hood.*

Roth had been lured to head 20th Century Fox films by Barry Diller in 1988 with a salary of $1 million and a deal that paid him 3 percent of Fox's film earnings. In 1990, thanks largely to *Home Alone,* he had earned $5 million. But by 1992, Diller had left the company to head the QVC cable shopping network, and Fox's studio operation was struggling under the weight of such losers as Bette Midler's megaflop *For the Boys.* Fox owner Rupert Murdoch and Roth had come to a parting of the ways, and Roth had turned to agent Michael Ovitz to find him a studio that would sign him to a production deal where he could make his own films.

The bidding eventually came down to Sony's Columbia Pictures unit, which was then looking to restart its struggling studio, and Disney. Eisner and Katzenberg had worked hard to sign Roth and had eventually paid dearly to get him, signing him for $1 million per film for the 25 films Disney wanted him to produce over the next five years. And he would get a healthy chunk of the profits.

Roth had put only a handful of films in place before his job changed. By mid-1994, Eisner asked him to step in to take over for Katzenberg. At the time, the studio was churning out a steady stream of animated blockbusters, and was approaching $1 billion a year in operating earnings. But Eisner worried that the studio's live-action operation was falling behind Warner Brothers, Paramount, and other studios. It was making too many losers like *Cabin Boy* and *More Money.*

The new Disney studio chief had raised eyebrows in Hollywood when he turned his back on the company's longtime philosophy of making cheap films and began to load up on pricier films and stars. He paid $3 million for the rights to an unpublished romance novel by a first-time novelist, Nicholas Evans, called *The Horse Whisperer,* and then signed Robert Redford to star in the movie.

But by mid-1995, the studio seemed to be on the mend. Roth's first film, a Michelle Pfeiffer film called *Dangerous Minds,* became the surprise hit of the summer and earned more than $70 million while producing one of the year's strongest sound tracks. The studio also had a major hit with the pricey Denzel Washington–Gene Hackman submarine drama, *Crimson Tide.*

By early 1995, however, the company was still searching for a new chief financial officer to take over from Richard Nanula, who had been moved over to head the company's fast-expanding Disney Store operation. Eisner had instructed Nanula to head the search for his own replacement, but increasingly the young CFO had turned to his own mentor, former Disney CFO Gary Wilson, for help. Wilson, still a member of the Disney board, was at the time cochairman of Northwest Airlines with his longtime friend Al Checchi.

In March 1995, Wilson suggested Stephen F. Bollenbach, the 53-year-old president of Host Marriott Corp., a spin-off from the Marriott hotel chain at which Wilson had worked in the early 1980s. Bollenbach was considered one of the premier CFOs of his day, having served as Marriott's CFO before organizing a 1993 financial maneuver that had split the company into two. The Host Marriott organization that Bollenbach headed owned 100 hotels and was the nation's largest operator of toll road and airport concessions, with facilities at 73 airports and along 14 major highways.

Bollenbach was also known throughout the finance industry as a proponent of the big deal. For 28 years after getting his graduate degree from the California State University at Northridge, Bollenbach had risen rapidly from the finance department of a local savings and loan to become a key player at casino and hotel company Holiday Corp. (now Promus), where he helped fend off the takeover advances in the mid-1980s of Donald Trump. He went on to work for Trump for two years, and engineered the restructuring of Trump's casino companies, after the billionaire was nearly forced into bankruptcy.

The easygoing, fast-thinking Bollenbach was just the type of CFO Eisner wanted. The two met for the first time at a Mighty Ducks hockey game at The Pond, the Anaheim arena at which the Disney-owned team played. They hit it off immediately, although Bollenbach had two major demands before he would take the job. He insisted on a contract that gave him 150,000 shares of Disney stock and a place on the Disney board. Eisner agreed to both, and on April 4 Bollenbach joined the Disney team. Three weeks later, at the next regularly scheduled Disney board meeting, both Litvack and Bollenbach were elected to the company's board of directors, bringing the board to 15 members.

Within a few months, Disney's two new board members would serve key roles in one of the largest acquisitions in corporate history.

❖

Eisner had remained fixated on buying the ABC parent company after coming within a few billion dollars of buying it in 1993. While he would joke later that he would only buy a company at which he had once worked, the former ABC programmer and Disney chief also knew that Cap Cities, with its bulging assets and streamlined financial operation, was the one company that could quickly add to Disney's value. Thanks to Larry Tisch, CBS was an overpriced company with years of rebuilding ahead of it. An NBC deal came with strings attached that Eisner couldn't tolerate.

Moreover, Cap Cities' fundamentals continued to improve mightily, according to Disney's financial experts. The network business alone, boosted by an increasingly strong advertising market, had jumped from a trough of $92 million in 1992 to $347 million in 1994, and was heading toward a $615 million gain in 1996. Moreover, the company's TV and radio station group, also enjoying the uptick in ad fortunes, were expected to increase operating earnings from $502 million in 1993 to close to $780 million by 1996. But the biggest winner of all, the Disney execs figured, would likely be ESPN.

The giant cable sports network, which already contributed a robust 20 percent of the company's earnings, was growing at an impressive rate. Moreover, revenues at the sports channel were projected to grow 18 percent to 20 percent in the future as new customers signed on from direct broadcast satellite users and the international market. Operating income was also projected to increase by 24 percent, to nearly $90 million by 1997. The year-old ESPN2 network, with over 20 million viewers, was already one of the fastest start-up cable channels in recent history. Both channels were making a heavy push into international areas, and were in the process of moving into India and Asia, places where Disney wanted to be as well.

Altogether, with more than 67 million households in the United States and nearly 150 million around the world already getting the service, Disney's financial experts were estimating that Cap Cities' 80 percent interest in the two sports services alone was worth more than $5 billion.

Moreover, ESPN could form the backbone of a expansive offering of other Disney cable services. With ESPN in its basket, Disney salespeople could promote the Disney Channel in Asian and South American markets that were only slowly warming to the Disney offering. ESPN could also play a significant role in the company's new expansion plans into sports. The company already had one joint venture with ESPN to build a sports bar at its Pleasure Island retail cluster in Orlando, and thought they could expand the concept elsewhere. Moreover, ESPN would allow Disney to promote its sports franchises, which included the Mighty Ducks hockey team, a growing sports facility in Orlando, and plans to buy the California Angels baseball team.

Then, there were ABC's diverse foreign operations, which included a 20 percent stake in the Japan Sports Channel, a half-interest in the Tele-München TV production company in Germany, a one-third interest in Hamster Productions in France, 23 percent of German network RTL, and 25 percent of the Scandinavian Broadcasting System. Those holdings were ideal for Disney, which by 1995 had pushed Disney-made TV shows into more than 100 countries and was anxiously eyeing a fast-exploding foreign market for American programs.

The Disney brain trust, which by April 1995 also included new CFO Steve Bollenbach and Sandy Litvack, met several times over the spring and summer of that year to work up projections. Frequently, those meetings took place in a private dining room on the sixth floor of the Team Disney building, under the arm of one of the giant terra-cotta statues of the seven dwarfs that symbolically held up the building. By the summer of 1995, Team Disney had narrowed a possible price tag for the company to $19 billion.

Eisner and Cap Cities chairman Tom Murphy had continued to keep in touch during the months that followed their near deal in 1993. Whenever possible, Eisner would call on him when in New York, and the Cap Cities chairman called his Disney counterpart on a regular basis, especially as the industry continued to consolidate. In March, the two had briefly discussed the notion of a deal once over dinner in New York. Again, Murphy insisted on Disney using its stock for the purchase, arguing that the combined companies would become a major entertainment power in an exploding industry. After years of protecting Disney's stock price, Eisner resisted, fearing a dilution that would erode the stock's upward spiral. But Eisner was weakening, and suggested that he might consider some combination of stock, cash, and possibly notes to swing the deal.

Both men came away from the table thinking a deal was, indeed, possible, if the method of payment could be agreed upon. By July, the Disney chairman decided to try again. Meeting with his brain trust at one of their lunches, new Disney CFO Bollenbach suggested that the company offer $19 billion for Cap Cities, the upper end of the range Disney's financial analysts had suggested, and put a combined cash and stock offer on the table. Eisner agreed.

The Disney executives planned to make the overture at the annual investment conference thrown in Sun Valley by Herb Allen. This year's session was to start on July 13, and Eisner, Litvack, and Bollenbach all made plans to attend. The Allen conference had a well-deserved reputation for being the crucible at which major deals got done. It was there that Ted Turner first decided to buy New Line Cinema, the independent film company, and where agent Michael Ovitz and Seagram Co. chairman Edgar Bronfman first contemplated Seagram taking a major stake in Time-Warner.

Eisner was scheduled to make a presentation to the assembled parties about Disney's upcoming plans during the second morning, on July 14. Afterwards, the Disney chairman went strolling through the conference center, specifically in search of Tom Murphy. The two Disney executives found Murphy, with major Cap Cities shareholder Warren Buffett, on their way to play golf. "We're wondering if the time is right for us to get this deal done," Eisner inquired. Murphy, as he had stated on previous occasions, said he was interested but only if Cap Cities shareholders could get shares in the new company. While Eisner told Murphy that an all-stock deal was still out of the question, the Disney chairman said he was willing to part with far more of the company's stock than he had agreed to in their previous talks.

That was enough for Murphy to agree to more in-depth conversations. A week later, on July 21, Eisner and Bollenbach headed to New York to meet with Murphy and Dan Burke, who was still a major shareholder in the company but had just retired as CEO. The meeting did not go well, at least at the outset. Murphy and Burke continued to insist on an all-stock deal. Eisner insisted that the Disney board would never consider such a major dilution. Instead, Eisner suggested the same kind of strategic alliance that NBC had offered to Disney the year before—the two companies would enter into an agreement by which Disney would produce a full slate of Saturday morning cartoons, three prime-time specials, and a weekly one-hour prime-time show.

At the time, ABC was a heavy buyer of programs from Disney anyway, paying Disney $81 million in license fees to produce *Home Improvement, Ellen,* and *Boy Meets World,* along with the rights to run Disney's movies. ABC's TV stations also paid roughly $9 million annually for the rights to air such Disney syndicated programs as *Live with Regis and Kathy Lee*. At the very least, Murphy figured, his bill for running some of the shows would go down. (Ironically, Cap Cities had three months earlier entered into a similar deal with Jeffrey Katzenberg's Dreamworks studio, by which each party put $100 million into a joint venture that would, among other things, provide Saturday morning programs for the ABC network.)

The meeting in New York ended with Murphy saying he would consider the idea of a joint venture. But for the next four days, the phone lines between Burbank and New York burned. With Bollenbach sitting in his office, Eisner continued to negotiate the price with Murphy. Finally, Eisner suggested that they simply split the difference. Eventually, Murphy agreed to a formula by which each of his shareholders would get a share of Disney stock, then trading at $57.38, and $65 in cash for each Cap Cities share. The final tab for the deal would be $19.08 billion, Bollenbach had calculated.

On July 25, Murphy called back to say that Buffett and Burke had both agreed to the formula. Eisner, obviously elated, still had work to do. Over the next two days, he called each of the company's 13 outside board members. Because it was summer, he had to track some of them down. Gary Wilson, enroute to an African safari, was tracked down in Tel Aviv. Roy Disney was on his boat in the Atlantic. On July 27, Eisner had approval from his board to take the next step and called Tom Murphy to say his team was ready to sit down and write the formal merger agreement.

By July 28, Litvack and Bollenbach headed to the New York offices of Dewey Ballantine, Litvack's former law firm and one of Disney's many outside lawyers. Camped out for the next four days in the office, executives from Disney and Cap Cities hammered out what would become a 125-page agreement for the deal. Until then, neither side had dealt with investment bankers, who usually structure such deals. (In fact, Eisner had insisted that the bankers stay out of the transaction, for fear that the traditionally chatty investment banking community would get wind of the deal early on and drive up Cap Cities' stock price.) Cap Cities called in Allen and Co., which turned over the deal to senior managing partner Enrique Senior, while Disney brought in one of its longtime investment bankers, Alan Schwartz at Bear Stearns.

By Sunday morning, July 30, when Eisner headed to New York, the agreement had been worked on for three days. During that period, the two sides had exchanged financial documents and agreed to certain bedrock provisions of the deal. Under the reorganization agreement, each Cap Cities shareholder could either convert each of their shares into a share of Disney and $65 in cash, or as much Disney stock as was available to them at the time. (Disney offered the all-stock provision for some investors in the event that some shareholders chose to sell their stock into the open market rather than back to Disney. If that happened, Disney would then be forced to allocate the remaining stock and cash to the existing shareholders.)

The largest shareholders in both companies, Sid Bass and Warren Buffett, turned out to be key players in the negotiations as each tried to look out for his best interests. At the time, Buffett's Berkshire Hathaway Inc., his Omaha-based holding company, owned 20 million shares of Cap Cities. That added up to 13 percent of the company, worth an estimated $2.5 billion in the Disney deal. After agreeing to the structure of the merger, Buffett pledged to vote his shares in support of the acquisition.

Tom Murphy was given a seat on the Disney board as well. As part of the deal, Murphy suggested that Cap Cities' current president, Bob Iger, stay on for five years as head of the same unit inside Disney. The contract Iger signed on July 31 pays him $1 million annually, with a $2 million bonus for the first year. Each year after that, he is scheduled to receive a "discretionary bonus" targeted at another $1 million annually, with the added amounts figured out by the board based on the rise in the new Disney operation's stock price. On top of that, Iger was given options to purchase 700,000 shares of the new company's stock, with 100,000 shares awarded each year through 2002.

The merger agreement also required Cap Cities to pay Disney a stunning $400 million in the event the deal was terminated. But even if the deal did fall apart, Eisner and company intended to get something for their troubles. The TV programming agreement, which Eisner had initially proposed to Murphy, would remain in effect unless Disney decided to terminate it. That agreement required ABC to purchase Saturday morning programs from Disney over a three-year period starting in 1996 that would fill the network's 8:00 A.M. to noon time period. Disney would also supply a weekly one-hour prime-time show that Eisner would host. And Disney would also deliver three one-hour specials each year for the network, made up of such subjects as "The Making of Pocahontas" or "Disneyland's 40th Anniversary."

❖

With the agreement complete, approval by the Disney and Cap Cities boards was almost anticlimactic. Eisner, Litvack, and Bollenbach, sitting in a Dewey Ballantine conference room with Sid Bass, convened a meeting by phone with most of the remaining Disney board. Alan Schwartz, the Bear Stearns managing director charged with heading the investment bank's efforts to write a fairness opinion, was there. So were the lawyers for Dewey Ballantine, Morton Pierce and Mark Baker, who had been in on the negotiations. Disney's strategic planning team, Larry Murphy, Peter Murphy, and Tom Staggs sat in, as did Disney assistant general counsel David Thompson. After a two-hour meeting, the Disney board approved the deal. The Cap Cities board took two days to complete its work. Allen and Company, which had also received a $2 million fee for its three days of crash work on the deal, had assessed a wide range of other media transactions that had taken place over the previous two years and found that the Disney deal fit somewhere in the middle. With the deal, Allen's analysis showed, the two companies would be a virtual powerhouse with cash flow of more than $4 billion. Allen went through a thorough analysis of Disney's operations, including its recently completed restructuring of Euro Disney, and detailed the upward mobility of Disney's stock price over the previous decade.

The board, wanting another day to sleep on what they had been told, asked Tom Murphy for more time to consider the deal. Murphy agreed, but asked them to reconvene the next morning for a breakfast meeting at 7:00 A.M. By 7:30, the Cap Cities board had given the impending merger its blessing.

That set in motion a fast-paced media blitz to get the word out. John Dreyer, Disney's top public relations executive, had flown into New York for the weekend and had enlisted the help of an ABC producer to remake Studio One, the ABC studio where *Prime Time Live* and other shows were telecast, for the press announcement. A banner with both companies' logos was ordered on Sunday afternoon, just as the Cap Cities board was beginning its first meeting, and Dreyer and others walked through the studio to determine where the chairs and podium were to be located.

By 7:30, when the Cap Cities board had given its approval, ABC's *Good Morning, America* was alerted to the announcement as well. By 8:00 A.M., Eisner and Tom Murphy appeared on the show with coanchor Charles Gibson to announce the deal to the world.

By 10:00 A.M., the two chairmen, along with major shareholders Warren Buffett and Sid Bass, were at a table set up in front of a swarm of reporters and camera crews in Studio One. "There are synergies under every rock we turn over," said an enthused Michael Eisner as he announced the blockbuster deal.

After the barrage of questions, Murphy and Eisner headed upstairs to the Cap Cities executive offices, where a series of one-on-one interviews followed with major publications. Then, the two men hopped Disney's corporate jet for Washington to do a segment on ABC's *Nightline* show, with Cokie Roberts sitting in for Ted Koppel. Then, they began the process of talking with congressional leaders and regulators to win federal approval for the deal. But even as the FCC and Congress began to tackle the chore, Eisner had another deal he needed to close: getting someone to help him run his giant empire.

❖

By 1985, Michael Ovitz, the 48-year old superstar talent agent and head of the Creative Artists Agency, was the acknowledged "most powerful man in Hollywood." His face peered out from the covers of *Business Week, Newsweek,* and the *New York Times* Sunday magazine, and regularly headed the superfluous lists of power brokers published annually by the likes of *Entertainment* and *Premiere* magazines.

Unlike Eisner and Katzenberg, both of whom were born into wealth and power, Ovitz had worked his way up from far more modest beginnings. Born in Chicago, the son of a liquor salesman, the gap-toothed agent grew up in a tract home in San Fernando Valley just outside Los Angeles. As a youngster, he had brushes with glamour—sneaking under the fence to see films being made at Republic Pictures's nearby lot and going to high school with future junk bond guru Michael Milken and actress-in-the-making Sally Field.

But while Milken was a yell leader and Field a cheerleader for the high school sports teams, Ovitz was content to stay in the background. He thought of becoming a doctor, and for a while majored in premedical studies at UCLA. But Hollywood soon beckoned, in the unlikely form of a job as a tour guide at Universal Studios and 20th Century Fox.

His next stop was the legendary mail room at the William Morris Agency, which spawned such Hollywood titans as David Geffen and Barry Diller. Ovitz, too, was elevated from envelopes to deal making when the head of the agency hired him as an assistant. Not long after, he was handling rock groups. After worrying about the drug use in that industry, he switched to representing television stars and producers like Aaron Spelling.

Packaging TV shows was an art that the Morris Agency had developed: By owning the rights to a show, as well as representing the top actors and directors, the agency would come to a network with a show all but made and force the network to pay to have it done. Ovitz learned his lessons well, and when he and four partners broke away in 1975 to start their own agency, he took the art of packaging to new heights.

Working from folding tables in their first offices, the new partners built the most powerful agency Hollywood had ever seen. By 1985, it represented just about every big name in the business, from directors like Steven Spielberg and Martin Scorcese to a galaxy of such stars as Robert Redford, Sylvester Stallone, Tom Hanks, and Barbra Streisand. It represented writers such as *Jurassic Park* author Michael Crichton and *Interview with a Vampire* creator Anne Rice.

Ovitz's power could be awesome. His agency had put together both the *Jurassic Park* and *Forrest Gump* movies, selling them as packages to executives at Universal and Paramount, and then collected when the fees for the directors, actors, and producers they represented started coming in.

At its height, CAA was said to be generating more than $300 million annually, with Ovitz, who ultimately owned 56 percent of the agency, taking home an estimated $35 million annually. But what CAA had given, it could also take away: When new Columbia Pictures chief David Putnam lashed out publicly at CAA client Bill Murray for demanding too much money, Ovitz held up the sequel to Columbia's *Ghostbusters* for months. Eventually, after Putnam left, Ovitz put together the deal for Putnam's successor Dawn Steel. Ovitz could maintain his power by helping to place executives in top places. He had represented Joe Roth when the Fox executive had jumped to Disney, and had negotiated NBC programming head Brandon Tartikoff's move to head Paramount Pictures.

By the early 1990s, however, Ovitz was already playing on a much larger field. He had taken CAA into the deal-making business, operating as an agent for such deals as the purchase of Columbia Pictures by Sony and

MCA's acquisition by Matsushita. In each case, representing the Japanese buyers, he pocketed handsome fees, getting an estimated $10 million alone for Sony's $3.4 billion Columbia purchase. CAA had stolen a big chunk of the Coke advertising account from McCann Erickson by offering flashy new ads that included soft-drink-swilling polar bears and a new hip "Always Coca-Cola" jingle. And, while Disney was allying itself with three of the seven Baby Bell phone companies to go into the TV distribution business, Ovitz had lined up three other Baby Bells for a rival network.

Ovitz fancied himself as another Lew Wasserman, the one-time talent agent who had risen to become Hollywood's reigning monarch by converting what had been the talent agency Music Corp. of America into the MCA entertainment empire that included the Universal Pictures studio, two theme parks, and a major record label. Like Wasserman, Ovitz wanted to run his own studio. He had his chances after Sony had purchased Columbia, but had turned down Sony USA chief Mickey Schulhof when the new Japanese owners wouldn't give the talent agent a piece of the studio as well as carte blanche power to run it.

By 1993, Ovitz had focused on Time-Warner, the sprawling entertainment giant that included Warner Brothers, cable TV holdings, HBO, *Time* magazine and *Sports Illustrated*. Ovitz was also friends with Seagram chief executive Edgar Bronfman, Jr., who had once been an aspiring movie producer. The two men also talked frequently about media issues, and in 1992 Ovitz had advised the liquor heir to invest in Time-Warner. By 1993, Seagram was heading toward a 15 percent stake in the entertainment colossus.

But in early 1995, Bronfman had set his sights on a different target. Matsushita had grown tired of operating MCA, which was then on the verge of taking a bath on the big budget film *Waterworld*. Seagram, eager to diversify its liquor business, had bid $5.7 billion to buy an 80 percent stake in the entertainment company, and Bronfman was looking for someone to run his empire. Ovitz was his man. But in an extraordinarily public bidding process for Ovitz, who prided his privacy, negotiations dragged on for weeks. At one point, the CAA chairman was offered a staggering amount of money, estimated with stock options to be worth more than $250 million. Eventually, when Seagram wouldn't give Ovitz the control he wanted to run the operation, the agent walked away again.

The negotiations with MCA may have been public. But behind the scenes, Michael Eisner was maneuvering to recruit Ovitz for Disney. For years, the two men had been the closest of friends. They had met years earlier when Eisner was buying TV shows for ABC and Ovitz was pitching them for his clients. Eisner had tried to hire Ovitz for ABC then and for Paramount years later. Their families sometimes vacationed together in Aspen, and on Eisner's birthdays, Ovitz took delight in finding different ways to surprise him. (One year, Ovitz threw the party a week early, telling Eisner they were going to a inexpensive restaurant with their families, then showing up at one of Hollywood's flashiest places with more than 200 people waiting.) When Eisner had his heart bypass operation, Ovitz took control at his bedside, shooing away Disney executives and taking the phone from Eisner's hand.

Michael Eisner had been forced to play two roles while Ovitz negotiated with Bronfman. On the one hand, he was being asked to give honest advise on the MCA offer, which was extraordinarily generous and would give Ovitz what he most wanted—the opportunity to run a company nearly as large and diverse as the one that Eisner himself was running. (Indeed, MCA's shopworn image was very nearly the equal to the broken-down Disney that Eisner had inherited a decade earlier.)

But Eisner wanted Ovitz to join him at Disney instead. The Disney chief had promised his wife Jane not long after his bypass operation that he would seek help running Disney. So, even while Ovitz was negotiating with Bronfman, Eisner continued to make his bid. He would offer the CAA executive, he told him, wide-ranging opportunities at Disney and generous stock options. Moreover, he would make it clear to the Disney board that, in the event that Eisner chose to step down or couldn't run the company, Ovitz would be the man to step in. "I think he saw me as a safety net," Eisner would say later. "He couldn't fail. If he couldn't get the deal done with Edgar, he always had me to fall back on."

By June, Ovitz's deal with MCA had fallen apart. Worse yet, it looked as if CAA was also starting to fall apart. During the talks with Bronfman, Ovitz had hoped that Seagram would also purchase his interest in the agency, valued at roughly $200 million. That, too, had become a sticking point in the talks. Moreover, the mood at MCA was growing increasingly downbeat. During his protracted talks with Bronfman, Ovitz had called several meetings of the 100-odd CAA agents to assure them he wasn't leaving. When it became apparent that he was, talk within Hollywood intensified that the stable of superstar CAA clients would feel abandoned and might bolt to International Creative Management, William Morris, or another agency.

Within days of Ovitz's backing out of the deal, things worsened. His longtime friend and partner, CAA cofounder Ron Meyer, had decided to take the top MCA job instead. (Ovitz had hoped to bring Meyer along with him to help run MCA, along with several other top CAA executives. When Ovitz's deal fell apart, Meyer took the president's job, leaving the top job, MCA's chairmanship, to be filled by Bronfman himself.)

Eisner called Ovitz not long after Meyers decided to take the MCA job. The time was right for him to make the move as well, the Disney chief told his old friend. This time Ovitz agreed, and the two began talking the specifics of the deal. It was a discussion that would take a few days, but in contrast to the MCA talks, Ovitz now seemed more motivated to make the move. His bridges at CAA had been burned. By necessity, Eisner had to let Ovitz in on the ongoing talks with Cap Cities, which had begun just after the two had first started negotiating in earnest and continued as the talks progressed. The weekend before Eisner was to fly to New York to make the announcement, the Disney chief laid out the entire Cap Cities deal for his new second-in-command at a meeting at Eisner's home in Bel Air.

Ovitz, as Eisner envisioned it, would serve as the executive charged with making sure the two companies would mesh. He would help ABC hire new executives and work on combining the two companies' various interests in programming, cable, and magazines. Moreover, Ovitz would spearhead the company's efforts to push into international markets with the Disney Channel and its TV programs.

The final details of Ovitz's employment were agreed upon during a weekend in Aspen in early August, and Ovitz's appointment was announced on August 14. All that was left was for the lawyers, Sandy Litvack for Disney and LA lawyers Robert Adler and Michael Rubel for Ovitz, to work out the final details. As Eisner and Wells had done with their contracts, Ovitz wanted the largest portion of his paycheck to come from bonuses and stock options. His base pay, however, would have to be $1 million annually. At the time Eisner was making only $750,000 in straight salary.

There were other differences. The agreements Eisner and Wells had signed had given them bonuses based on a formula tied to the level of earnings the company achieved. (In Eisner's case, the board had agreed in his 1989 contract to pay him 2% of the amount Disney's income exceeded a specified limit. In 1995 that meant a $8 million bonus.) Ovitz did not want to be limited, especially if the work he did wouldn't bear fruit in terms of profits until some years down the road. As a result, Ovitz would be eligible each year for a bonus, which would be decided by the Disney board's compensation committee. (The committee is made up of outside board members that included actor Sidney Poitier, former Disney chairman Ray Watson, and Spanish publisher Ignacio E. Lozano, Jr.)

Like Eisner, though, Ovitz stood to make the largest chunk of his salary through the stock options that had zoomed in value during the Eisner years at Disney. Ovitz's stock options were hardly as generous as Eisner's, whose contract called for options to 8 million shares. Eisner had cashed in stock options for hundreds of millions of dollars in previous years, and in 1995 was granted 97,445 shares of stock worth an additional $5.9 million. Ovitz's contract called for him to be granted 1 million shares of Disney stock annually. And because the options were priced at $57 a share, the price when the new Disney president's contract was signed, Ovitz could potentially reap many millions as well. (Indeed, by the time the ABC deal closed in early January, Disney's stock had climbed past $60 a share, earning Ovitz a paper profit of $15 million after being on the job for a mere three months.)

Ovitz would also receive a $10 million bonus in the event that the company didn't renew his option at the end of the five-year deal. But to compensate for the fortune that Ovitz was likely to receive, Disney took steps to make sure he wouldn't bolt before the end of his contract, which expires on September 30, 2000. Under the agreement, Ovitz would receive the first 3 million shares in yearly increments of 1 million but had to be working on June 30th of any year to receive his stock options for that year. And he couldn't touch the remaining 2 million shares until the year after his contract expired, getting a million in 2001 and another million in 2002. And he couldn't get any of the 2 million unless he was still working at the company at that time.

Ovitz's tenure at the company was scheduled to begin on October 1, 1995. That was designed to give him time to arrange an orderly transition at CAA and to arrange to sell his 56 percent stake to the agency's top agents. But while Ovitz was taking those steps, he was also very obviously a presence at the Walt Disney Company. Working from what had been Frank Wells's conference room, the Disney executive was fast becoming acquainted with how the company worked.

In August, just days after his announced hiring, the new Disney president was in Jackson Hole, Wyoming, attending a meeting of Disney's consumer products division. Later that month, he was on his way to Europe for meetings on Euro Disney and the company's growing international operations. At Disney, he and Eisner were already being called "the two Michaels."

❖

The two Michaels, Eisner and Ovitz, had gone to New York on February 21, just days after the Federal Communications Commission had given Disney's merger with Cap Cities its final approval, to calm the fears among ABC's news crew that the network's new owners planned massive changes that would infringe upon the news organization's freedom and objectivity. But Eisner and Ovitz had other nerves to calm as well. Speaking to ABC's 224 affiliates, who were meeting at the Fairmont Hotel in Dallas, Disney's top executives beamed a message via a telephone hookup from the same Studio One facility in New York where Eisner and Tom Murphy had first announced the megadeal.

Things had worsened at ABC since the deal. At the time of the transaction, ABC was comfortably ahead of NBC in the ratings war. By February, NBC had poked into the ratings lead, propelled by such highly rated shows as *Seinfeld, Friends,* and *ER.* Meanwhile, such long-time ABC ratings champs as *Roseanne* and *Coach* were fading. Overall, ratings were off by 8 percent from a year earlier, while ratings for such key advertising groups as 18–49-year-old women had fallen even further. Worse yet, one of NBC's top new shows, *3rd Rock from the Sun,* had landed at the rival network after ABC had dropped the show from its lineup.

The lost audience, plus a suddenly weaker advertising market, had saddled ABC with a 3 percent decline in operating earnings for its final quarter as an independent company. Telecasting from Studio One, Disney's executives were quick to say that, they, too, were concerned about the drop. "This is not satisfactory," said Ovitz, who had pledged to make changes.

In fact, Ovitz was already hard at work at doing just that. A week earlier, he had contacted Jamie McDermott, the 31-year-old NBC programming executive who was credited with finding *Friends* and *Mad About You* for that network. McDermott had wanted to move up at NBC but had been blocked when the network gave program chief Warren Lit-tlefield a contract extension. Ovitz stepped in after McDermott had al-ready contacted ABC chief Iger.

Ovitz wanted McDermott to replace Ted Harbert, ABC's longtime programming chief, who would move upstairs to a different job. (Harbert had not helped himself by being the executive who had turned away *3rd Rock from the Sun.*) The problem was that McDermott, whose contract ran out in May 1997, couldn't win her release from NBC in time for the ABC affiliates' meeting. Instead, she and her bosses decided she would take a leave of absence until June 15, well past the time when she could help ABC with its upcoming schedule, before she would be allowed to join Disney. (On June 17, 1996, ABC announced the hiring of McDer-mott, who was now using her married name of Tarses. She was named president, and Harbert became chairman of ABC's entertainment unit.)

The problems at ABC overshadowed what had been a spectacular 1995 for Disney overall. For the year, the company had earned a record $1.38 billion, a 24 percent hike over the previous year, as revenues jumped past $12 billion for the first time in the company's history. The loss from its Euro Disney holdings had been slashed to $35 million by the restructuring. Elsewhere the company was hitting on all cylinders. The studio, propelled by the 30 million copies of *The Lion King* the company shipped and the syndication of *Home Improvement,* had operating earnings alone of $1.07 billion. A rebound in attendance boosted theme park earnings by 26 per-cent, while the company opened 105 new Disney Stores during the year and were operating 429 worldwide. Overall, the consumer products unit was up by 20 percent, with the growth in merchandise tied to *The Lion King* and *Pocahontas* helping to propel the growth.

Moreover, as the ABC acquisition showed, the company seemed to have recovered the vitality that many thought it had lost during the terri-ble 1994 period that followed Wells's death and Katzenberg's departure. Construction had been completed on Celebration, the 5,000-acre com-munity at Walt Disney World that would eventually be home to 20,000 people. The company had opened the Disney Institute, and was in the midst of final negotiations with the Oriental Land Company on building a second theme park alongside the still immensely profitable Tokyo Disney-land. The new park, which would use some of the nautical themed rides that had been planned for Long Beach, was to be called Tokyo DisneySea.

The company was moving into new areas as well, including a cruise ship line and timeshare apartments at Hilton Head, South

Carolina and Vero Beach, Florida. In late 1995, the company agreed to purchase a 25 percent interest in the California Angels baseball team, with an option to buy the remaining interest at a later date from long-time owner Gene Autry. And there were continued rumors that Disney, already the owner of a professional hockey team, was contemplating the purchase of the Los Angeles Clippers basketball team and might bid on a franchise for professional football for Anaheim.

Based on the spectacular success of its Broadway adaptation of *Beauty and the Beast*, the company also planned to spend $32 million to remodel the ancient New Amsterdam Theater by early 1997. With the theater as its main venue, Disney planned to stage a new show a year. Among those being contemplated were shows based on *The Lion King* and *Mary Poppins*, and another based on the opera *Aida* with music by Elton John.

Elsewhere in the Disney empire, things were also picking up. At the studio, which finished 1995 with the largest market share in the industry, things continued on an uptick. *Mr. Holland's Opus*, starring Richard Dreyfuss as a high school music teacher, earned more than $70 million. Disney also had another big hit in *Up Close and Personal*, which starred Robert Redford and Michelle Pfeiffer. By Christmas, its computer-animated film *Toy Story* was heading over $100 million in the United States alone. And down the road, the studio lined up such high-priced talent as Robin Williams to star in a comedy, *Jack*. The company also had films starring Nicholas Cage, Whoopi Goldberg, Mel Gibson, and Denzel Washington on its upcoming list. (In a major move away from the Katzenberg philosophy of increasing production, however, Disney decided to cut its film production nearly in half, as Hollywood profits continued to be eroded by production.)

The animation unit, being run now by Peter Schneider, also had a full plate. Its 1996 offering, a musical version of *The Hunchback of Notre Dame*, opened strongly and went on to gross more than $70 million. The company was already working on its next offering, *Hercules*, and *The Legend of Mulan*, based on a Chinese folk story.

The presence of Michael Ovitz was being felt increasingly throughout the company as well. Within days after Ovitz started at the company, the studio signed actor Sean Connery, an Ovitz client whom the agent signed for an $8 million payday to do *Rising Sun*. Other Ovitz clients followed in short order, including Steven Spielberg's husband-and-wife producer team, Kathleen Kennedy and Frank Marshall.

Martin Scorsese also signed on, leaving Universal Studios after nine years there to sign a two-year, $10 million deal to make his next three films for the company.

Moving Disney into new areas, the former agent brought Creative Artists' advertising component to the company, along with its Coke account. Kevin Gasser, a top CAA music agent, was recruited as a top executive at Disney's struggling Hollywood Records unit.

Ovitz was also put in charge of the "Jeffrey situation," as company insiders came to call the still unresolved issue of whether Katzenberg would sue the company over the percentage of profits he believed were still owed to him. Ovitz had taken on the chore of trying to negotiate a settlement to a lawsuit that Katzenberg continued to consider in early 1996. If nothing else, it was a constant reminder of the turmoil in 1994 that had taken up so much of Eisner and his team's time.

(On April 10, 1996, Katzenberg filed suit in L.A. County court, seeking $250 million in back wages, which he says was owed to him under a contract provision that paid him 2 percent of the earnings Disney generated from certain studio films and TV shows. In its response, Disney said that Katzenberg forfeited the bonuses by leaving his contract before its scheduled expiration date.)

But it was ABC that continued to take most of Team Disney's time and attention in early 1996. To win formal approval from the FCC, Disney had to agree to sell KCAL, the local Los Angeles TV station it had bought in 1987 for $320 million. On May 13, 1996 Disney sold the station for $368 million to Young Broadcasting, a major TV station group that already had six ABC affiliates. Because Cap Cities also owned a 14% interest in Young, Disney maintained some ownership in the station.)

Within days of completing the deal, Eisner sent Steve Burke, the company's top troubleshooter, from Euro Disney to work with Bob Iger as executive vice-president of the former Cap Cities unit. (The move also was tinged with irony, since Burke's father was the same Dan Burke who helped create Cap Cities in the first place.) Gilles Pelisson, a longtime associate of Euro chairman Philippe Bourguignon, succeeded Burke at the Paris theme park.

To expand the new cable properties that Disney inherited in the Cap Cities deal, Geraldine Laybourne, the one-time school teacher who had built the Nickelodeon channel into a worthy challenger for the Disney Channel, was lured from Viacom. Her mandate was to expand Disney's holdings in Lifetime, Arts and Entertainment, and the Disney Channel by launching new programs, including those aimed at teenagers. (ESPN, and

all of Cap Cities' sports programs, were put under ESPN head Steve Born-
stein.) To help her, Laybourne hired Anne Sweeney, who had run the fx
channel for Fox, to run the Disney Channel.

The integration of Disney and ABC also moved ahead quickly, as
more and more Disney-produced programs found their way to the network. As required under its programming agreement with Disney, ABC
announced a new Saturday morning TV schedule the week before the
deal was completed that included three new Disney-produced shows—
two of them, *The Jungle Cubs* and *The Mighty Ducks*, designed to help
promote other Disney properties. Disney soon announced that it was
purchasing Jumbo Pictures, which produced the other new ABC morning show, *The Brand Spanking New Doug.*

In an attempt to boost ratings, ABC also shuffled its prime time
lineup and added a new Disney show in the process as well, *Buddies,*
about a black man and white man who are best friends. The network resigned the Carsey-Werner team to make *Roseanne,* its faded hit, but in
classic Disney style cut the price it was willing to pay to $2 million an
episode from the $3 million the network had paid the year before.

More Disney shows were also destined to appear on the ABC network. In the weeks that followed the formal merger agreement, Disney-
made movies began to appear more frequently in prime time on Saturdays
evenings. And, as ABC executives began to make plans for the season that
would begin in September 1996, they ordered five pilots from Disney—
more than any other studio other than Warner Brothers, from which it
also ordered five pilots. (ABC also had a financial interest in two other studios, Dreamworks and Brillstein/Grey, and, together with the Disney-
made programs, that gave Disney an interest in 12 of ABC's 29 pilots.)

If the pace of the changes Disney was bringing to Cap Cities startled Hollywood, it was playing well on Wall Street. Within one three-day
period in early March, a month after the merger was completed, Disney's stock jumped nearly 5 percent, to almost $69 a share, a pace nearly
double the rest of the Dow Jones Industrial Average. It no doubt helped
that Warren Buffett announced that he intended to retain the maximum
amount of Disney stock his former Cap Cities holdings would allow—
giving him roughly 3 percent of the company's stock. A week later, the
bond market jumped in, snapping up a record $2.6 billion in corporate
bonds that Disney issued to help it finance its Cap Cities purchase. "It's
the quality media stock today," Sanford C. Bernstein & Co. analyst Tom
Wolzien told *Variety.*

❖

Sitting in the Team Disney building at Burbank, Michael Eisner looked over an expanding Disney empire as vast as it was different from The Walt Disney Company he inherited. Instead of falling profits and unwanted suitors, the company was a $19 billion behemoth. The once sleepy studio was now turning out such hits as *The Rock*, the Sean Connery–Nicholas Cage action film that grossed more than $100 million in the summer of 1996. The theme parks, including the restructured Paris venture, were once more among the happiest places on earth, at least for Disney shareholders. And, with the world's media giants vying for position, Disney owned one of four major American broadcast networks.

The acquisition of Cap Cities would hardly be the end of the Disney story. Even as Eisner and Michael Ovitz were struggling with a suddenly weakened ABC network, they were planning new initiatives to expand the Disney empire. Reports continued to circulate that Disney would buy a major record company, possibly British label EMI. Ovitz spent much of his first few months on the job shuttling between Burbank and Beijing. Down the road, a theme park located somewhere within the borders of the Communist giant was seen as a virtual certainty. Elsewhere in the company, Disney Imagineers were hard at work on the next generation of amusements, looking both at giant rides and at virtual reality games that could fit into neighborhood arcades.

The cast had changed since Michael Eisner had arrived in Burbank: Frank Wells was gone, as were Jeffrey Katzenberg, Gary Wilson, Richard Frank, and the dozens of others who had brought with them their unique energies and talents. But the mission at The Walt Disney Company lived on. As Walt had done before him, Michael Eisner had harnessed creative talents capable of bringing forth unique assets that would stand the test of time and competition. There was only one *Beauty and the Beast*, only one Euro Disney, and only one Mighty Ducks hockey team. Others would try, and inevitably fail, to copy the Disney formula.

The world would continue to change, and Disney would be forced to change with it. By the 21st century, telephone companies are predicted to offer television over their wires. Satellites will transform sports viewing in the United States and abroad. People will continue to want (and need) to be entertained, informed, and challenged, and the competition for their business will be intense. But, after a decade of restoring and enlarging an American icon, no company seems as capable of meeting that challenge as The Walt Disney Company.

Notes

❖

Introduction

Interview with Sid Bass, May 30, 1990.

Walt Disney Productions annual report, 1983, p. 45.

Ibid., 1976, 1979, and 1983.

Ibid., 1984, p. 20.

"North American Theatrical Film Rental Market Shares: 1970–1989," *Variety*, January 11, 1990, p. 4.

Chapter 1

Bob Thomas, *Walt Disney: An American Original* (New York: Simon & Schuster, 1976), p. 78.

Walt Disney Productions Archive.

John Taylor, *Storming the Magic Kingdom* (New York: Alfred A. Knopf, 1987), p. vii.

Thomas, op. cit., p. 137.

Ibid., p. 99.

Ibid.

Walt Disney Productions annual report, 1940, p. 10.

Ibid., p. 260.

Alex McNeil, *Total Television* (New York: Viking Penguin, 1984), pp. 899–900.

Taylor, op. cit., p. 9.

Walt Disney Productions annual report, 1974, p. 23.

Ibid. 1973–1979; p. 12; p. 16.

Interview with Roy Disney, March 14, 1990.

Interview with Roy Disney, April 26, 1990.

Walt Disney Productions annual report, 1979.

Ibid., 1983, p. 32.

Ibid., 1982.

Interview with Stan Kinsey, April 4, 1990.

Ibid.

Interview with Ron Miller, April 26, 1990.

Interview with Ray Watson, April 16, 1990.

Interview with Ron Miller, April 26, 1990.

Ibid.

Taylor, op. cit., p. 1.

Interview with Roy Disney, March 14, 990.

Taylor, op. cit., pp. 51–52.

Ibid., pp. 185–86.

Interview with Al Checchi, April 14, 1990.

Interview with Rich Frank, May 17, 1990.

Interview with Ray Watson, March 14, 1990.

Interview with Sid Bass, May 30, 1990.

Interview with Michael Eisner, August 27, 1990.

Ibid.

Interview with Sid Bass, May 30, 1990.

Chapter 2

Minutes, Walt Disney Productions board of directors meeting, September 22, 1984.

Ibid.

Interview with Stanley Gold, June 8, 1990.

Tony Schwartz, "Hollywood's Hottest Stars," *New York*, July 30, 1984, p. 31.

Variety, January 11, 1990, p. 4.

Alex Ben Block, *Outfoxed* (New York: St. Martin's Press, 1990), p. 51.

Interview with Jerry Zucker, April 10, 1990.

Schwartz, op. cit., p. 30.

Interview with Michael Eisner, March 12, 1990.

Chapter 3

The Wall Street Journal, September 17, 1984.

Interview with Sid Bass, May 30, 1990.

Ibid.

Tony Schwartz, "Hollywood's Hottest Stars," *New York*, July 30, 1984, p. 24.

Interview with Sid Bass, May 30, 1990.

Ibid.

Ibid.

Ibid.

These numbers were confirmed by the Orlando/Orange County Convention and Visitors Bureau.

Interview with Sid Bass, May 30, 1990.

Ibid.

Ibid.

Ibid.

Ibid.

Ibid.

Ibid.

Ibid.

John Taylor, *Storming the Magic Kingdom* (New York: Alfred A. Knopf, 1987), p. 238.

Michael Cieply, "Disney Faces Calm Period as Bass Group Buys Out Jacobs Stake for $58.1 Million," *The Wall Street Journal*, October 5, 1984.

Interviews with Sid Bass, May 30, 1990 and Michael Eisner, August 27, 1990.

Laura Landro, "Cablevision to Pay $75 Million for Rights to Offer Disney Channel to Its Subscribers," *The Wall Street Journal*, October 10, 1984.

Chapter 4

Interview with Graef "Bud" Crystal, April 7, 1990.

Interview with Stanley Gold, June 8, 1990.

Interview with Ray Watson, April 14, 1990.

Interview with Michael Eisner, August 24, 1990.

Employment contracts between Walt Disney Productions and Michael Eisner and Frank Wells, amended and restated, September 22, 1984.

Walt Disney Productions proxy, 1986, p. 16.

Ibid., proxy, 1985, p. 23.

Aljean Harmetz, "The Man Who Makes Disney Run," *The New York Times Magazine*, February 7, 1988, p. 51.

Ibid.

Interview with Stan Kinsey, April 4, 1990.

Ibid.

Ibid.

Interview with Sid Bass, May 30, 1990.

Ibid.

Ibid.

Interview with Michael Eisner, August 24, 1990.

Walt Disney Productions proxy statement, January 6, 1986, p. 12.

Interview with Eisner, March 12, 1990.

Ibid.

Interview with Stan Kinsey, April 4, 1990.

Interview with Steve Beeks, March 4, 1990.

Interview with Richard Berger, March 27, 1990.

Chapter 5

Walt Disney Productions annual report, 1983, p. 46; 1984, p. 8.

Ibid., 1984, p. 8.

Ticket information provided by Walt Disney Productions.

Interview with Al Checchi, April 14, 1990.

Walt Disney Productions annual report, 1984, p. 47.

Interview with Jack Lindquist, June 4, 1990.

Ibid.

Walt Disney Productions annual report, 1984, p. 47.

Interview with Richard Nunis, April 3, 1990.

Ephraim Katz, *The Film Encyclopedia* (New York: Putnam Publishing Group, 1979), p. 740.

"Top 100 All-Time Film Rental Champions," *Variety*, January 11, 1989, p. 26.

Stephen J. Sansweet, "Disney's 'Imagineers' Build Space Attraction Using High-Tech Gear," *The Wall Street Journal*, January 6, 1987, p. 1.

Interview with Frank Wells, June 25, 1990.

Randy Bright, *Disneyland: The Inside Story* (New York: Abrams, 1987), p. 230.

Stephen J. Sansweet, *The Wall Street Journal*, January 6, 1987, p. 1.

Ibid.

Ibid.

Interview with Jack Lindquist, June 4, 1990.

Michael Burkett, "Sneaking a Peek at Disneyland's 'Captain EO,' " *The Orange County Register,* September 15, 1986.

Letter from Frank G. Wells to John L. Tishman, Tishman Realty & Construction Co., Inc., et al., dated December 11, 1985.

S. G. Warburg and Walt Disney Productions annual report, 1984, p. 8.

Walt Disney Productions, 10-K report to the Securities & Exchange Commission, 1984, p. 2.

Orlando/Orange County Convention and Visitors Bureau.

Tishman Realty & Construction, et al. v. Walt Disney Productions, et al., Case No. 86–1518, filed February 4, 1986.

Interview with Michael Eisner, August 24, 1990.

Walt Disney Productions archive.

Walt Disney Productions annual reports, 1983, p. 40; 1984, p. 42.

Walt Disney Productions annual report, 1987, p. 44.

Ed Bean, "Delta to Announce Pact with Disney World," *The Wall Street Journal,* January 30, 1987.

Walt Disney Productions annual report, 1985, p. 34; 1987, p. 38

Ibid., 1987, p. 6

Ibid., pp. 37, 39.

Interview with Jack Lindquist, June 4, 1990.

Chapter 6

Interview with Michael Eisner, August 24, 1990.

Interview with Richard Berger, March 27, 1990.

Interview with Michael Eisner, March 12, 1990.

Nancy Collins, "Bette Midler: The Cheese-Bomb American Crapola Dream," *Rolling Stone,* December 9, 1982, p. 15.

Jule Salamon, "Jeffrey Katzenberg: Disney's New Mogul," *The Wall Street Journal,* May 12, 1987, p. 32.

Motion Picture Association of America, *U.S. Economic Review,* 1988, p. 6.

Aljean Harmetz, "Who Makes Disney Run?" *The New York Times Magazine,* February 1988, p. 29.

Ephraim Katz, *The Film Encyclopedia* (New York: Putnam Publishing Group, 1979), p. 360.

David Ansen, "A Wise Guy's Resurrection," *Newsweek,* August 10, 1987, p. 56.

Interview with Michael Eisner, March 12, 1990.

Interview with Sam Cohn, May 15, 1990.

Down and Out in Beverly Hills, production notes.

Andy Pasztor et al., "Hutton Unit Pleads Guilty in Fraud Case," *The Wall Street Journal,* May 3, 1985, p. 3.

Interview with Roland Betts, May 9, 1990.

Interview with Michael Eisner, March 12, 1990.

Interview with Roland Betts, May 9, 1990.

Silver Screen Partners II prospectus, April 17, 1985, pp. 2, 4, 18.

Interview with Roland Betts, May 9, 1990.

Ibid.

Interview with Frank Wells, June 25, 1990.

Interview with Tom Bernstein, May 9, 1990.

Ibid.

Interview with Robert Cort, June 1, 1990.

Walt Disney Productions press release, May 7, 1982.

Laura Landro, "Unit Says 2 Officials Quit in Ethical Matter," *The Wall Street Journal,* June 6, 1984.

Wade Lambert, "Grand Jury Indicts 2 Former Officials of Paramount Unit," *The Wall Street Journal,* April 30, 1990, p. A9.

Interview with Ray Watson, April 16, 1990.

Ibid.

New York Magazine, March 10, 1986, p. 42.

Joseph Gelmis, "Living on the Down Side of the Good Life," *Newsday,* January 31, 1986, weekend edition, p. 3.

"Walt Disney Declares 4-for-1 Stock Split, Eight-Cent Dividend," *The Wall Street Journal,* January 14, 1986.

Chapter 7

Interview with Robert Cort, June 1, 1990.

"Top 100 All-Time Film Rental Champs," *Variety,* January 11, 1989, p. 26.

Walt Disney Company annual report, 1988, p. 45.

Ibid., 1987, p. 1, 17.

Ibid.

Mike Clark, *USA Today,* October 17, 1986.

Vincent Canby, *New York Times,* October 17, 1986, p. 16.

David Ansen, *Newsweek,* October 15, 1986, p. 75.

Interview with Robert Cort, June 1, 1990.

Ibid.

Interview with Robert Levin, May 22, 1990.

Ibid.

Good Morning, Vietnam production notes.

Martin Burke v. The Walt Disney Company and Touchstone Pictures, filed November 16, 1988 in California Superior Court, Case No. C 706826.

Donna Rosenthal, "Cadillac Man Finds a New Life," *Los Angeles Times,* May 1, 1990, p. F6.

Interview with Robert Levin, May 22, 1990.

Ibid.

Variety, January 11, 1990; Motion Picture Association, *U.S. Economic Review,* 1988, p. 1.

Chapter 8

Interview with Ron Miller, April 26, 1990.

The Walt Disney Company Archive.

Walt Disney Productions annual report, 1966, p. 3.

Interview with Michael Eisner, March 12, 1990.

Kim Masters, "What's Up, Doc," *Premiere,* July 1988, p. 32.

Walt Disney Productions annual report, 1983, p. 18.

Silver Screen Partners III, L.P. prospectus, October 7, 1986, p. 27.

Ibid.

Adam Eisenberg, *Cinefex,* p. 11.

Kim Masters, *Premiere Magazine,* p. 37.

Michael Reese, *Newsweek,* p. 54.

Walt Disney Company press releases.

"North American Theatrical Film Rental Market Shares: 1970–1989," *Variety,* January 11, 1990, p. 4; Motion Picture Association of America, *U.S. Economic Review,* 1988.

Interview with Roy Disney, March 14, 1990.

Ibid.

Ibid.

"Sears and Disney Agree on a Mickey Mouse Deal," *The Wall Street Journal,* November 19, 1987.

Interview with Bert Fields, *American Film Magazine,* December 1989, p. 48.

Motion Picture Association of America. *U.S. Economic Review,* 1988, p. 6.

Interview with Bert Fields, op. cit.

Anna Quindlen, "Tracy, Tracy—Aaugh!," *New York Times,* June 24, 1990, p. 21.

Jack Mathews, "A Day and Night with Warren Beatty," *Los Angeles Times,* June 10, 1990, p. 6.

Jim Emerson, "Back with a Simple Vision," *Orange County Register,* June 12, 1990, Show Section, p. 1.

Claudia Eller, "'Tracy' Expenses Revealed in Profit/Loss Statement," *Variety,* October 15, 1990, p. 1.

Chapter 9

Interview with Ronald Miller, April 26, 1990.

The Walt Disney Company, *Buena Vista Home Video: A Ten-Year History,* p. 1.

Report by Robert J. Race, Reliance Group, April 18, 1984, pp. 2, 6.

Interview with Sid Bass, May 30, 1990.

Richard Simon, Goldman Sachs investment report, March 10, 1987, p. 6.

Walt Disney Productions annual report, 1983, p. 46, 23.

Interview with Richard Frank, May 17, 1990.

Ibid.

Ibid.

Video Marketing Newsletter, January 4, 1988, p. 5.

Buena Vista Home Video press release, March 31, 1988.

Ibid.

The Walt Disney Company annual report, 1986, p. 46.

Ibid., p. 19.

Walt Disney Productions annual report, 1984, p. 1.

Walt Disney Productions annual report, 1983, pp. 22, 32.

Ibid. 1984, p. 13.

Interview with Ronald Miller, April 26, 1990.

Morgan Stanley, "Project Fantasy," report to the board of Walt Disney Productions, May 4, 1984.

Laura Landro, "Cablevision to Pay $75 Million for Rights to Offer Disney Channel to Its Subscribers," *The Wall Street Journal,* October 10, 1984, p. A-12.

"Who's News: Walt Disney's Jimirro, President of 2 Units, Quits Unexpectedly," *The Wall Street Journal,* June 19, 1985, p. B-6.

Interview with John Cooke, June 2, 1990.

Ibid.

The Walt Disney Company annual report, 1988, p. 14.

Ibid, p. 45.

Video Marketing Newsletter, July 27, 1987, p. 1.

Channels Magazine, February 1990, p. 78.

Nielsen Media Research, week of October 10, 1989.

Debra Goldman, "War in the Afternoon," *Adweek*, June 11, 1990, p. 32.

Walt Disney Productions 1984 annual report, pp. 14, 20.

Walt Disney Productions 1984 annual report, p. 20.

Walt Disney Productions 1984 annual report, p. 16.

The Walt Disney Co. 1987 annual report, p. 22.

Ron Miller interview, April 26, 1990.

Steve Burke interview, June 21, 1990.

Bob Pool, "Reagan Joins the Christmas Rush," *The Los Angeles Times*, December 9, 1989, Metro, p. 1.

The Walt Disney Company 1989 annual report, p. 49.

John Frook, "Firms Spin Off New Record Labels in Search of Market Share," *L.A. Daily News*, August 27, 1990, Business, p. 5.

Chapter 10

Interview with Dick Nunis, April 3, 1990.

Ibid.

Interview with Ronald Miller, April 26, 1990.

Richard Simon, Goldman Sachs research investment report, March 10, 1987, p. 3.

Interview with Michael Eisner, March 12, 1990.

Ibid.

Interview with Paul Junger Witt, April 2, 1990.

Interview with Dick Nunis, April 3, 1990.

Interview with Leonard Goldenson, August 24, 1990.

Interview with Rich Frank, May 17, 1990.

Ibid.

Ibid.

Ibid.

Ibid.

Interview with Michael Eisner, March 12, 1990.

Alex McNeil, *Total Television* (New York: Viking Penguin, 1984), p. 710.

Alex Ben Block, *Outfoxed* (New York: St. Martin's Press, 1990), p. 203.

The Walt Disney Company annual report, 1987, p. 19.

Interview with Garry Marshall, April 2, 1990.

Interview with Rich Frank, May 17, 1990.

Interview with Michael Eisner, March 12, 1990.

Chapter 11

Ephraim Katz, *The Film Encyclopedia* (New York: Putnam Publishing Group, 1979), p. 803.

Ibid.

MGM/UA Communications Co. prospectus 1989.

From a declaration by Frank Rothman, *MGM/UA Communications Co. and MGM Grand, Inc. v. The Walt Disney Co.,* California Superior Court, Case No. C686329.

Bob Thomas, *Walt Disney: An American Original* (New York: Simon & Schuster, 1976), p. 226.

Interview with Richard Nunis, April 3, 1990.

Interview with Frank Wells, June 25, 1990.

Interview with Martin Sklar, April 18, 1990.

Interview with Frank Wells, June 25, 1990.

From a declaration by Frank Davis, *MGM/UA Communications Co. v. The Walt Disney Co.,* op. cit.

Agreement between MGM/UA Entertainment Co., United Artists Corp., and Walt Disney Productions, dated June 27, 1985.

Letter from Martin Sklar to Bill Dennis, MGM vice-president of licensing and merchandising, September 4, 1986.

Op. cit.

Peter Bart, *Fade Out: The Calamitous Final Days of MGM* (New York: William Morrow & Co., 1990), p. 277.

Ibid.

MGM/UA Communications Co. and MGM Grand, Inc. v. The Walt Disney Co., op. cit.

Walt Disney Productions press release, July 8, 1985.

Ibid.

Ibid.

Vicki Vaughan, "MCA Smells a Rat in Disney's Plans for Studio Tour," *Orlando Sentinel,* May 15, 1985, p. A-1.

Michael Cieply, "Disney's Plan to Build Cities on Florida Tract Could Shape Its Future," *The Wall Street Journal,* July 9, 1985, p. 1.

Ibid.

Ibid.

Charles Leerhsen, "Kongfrontation," *Newsweek*, June 11, 1990, p. 67.

Ibid.

Ibid.

Michael Cieply, "MCA Inc. Says Disney Is Trying to Sabotage Plans to Build Facility," *The Wall Street Journal*, May 21, 1985, p. B23.

Ronald Grover, "Theme Parks: This Slugfest Is No Fantasy," *Business Week*, March 23, 1987, p. 38.

Ike Flores, Associated Press article printed in *Los Angeles Herald Examiner*, January 4, 1987, p. A-6.

Greg Braxton, "MCA Admits Attack on Disney Backlot Plan," *Los Angeles Times*, November 12, 1987, p. 8, Metro Valley edition.

Letter to Robert R. Ovrom, executive director of Burbank Redevelopment Agency, from Alan Epstein, vice-president of Disney Development Company, April 8, 1987.

Charles Leerhsen, "How Disney Does It," *Newsweek*, April 3, 1989, p. 48.

Richard Corliss, "Universal's Swamp of Dreams," *Time*, June 18, 1990, p. 64.

Chapter 12

"Disney Grins and Bears Canadian Pooh Statue," *The Associated Press* (reprinted in *Los Angeles Daily News*), September 30, 1989.

Interview with Michael Eisner, March 12, 1990.

Interview with Peter Nolan, July 22, 1990.

Vicki Vaughan, "Disney Warns Union Members," *Orlando Sentinel*, November 11, 1988, p. B-1.

Interview with Jeffrey Katzenberg, July 27, 1990.

Interview with Robert Cort, June 1, 1990.

Ibid.

Interview with Garry Marshall, April 2, 1990.

Jeffrey Katzenberg, press conference, April 10, 1990.

Paul Richter, "Disney's Tough Tactics," *Los Angeles Times*, Business section, July 8, 1990, p. D-1.

Interview with Jerry Zucker, April 10, 1990.

Ibid.

Ibid.

Will Tusher, "Disney Claims Kirkpatrick Breach," *Variety*, August 31, 1990, p. 1.

Laura Landro, "U.K. Firm Seeks Movie Rights from Columbia," *The Wall Street Journal*, November 30, 1988, p. B-8.

Sky Television, PLC v. The Walt Disney Company, et al., filed at the Superior Court for the County of Los Angeles, Case C724117, May 15, 1989.

Ibid.

Interview with Rich Frank, May 17, 1990.

Ibid.

Sky Television, PLC, v. The Walt Disney Company, et al., op cit.

Ibid.

Ibid.

Sky Television, PLC, v. The Walt Disney Company, et al., op cit.

Ibid.

Interview with Larry Murphy, June 7, 1990.

Metrocolor Partners v. The Walt Disney Company, filed at the Superior Court for the County of Los Angeles, Case C734625, August 17, 1989.

Ibid.

Laurie A. Krock and Glenn H. Epstein, "Disney Sues Property Appraiser's Office—Again," *News Gazette* (Osceola, Florida), September 23, 1990, p. A-3.

Ibid.

Michael Griffin, "Disney May Help Orange Get a Loan," *Orlando Sentinel*, May 30, 1990, p. A-1.

Richard Turner, "Well, Nobody Ever Claimed She Had a Sense of Humor," *The Wall Street Journal*, April 3, 1989, p. 1.

Public statement by Frank Wells, March 30, 1989.

Bruce V. Bigelow, "Disney Sues Academy over Unauthorized Use of Snow White," Associated Press article, March 30, 1989.

Bob Thomas, *Walt Disney: An American Original* (New York: Simon & Schuster, 1976), p. 271.

Interview with Frank Wells, June 25, 1990.

The Walt Disney Company annual report, 1988, p. 24.

"Disney in Copyright Spats with Day Care Center," Associated Press article, April 30, 1989.

Paul Richter, "Disney's Tough Tactics," *Los Angeles Times*, July 7, 1990, p. D-1.

Interview with Frank Wells, June 25, 1990.

Richter, op. cit.

Ibid.

Interview with Rich Frank, May 17, 1990.

Richter, op. cit.

The Walt Disney Studio press release, February 21, 1990.

Chapter 13

Bruce Nussbaum, "Deal Mania," *Business Week*, November 24, 1986, p. 75.

Laura Landro and Dennis Kneale, "Mega-Media. Entertainment Giants Are Now All the Rage, But Is Big Any Better?" *The Wall Street Journal*, June 9, 1989, p. 1.

The Walt Disney Company annual report 1987, p. 47.

Ibid., p. 37.

Ibid., p. 32.

Interview with Michael Eisner, March 12, 1990.

Ibid.

Bill Abrahams and Johnnie L. Roberts, "General Electric to Acquire RCA for $6.28 Billion," *The Wall Street Journal*, December 12, 1985.

Interview with Gary Wilson, April 21, 1990.

The Walt Disney Company annual report, 1986, p. 37.

Interview with Gary Wilson, April 21, 1990.

Ibid.

Ibid.

The Walt Disney Company press release, November 28, 1989.

Interview with Sid Bass, May 30, 1990.

Ida Picker, "Financial Magic for the Magic Kingdom," *Corporate Finance*, October 1989, p. 256.

The Wall Street Journal, March 30, 1988, p. 17.

Interview with Charles E. Cobb, Jr., May 3, 1990.

Interview with Gary Wilson, April 21, 1990.

Tony Ettore, *Arvida, A Business Odyssey* (Coral Springs, Florida: ECI Publication), 1990, p. 69.

The Walt Disney Company annual report, 1987, p. 27. Agreement between The Walt Disney Company and Arvida Acquisition Associates, Ltd., dated January 29, 1987, Appendix: Arvida Corp. divisional income statements and cash flow, 1985–1996.

Agreement between The Walt Disney Company and Arvida Acquisition Associates, Ltd., dated January 29, 1987.

Letter agreement between Arvida/JMB Partners, L.P., and JMB Realty Corp., and The Walt Disney Company, dated September 10, 1987.

Ettore, op. cit. p. 77.

The Walt Disney Company v. Robert E. Anderson, et al., filed in the United States District Court, Middle District of Florida, April 10, 1987, Case 87-309-Div-J-12.

Settlement Agreement and General Release between Charles E. Cobb, Jr., and The Walt Disney Company, June 8, 1987.

Gregory Stricharchuk, "Westinghouse Ends Accord to Purchase GenCorp's Los Angeles Television Station," *The Wall Street Journal*, January 30, 1987, p. A-6; Bill Abrams, "GenCorp's RKO Alleges in an FCC Filing Two Ex-Aides Directed Ad Overcharges," *The Wall Street Journal*, August 15, 1984, p. C-3.

Interview with Rich Frank, May 17, 1990.

Interview with Frank Wells, June 25, 1990.

Interview with Larry Murphy, June 7, 1990.

Chapter 14

Todd Vogel, "Vestron Is Now Starring in Its Own Cliffhanger," *Business Week*, July 17, 1989, p. 66.

Motion Picture Association of America, Inc., economic review, 1988, p. 6.

Variety, January 11, 1990, p. 4.

The Walt Disney Company annual report, 1989, p. 49.

Motion Picture Association of America, op. cit., p. 6.

Richard Turner, "Disney Strategy to Increase Film Output Gets First Test in Spider Thriller-Comedy," *The Wall Street Journal*, Marketplace section, July 13, 1990, p. 1.

Arachnophobia production notes, p. 29.

"North American Theatrical Film Rental Market Shares: 1970–1989," *Variety*, January 11, 1990, p. 2.

Interview with Garry Marshall, April 2, 1990.

Ibid.

Ibid.

Ibid.

Ibid.

Ron Givens, "Tracking *Pretty Woman*," *Entertainment Weekly*, March 23, 1990, p. 63.

Hollywood Reporter, March 27, 1990 and June 12, 1990.

Figures provided by The Walt Disney Company.

Advertising Age, September 26, 1990, p. 55.

Interview with Robert Cort, June 1, 1990.

The Walt Disney Company annual report, 1989, pp. 23, 49; 1990 annual report, p. 38.

Interview with Roland Betts, May 9, 1990.

Ibid.

Interview with Michael Eisner, March 12, 1990.

The Walt Disney Company annual report, 1989, p. 46; 1987, p. 42.

Variety, January 4, 1991, p. 1.

Chapter 15

Press conference, Disneyland Hotel auditorium, Jan. 12, 1990.

Michael Eisner press conference, Swan Hotel, Jan. 14, 1990.

The Wall Disney Company annual report, 1991.

Associated Press, "Disney President Pelted with Eggs at Stock Announcement," October 5, 1989.

S. G. Warburg Securities and Co., International Offering of Shares for Euro Disneyland SCA, October 5, 1989, p. 36.

Associated Press, "Disney Stock Up Sharply on Euro Disneyland Demand," Oct. 9, 1989.

Warburg offering.

Peter Gumbel and Richard Turner, "Mouse Trap: Fans Like Euro Disney But Its Parent's Goofs Weigh the Park Down," *The Wall Street Journal*, March 10, 1994, p. A 1.

Ibid.

Ibid.

Interview with Michael Eisner, February 16, 1996.

Ibid.

Gumbel and Turner, *The Wall Street Journal*, March 10, 1994, p. A 1.

Ibid.

Ibid.

Richard Nanula interview, March 8, 1996.

"Euro Disney Expects a Loss for Fiscal Year," *The Wall Street Journal*, Feb. 12, 1993. Pb. B 4D.

Euro Disney S.C.A. press release, April 4, 1994.

Mark Milner, "Euro Disney Picture Still Looks Out of Focus," *The Guardian*, Nov. 4, 1994, p. 19.

Euro Disney S.C.A. 1994 annual report.

Stanley Gold interview, June 8, 1990.

Ron Miller interview, April 26, 1990.

Walt Disney Productions 1976 and 1979 annual reports, pp. 6 and 12.

Walt Disney Productions 1978 annual report, p. 14 and Disney company executives.

Walt Disney Productions 1984 annual report, p. 42.

Warburg, International Offer of Shares, Oct. 5, 1989, p. 65.

Interview with Michael Eisner, February 16, 1996.

Nanula interview, March 8, 1996.

Ibid.

Ibid.

"Euro Disney May Have to Close — Walt Disney Chairman," *Le Monde,* January 2, 1994.

"Disney, Euro Disney and Bank Committee Present Broad Financial Restructuring Plan," *PR Newswire,* March 14, 1994.

Euro Disney S.C.A. 1994 annual report.

John Rossant, "The Prince," *Business Week Magazine,* Sept. 25, 1995, p. 89.

"Euro Disney Announces International Investor to Acquire 13 to 24 Percent Stake," *PR Newswire,* June 1, 1994.

Nanula interview, March 8, 1996.

Ibid.

Euro Disney S.C.A. 1994 annual report.

Euro Disney S.C.A. press release, Nov. 15, 1995.

The Walt Disney Co. press release, Dec. 12, 1991.

Matt Lair and Chris Woodyard, "Disney Proposes Big Cut in Westcot Plans," *The Los Angeles Times,* August 12, 1994.

Richard Nanula interview, March 8, 1996.

"Plans Unveiled for 'Disney America' near Washington, D.C.," *PR Newswire,* November 11, 1993.

"Disney Chairman Describes Vision for American History Park," Disney press release, June 21, 1994.

"Disney to Seek New Site for Proposed Theme Park," Disney Press Release, Sept. 29, 1994.

Chapter 16

Corie Brown, "The Third Man," *Premiere,* November 1994, p. 111.

"Disney Chairman Eisner Will Assume Additional Duties and Title of President," Disney press release, April 4, 1994.

Ibid.

The Walt Disney Company 1994 annual report, p. 6.

Michael Eisner interview, Feb. 16, 1996.

John Huey, "Eisner Explains Everything," *Fortune*, April 17, 1995, p. 44.

The Walt Disney Company 1990 proxy statement, p. 18.

"Nanula to Lead Disney Stores," Disney press release, Nov. 8, 1994.

Ken Auletta, "The Human Factor," *The New Yorker*, September 26, 1994, p. 53.

Ibid.

Kim Masters, "A Mouse Divided," *Vanity Fair*, November 1994, p. 169.

Michael Eisner interview, Feb. 16, 1996.

Kim Masters, "A Mouse Divided," *Vanity Fair*, November 1994, p. 169.

Ibid.

Ken Auletta, "The Human Factor," *The New Yorker*, Sept. 26, 1994, p. 61.

Ibid.

Ibid.

Ibid, p. 62.

Kim Masters, "A Mouse Divided," *Vanity Fair*, November 1994, p. 170.

Ken Auletta, "The Human Factor," *The New Yorker*, Sept. 26, 1994, p. 62.

Ibid.

Michael Eisner interview, Feb. 16, 1996.

The Walt Disney Co. press release, July 16, 1994.

Ken Auletta, "The Human Factor," *The New Yorker*, Sept. 26, 1994, p. 64.

The Walt Disney Company press release, July 16, 1994.

Richard Turner, "Top Disney Aide Isn't Given Edge to Be President," *The Wall Street Journal*, July 20, 1994, p. A3.

Ken Auletta, "The Human Factor," *The New Yorker*, Sept. 26, 1994, p. 64.

Ibid.

The Walt Disney Co. press release, August 24, 1994.

Ibid.

Kathryn Harris, "Eisner Speaks out on Katzenberg Departure," *The Los Angeles Times*, Sept. 26, 1994.

Ken Auletta, "The Human Factor," *The New Yorker*, September 26, 1994, p. 66.

Ibid.

"Dream Team" press conference, Peninsula Hotel, October 24, 1994.

"Richard Frank to Leave Disney; Dennis Hightower Named President of TV Unit," The Walt Disney Co. press release, March 13, 1995.

Chapter 17

The Walt Disney Co., 1993 annual report, p. 4.

Richard Nanula interview, March 8, 1996.

The Walt Disney Co., proxy, November 13, 1995, p. 14.

Ibid, p. 23.

Ibid, p. 67.

Richard Nanula interview, March 8, 1996.

Richard Nanula interview.

Subrata N. Chakravarty, "We Bought, We Leveraged, We Improved," *Fortune*, November 7, 1994, p. 196.

Ibid.

Elizabeth Jensen and Richard Turner, "Disney Weights $5 Billion Offer for GE's NBC unit," *The Wall Street Journal*, September 14, 1994, p. A-3.

Ibid.

The Walt Disney Co. press release, April 24, 1995.

Edward Klein, "Mighty Joe Roth," *Vanity Fair*, February 1993, p. 165.

Ibid, p. 169.

James Sterngold, *The New York Times*, August 18, 1995.

The Walt Disney Co. press release, April 4, 1995.

The Walt Disney Co. press release, April 24, 1995.

Wayne Walley, "Cross-pollination," *Electronic Media*, August 7, 1995, p. 3.

The Walt Disney Co., proxy for special shareholders meeting, January 4, 1996, p. 23.

Michael Eisner interview, February 16, 1996.

The Walt Disney Co., proxy, November 13, 1995, p. 23.

Ibid.

Ibid, p. 106.

Ibid.

Ibid, p. 7.

Ibid, p. 42.

Agreement and Plan of Reorganization, dated as of July 31, 1995, between The Walt Disney Company and Capital Cities/ABC, Inc.

Ibid, p. 32.

Wayne Walley, "Cross-pollination," *Electronic Media*, August 7, 1995, p. 3.

Johnnie L. Roberts, "King of the Deal," *Newsweek*, June 12, 1995, p. 44.

Michael Eisner interview, February 8, 1996.

Employment Agreement between The Walt Disney Company and Michael S. Ovitz, dated October 1, 1995.

Employment contract between The Walt Disney Co. and Michael Ovitz.

Employment contract between The Walt Disney Co. and Michael Ovitz.

Employment Agreement between The Walt Disney Co. and Michael S. Ovitz.

Ibid.

Daily Variety, February 7, 1996, p. 8.

Capital Cities/ABC 10Q Earnings Statement, February 1, 1996.

The Walt Disney Co. 1995 annual report.

Ibid.

Adam Sandler, "CAA, MEG Groups U2 Tour Finalists," *Daily Variety*, March 11, 1996, p. 1.

Daily Variety, February 22, 1996, p. 22.

Steve Coe, "It's Disney Morning on ABC," *Broadcasting and Cable*, February 5, 1996.

Sally Hofmeister, "Disney Cranks to Meet Its TV Mandate," *The Los Angeles Times*, March 29, 1996, p. D-4.

Martin Peers, "Mouse Roars on Wall St.," *Variety*, March 14, 1996.

INDEX